THE BORGIAS

The Rise and Fall of a Renaissance Dynasty

O PASTOR·DEGNIO·ALMIO·POPOL·XPIANO
A TE·DI SIENA·ORMAI·LA CURA·RENDO
FA·CH ALLEI·VOLGA·OGNI·TUO·SENSO·HUMANO
STUS III · SANUS·PETRI·DESENI·PIXIT

THE BORGIAS

The Rise and Fall of a Renaissance Dynasty

MICHAEL MALLETT

BARNES & NOBLE, Inc.
NEW YORK
PUBLISHERS & BOOKSELLERS SINCE 1873

First published in the United States, 1969
by Barnes & Noble, Inc.

Printed and bound in Great Britain
by William Clowes & Sons Ltd
London & Beccles

CONTENTS

ILLUSTRATIONS

TEXT FIGURES

GENEALOGICAL TABLES

INTRODUCTION

It is said that when asked to enumerate the most illustrious Popes, Sixtus V replied: 'St. Peter, Alexander and ourselves', and Urban VIII when confronted with the same question, offered: 'St. Peter, St. Sylvester, Alexander and me.' That two later Popes of considerable standing should have singled out the notorious Rodrigo Borgia, Alexander VI, in this way requires some explanation other than the traditional, lurid pictures of the lives and loves of the Borgias with which English-speaking audiences have been sated.

It is my intention therefore in this book to present as wide a spectrum as possible of recent views about the Borgias in an attempt not to rehabilitate them but to explain them. To explain why they were so hated, so feared and so maligned; to explain what they were doing which so upset the Renaissance Italians as to bring down the whole weight of contemporary humanistic and later historical censure upon them. Jacob Burckhardt in his *Civilisation of the Renaissance in Italy* remarked that in that period 'no one could escape calumny and the most exemplary virtue provoked the worst detraction'. With the Borgias of the late fifteenth century it was their vices rather than their virtues which were exemplary, but it remains true nevertheless that it was with calumny that their enemies fought them, calumny which has been allowed to distort the picture of their activities ever since.

The achievement of the Borgias was that of a Spanish noble family of moderate standing, noted in the province of Valencia as soldiers and local gentry, who succeeded in inserting themselves into the upper echelons of Renaissance European society. By the somewhat fortuitous election of one member of the family to be Pope, Calixtus III, the way was prepared for a successive Pope, Alexander, for eleven Borgia cardinals in the space of two and a half centuries (and at least four others closely related to the family), and for princes and dukes in Naples, central and northern Italy, France, Spain and the New World.

The elevation of relatively obscure papal families was a feature of the Italian social scene, particularly in this period when economic and bureaucratic expansion had made society more mobile, but by nature papal patronage and influence were ephemeral. Few papal families succeeded in establishing a permanent position of influence even in Italy, and the Borgias achieved much more than this. But that achievement infuriated the families whom they were elbowing aside; the Roman aristocrats of the Orsini and Colonna families were stripped of their estates and driven into exile to make way for Borgia Dukes; the *condottiere* princes of central Italy, who had often themselves only recently and with much effort won their lordships, were humiliated and ousted. All this was the work of Spaniards, or to be more exact Catalans, a race hated and despised in Italy since before the days of Dante for their greed and avarice.

This was, of course, not the whole story. Alexander VI was both a handsome and sensual libertine, and a vigorous and unscrupulous politician. His court, despite certain surprising ascetic features, was that of a Renaissance prince; his policies were those of a Renaissance Pope. The protection of the temporal interests of the Papacy, the strengthening of central authority within the Papal States, and the extension of the network of papal diplomacy were for him of more immediate concern than reform of the Church and the maintenance of spiritual standards. At a time when the states of Italy were falling one after another under the control of France or Spain, the Papacy managed to preserve its territorial integrity by a diplomacy of duplicity and betrayal, and also played its part in the destruction of the Italian state system by dispossessing many of the semi-independent lords who had established themselves within the Papal States. These achievements earned for Alexander and his family the hatred of rulers and the distrust of politicians all over Italy, while his failure to face the problems of reform, and the ostentatious worldliness of his court, earned him the contempt and vituperation of reformers.

Alexander VI died surrounded by an atmosphere of hatred and fear; a hatred so violent that Julius II and all his successors refused to occupy the Borgia apartments in the Vatican which were left neglected until the nineteenth century. It was this hatred which led the same Julius to torture confessions of crimes, supposedly committed at the command of the Borgias, out of Alexander's servants, and to eradicate as far as possible every evidence of Borgia achievement. Julius, as Cardinal Giuliano della Rovere, had been Alexander's chief rival during his lifetime; first a rival in the papal election, and then the leader of those cardinals who sought to depose him with French help. He had passed most of Alexander's pontificate in exile, stripped of many of his benefices, his boundless energy and ambition shackled by the success of his rival. It was Julius perhaps more than any other single person who set the tone of contemporary and later attitudes towards the Borgias.

But what Julius with his anti-Borgia activities had started, the humanist propagandists of the Italian princes and the local chroniclers of the cities of the Papal States completed. There are few of the contemporary observers and early sixteenth century commentators, whose reports and writings form the narrative sources for an account of the second Borgia pontificate, who can be described as entirely objective. Among the chroniclers Stefano Infessura was a partisan of the Colonna and a violent anti-papalist whose writings did much to destroy the reputation of Sixtus IV as well as Alexander. Matarazzo, the Perugian, was a client of the Baglione family and an opponent of papal government. Sigismondo de' Conti, a Curia official and therefore in sympathy with papal policies, was among the fairest reporters; but he was also a humanist historian to whom literary style and the introduction of apposite classical example were sometimes more important than factual accuracy. Then there were the Neapolitan publicists Sannazzaro and Pontano who poured out invective against the Pope who had abandoned their King to the mercy of foreign invaders. Ottaviano Ubaldini, who said of Alexander, 'Judas sold Christ for 30 denari; this man would sell him for 29', was a protégé of Guidobaldo da Montefeltro, Duke of Urbino, who was dispossessed by the Borgias. Guido Posthumus, another influential humanist critic, was employed by Giovanni Sforza, the divorced husband of Lucrezia Borgia and the author of charges of incest against her. There was the more influential Paolo Giovio, an employee of Orsini, Colonna and Medici patrons; Marin Sanuto, the Venetian diarist, into whose vast collection went every scrap of rumour and gossip about the Borgias whose policies caused so much alarm in Venice; and his fellow countryman, the diplomat Giustinian, who had learnt at first hand to distrust the Borgias, but admitted that it was easy to misinterpret their motives. Ambassadors, like Giustinian and his fellow Cataneo, the Mantuan, and Boccaccio, the Ferrarese, provide much of our information about Rome and the Borgias, but their reports were frequently flavoured by the political attitudes of the states which they represented and by their assessment of what their masters would like to hear.

High on the list of effective contemporary pamphlets comes the Savelli Letter, written anonymously for the benefit of Silvio Savelli, a Roman baron exiled by the Borgias. This was a tract, the extravagant invective of which made Alexander smile when it was read to him; but the echoes of its charges are to be found in many subsequent accounts. Another important source for the period is the diary of Johannes Burchard, the papal master of ceremonies. Burchard was a small-minded and prudish German, obsessed by his own failure to gain preferment, who gives us much valuable information on the daily life of the court, but who at the same time cannot be expected to have been either well-informed about Borgia policies or in sympathy with Borgia moral standards.

Finally, and most influential of all, came the Florentines, Niccolò Machiavelli and Francesco Guicciardini. Machiavelli's dispatches, although containing some of the most favourable contemporary descriptions of the Borgias, were often tinged with distortion designed to influence Florentine policy, and his later treatises have a polemical quality which at times twists the true facts. On the other hand Guicciardini, writing at a distance about events which he had often not witnessed at first hand, allowed his Florentine patriotism and his strong anti-clericalism and anti-papalism to make his fine *History* a repository for some of the most virulent and least well authenticated of the Borgia legends.

However even if we could write off everything reported in these sources as calumny, and of course we cannot, the fact that Alexander was so violently attacked made an enormous impact at a time when papal authority and Catholic unity was under such heavy fire. It is often difficult for the historian to accept that the public image, however distorted it is, may be of more historical significance than the real, often more complex, situation.

These are some of the pitfalls which confront the Borgia historian and which can easily frighten him into the abyss of unrealistic rehabilitation on the other side of the narrow path of objective historical truth. This path is even narrower and harder to find than usual on this subject, and it would be optimistic and pretentious to imagine that this modest contribution has succeeded entirely in finding it. Although the more obvious documentary sources of Borgia history have long since been investigated by historians in addition to the narrative sources described here, there remains much which might be discovered in the local administrative and financial records of the Papal States about Borgia government and internal policy. Such research would test, amplify, and probably to some extent reject, some of the tentative ideas suggested here.

In this book in the interests of space and in order to maintain the pace of the narrative for the ordinary reader and the busy student, I have tried to keep the notes to a minimum. But if a historical work is to be of any real value to a serious reader there must be some indications of further reading and some support for more unusual and radical ideas. I have therefore provided some notes of a purely bibliographical nature and have attempted to support with references some of the more novel ideas which readers will find in this book. I have also when occasion demanded referred in the notes to outdated and discarded theories about the Borgias which can no longer figure in the narrative without unduly encumbering it. Finally I have provided the original versions of some of the less well known quotations which appear in the text in translation.

I have also tried to further my aim of bringing before an English-speaking audience some of the recent ideas and discoveries of Borgia research in other languages, by adding an extensive bibliography which I hope will be of value to both scholars and students.

When referring to the Borgia family I have adopted a convention of using the Spanish version of the name—Borja, and of Christian names, for those members of the family who remained primarily connected with Spain. On the other hand Alexander and those of his immediate family whose activities are more a part of Italian history than Spanish, I have described by the more familiar Italian versions of their names. My only departure from this convention is with San Francesco de Borja whose major role in the history of the Catholic Church and of the Jesuits has made him better known to English and American readers as St. Francis Borgia, and it is thus that I have described him.

In venturing into this highly controversial field I owe a great debt to those friends and scholars who have generously given their time to reading and commenting on the manuscript at various stages. In this connection I want particularly to thank Professor Nicolai Rubinstein, Professor John Hale, and Mr. John Larner whose comments and suggestions have saved me from many errors. Those from which they have not saved me, and they are still no doubt many, must be attributed to my own obstinacy. I must also thank Mr. John Huntington of The Bodley Head who has patiently prepared an untidy and often illegible manuscript, and to whom is mainly due any pleasure which the reader may derive from the presentation of this book. Finally both for invaluable help in collecting the illustrations and preparing the maps, and for her unfailing patience in coping with a frequently irritable and preoccupied husband while the book was being written, I want to thank my wife.

CHAPTER ONE

THE RENAISSANCE PAPACY

When Martin V rode into Rome in September 1420 he received a ragged but heartfelt welcome from the Romans. Apart from two brief interludes in the 1360s and the 1370s, there had not been a Pope resident in the Holy City since the beginning of the previous century who had commanded general recognition throughout western Christendom. For much of that time the Lateran and Vatican palaces had stood empty as the Popes had moved their court to Avignon, and for the last forty years although there had been a Pope in Rome the Great Schism had ensured that large parts of Europe did not recognise his authority. It was therefore as the personification of the restoration of Catholic unity, and as the first of a new series of Popes, the Renaissance Popes, that Martin V was welcomed to Rome.

By 1420 the great medieval conflict between Popes and Holy Roman Emperors for ultimate authority over Christendom was long since over. The victory appeared to have been convincingly won by the Papacy in the thirteenth century when Frederick II, the 'wonder of the world', had died a frustrated man, and his heir had been convincingly defeated by the papal forces at the battle of Tagliacozzo. From these moments the papal idea of the Pope as God's supreme vicar on earth in both the spiritual and temporal spheres, claiming the right to the homage of the princes of Europe, seemed to have triumphed. But already the Europe over which the Popes appeared to have won control was changing rapidly. When Boniface VIII sought to formalise the papal theory of sovereignty in his Bull *Unam Sanctam* in 1302, he met opposition not from the Emperor but from the rising power of the national monarchies of Western Europe. It was the ambassadors of the King of France who were said to have slapped the Pope's face at Anagni thus demonstrating their rejection of his claims. Two years later a French Pope, Clement V, was elected and it was not long before French influence had succeeded in establishing the papal court at Avignon.

The abandonment of Rome by the Popes in the fourteenth century was not such a surprising move as it appears. Many medieval Popes had spent little time in the city, and not a few had at one time or another sought refuge in France when pressure on them in Italy had been too great. Nor should the Avignonese Popes be written off completely as puppets of France. Many of the Popes of the fourteenth century were university-trained men who set about the organisation of papal administration along more efficient and more highly centralised lines. It was in Avignon that the Curia became the most sophisticated civil service in Europe in its day. The collection of papal revenues was improved as it needed to be with the ever-increasing cost of papal government. The Popes began to build themselves the great palace at Avignon, to some extent the symbol of their independence and authority.[1]

But nevertheless the prestige of the Papacy inevitably suffered in this period. The improvements in the central administration and the increased fiscal pressure caused widespread alarm; bishops feared for their independence, the laity feared for their pockets, kings feared for their national revenues. This fear and suspicion was increased when it was felt that the Pope and his administration were becoming too closely attached to one nation, a nation with which England was at war and the Empire on terms of permanent distrust.

Despite the independent position which the Avignonese Popes were to some extent maintaining, there was no escaping the facts that it was to the Kings of France that massive papal loans went, and that 113 of the 134 cardinals appointed by those Popes were Frenchmen. In these circumstances anti-papalism and anti-clericalism were inevitably exacerbated by rising national feeling.

By the 1360s there was a clear desire on the part of the Popes, French though they continued to be, to escape from this situation. Avignon, threatened by roving companies of unemployed soldiers during the lulls in the Hundred Years War, was no more secure than Rome had been. In 1367 Urban V moved his court briefly back to Rome; but by now accustomed to the civilised surroundings created in Avignon he was appalled by the primitive and disturbed conditions in Rome. He returned to Avignon to die and it was left to his successor Gregory XI to carry out a more permanent move.

So in 1377 the Roman papacy was re-established and a year later on the death of Gregory the first conclave for over seventy years was held in Rome. But the majority of the cardinals were still French and although, intimidated by the Roman populace clamouring for an Italian Pope, they elected the Neapolitan Urban VI, they very quickly renounced their decision and withdrew from Rome. Urban, a neurotic and violent man, created twenty-five new Italian cardinals to replace his dissident College and the latter declared his election void and chose one of their number, Robert of Geneva, to be Clement VII. After a brief civil war Clement and his Avignonese cardinals gave up their attempt to depose Urban by force and returned to Avignon. The Schism had begun.

This was a schism dictated by personal and political factors rather than doctrinal ones and it was highly damaging to the prestige of the Papacy. The whole concept of the universal church was destroyed as two supreme pontiffs struggled for control, aided by political factions. The division of Europe followed political lines: England and Germany, politically opposed to France, supported the Roman Pope regardless of the equivocal activities of Urban who tortured and murdered cardinals who opposed him; Scotland, Spain and the Angevin dynasty in Naples supported the French Pope. Many sees had bishops appointed by both Popes, and even the great religious orders were split as generals were appointed from both sides. Much needed reform of the Church was indefinitely delayed, and as each Pope attempted to make the half of the papal revenues which he controlled pay the whole cost of his administration, fiscal exactions were increased and the unpopularity which these caused grew. The Church like other great landowners suffered severely in the second half of the fourteenth century from falling grain prices and the reduction of the rural labour force. Thus the revenues of the Church were declining both from the Church lands and from the spiritual taxes just at the moment when expenditure was increasing.

The situation was clearly intolerable and it was not long before pressure began to build up for the restoration of a unified Papacy. The election of the authoritarian Spaniard Pedro de Luna to the Avignonese throne as Benedict XIII offended France; the University of Paris declared against him and his French revenues were cut off. The complete confusion in the Papal States as the bankrupt Roman Popes struggled for authority disillusioned the Italians. The cardinals on both sides were anxious for a solution, but the main stumbling block was the two Popes themselves who dreaded the loss of authority which reunification would inevitably bring to one of them. In this situation it was to a General Council of the Church that men turned to heal the Schism; a Council that was to be no longer the instrument of the Papacy as the earlier Councils of the Church had been, but a Council fortified by a new body of theories which had grown up in the fourteenth century.

The emergence of representative institutions in the increasingly self-sufficient states of Western Europe, the breakdown of medieval concepts of universalism and the growth of anti-clericalism all contributed to the growth of the new conciliar theory. The idea that the ultimate authority in the Church should be a Council representing not just the clergy of all Christendom but also the laity, and that such a Council should have the power to depose an erring Pope was an attractive one at the time of the Schism. Its formulation was assisted by the writings of John of Paris and Marsilio of Padua during the fourteenth century, and hardened under the influence of men like Pierre d'Ailly and Jean Gerson during the conciliar period itself. Thus the solution to the Schism seemed to threaten a permanent reduction of the Pope's prestige by the establishment of a constitutional papal monarchy.

The first of the fifteenth-century councils met at Pisa in 1409. It was not well attended and its decisions to depose the two existing Popes and elect another, Alexander V, although commanding general support, did not carry sufficient weight to bring a permanent solution. Neither Gregory XII in Rome, nor Benedict XIII now in Spain, accepted their deposition and so Christendom had three Popes. It was therefore the next Council held at Constance between 1414 and 1418 which took the first effective steps towards healing the Schism. Part of the conciliar idea stated at Pisa was that Councils should meet at regular intervals, and the Council of Constance was therefore well prepared and well attended. Alexander V's successor as 'conciliar' Pope, John XXIII, had issued the formal summons to the Council and had hoped that it would confirm his position and accept his leadership. But the precedents set at Pisa, the urgent need for reform, and the continued resistance of the surviving Popes ensured the temporary triumph of the conciliarists. John fled from Constance and opened the way for his own deposition and the confirmation of those of his rivals. The council, torn between a desire to press on with reforms and the need to elect a new Pope who could command general support, eventually proceeded with the latter and at a special conclave Cardinal Oddo Colonna was elected and took the title of Martin V.

Martin V can be justifiably described as the first of the Renaissance Popes, and the period which lay between his entry into Rome and the sack of that city by Charles V's troops in 1527 as the Renaissance Papacy.[2]

It was not the extent to which these Popes were associated with the intellectual and cultural trends of the Renaissance which gives meaning to the term the Renaissance Papacy, as such involvement and interest varied greatly from Pope to Pope. But the similarity of the problems which they faced, and the emergence of a continuity in their response to those problems and in their interpretation of the concept of papal monarchy, linked Martin V and his successors. Martin V was faced with the problems of re-establishing papal prestige, of re-asserting papal supremacy against conciliar theories and emerging national churches, of reimposing papal control over the Papal States, and of maintaining the independence of the Papacy from any external political forces. His solution in a world where secular values were of increasing importance was to concentrate on establishing the temporal power of the Papacy. The prestige, independence and ultimate spiritual supremacy of the Pope were to depend on a secure and well administered territorial state, on independent finances, on a well-trained civil service, on diplomacy and on military strength. Once the prestige of the Pope was re-established then he could think of promulgating effective reform; but Martin V and all of the Popes who followed him in the next century proved themselves consistently alien to conciliar theories or to any repetition of what they saw as the weakness and dependence of the Avignonese Popes.

For both Martin and his immediate successor, Eugenius IV, the task of recovery was a difficult one. The Spanish antipopes in the person of Clement VIII did not finally capitulate until 1429, and it was not until 1449 that the third of the great Councils, that of Basle, finally broke up in disorder and the cause of papal supremacy seemed to be once more secure. All the Councils had suffered from internal national rivalries, from the opposition of ecclesiastical vested interests to specific programmes of reform and to lay influence, and from a tendency towards idealistic rather than practical policies. Eugenius IV with the aid of his experienced Curia was able to play on these divisions, to win for himself the credit for the apparent healing of the breach with the Orthodox Church at the Council of Florence, and to come to agreement with the various princely supporters of the conciliar movement in a series of concordats.

The policy of negotiating with each nation separately over ecclesiastical grievances and reform had been employed by Martin V as a means of breaking up the Council of Constance. It had the advantage for the Popes of dividing the opposition to papal authority and of limiting the extent of concessions to local independence. At the same time the policy did encourage the growth of national churches and initiated a process of negotiated reduction of papal influence. The concordats agreed by Martin V were largely concerned with restricting papal rights of reservation of and provision to benefices, and with limiting ecclesiastical dues payable to Rome and appeals to Rome. These concordats, and later negotiations such as the Concordat of Vienna agreed between Nicholas V and the Emperor in 1448, were not particularly effective as reforming instruments. They were politico-religious treaties which tended to transfer some authority from Pope to princes, thus winning the latter away from the cause of more far-reaching reform. The recognition of national churches implied in these negotiations sometimes encouraged unilateral action by the churches themselves as in the Pragmatic Sanction of Bourges by which the French clergy with the support of the Crown placed very extensive limitations on papal authority in France. But the Pragmatic Sanction itself became a subject of negotiation and diplomatic manoeuvring between the Popes and Louis XI, so that its revocation became a bargaining counter for papal support in French foreign and dynastic policy. During the fifteenth century with the interest of the Popes turned towards temporal power, it was increasingly the case that Church reform and ecclesiastical authority became pawns in papal diplomacy.

In keeping with the shift to a secular diplomacy, papal nuncios were rapidly ceasing to be ecclesiastical envoys and becoming ambassadors. The Papacy contributed greatly to the development of international diplomacy and the Pope's nuncios, like the representatives of other Italian states, were becoming resident ambassadors towards the end of the fifteenth century. Alexander VI, the most active diplomat of all the Renaissance Popes, played a major part in this trend and by the end of his pontificate resident nuncios were established in Spain, France, England, Venice, and the Empire.[3]

Dangerous as these developments were for the cause of reform, they played their part in the victory of the Renaissance Popes over the conciliar movement. Alfonso V of Aragon was won away from the cause of the Council of Basle at the Treaty of Terracina; the Emperor Frederick III by the Concordat of Vienna. By 1450 it could be said that the papal monarchy was restored. In that year Nicholas V held a triumphant Jubilee; pilgrims and cash poured into Rome and assisted in the rapid transformation of the city into a suitable capital for the Renaissance Popes. In the same year Juan de Torquemada produced his *Summa de Ecclesia* which was a complete and violent restatement of the doctrine of papal supremacy. Then in 1452 Frederick III visited Rome and was the last Emperor to be crowned in Rome by the Pope. Eight years later Pius II seemed to consolidate the victory with his Bull *Execrabilis* declaring any appeal to a General Council as a superior authority to the Pope to be anathema. The fact that Nicholas was a scholar of humble origins and Pius an ex-conciliarist indicates that the Renaissance Popes were not just autocrats determined to ride roughshod over any opposition to their authority. Their belief in the rightness of their cause was uncompromising; they were practical men and in this perhaps they enjoyed an advantage over the conciliarists who tended to be idealists.

In one sense the Popes of the second half of the fifteenth century did not appear to be very practical and this was in their constant attempts to launch a crusade against the triumphant Turks. No Pope of this period was more earnest in this endeavour than Nicholas V's successor, the first Borgia Pope, Calixtus III. For three years, as we shall see, he devoted his failing strength to trying to stimulate the crusading movement. Following him Pius II died on the eve of leading a forlorn venture to the Eastern Mediterranean. Hopes of a crusade played their part in the election of both the wealthy and influential Venetian Paul II and the Franciscan friar Sixtus IV. Even Alexander VI paid at least lip service to the same ideal. But the crusading ideal in the fifteenth century was already an optimistic, and unrealistic, one. The demographic and economic crises of the fourteenth century had temporarily reversed the expansionist urge which had played so great a part in the era of the crusades. Nor were the princes of Europe any more prepared to answer the Pope's call to a crusade than they were to allow him to receive taxes from their kingdoms or install bishops in their cathedrals. Yet the Renaissance Popes by taking the initiative against the Turkish threat were both responding to an urge that was still widely felt, and were also specifically claiming that position as leaders of Christendom which they still felt to be theirs. The call to a crusade, idealistic as it may have seemed, was itself an assertion of papal leadership and those who failed to respond to it were placed to some extent in an inferior bargaining position.[4]

But however anxious the Renaissance Popes were to assert their supremacy on a wide front, it was the establishment of their position as Italian princes which in practice occupied most of their energies. At a moment when the Italian state system was stabilising itself round a group of larger states whose strength to some extent balanced each other out, the Popes as the rulers of a large part of Central Italy stretching from the Tyrrhenian Sea to the Adriatic were inevitably committed to play a part in Italian politics.[5] Their first concern in their relations with the other Italian states was the protection of the frontiers of the Papal States. To the south lay the Kingdom of Naples, the object of dispute between the Kings of Aragon and the Dukes of Anjou. Naples was a fief of the Papacy which gave the Popes added reason for a close interest in Neapolitan affairs, and throughout the long struggle between Aragonese and Angevin relations with Naples were at the forefront of papal diplomacy. The Popes of the fourteenth century tended to support the Angevins but were never averse to giving assistance to their rivals if the Angevin rulers seemed to be becoming too independent or hostile. The constant aim of papal policy was in fact to keep Naples impotent or as far as possible subservient. The emergence of Alfonso V of Aragon as successful claimant to the Neapolitan throne in 1442 was obviously potentially dangerous, as at this moment the Aragonese empire was reaching the limit of its expansion. Alfonso was the ruler of Sicily and Sardinia as well as Aragon, Catalonia and Valencia. The appearance of such a ruler in Naples was just the threat which the Popes always sought to avoid, but Eugenius IV realised that Alfonso's support in his conflict with the Council of Basle was crucial and so he accepted the situation. Calixtus III attempted to undermine the Aragonese position in Naples by refusing recognition to Alfonso's illegitimate son Ferrante and giving encouragement to the Angevins. But with the failure of the Angevin line and the passing of Angevin claims to the Kings of an increasingly united France the alternative to the Aragonese in Naples was becoming an ever more dangerous power. Innocent VIII offered support to the dissident Neapolitan barons as an alternative means of weakening his southern neighbour, and both he and his predecessor, Sixtus IV, linked their own families by marriage with that of the Aragonese in Naples as an additional means of gaining security.

On the northern frontiers of the Papal States there was no one single power which posed the same problem as did Naples to the south. Florence was traditionally Guelph but there were nevertheless two serious clashes between the Popes and the Tuscan republic. In 1375 the War of the Eight Saints broke out as Florence, becoming increasingly aggressive in her attempts to dominate Tuscany, clashed with the energetic vicars of the Avignonese Popes trying to establish control in the Papal States. The Pazzi War of 1478–80 was primarily caused by Sixtus IV as he endeavoured to extend the influence of his family northwards. With Venice whose frontier marched with that of the most distant and turbulent area of the Papal States, the Romagna, papal diplomacy pursued a shifting policy. Despite growing Venetian interest in the Romagna, the Renaissance Popes, two of whom were Venetians, tended to seek to preserve good relations with Venice. Venetian help was vital for any crusading project, and it was in alliance with

Venice that Sixtus IV sought to subdue one of the more independent of his vassals, the Duke of Ferrara. On this occasion by 1483 Sixtus was forced to renounce his plans and abandon his Venetian alliance by the other Italian powers.

Papal relations with the last of the major Italian states, the Duchy of Milan, were controlled less by immediate concern for territorial security and more by the general situation of Italian politics. The alliance of the Lombard communes had always been sought by medieval Popes as an advance shield against Imperial armies crossing the Alps, and in the fifteenth century the key to Italian security from foreign invasion lay in a strong and confident Milanese duchy. Thus the Renaissance Popes, particularly as long as Francesco Sforza was alive, tended to seek a good understanding with Milan. A peaceful Italy, free from foreign influence and secure from foreign invasion, emerged as the main diplomatic aim of the Renaissance Papacy. In this situation the security of the Papal States was assured, and the Pope, rather than resort to arms, could claim to be the arbiter in Italian quarrels. Nicholas V was prominent in the negotiations for the Italian League in 1454 which brought temporary peace to Italy, and Calixtus III raged at those who sought to disturb that peace. Pius II reversed the Angevin tendencies of his predecessor and sought, in alliance with Francesco Sforza, to restrain the growth of French influence in Italy. Under Sixtus IV the Pope's image as a pacifier and arbitrator became rather distorted, and Innocent VIII although suited temperamentally to the role was too ineffective to carry it out. The continued presence of foreign armies on Italian soil after 1494 altered the context of the problem, and both Alexander VI and Julius II became concerned with giving the Popes a role as the leaders of an Italian resurgence which would drive the foreigners out of Italy.

This close involvement in Italian politics meant that the Renaissance Popes had to be politically and militarily strong.

The Papal States, on which the papal claim to be an Italian power rested and the protection of which played so great a role in papal policies, needed to be securely administered. The Popes depended increasingly on the Papal States both for the personnel of their armies and for the money with which those armies were paid. As direct papal authority outside Italy declined and the proceeds from the spiritual revenues of the Church diminished, so the temporal revenues collected by the Popes as rulers of the Papal States became vitally important. It was on well paid *condottieri*, on good artillery, on locally raised militia infantry, that papal authority was coming to depend in the second half of the fifteenth century. The spiritual weapons like excommunication and interdict were still used but often for political purposes. The path of reform which might have led to a recovery of spiritual authority seemed too difficult a one for Popes who already lacked that authority. The Renaissance Popes were not unaware of the need for reforms of the Church, and they included amongst their number truly pious men; but apart from piecemeal reforms largely concerned with the religious orders they were able to achieve little in this direction.[6]

It is within the ranks of these Popes and against the background of these developments that we have to view the activities of the two Borgia Popes, Calixtus III and Alexander VI. As Popes they were princes of Renaissance Europe and rulers of a Renaissance state, and right or wrong though the decision to accept this trend may have been, it was a decision taken consistently by all the Popes between 1420 and 1527. The Throne of St. Peter was no place for a mystic, and at no time was this more true than in the fifteenth century.

CHAPTER TWO

THE PAPAL STATES IN THE FIFTEENTH CENTURY

A fifteenth-century traveller wishing to visit Rome had several choices of route open to him. He could go by sea landing either at Civitavecchia, a port the activity of which expanded rapidly after 1460 with the exploitation of the newly discovered Tolfa alum mines, or at Ostia at the mouth of the Tiber. A galley at certain times of the year could even take him up to the walls of Rome itself where he would probably disembark at S. Paolo fuori le Mura and enter the Holy City on foot. But sea voyages were still regarded with considerable trepidation by travellers, not so much because of any strong possibility of disaster but because they necessitated great discomfort and tended to be of uncertain duration.

Therefore a vast majority of the travellers approaching Rome came by road. If they were pilgrims from the north hurrying towards the Holy City they would come down the most direct route, the old Via Cassia through Tuscany. The coast road, the Via Aurelia, was little used by international traffic as it passed through the malaria infested swamps of the Maremma. Even travellers from Genoa and Pisa would strike inland and join those from Bologna and Florence as they passed through Siena. Siena was still an independent republic despite the progress of Florentine imperialism which had absorbed nearly all the other Tuscan cities, but towards the end of the century it was falling under the domination of the Petrucci family in the person of the intelligent and unscrupulous Pandolfo. From there the pilgrims would cross the frontier into the Papal States under the watchful eyes of the castellan of the towering frontier fortress of Radicofani and ride on through the papal cities of Acquapendente and Viterbo, across the brigand infested ridges of the Monti Cimini and down into the Roman Campagna. So far they would have been crossing the province of the Papal States known as the Patrimony of St. Peter, administered by a rector or legate resident in Viterbo, but now they would be entering the District of Rome governed, at least in theory, from the Capitol in Rome. The road was bad, the air insalubrious, the countryside apparently deserted. But the scarcity of population was more apparent than real; the inhabitants of this area had long since withdrawn from the main roads and settled in isolated, well-defended villages hidden in the ravines of this deceptively barren volcanic landscape. The villages under their feudal lords enjoyed a vitality which would have surprised the traveller who was scarcely aware of their existence, and an independence of Rome which belied their proximity to the city. The last forty mile stage of the pilgrimage would have seemed like the longest and most unpleasant, until climbing out of the marshy Baccano crater the pilgrims could see laid out some twenty miles in front of them the towers and walls of their goal.

But if the traveller was in no hurry and wished perhaps to gain a more comprehensive idea of the extent of the temporal domains of the Pope, he could travel from Bologna to Rome without ever leaving the Papal States. Bologna and Ferrara were the northernmost cities of the Papal States. Ferrara, ruled by the Este family as perpetual vicars of the Church, enjoyed as did the other vicariates a considerable degree of autonomy; Bologna, although in theory a papal city governed by a legate, had become by the end of the fifteenth century a preserve of the Bentivoglio family. From Bologna the great

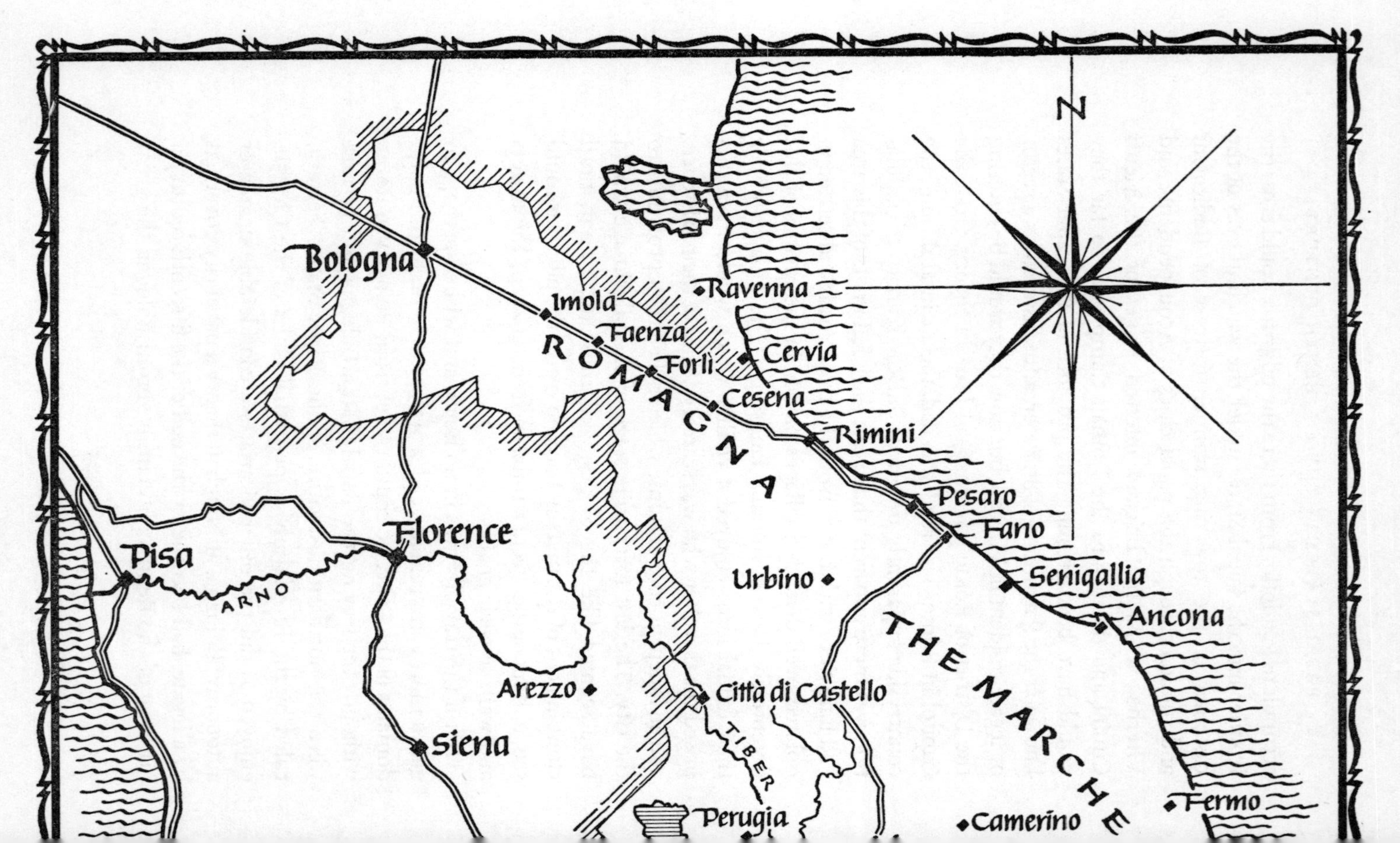
N
Bologna
Imola
Faenza
Forlì
Cesena
Ravenna
Cervia
Rimini
Pesaro
Fano
Senigallia
Ancona
Fermo
Camerino
ROMAGNA
THE MARCHE
Urbino
Florence
Pisa
ARNO
Arezzo
Città di Castello
TIBER
Siena
Perugia

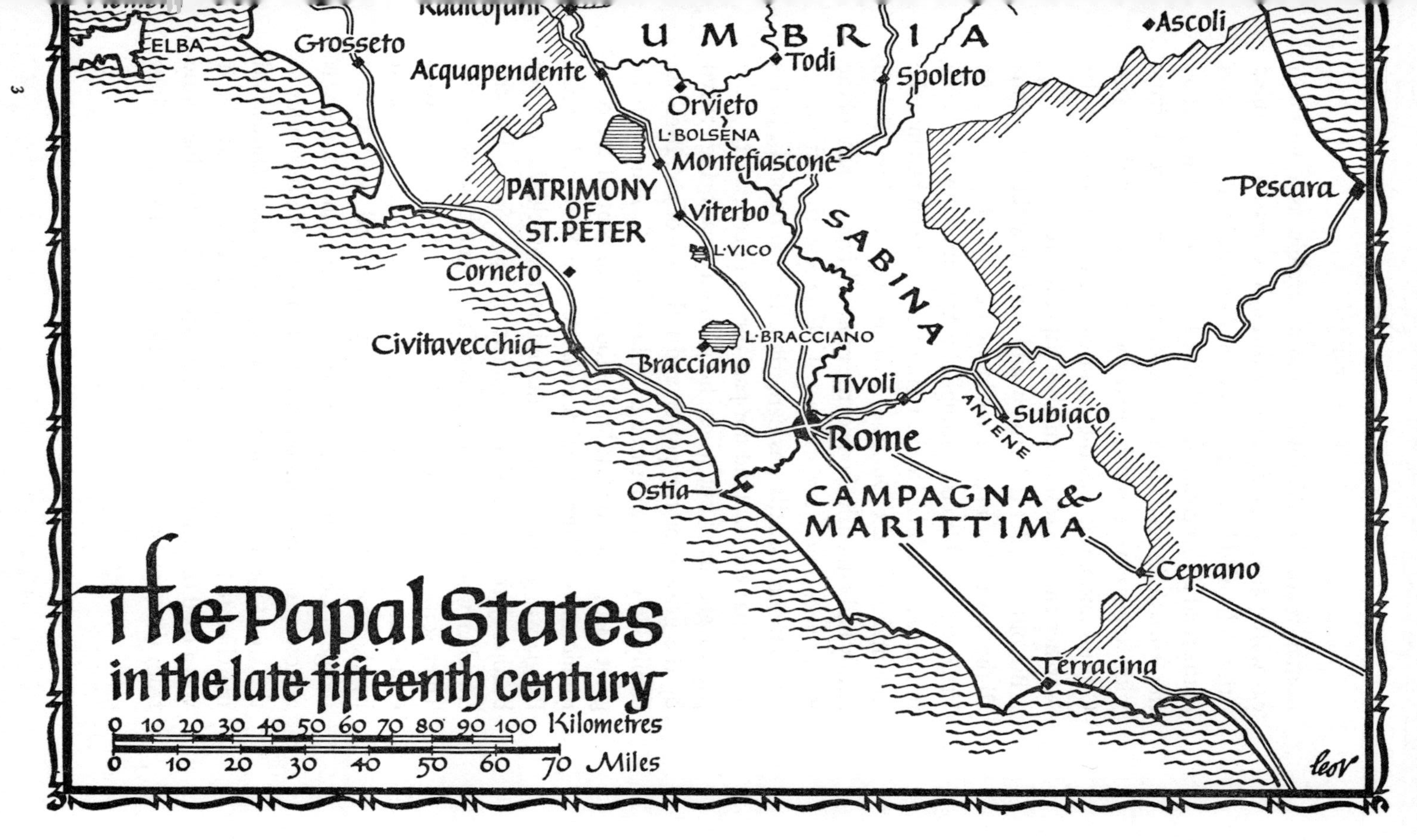
UMBRIA
Ascoli
ELBA
Grosseto
Acquapendente
Todi
Spoleto
Orvieto
L·BOLSENA
Montefiascone
Pescara
PATRIMONY OF ST.PETER
Viterbo
SABINA
L·VICO
Corneto
L·BRACCIANO
Civitavecchia
Bracciano
Tivoli
ANIENE
Subiaco
Rome
Ostia
CAMPAGNA &
MARITTIMA
Ceprano
Terracina
The Papal States
in the late fifteenth century
0 10 20 30 40 50 60 70 80 90 100 Kilometres
0 10 20 30 40 50 60 70 Miles
leov

Roman road, the Via Emilia, ran as straight as a die south eastwards across the Romagna through a series of fortified cities each ruled by a vicar in the name of the Pope. At the end of the road lay Ancona, after Venice the busiest Italian port on the Adriatic. Ancona and the trade links across the Adriatic with Ragusa were much used by Florentines trading with Constantinople. It was the main city in the province of the Marches and the seat of another papal legate.

But our traveller to Rome would not follow the Via Emilia all the way to Ancona; at Fano he would turn off inland on the Via Flaminia which cut through the Appenines down into the province of Umbria. On the right as the road climbed into the mountains was the Duchy of Urbino where the Montefeltro family had established one of the most cultivated courts of the Renaissance but were still papal vicars. On the left out of sight among the hills was Camerino. Then in front the plains of Umbria; the road did not pass through Perugia where the papal legate lived but where his authority was being eroded by the growth of the power and influence of the Baglione family. It ran down through Foligno and Spoleto with its great castle built by Cardinal Albornoz to control the communications of the Papal States. Here in Spoleto Lucrezia Borgia was governor for a time and in this castle she and her brother Jofrè spent some months in 1499. So at last the traveller would enter the Roman Campagna by crossing the Tiber some forty miles above Rome. The fortress of Civita Castellana guarded this crossing, the fortress which was held by the Borgias for most of thirty years and was the last refuge of Cesare in 1503. The road from there into Rome was almost as desolate and depressing as the Cassia ten miles to the west; but it was the road along which Constantine had marched to his great victory at the battle of Ponte Milvio. It was a road on which the constant expectancy of seeing Rome from the crest of each successive ridge alleviated the tedious and uncomfortable journey. Along this road the traveller would reach Rome, coming down the last slope towards Ponte Milvio rebuilt and refortified by Nicholas V and Calixtus III, and making his way along the last stage of the Flaminia to the Porta del Popolo, the northern gate of the city.

If he wished to continue his journey southwards and see the last province of the Papal States, Campagna and Marittima, the traveller would once again avoid the unhealthy coast and the Pontine marshes and keep to the inland road through the Alban Hills and the castles of the Roman Colonna and Gaetani families. The journey to the Neapolitan frontier at Ceprano was not a long one and most of the lords of this area tended to be allied with Naples, so it was towards this frontier that the Popes of the fifteenth century looked with the greatest apprehension.

The nominal extent of the Papal States had remained constant since the end of the eighth century when the personal estates of the Pope round Rome had been united with a vague political and administrative control over the outlying provinces as a result of an alliance with the Frankish conquerors of the Lombards. Pepin and Charlemagne had consented to what amounted to a division of Italy with the Popes, and it was the so-called donation of Pepin rather than the forged donation of Constantine which was the real authority for papal control over Central Italy. But control was not fully established until Innocent III acquired the March of Ancona and the Duchy of Spoleto. He then divided the area into provinces and established the provincial government of rectors.[1] Within the framework of this provincial government there was a place for locally summoned Parliaments and for a considerable degree of communal autonomy for the larger cities. It was these communal liberties which were to a large extent usurped throughout Italy in the late thirteenth and early fourteenth centuries by the emerging *signori*. The Papal

States were no exception to the general tendency towards autocratic government, and it was this trend rather than any dramatic breakdown of papal administration during the absence of the Popes in Avignon which led to a number of 'tyrants' setting themselves up in the outlying papal cities. The fourteenth century was in fact a period of steady strengthening of papal administration in so far as the disturbed state of Italy allowed this. Much of the resources of the Avignonese papacy were spent on this task and a number of able soldier administrators were employed of whom Cardinal Albornoz and Cardinal Robert of Geneva were the outstanding. The work of Albornoz is particularly well known as it was his *Constitutiones Aegidianae* which codified the administrative law of the Papal States, and it was he who sought to control and formalise the growth of the *signori* by the creation of the system of the apostolic vicariates. By this system the *de facto* master of a papal city was recognised as ruler in return for the annual payment of a *census*. The vicars were naturally expected to rule well in the Pope's name and to answer a papal call to arms, but they collected all the revenues from the city and were sometimes able to get their vicariate extended for life and in exceptional cases made hereditary in their families. The vicariate system was widely employed in the Romagna and was the type of government inherited by the Renaissance Popes.[2] But it was essentially a compromise devised by Albornoz as a means of avoiding the complete alienation of the cities while he was not strong enough to crush the *signori* by force. It was a denial of the central authority of the Pope and a permanent check on any attempts to improve the financial structure of papal temporal government. Furthermore it became intolerable when the vicars nearly all of whom were *condottieri* became attached by contract to other Italian powers. Therefore it was the policy of all the Renaissance Popes to try to erode the powers of the vicars either by force or by tying their states more closely to the Papacy by marriage.

The Este family in Ferrara were the most firmly established of the vicars and attempts to overthrow them by Sixtus IV proved unsuccessful. They behaved very much as independent princes and were sufficiently powerful to act as a useful buffer against Venetian advance. To the south lay Forlì and Imola which were recovered from their vicars by Martin V but subsequently allowed to return to the hands of the former rulers.[3] Sixtus IV married his nephew, Girolamo Riario, to Caterina Sforza and conferred the united vicariate of the two cities on him. After the death of Sixtus and then the murder of Girolamo in 1488, Caterina Sforza continued to rule the two cities in the name of her Riario children. She was a violent, vengeful woman whose activities are often mistakenly taken to represent the typical behaviour of all the vicars.[4] Sandwiched between these two cities on the Via Emilia was the vicariate of the Manfredi in Faenza. The Manfredi were old established vicars who enjoyed the friendship and protection of Florence. Cesena, the next city along the road, was recovered for the direct government of the Church after the death without heirs of the vicar, Malatesta Novello, in 1465.[5]

In Rimini the main Malatesta line retained their vicariate throughout the fifteenth century despite the efforts of both Pius II and Paul II to evict them.[6] The Malatesta were noted *condottieri* and enjoyed considerable support from the other Italian powers in their struggles with the Popes, but it was galling in the extreme for the Renaissance Popes to be powerless to impose their will on their supposed vassals. The last of the Romagna vicars were the Sforza in Pesaro. Francesco Sforza had been ruler of Pesaro before he became Duke of Milan, and he passed his vicariate on to his brother Alessandro from whom it passed eventually to Giovanni Sforza to whom Lucrezia Borgia was married in 1493.

On the fringes of the Romagna there were a number of smaller vicariates and semi-independent lordships of a less official status. In Città di Castello the Vitelli family were in command; in Camerino the Varano. Fermo was ruled by Oliverotto Euffreducci by the end of the century and in Senigallia another nephew of Sixtus IV was installed as the son-in-law of the Duke of Urbino. Finally the Montefeltro Dukes of Urbino were rulers of a considerable state and rivalled the Este for the magnificence of their court and their independence of their nominal overlord, the Pope.

The use of the word 'tyrant' to describe these men is somewhat misleading. Their authority was often considerably restricted by the extent of the survival of communal institutions in their cities and by their need for popular support to preserve their positions. These were in fact more potent restraints on them than the papal overlordship which they scarcely acknowledged and on account of which they rarely paid the expected *census*. They were by no means all the arbitrary and hated tyrants described by Machiavelli in his *Discourses*;[7] some like the Montefeltro, Este and Manfredi seem to have been efficient and conscientious rulers; many were famous patrons of the arts like Sigismondo Malatesta, the patron of Alberti, and Federigo da Montefeltro who employed Piero della Francesca. But they were all obstructions to that centralisation of administration in the Papal States which was the aim of the Renaissance Popes. Just as Louis XI of France sought to break up the apanages, just as Edward IV and Henry VII battled with the Marcher Lords, so did the Renaissance Popes press on the vicars taking every opportunity to restrain or if possible to oust them. But before the election of Alexander VI the policy had been unconcerted and rarely successful; little impression had been made on the position of the vicars in a series of spasmodic assaults and indecisive intrigues. The Romagna remained the weak point of the Papal

States, loosely controlled and wide open to foreign influences.

In the other provinces of the Papal States the authority of the Popes was stronger once Martin V had confronted the task of restoring law and order after a disastrous period of fifty years between a series of rebellions against the papal governors, mostly Frenchmen, in the 1370s and the restoration of a unified Papacy after the Council of Constance. The rectors, or legates as they often came to be called as cardinals were appointed to the provincial governorships, were assisted by elaborate administrations which reproduced in miniature that of the Curia in Rome. They had more or less complete judicial authority in their provinces, and were assisted by a treasurer who handled the provincial revenues. In addition to the provincial governments a number of cities and districts had rectors or governors appointed direct from Rome. In such cases there was often a confusion of authority as such a local governor, although nominally dependent on the provincial legate, was often also directly supervised from Rome. Such a situation was the result of the inherent particularism which affected fifteenth-century Italy, and this and the disorder caused by factional jealousies were still, despite the elaborate machinery of papal government, the key factors in the internal politics of the Papal States.

One of the main concerns of the Popes in extending and strengthening their authority in the Papal States was financial. Each provincial treasurer, having paid the expenses of provincial government, was expected to send any surplus to the Apostolic Camera in Rome, the central treasury of the Papacy.[8] The taxes which were collected by these treasurers varied from province to province, but in all the provinces by the fifteenth century either a tithe or a hearth tax was collected, sometimes both. Every community had its assessment; every household had to pay its share. In addition the treasurers collected the proceeds of the special tax on the Jews and all the judicial fines imposed by the legates and their courts. The other sources of temporal income were controlled directly by the Apostolic Camera through tax farmers. These included the customs revenue and gate tolls of the main cities, the salt monopolies, grain export licences, and the transhumance dues payable on herds of livestock which were moved every spring and autumn long distances from winter pasture up into the hills and then back again. The Camera also received the *census* payments direct from the vicars. Finally the city of Rome through its customs and tolls contributed about one-fifth of the total temporal revenues of the Apostolic Camera.

To have some idea of how important these temporal revenues were becoming to the Papacy and how crucial it therefore was to establish control over the Papal States from which these revenues were raised, we must look briefly at some figures. During the 1370s the income of the Papacy varied between 200,000 and 300,000 florins; of this sum about one quarter or less was temporal revenue. At the time of Martin V in the 1420s the total income had dropped to about 170,000 florins but very nearly half of this, 80,000, was contributed by the Papal States. The Schism had had a disastrous effect on the spiritual revenues and it says much for the success of the policy of the Renaissance Popes that by 1480 total income seems to have risen to about 290,000 florins. By this time temporal revenues had doubled since the 1420s to about 170,000 florins a year. Spiritual revenues were also increasing again, but through the growth of the sale of offices and indulgences and through increased fees for appeals and requests to the Pope, rather than through the traditional spiritual taxes like annates, first fruits and Peter's Pence which now provided less than one seventh of the total income.

This dramatic increase in the temporal revenues was in large part the result of the discovery of the alum mines at

Tolfa. Alum was a vital commodity in both the cloth and tanning industries; it was used for cleaning the wool and the leather. The main source of supply for medieval Europe was the Genoese controlled mines in western Turkey. The occupation of these mines by the Turks led to a great increase in the price of Turkish alum, and the Popes among others launched a drive to discover new sources of alum. As far as the Popes were concerned economic self interest was linked to religious fervour in that the discovery of a reliable source of alum in the West would avoid the necessity of trading with the infidel. Thus when in 1462 Giovanni di Castro discovered alum in the Tolfa mountains behind Civitavecchia, efficient exploitation of the deposits became a matter of first priority. The first big contracts for the distribution of the alum were given to the Medici, and it was made incumbent on Christians to buy papal rather than Turkish alum.[9] Sixtus IV subsequently transferred the alum contracts to his own co-nationals, the Genoese, and by 1480 the Apostolic Camera was enjoying an additional income of 50,000 florins from this source, almost one third of the total temporal revenues.[10] In theory the Tolfa receipts were put into a special fund for crusading purposes, but even if this division was rigorously observed it clearly released other revenues for domestic purposes. By the 1480s Sixtus was spending 100,000 florins a year, or over a third of his total revenues, on his army, but even so the improvement in his finances made possible the great artistic projects for which his pontificate is famous.

The Tolfa mines lay in the District of Rome and their protection was obviously of great importance to the Popes. This was therefore an additional reason for suppressing disorder and establishing political control round the city. The main source of disorder was the deeply entrenched position of the Roman nobility in this area, and it was the Anguillara family who displayed their defiance of the Pope by sacking the mines in the 1460s. Paul II took violent counter measures against the family, seizing their castles and breaking up their estates.

This was one of several similar outbursts by the Renaissance Popes against their turbulent nobility, for just as the independence of the vicars of the Romagna was a barrier to good papal administration so was the special position of the Roman barons. While the former owed their strength to the fact that they operated at the furthest distance from Rome, the latter had profited from their proximity to Rome. Their strength had been built up by natural feudal processes and by the extent to which successive Popes had relied on them as soldiers and Roman leaders. At one stage they had played a major part in the election of the Pope and throughout the thirteenth and fourteenth centuries they had been building up a position as the lords of the Roman Campagna. The estates round Rome which at one time had belonged largely either to the Pope directly or to the great Roman monasteries were by the end of the fourteenth century almost entirely in the hands of the Roman nobility. The nepotistic Popes of the late thirteenth century had advanced different families in turn so that Rome became surrounded by great baronial estates, to some extent balanced against each other but at the same time united in their resistance to any central authority. To the north of Rome lay the estates of the Prefects of Vico, hereditary Prefects of Rome and dominant in an area stretching from Civitavecchia across to their stronghold at Vico. Between them and Rome lay the estates of the Orsini and Anguillara families. Astride the Tiber and covering the Sabina were the Savelli. To the east and south-east of Rome the Colonna were dominant, while due south astride the roads to Naples lay first the Conti and then beyond them the Gaetani.

The consequences of this situation were disastrous. The roads into Rome were all controlled by the barons which at the best meant the imposition of unofficial tolls on travellers and merchandise, and at the worst meant armed pillage of the essential lines of communication. The feuds amongst the barons meant constant disorder and serious disruption of the Campagna which was supposed to provide food supplies for the city. The inhabitants of the area were ruled almost independently by their feudal lords and it was difficult for the Pope even to raise troops without the consent of the barons. The great families still participated in papal elections through the cardinalates which were distributed to their members as if by right, and through the armed forces which they assembled at each conclave. They also sold their services both as soldiers and political allies to the Pope's enemies, particularly Naples, and did not hesitate to join foreign armies in attacks on Rome. It was in alliance with the Colonna that the French had acted against Boniface VIII in 1303, and in alliance with the Gaetani that the Avignonese cardinals had rejected Urban VI in 1378.

The early Renaissance Popes, financially and militarily weak, relying on the barons themselves to provide much of the leadership and the manpower for papal armies, were at a serious disadvantage in dealing with this situation. Their method had to be at first to play one family off against another, to destroy one at the cost of strengthening the others. Martin V, a Colonna himself, used his family to attack the Orsini and left a legacy of Colonna predominance to Eugenius IV. Eugenius reversed the situation and with the aid of the Orsini and his warlike cardinal Vitelleschi destroyed the power of the Prefects, allies of the Colonna, and razed their fortress of Vico to the ground forever. But this was not before an alliance of the barons had exiled the Pope from his capital for eight years. Nicholas V managed to bring some peace to the Campagna, but Calixtus, anxious though he was for peaceful conditions at home in which to further the cause of his crusade, was drawn into a violent conflict with Orsini, the echoes of which were still reverberating when his nephew Rodrigo became Pope thirty-five years later. Paul II rooted out another of the families, the Anguillara, but again at the cost of strengthening the Orsini who now completely dominated the area north of Rome. It was said that Virginio Orsini from his stronghold at Bracciano could call on the support of 10–20,000 vassals.[11] Sixtus IV and his nephew, Girolamo Riario, allied themselves with the Orsini, but on his death the Colonna swept back into the ascendancy with the support of Innocent VIII.

Within the city of Rome itself the establishment of papal control was achieved rather earlier than it was in the surrounding district. There were long traditions of both aristocratic and republican government in Rome. The office of Prefect, by now a hereditary title, represented to some extent the former tradition; that of the Senator, at some times the leader of an aristocratic senatorial class, at others elected by popular vote, seemed to combine both traditions. But by the beginning of the fourteenth century the appointment of the Senator was subject to papal approval and the statutes of the city, although appearing remarkably democratic, were ratified by the Pope and liable to arbitrary alteration.[12] Rome had never developed any large scale commercial or industrial activity; it remained, as it had been in classical times, a great parasite. As Mommsen put it: 'there has perhaps never existed a great city so thoroughly destitute of the means of support as Rome; importation on the one hand, and domestic manufacture by slaves on the other, rendered any free industry from the outset impossible there'.[13] The same still applied in the late Middle Ages. All food supplies and manufactured goods were imported; Rome herself produced nothing. The results of this were twofold. In the first place the city was entirely dependent on the presence of the Pope and the papal court for its economic life. The revenues of the Papacy took the place of the tribute of the Empire as Rome's means of support. The Popes now provided the bread and the circuses which made life in Rome supportable. Hence there was an inevitable tendency towards subordination to papal rule which offset all the idealistic republican ardour of Cola di Rienzo in the fourteenth century and Stefano Porcari in the fifteenth. Secondly this lack of an independent economic life meant the lack of a middle class; that class which by its independence and size was bringing stability to the cities of northern Italy. Thus in Rome there was a great gulf between the aristocracy whose interests increasingly lay in their estates outside Rome and whose opposition to papal power within Rome was steadily bought off, and an artisan and working class which was incapable of resistance to papal pretensions.

The return of the Popes to Rome in 1420 set the seal on this growing papal authority in the city. The papal vice chamberlain became in practice the governor of the city and by the end of the fifteenth century he was titular governor also. The Senator, a papal nominee, took his orders from the vice chamberlain, and the finances of the city were integrated with those of the Papacy as a whole. A communal administration continued to function on the Capitol but most of the officials were appointed by the Pope. The marshals and the judges were papal officials and many lived in the Vatican; the guardians of the walls were paid by the Pope.

So the Holy City became transformed from an independent medieval commune, in which the Pope to some extent appeared a guest with his influence and authority confined to the Borgo round St. Peter's and the Vatican, to the unified administrative capital of a considerable territorial state. In keeping with this transformation the city began to change in its appearance.

The Rome to which Martin V had returned in 1420 was a desolate city.[14] Its population had shrunk to about 25,000 and only small areas of the great extent of ancient Rome enclosed by the walls of Marcus Aurelius were still occupied. The inhabitants of late medieval Rome were mostly huddled in the bend of the Tiber round the Pantheon, the ruins of the stadium of Domitian soon to become the Piazza Navona, and the Campo dei Fiori. Scattered houses were to be found on the slopes of the Capitol and the slopes of the Esquiline facing the Forum, but most of the seven hills were gardens and vineyards. The Forum itself was a cattle pasture. The area round the Lateran had been sacked in the previous century; the Palatine was abandoned; the Aventine occupied only by the old monastery of SS.Alessio and Bonifacio. Trastevere on the opposite bank of the Tiber was fairly thickly populated, but the Borgo round the Vatican had suffered severely from piratical raids, being exposed on the coast side of the city. With the steady decline of the population many of the churches had fallen out of use and were neglected; little had been spent on their upkeep by the Avignonese Popes. The palace of the Senator, burnt at the time of Cola di Rienzo's revolution, had never been restored. There were no great private palaces, as the nobility preferred to live in grim fortified strongholds fashioned out of the ruins of the great public buildings of Imperial Rome. There were no wealthy merchants to lead an architectural revival. Only one aqueduct had been left intact by the Goths a thousand years before, and this, the Acqua Vergine, was erratic and often ineffective. It was this as much as anything which had led the medieval population to concentrate in the unhealthier areas near the river, the only reliable source of water. Only three bridges across the river survived: the Ponte Sant'Angelo linking the Borgo with the rest of the city and dominated by the papal fortress Castel Sant'Angelo; the bridges linking the Isola Tiberina with both banks; and the bridge of the Senators, now the Ponte Rotto, which collapsed in the next century.

The great walls of the city had been maintained during the Middle Ages, although the defence of so vast a circuit must have been beyond the capabilities of so small a population, and the continued restoration of the walls was one of the tasks which received priority from the Renaissance Popes. All the Popes from Martin V onwards also devoted their energies to restoring the churches. Cardinals, once more resident in Rome, were encouraged to restore their titular churches and each pontificate produced a new crop of restorations with all the accompanying commissions for sculptors and painters that these involved. The cardinals in their new role as 'princes of the Church' began to build the great palaces which Rome lacked. The Palazzo San Marco [now Venezia], built by Paul II while still a cardinal and occupied by him while Pope, was the outstanding example; but the palaces of Cardinals Nardini, Borgia, Giuliano and Domenico della Rovere, and Raffaele Riario, marked the gradual evolution of a distinctive Roman Renaissance style of domestic architecture which reached fruition in the work of Bramante and Michelangelo.[15]

Meanwhile Nicholas V restored the Acqua Vergine and created the first Trevi Fountain at its end where three roads (*tre vie*) met. Sixtus IV built the Ponte Sisto and paved the Piazza Navona and the Campo dei Fiori, turning them from untidy fields into busy market places. The moving of the main market of the city from the foot of the Capitol to the Piazza Navona was yet another indication of the declining importance of the communal administration. Many of the streets were paved for the first time and the medieval arcades, which made the streets so narrow and so dangerous in times of factional disturbance, were pulled down. Much of this work was done by the *maestri delle strade*, a group of communal officials who had functioned spasmodically during the Middle Ages, but were now revived with added powers by the Popes. The *maestri* could impose fines on those who dumped rubbish in the streets or refused to pull down unsafe houses; they could commandeer houses for development and order citizens to assist in the paving of streets.

The results of a century of rule by the Renaissance Popes were remarkable. Long before Sixtus V and the well known formalisation of the planning of papal Rome, the city had begun to take on an appearance worthy of a capital. By 1500 Rome was beginning to become a city of domes instead of medieval towers; the classicism of Bramante and the San Gallo family was replacing the disordered severity of the medieval styles. By 1526 the population had risen to 55,000

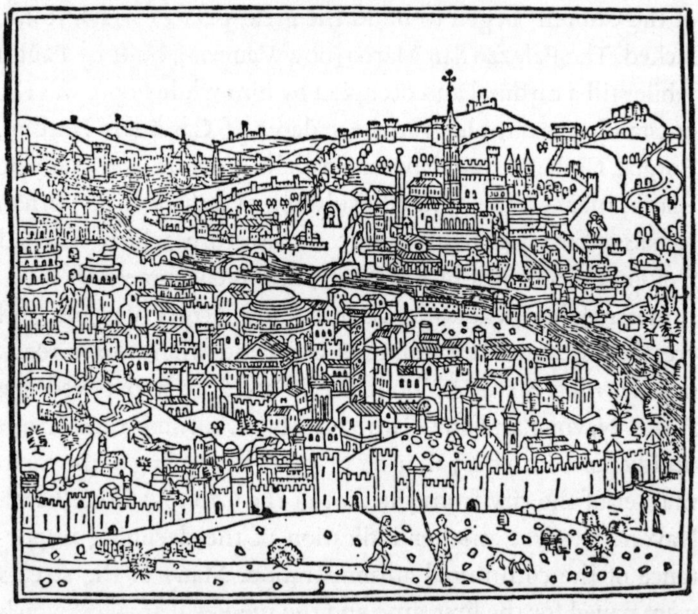

Rome about 1480; this woodcut from Jacopo Filippo Foresti da Bergamo, *Supplementum Chronicarum* (Venice, 1486) is one of the earliest views of the city. The detail from the area of the Pincio across to St. Peter's in the background is remarkably well observed.

and it was a population which included not only the great numbers of wealthy Curia officials, many of whom were foreigners, but also bankers, merchants and industrialists.

1 Rodrigo Borgia, Pope Alexander VI; detail of *The Resurrection* by Pinturicchio in the Borgia Apartments. This portrait was painted in 1493 and gives a good impression of the physical vigour and commanding personality of Rodrigo at the age of 62.

2 St. Peter's and the Vatican in the early sixteenth century; the drawing by Martin van Heemskerck gives an indication

The first sumptuary laws were imposed in 1473, an indication of the rising economic standards of the city as well as a desire to restrain ostentatious display in the capital of the Church.[16]

Eugenius IV was the last Pope who was forced to flee from Rome until the days of Napoleon. After his restoration the Popes were masters in their capital although it was still some time before they could claim to be masters in their state as a whole.

CHAPTER THREE

THE VATICAN AND THE PAPAL COURT

In 1489 Lorenzo the Magnificent succeeded in getting his son Giovanni created a cardinal at the age of thirteen by Innocent VIII with the proviso that he could not take his seat in the College for three years. When this time had elapsed the young cardinal set out for Rome and was soon followed by a letter of instructions and advice from his father, which not only embodied a very shrewd assessment of the papal court but also typified contemporary attitudes towards it.[1] For Lorenzo, while describing Rome as 'the very focus of all that is evil', schemed to get his young son established there because of the advantage that a cardinalate could be both to his family and to Florence. He was thus conforming to that secularising trend which was making Rome what he professed to abhor.

Just as the Popes of the Renaissance were growing more like the temporal princes of Europe, so their court was beginning to resemble those of their fellow sovereigns. With the growth of the papal civil service more and more of the personnel were laymen. Foreign ambassadors, bankers, soldiers, and artists thronged the Vatican apartments while the clerics frequently remained so only in name as their interests lay more in humanistic learning, in diplomacy, or in papal administration than in pastoral duties or in personal righteousness. The cardinals who remained the leaders of this court were frequently chosen for reasons other than Christian suitability. Many were the sons of princes, or ambitious relatives of

Popes, and as such were often eminently suited to play their part as princes of the Church. The Vatican had become a centre of temporal government and international intrigue as well as the headquarters of the Catholic Church.

Inevitably this secularisation brought a tendency towards sumptuousness and worldly style in the life and particularly in the entertainments of the Vatican court. Most of the Renaissance Popes managed to maintain a considerable degree of personal austerity for themselves and their immediate entourage. But prestige demanded that prominent visitors were properly entertained and that there was a magnificence and style to the outward appearance of the court. Cardinals who were accustomed to such a life were not lacking and they were entrusted with the main burden of entertaining princely visitors to Rome. Lorenzo de' Medici, the theme of whose letter to his son was moderation in all things, remarked that 'it is better for you to entertain your friends at home than to dine out often'. But increasingly secular entertainment began to intrude into the Vatican itself. Paul II, himself an ex-merchant and a Venetian aristocrat, continued to entertain in the Vatican and in the Palazzo San Marco as Pope as he had done as cardinal. It is probable that women first began to make their appearance in Vatican society during his pontificate. Earlier than this in 1457 Lucrezia d'Alagno, the mistress of Alfonso V, had been formally and respectfully received by Calixtus III when she came to Rome to attend the funeral of her brother Cardinal Piscicello.[2] Both the son, Franceschetto Cibo, and the grand-daughter, Battistina, of Innocent VIII were married in great state in the Vatican. Franceschetto married a daughter of Lorenzo de' Medici, a dynastic alliance which merited a splendid and triumphant display.[3]

That the Pope should have children who could be the objects of such secular festivities was no longer a matter of surprise to many people. Clerical immorality was one of the principal targets of the reformers and, although there was inevitably an element of exaggeration in their attacks, the mistresses and bastards of priests and prelates were common figures particularly in Italy. In the Renaissance there was a general disregard for the stigma of illegitimacy and this was extended to the children of the clergy. St. Francis Borgia was the great grandson of a Pope on his father's side and the grandson of an archbishop (himself the illegitimate son of a King) on his mother's but no one considered this any bar to him becoming General of the Jesuits. This was despite the fact that the Jesuits were in the sixteenth century the main defenders of the principle of clerical celibacy. There was a strong movement within the Church which was expressed at the Council of Trent, and of course was effective in the Reformed churches, to end the ban on clerical marriage. This was a natural tendency when the priesthood was becoming as much a lucrative profession as a matter of calling, and the sons of princes and nobles who entered the Church were scarcely expected to conform to strict ecclesiastical standards. Of the Renaissance Popes, Pius II and Julius II as well as Innocent VIII and Alexander VI certainly had children; Calixtus III, Sixtus IV and Pius III were all suspected, probably unjustifiably, of having them. Indeed Gregorovius credited Pius III with twelve children, but these seem to have been the progeny of imaginative and scurrilous chroniclers rather than of the Piccolomini Pope whose reputation was otherwise high.[4] For although this increasingly secular trend in ecclesiastical life, particularly at the upper levels, was to some extent natural and accepted by many, it was also widely and vociferously deplored. It was deplored by the conservative and traditional elements in the Church, and by the more spiritual of its leaders; but it was also deplored for less worthy reasons, out of fear for the growing political strength of Rome, and out of jealousy.

It was political opposition and jealousy which motivated

some of the more bitter attacks of the humanists on the Renaissance Popes. Propaganda was part of the stock in trade of humanist writers and they were employed for this purpose by the political opponents of the Renaissance Papacy. However the attacks of Filelfo and Vespasiano da' Bisticci on Calixtus III, and of Platina on Pius II and Paul II were prompted by more personal motives, by loss of patronage and by exclusion from the Vatican court. For the Popes of the Renaissance as well as being the creators of an ecclesiastical state had made themselves leaders of international culture. Eugenius IV during his long exile in Florence had imbibed to some extent the spirit of Florentine humanism, and Nicholas V was a product of the Florentine intellectual environment. The interests and patronage of Nicholas together with the rapid expansion of the opportunities in the Curia and in the households of cardinals for secretaries and chancellery clerks quickly attracted a new intellectual life to Rome. Lorenzo Valla, Filelfo, Alberti, Gianozzo Manetti, Flavio Biondo and Poggio Bracciolini were just a few of the intellectual figures who were attracted to Nicholas V's court.

Humanist ideas of the moral value of the active secular life and humanistic concern to reveal the greatness of ancient Rome were of increasing relevance to the Renaissance Popes. But at the same time, the pagan interests and sceptical attitudes of some of the humanists were not approved of by the more conservative Roman ecclesiastics. Papal patronage of the humanists was therefore intermittent. Calixtus III had none of his predecessor's passionate enthusiasm for the classics and preferred to spend his money on the crusade. Pius II, himself a distinguished humanist, was perhaps depressed by the mediocrity of many of those who clamoured for employment, and was also devoted to the crusading ideal. He was a great disappointment to the humanists and suffered from the bitter pen of Platina.[5] The same writer also attacked Paul II who reduced the number of curial sinecures available to the humanists and broke up the Roman Academy which he suspected of being a socially dangerous and revolutionary clique. But Sixtus IV allowed the Academy to revive and made Platina Vatican librarian. Inevitably, regardless of the tastes and interests of individual Popes, the Vatican, with its ever growing need for educated servants and the multiplicity of the patronage dispensed by the cardinals and senior prelates, began to assume new importance as an intellectual centre.

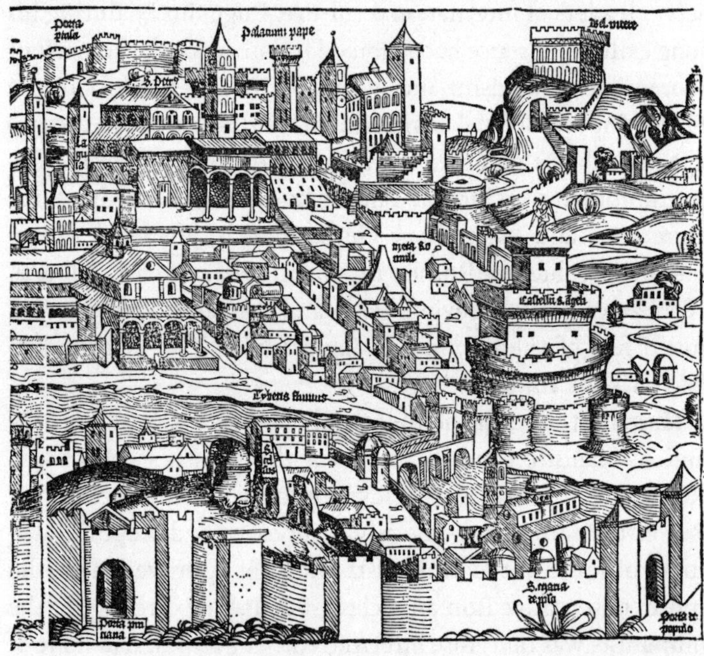

Rome in 1492; detail from Hartmann Schedel's woodcut for the Nuremburg Chronicle. Schedel was present at the coronation of Alexander VI and wrote a favourable report on the new Pope.

The role of the Renaissance Popes as patrons of the visual arts was a less ambiguous one.[6] The restoration of many of Rome's churches by Martin V brought commissions to Gentile da Fabriano, Pisanello, and Masaccio, while Eugenius IV made a conscious attempt to attract the Florentine culture, to which he had become attached, to Rome. Donatello and Fra Angelico arrived to work at the Pope's command, and Filarete's bronze doors with all their reminiscences of Ghiberti's Baptistery doors were set up in St. Peter's. But it was Nicholas V who formulated a wider justification for papal patronage. 'If the authority of the Holy See was visibly displayed in majestic buildings . . . all the world would accept and revere it. Noble edifices combining taste and beauty with imposing proportions would immensely conduce to the exaltation of the chair of St. Peter',[7] was Manetti's version of the Pope's exhortation to his cardinals on his deathbed. Discriminating patronage, fine building projects and a distinguished artistic and literary circle were essential components of political and social prestige in the Renaissance, and the Popes consciously sought to make them both auxiliaries and symbols of papal supremacy.

Nicholas V had great projects for the creation of a Vatican city in the Borgo; a functional well-planned living quarter for all the officials and dependents of the Curia.[8] At the centre of this ambitious scheme were to be an enlarged Vatican palace which with its fortification would reflect the power and supremacy of the Pope, and a great new St. Peter's, a true symbol of the majesty of the Church which could house the vastly increased numbers of pilgrims who were coming to Rome in the Jubilee years. In the time available to him Nicholas made little progress with these plans. He built a new wing of the Vatican palace, the wing which houses the Borgia apartments, and the great tower bastion which dominates the Porta S. Anna. Fra Angelico and Benozzo Gozzoli decorated the Pope's chapel in that Renaissance courtly style which was to characterise so much of the work done for the Popes, and to be continued by Pinturicchio in his work for Alexander VI. But no start was made on the three new buildings which were to house all the Curia offices, or on the theatre which was intended to be an integral part of the project. Similarly, although the building of an extended choir behind the apse of old St. Peter's was started, it was to be more than a century before Nicholas' vision of a church which would be the greatest in the world was fulfilled.

After Nicholas, progress with the improvement of the Vatican was almost continuous if at times slow. Pius II set up the statues of St. Peter and St. Paul dominating the steps of St. Peter's and began building the Benediction Loggia in front of the basilica.[9] Paul II was more interested in the Palazzo San Marco as a papal residence and in his antique collection which he kept there, but Sixtus IV with the building of the Sistine chapel and the decoration of its walls by the leading Florentine painters took another step forward in the beautification of the papal palace.[10] The Belvedere pavilion was the work of Innocent VIII,[11] while Alexander VI, as we shall see, contributed the Borgia tower and the decoration of the Borgia apartments; he also completed Pius II's Loggia. With Julius II the work began to go ahead at the speed and in the directions which Nicholas V had dreamed of. The creation of the Cortile del Belvedere, the Sistine ceiling of Michelangelo, the decoration of the Stanze above the Borgia apartments by Raphael, and the final decision to rebuild St. Peter's completely with the start made on this by Bramante, were all projects worthy of the sweeping conceptions of Nicholas V.

The need for an enlarged Vatican palace was almost as urgent as the need for a new St. Peter's by the middle of the fifteenth century. The papal bureaucracy was steadily expanding partly in response to a growing amount of business and partly as sinecures were created and sold to raise money. Part of the staff of the Chancellery probably moved out of the Vatican when Rodrigo Borgia as Vice-Chancellor built his new palace across the river. Certainly the palace seems to have passed with the office of Vice-Chancellor after 1492 which suggests that a part of the accommodation was given over to offices. The Chancellery was the largest of the Curia departments and by the end of the fifteenth century was issuing 10,000 letters a year.[12] Under the direction of the cardinal Vice-Chancellor the protonotaries acted as secretaries at the meetings of consistory and issued Bulls conferring benefices, the abbreviators prepared all letters and Bulls, and the scriptors prepared legal documents, while a host of lesser clerks did the work of copying all documents into the registers.

Alongside the Chancellery and often overlapping with it in functions was the Apostolic Camera which handled the financial affairs of the Curia. The Camera was presided over by another cardinal, the Chamberlain, and all orders for payments from the Camera originated with him. The actual control of the accounts was in the hands of the Treasurer who during the fifteenth century steadily assumed responsibility for the daily running of the Camera. The third figure of importance in the financial administration was the papal banker, the Depository General, who handled the cash and paid out on the orders of the Chamberlain or the Treasurer. As papal finances became increasingly a matter of credit transactions with revenues mortgaged in advance for loans and services rendered, the position of the papal banker became more important. The clerks of the Camera who worked under the Treasurer were a select and highly qualified group from which many of the most responsible posts in the papal administration were filled. But the Camera also had its notaries and scriptors who handled a considerable section of papal correspondence dealing with financial affairs.

By the fifteenth century not all the papal income was paid to the Camera. By this time a secret treasury had been established under the control of a private treasurer and into which the fees charged on the issue of Bulls were paid, as well as small windfalls to the Pope like gifts, legacies, etc. This money was immediately available for the Pope's use without having to go through the accounting procedures of the Camera or to pass under the nose of the Chamberlain.[13] There also grew up in the fifteenth century the department of the Datary which was in theory responsible for the dating and taxing of all letters and favours, but which came to control the sale of all venal offices. The Datary himself was not a cardinal and his appointment, and presumably his funds, were much more closely under the control of the Pope than was that of the Chamberlain.[14]

Two other departments of the Curia deserve brief mention; the office of the apostolic Penitentiary, a cardinal with a considerable staff responsible for the issuing of absolutions and remitting penances in cases reserved to the Pope; and the Roman Rota, the final court of appeal both in ecclesiastical cases and in judicial cases from the Papal States. The Rota was composed of twelve judges or auditors presided over by the Vice-Chancellor.

One of the most striking things about the organisation of the Curia was the influential position of certain cardinals at the heads of the various departments. The College of Cardinals were traditionally the advisors of the Pope, and the Pope meeting with the cardinals in Consistory formed the supreme council of the Church. But the emergence of the cardinals as heads of the departments of the papal bureaucracy was a relatively recent development. This step forward was part of a general improvement in the position of the cardinals *vis-à-vis* the Pope during the fourteenth century. For the first time in the conclave of 1352 and in many conclaves thereafter election capitulations had been drawn up and agreed by all the cardinals before they proceeded to the election of the new Pope. These capitulations were intended to be limitations imposed on the actions of the future Pope, on the whole for the benefit of the cardinals.[15] They always included such demands as the right of the College of Cardinals to be consulted in all important matters of policy including the conduct of papal diplomacy and the alienation of Church property; they laid down that the Pope should not leave Rome without the consent of the cardinals, that the College should not consist of more than 24 members, and, in the later fifteenth-century capitulations, that the income of the poorer cardinals should be made up to a reasonable figure out of Camera funds. The election capitulations were rarely effective and were frequently specifically revoked by the Pope, once elected, on the grounds that they were contrary to the best interests of the Church. But they represented the view of the College of Cardinals as to how the Church should be governed, which was essentially by an oligarchy. The Councils of the first half of the fifteenth century tended to support the cardinals as a permanent counter balance to papal authority, and incorporated in their reforms such ideas as limitations on the number of cardinals and the need for international representation among the cardinals.

There was then a continuous conflict between Pope and cardinals in the fifteenth century, between the monarchical and oligarchic views of Church government. The cardinals through the capitulations, through the actual choice of Pope, through their control of the great offices of state, and through their political influence sought to restrain the recovery of papal monarchy or at least to make themselves active components of it. The Popes, on the other hand, by expanding the size of the College, by inserting their own relatives into it and by tacit rejection of the election capitulations, managed gradually to strip the cardinals of their real power although at the same time encouraging them to take on more of the trappings of power.

The cardinals vigorously resisted increases in their numbers. They claimed the right to be consulted about all new nominations and most of the Renaissance Popes formally conformed with this demand, but the creation of cardinals was frequently announced in the teeth of bitter opposition from the College. The cardinals feared both the loss of influence which an increase in their numbers would bring, and a loss of revenue as much of their income was derived from sharing revenues which were settled on the College as a whole. A proportion of the service taxes was set aside to be shared amongst the cardinals, and when the number of cardinals rose from about twenty at the time of Martin V to over forty by the turn of the century, this had an inevitable effect on the economic position of individual cardinals.[16]

At the same time as the numbers of the College increased there was a tendency towards its Italianisation. All but three of the Renaissance Popes were Italians as was inevitable as the Pope became an Italian prince, and the cardinals they created tended to be for most part Italians. This secured both a more pliable College and political allies in Italy. Attempts to restrain this tendency by the foreign Popes, and two of these were the Borgia Popes, and return to the original conception of an international College were again vigorously resisted. At the conclave of 1455 eight of the fifteen cardinals were not Italians, but by 1492 only two of the twenty-three electors could claim this distinction. Of the sixty-four cardinals created by the four Italian Popes between 1458 and 1492, forty-three were Italians.

Lorenzo remarked in his letter to his son that 'the College of Cardinals is at this moment so poor in men of worth. . . . I remember the day when it was full of learned and virtuous men'. That the character of the College had changed considerably in the fifteenth century was beyond dispute but that this change had taken place during the relatively short life of

Lorenzo, born in 1449, is less true. From the time of the restoration of Martin V the appointment of cardinals had depended increasingly on secular factors. Apart from anything else the higher clergy from whom many of the cardinals were drawn were becoming involved in temporal affairs. Even the best of the Renaissance cardinals tended to be men who had played a part in papal diplomacy or papal administration. They were joined in the College by the younger sons of Italian princes, representatives of the Roman baronial families and relatives of successive Popes. Of the thirty-four cardinals appointed by Sixtus IV six were members of his own family, five could be described as members of Italian ruling families, and five were representatives of the great Roman families. Eleven of the thirty-four were non-Italians mostly appointed at the request of foreign princes, and these men also tended to be courtiers as much as prelates.[17]

The way of life of many of these cardinals was princely and splendid, and this tendency was encouraged by the Popes. Men of wealth and taste were useful adornments to the papal court and it was hoped that the superficial advantages of the cardinalate might compensate and mollify the cardinals for the loss of real power which they were suffering.

Paul II dressed his cardinals in red, and all the Renaissance Popes used them as legates and nuncios; but as the size of the College grew it was a small group of close advisers made up of cardinal nephews and curial officials who were not cardinals which became the real inner council of the Church.

Inevitably most fifteenth-century cardinals became increasingly concerned about their economic standing, about the incomes which were to pay for this new social status. Again as the College grew in size their receipts from the common funds declined; election capitulations began to insist on a minimum income for cardinals. In such a situation pluralism flourished, the cardinals came to rely on the accumulation of bishoprics and lesser benefices for the maintenance of their standards of living. The practice grew up of giving wealthy abbeys to cardinals '*in commendam*', implying a sort of protectorate over the abbey for a cardinal in return for a share of its revenues. Cardinals, particularly non-Italian cardinals, were beginning to gain lucrative positions as semi-official 'protectors' of individual national interests at the papal court. All this was again encouraged by the Popes as a means of distracting cardinals from demands on the central funds of the Church.

By the end of the fifteenth century there was wide acceptance in Italian courtly circles of the cardinal as a prince of the Church and a magnificent courtier. The courtly treatises of Paolo Cortese and Baldassare Castiglione both applaud the trend and describe with satisfaction the way of life of the more worldly cardinals.[18] Lorenzo de' Medici when he advised his son to 'spend your money rather on a well appointed stable and servants of a superior class than on pomp and show. Silks and jewels are for the most part unsuitable for you, but you should possess some valuable antiques and handsome books', was seeking to draw a *via media* between the 'Scylla of sanctimoniousness and the Charybdis of profanity'. But that even a moderate course should suggest that a cardinal should concern himself with stables, antiques and handsome books is indicative of the changes which had taken place in the College.

But it would be wrong to see all the cardinals of the fifteenth century conforming to this secular pattern. Throughout the century there was a clear split between the worldly cardinals and those whose appointments and whose way of life were more traditional. The cardinals of Nicholas V who must have been the first that Lorenzo could have remembered were just as much divided as those of Innocent VIII. On the one side there were Cardinals Carvajal, a model of Christian virtue with twenty-two important legations behind him; Torquemada, the austere and brilliant theologian; Bessarion, an ex-monk and the exponent of Christian humanism; Capranica, humanist and reformer; and not least Alonso de Borja, the leading canon lawyer of his day and a man of unimpeachable reputation. But on the other side there were Cardinals Scarampo, the violent but effective soldier; Pietro Barbo, a rich aristocrat, and d'Estouteville, related to the French royal family and the richest cardinal of his day. Even in 1490 the College still contained men of the stamp of Carafa, Marco Barbo and Piccolomini whose opposition to the worldly ways of their colleagues was forthright and frequent.

One of the best known features of the Renaissance Papacy was its nepotism. There was of course nothing new about Popes taking advantage of their opportunities to advance their own families. It was the late thirteenth-century Popes who had created the predominant position in Rome of the families to which they belonged. But the Popes of the Renaissance carried on the practice to an extreme degree. With their new found temporal authority the opportunities for patronage were much greater; there were more and a greater variety of posts at their command. In the troubled environment of the fifteenth-century Papacy, faced with unruly and disloyal subjects and with suspicious and obstructive cardinals, it was natural that successive Popes should seek to place their own creatures in key positions, to surround themselves with men on whose loyalty they could rely. There thus arose a spoils system which, although it helped temporarily to strengthen papal authority and to bring stability in each individual pontificate, led to a disastrous discontinuity right through the papal administration at the death of each Pope.

The College of Cardinals where appointments were for life and where temporal rewards were greatest was the obvious target for the nepotist Popes. All the Renaissance Popes except Nicholas V appointed relatives, frequently nephews, to the

College and relied on these appointments to weaken the opposition of the College. Martin V elevated one Colonna nephew, Eugenius IV advanced two of his family to the College, Calixtus two, Pius II two, Paul II three, Sixtus IV six, Innocent one, Alexander VI at least eight, and Julius II four. In 1492 no fewer than nine of the twenty-three cardinals who attended the conclave were relatives of previous Popes. Five of the Renaissance Popes were themselves nephews of Popes.

Apart from the ultimate dignity of cardinal, bishoprics and benefices were poured on the papal relatives usually in connection with high offices in the Curia. The purely secular side of papal administration provided opportunities for those papal relatives who were not committed to the ecclesiastical life. Pedro Luis Borja, the nephew of Calixtus, was Captain General of the Church, governor of the Patrimony and of many papal fortresses; Antonio Piccolomini, nephew of Pius II, was governor of Castel Sant'Angelo, and as the husband of an illegitimate daughter of Ferrante of Naples was Duke of Sessa and Amalfi, and Chief Justice of the Kingdom of Naples. Sixtus IV in addition to creating six of his relatives cardinals had the support of Leonardo della Rovere, son of his brother Bartolomeo, who was Prefect of Rome and married to another illegitimate daughter of Ferrante with the title of Duke of Sora; of Giovanni della Rovere who succeeded his cousin Leonardo as Prefect and was vicar of Senigallia and married to the daughter of the Duke of Urbino; and of Girolamo Riario, brother of cardinal Pietro Riario, who became Captain General of the Church and vicar of Imola and Forlì. There were in addition at least four members of the Della Rovere family who held important provincial treasurerships. Supporting Innocent VIII besides his son Franceschetto, married into the Medici family and lord of the famous Cibo castles, was the Pope's brother Giovanni who was Captain General.

Alexander VI was certainly the greatest nepotist of all, but

3 Cardinal Giuliano della Rovere; detail from *Sixtus IV and his court* by Melozzo da Forlì in the Vatican Pinacoteca.

4 Cardinal Francesco Piccolomini, later Pius III; an engraving by Marcantonio Raimondi.

5 Bracciano Castle; the castle was rebuilt in its present form by Napoleone Orsini about 1480; traces of the medieval castle can be seen in the courtyard.

as one of the only three foreign Popes of the period he had the greatest need of the support of his family. Already by the time he became Pope the trend from nepotism to organised papal dynasticism was apparent. Valuable as the immediate services which well placed relatives could render were to the Popes themselves, there was always in addition the desire to make the position of those relatives secure so that they could survive the death of their papal patron. The Popes, as European sovereigns, were inevitably affected by the desire to give the fortunes of their families that permanence which those of their contemporary rulers enjoyed. Thus the marriage of papal nephews into the Italian princely houses was not just a diplomatic, but also a dynastic manoeuvre, and the installation of papal relatives as vicars of the Church served dynastic as well as administrative ends. By these methods Sixtus IV was able to raise the Della Rovere family from being humble Ligurian fishermen to a secure place amongst the princes of Italy. Through Giovanni della Rovere's marriage into the Montefeltro family, the heirs of the Duke of Urbino bore the name of Della Rovere, and with a strong family group established in the College of Cardinals there was the possibility of another Della Rovere Pope, or indeed a succession of Della Rovere Popes.

Finally the particular favours accorded by Renaissance Popes were not confined to their own families. The justifications for nepotism could be equally well applied to the advancement of friends, dependents and co-nationals of the reigning Pope. All such men were likely to be more reliable servants to the newly elected Pope than would be those of his predecessor. Thus following the hated Catalans who surrounded Calixtus III came the Sienese followers of Pius, the Venetian adherents of Paul, and the Genoese who flocked to the Vatican in 1471 when Sixtus IV became Pope. The death of each Pope sparked off a spontaneous outburst in Rome against the fellow countrymen of the dead Pope, and a reign of terror, as much as more formal processes of replacement, opened the way for the partisans of the victor at the succeeding conclave. In this context, given the particularism of Renaissance Italy, it mattered little to the Romans whether the hated papalist was a Genoese or a Catalan; he was the representative of a favoured and alien group.

This then was the Papacy which Alexander VI represented and some description of it serves as an explanation rather than a justification of Borgia Papacy. The Catholic Church of the late fifteenth century had two faces; on the one hand there was the growing secularisation of the Church establishment and the acceptance by a section of opinion of this new temporal involvement; on the other there was a trend to a more spiritual and personal religion, a yearning for reform of the Church, a growing concern at the new positions adopted by the Church. Alexander VI represented more clearly than any other of the Renaissance Popes the former, and Savonarola, his contemporary and opponent, the latter. It was this dichotomy which was to prepare the ground for the Reformation, and Alexander as the epitome of the Renaissance Pope must bear his share of the responsibility for the schism in the Church.

CHAPTER FOUR

CALIXTUS III

When Alonso de Borja, Cardinal priest of Quattro Coronati and Bishop of Valencia, emerged from the conclave of 1455 as Pope Calixtus III, the dynastic significance of the event was by no means apparent. The new Pope had been living quietly in his palace on the slopes of the Caelian hill for eleven years, but apart from his familiar title—'Il Valentino', and a general air of legalistic sanctity, the Italians knew little of him. Gradually, however, interest in his origins and his family grew, and theories and rumours which spread conflicted as much as did information about current Borgia activities.

Both Calixtus and his nephews believed firmly that the Borja family could claim royal descent from ancient kings of Aragon. This seems to have been a long standing family tradition, and not a recent invention to justify dynastic ambitions in Italy and subsequent matrimonial negotiations with the royal families of Europe. Hostile Italian chroniclers tended to think otherwise and poured scorn on the idea that the Borgias might be descended from Don Pedro de Atares, lord of Borja and elected King of Aragon in the twelfth century. Don Pedro had taken the title of Lord of Borja after being forced to resign the Aragonese crown. Borja, an important communications centre in the Ebro valley, was also the original home town of the Borgias but the name 'de Borja' meant no more than this, and there is no certain evidence, apart from family tradition which is not necessarily to be scorned, that the Borgias were in fact descended from the leading family in Borja.[1]

The known ancestry of the fifteenth-century Borgias can be traced back as far as the Aragonese conquest of Valencia from the Moors in the first half of the thirteenth century. Esteban de Borja and other members of his family followed King James I of Aragon in his campaign and after the successful conquest of Valencia and its hinterland in 1240, Esteban was granted the right to distribute the newly conquered land round Jativa to his family and followers. Jativa is a small fortified hill town of Roman origin which overlooks the Valencian plain away to the south of the city itself. The grant to Esteban ensured that the Borja family became the chief family in Jativa, and guaranteed their position as influential local nobility. Throughout the fourteenth century members of the family served as *jurados* or councillors of Jativa and Rodrigo Gil de Borja, the grandfather of Alexander VI, was in high favour with Pedro IV of Aragon, and married Doña Sibila de Oms of a distinguished Catalan family.

The family therefore do not seem to have been either upstarts, in the strict sense of the word, or alternatively robber barons as was sometimes suggested in Italy. They do seem, however, legendary royal ancestry apart, to have been of modest aristocratic lineage and their dynastic ambitions and successes in the second half of the fifteenth century did represent a dramatic change in the family fortunes.

Alonso de Borja, to whom the change was largely due, came from a younger branch of the family, and his father Domingo de Borja was a small landowner and country gentleman who lived at Torre del Canals near Jativa. Once again Italian tradition has described Domingo as a humble farmer, but his clearly established relationship to the undoubtedly noble Borjas of Jativa, and the good matches which he was able to arrange for his daughters are clear evidence that contemporary reports are unreliable. Domingo married Francina Martì from a Valencian family which had settled in Jativa, and one of his daughters, Juana, married into the same family. Another daughter, Catalina, married Baron Juan de Mila and a third daughter, Isabella, married the heir to the main Borja line, Jofrè, the son of Rodrigo Gil and Sibila. Alonso's fourth sister, Francisca, entered a convent.

Alonso himself was born on 31 December 1378, the year of the Great Schism which he was to play some part in ending. He was baptised in the parish church at Jativa and seems to have slipped rather casually into an ecclesiastical career.[2] He did not finally become a priest until he was raised to the bishopric of Valencia in 1429 and his reputation was made as a canon lawyer. He embarked on this career as a law student at the University of Lerida at the age of fourteen; there he took doctorates in both canon and civil law and later became a lecturer. It was not until he was thirty, in 1408, that he received his first ecclesiastical benefices. By this time his learning had attracted the attention of two of the leading Spanish ecclesiastics of the day. Pedro de Luna, the Spanish Pope Benedict XIII, who was ultimately to resist the decisions of the Council of Constance and earn the title of anti-pope, made him assessor of the 'bayle' of the diocese of Lerida and later, in 1411, canon of the cathedral of Lerida. St. Vincent Ferrer, on the other hand, is reputed to have prophesied a great future for the young jurist and even to have foretold his eventual elevation to the See of St. Peter. Certainly it was Alonso de Borja, as Calixtus III, who was personally responsible for the canonisation of St. Vincent in 1455.

While canon of Lerida cathedral Alonso also acted as 'official' of the diocese, and the surviving records of the cathedral reveal his punctilious and often influential attendance at chapter meetings. In 1416 he was chosen as official delegate of the diocese to the Council of Constance, an indicatoin of proposed submission to the decisions of the Council and abandonment of Benedict XIII, Alonso's former patron. It seems however that this mission was not carried out as the accession of Alfonso V of Aragon and a temporary reversal of royal policy toward the Council and its elected Pope, Martin V, intervened. However it is interesting to find even at this stage Alonso appearing as a protagonist of a united Papacy. Although he did not go to Constance, Alonso did in the same year represent his chapter at the junta of the Aragonese church in Barcelona which discussed the attitude to be adopted toward the Council, and it was probably here that he first caught the eye of King Alfonso. However it was in the next year, when he was sent by his chapter to negotiate with royal officials over the finances of the diocese of Lerida, that he first appeared at the royal court and was immediately taken into the royal service. From this time until 1444 when he took up residence as a cardinal in Rome, Alonso was the secretary and chief councillor of one of the most active and intelligent of contemporary European monarchs.

Alonso's first important mission on behalf of his new master was to negotiate with the papal legate, Cardinal Adimari, Archbishop of Pisa, who had been sent by Martin V to secure the submission of Aragon to his election. This was in 1418 and Alfonso V with his eye already on a Neapolitan kingdom was soon persuaded that his best interests lay in supporting the Pope in Rome, and he agreed to press Benedict XIII to resign. We can be sure that Alonso de Borja played a great part in influencing this decision because not only was concern for Church unity and papal supremacy the dominating passion of his life, but also in this particular instance he was rewarded for his part in the negotiations by Martin V. He was made a canon of Barcelona cathedral and rector of the church of St. Nicholas in Valencia.

It was not only in ecclesiastical affairs that Alfonso V relied on his new secretary. Alonso was quickly involved in the protracted quarrels and negotiations between the King of Aragon and other monarchs of the peninsula, his brother John of Navarre and his cousin John of Castile. In 1420 when Alfonso first went to Naples Alonso de Borja was left on the Council of Regency in Aragon as vice-chancellor. Between 1420 and 1423 he was also vice-chancellor of the University of Lerida, but royal affairs occupied more and more of his time and in 1423 he resigned both the vice-chancellorship and his canonry in Lerida, and the city in which he had built up his great reputation as a jurist was to see him no more. It is significant that the accumulation of benefices and worldly wealth meant little to Alonso de Borja. Unlike most of the high ecclesiastics of his day he eschewed as far as possible pluralities and absentee livings for himself, and his prompt resignation of his Lerida benefices is indicative of his attitude throughout his life.

As early as 1421 Alfonso V was proposing to the Pope that his secretary and vice-chancellor should be made a cardinal, but the suggestion had all the appearances of a political manoeuvre and was justifiably ignored. The coveted red hat, when it was to be conferred twenty-three years later, was conferred for services to the Church, and not for those to a secular prince. For the time being Alonso appeared to be content with his modest benefices and with the post of administrator of the diocese of Majorca which he received in 1424.

Major ecclesiastical preferment was finally to come Alonso's way in 1429 as a reward for his diplomatic success in securing the resignation of the Spanish anti-pope Clement VIII, successor of Benedict XIII. A new papal legate, Cardinal de Foix, prompted a further effort to gain the resignation of the obdurate anti-pope who since his election in 1424 had shut himself up in the rocky fortress of Peniscola. Alonso de Borja with one companion made the journey on behalf of both his king and Martin V to persuade Clement to renounce his claims. His mission was finally successful; Clement VIII formally resigned in August 1429 and was given the bishopric of Majorca. The Great Schism was ended and the unity of the Church on which the strength of the Renaissance Papacy was based was restored. Alonso had played no small part in this success and his reward was the bishopric of Valencia. The jurist, diplomat, royal councillor and ecclesiastical administrator was now firmly embarked on the course which was to lead twenty-six years later to the papal throne.

Alonso's new task, to which he was only able to devote himself personally for less than three years before he departed for Italy with Alfonso, was a formidable one. The diocese of Valencia had been the last stronghold of the Schism; religious disunity and perplexity were strong and techniques other than those of the dispassionate and tireless administrator were required to redirect the natural religious ardour of the Valencians. Alonso realised the value of splendid ceremonies for his purpose and began to display that theatrical flair which was to become identified with his family. Veneration for the Virgin Mary and the early female martyrs was traditional in Valencia, and this he sought to restore. With great ceremony the bones of St. Louis of Torlosa were brought to the cathedral and work on building a special chapel for the relics was started, and completed in 1486 by Rodrigo Borgia.

But in 1432 royal affairs took precedence once more and Alonso was summoned to follow his master to the Kingdom of Naples where the steady Aragonese pressure to gain a foothold was beginning to bear fruit. He was only to return twice to Spain and on each occasion, in 1436 and 1437, he was more occupied with royal business and disputes with the neighbouring Spanish kingdoms than with his diocese.

We know relatively little about Alonso's life and activities during the next ten years in Italy. One of the objects of his

1436 visit to Spain was to bring back Alfonso's illegitimate son Ferrante and to assume a role as one of the tutors to the future Neapolitan king. It was also to Alonso that the task of re-organising the judicial system and the courts of Naples fell after Alfonso had finally won control of the Kingdom. The Sacro Consiglior, or tribunal of Santa Chiara, was established as a part of this reorganisation, and Alonso was until 1444 president of this, as well as of the Royal Council.[3] We do know however that relations between the Bishop of Valencia and his royal master were not always easy in this period. Already Alonso was beginning to show that independence of his king which was to be so marked a feature of his pontificate. When Alfonso, in an attempt to force the Pope to recognise his title to Naples, dallied with the idea of supporting the Council of Basle and the anti-pope Felix V, Alonso Borja refused to represent his master at the Council. He was horrified at the thought of a new schism. On the other hand after Eugenius IV had gained a partial victory over the Council of Basle by reconvening it in Florence in 1439 to discuss the union of the Western and Eastern churches, it was Alonso Borja who led the Aragonese deputation to Florence. There he met Cardinals Bessarion and Cesarini and had his first contacts with the papal court and with the new atmosphere of intellectual and cultural patronage which pervaded in Florence and was to triumph in Rome under Nicholas V. The austere Spaniard was often later derided and criticised by the humanists for his apparent lack of interest in their ideals and aims, but in 1439 he seems to have made a reasonably favourable impression in Florence and there was once again talk of his elevation to the Sacred College.

Alonso was not one however to be bribed into abandoning his master by ecclesiastical preferment, and it was not until the breach between Pope and King had been finally healed that he accepted the red hat. With Alfonso's final triumphant entry into Naples in 1442 it became impolitic for Eugenius IV to postpone any longer his recognition of the change of dynasty in the Neapolitan kingdom. Furthermore the Pope's own implicit victory over the Council of Basle made Alfonso aware that it was only by direct negotiation with Eugenius himself that he would get the recognition that he needed. Thus in 1443 Alonso Borja and the papal negotiator Cardinal Scarampo were quickly able to arrive at an agreement which was embodied in the Treaty of Terracina.[4] This treaty, in which Alfonso finally abandoned his tentative support of the Council of Basle and recognised Eugenius IV, was a major step forward in the triumph of the rising Renaissance Papacy over the conciliar idea. The adherence of the powerful ruler of the Aragonese empire to the Roman Pope was a crippling blow to the Council. At the same time papal recognition for the Aragonese in Naples, although later briefly reversed by Calixtus III himself, represented a decisive moment in Neapolitan history and a fatal blow to the Angevin hopes. In addition to this mutual recognition, Alfonso agreed to assist in a crusade and in protecting the Papal States from Francesco Sforza, while Eugenius invested Alfonso with the two jealously guarded papal cities of Benevento and Terracina for the duration of his life.

The importance of this treaty in the history of both the Renaissance Papacy and the Neapolitan kingdom is manifest, and the reward to one of its principal architects was justly deserved. In 1444 Alonso Borja was nominated cardinal and in the next year he took up residence in Rome in his urban parish of Quattro Coronati. That a cardinal elevated primarily for politico-religious services and to flatter and please a secular prince whose chief minister he was, should immediately elect to come to Rome must have caused some surprise. But Alonso Borja was never one to enjoy absentee honours; his political activity had in large part been devoted to ensuring the supremacy of a united Church, and now that in a certain sense a seal had been set on this task with the Treaty of Terracina, he was ready to devote himself to a more clearly religious life. It might be said that for a man of sixty-six this represented his retirement after an active and important career, but at the same time Alonso himself is reputed never to have forgotten the prophecy of St. Vincent Ferrer that he would eventually become Pope. The move to Rome may have represented for him a step nearer this goal, and although little in his character would lead one to ascribe overwhelming ambition to Alonso Borja, he no doubt looked on this preferment and this move as a step in his destiny.

However during his eleven years in Rome as a cardinal Alonso seems to have played little part in the government of the Church. He was described as being immune to flattery and corruption and one gets the impression that he led a quiet and secluded life. There is no mention of him playing any notable part in the conclave of 1447 when Nicholas V was elected. He devoted his energies to the restoration of the cloister and the cardinal's palace of Quattro Coronati, and the endowment of hospitals. He was noted for his care of the poor and the needy. His health was already failing by this time, but in Rome he quickly gained a reputation for moral purity and integrity. The life he led was very austere compared to that of some of his fellow cardinals, and he always held himself apart from all factions within the Sacred College. He drew a net income of about 6,500 Aragonese pounds from his diocese of Valencia after diocesan expenses had been paid, and this would have been more than sufficient for the limited expenses of his chosen way of life as a cardinal.[5]

That such a man, living a relatively isolated life in a city which was in many ways becoming increasingly alien to his natural austerity, should surround himself with members of his own family and servants of his own race is scarcely surprising. Such behaviour on the part of a cardinal would have aroused little comment and could scarcely be described as a failing. That undue nepotism and a tendency to favour Catalans were to be serious charges levelled at Alonso as Pope are questions that will be discussed in their proper place. But without doubt this feature of his character and daily life were already fully established during the period of his eleven years residence in Rome as a cardinal. It is not entirely clear at what stage his nephews joined him in Rome, but his passion for his family and his determination to share with them the fruits of his own success are clearly documented. Equally apparent is the growth of a Catalan predominated household which was to form the basis of the papal household established in the Vatican after 1455.

In addition to his nepotism it has been stated by some historians that Alonso Borja was the father of Francesco Borgia who was created a cardinal in 1500 by Alexander VI. The story seems to have originated with Ciaconius, the papal historian who was both extremely hostile to the Borgias and guilty of propagating some notorious errors about them.[6] In this case all that we know of Alonso's character and reputation would seem to discredit the charge, and the possibility that this widely respected, rather ascetic figure should have fathered a child in his advancing years seems a remote one. Certainly it would require some more concrete evidence than the word of Ciaconius and the vague physical similarities observed between Alonso and the presumed portrait of Francesco by Pinturicchio in the Borgia apartments to place the matter beyond doubt.[7]

To understand how it was that the death of Nicholas V and the subsequent conclave brought this reserved and ageing Spaniard to the papal throne, it is necessary for a moment to consider the general state of affairs in Italy. In the first place

Constantinople had just fallen to the Turks. Although the cultural and even the political impact of this event have often been exaggerated, there can be no doubt that a ripple of shock went through Europe as the news of the final fall of the Byzantine Empire spread. Venice was particularly alarmed and the advance of the Turks was one of the factors which contributed to the rapid conclusion of the peace of Lodi between Venice and Milan, and to the subsequent attempt at a general pacification of Italy with the formation of the Italian League. Nicholas V had played his part in these events, calling for an end to Italian wars and a restoration of Christian unity in the face of the Turkish threat. But while there was a general degree of unanimity about the need for a crusade at the conclave of 1455, there was also a heightened atmosphere of rivalry between the Orsini and Colonna factions which split the Italian cardinals. The support given to these factions by the individual Italian states reflected the growing importance of papal elections in Italian politics, but in this case the Italian cardinals were still in a minority and it was this more than anything else that contributed to the ultimate choice.

Fifteen cardinals assembled on 4 April 1455 to choose Nicholas' successor.[8] Seven were Italians, and the remainder were made up of four Spaniards, two Frenchmen and two Greeks, Bessarion and Isidore. Cardinals Barbo and Capranica were the principal Italian contenders, the former supported by Venice, Naples and the Orsini, the latter by the Colonna. Among the non-Italian cardinals Bessarion was the most favoured candidate, but he was bitterly opposed by the French. The outcome therefore was the inevitable compromise. With the non-Italians primarily concerned to choose a potential crusader, and the Italians reluctantly reconciled to accepting an elderly foreigner who was known to be above party factions, the choice of Alonso Borja became an obvious one. But if he had many of the characteristics of a compromise pope, age, failing health and neutrality, Alonso was also a skilled diplomat, a passionate believer in papal supremacy, and a product of the severe Spanish crusading tradition. It was not long before the Italians began to regret their acceptance of a Spanish Pope. Although almost permanently bedridden with gout, and conducting the affairs of the Church from a shuttered and candle-lit bedroom, the new Pope showed an energy and independence which filled his electors with dismay.

The elaborate coronation ceremony itself was enough to try the strength of all but the fittest of newly-elected Popes. After high mass in St. Peter's, Calixtus robed in white rode in procession to the Lateran. He was escorted by eighty bishops and all the officers of the government of Rome with the standards of the quarters of the city. By custom the Jewish community awaited him near Monte Giordano to do homage, and their rabbi presented a richly bound Book of the Law to the new pontiff. Calixtus took the present and then let it fall to the ground saying 'We recognise the Law; but not the interpretation which you give it.' He then turned his back on the ensuing unseemly scramble for the luxurious volume and went on his way to the Lateran.[9] This was a traditional reply in a traditional ceremony; but the accounts of it leaves us with an impression of the vigour and dedication which Alonso could still display at the age of seventy-seven, and in the middle of a long and exhausting day.

One of the first acts of Calixtus III was the canonisation of Vincent Ferrer, whose prophecy and example had meant so much to him. This was followed by an even more important act of papal 'preferment', the rehabilitation of Joan of Arc. The motive behind this seems to have been to please the French and unite them behind the crusade which Calixtus was determined to launch. For it was towards the idea of a crusade that his main efforts were to be directed. Having taken a solemn vow soon after his election to devote his failing strength to the defeat of the Turks and the recovery of Constantinople, he lost no time in sending out legates to all parts of Europe to stir up enthusiasm for the crusade. Thirty-eight volumes in the Vatican archives are filled with his Bulls and correspondence on the subject. He ordered that all the church bells in Christendom be rung every midday to remind Christians of their duty to pray for the success of the Crusade.[10]

Unfortunately his energy and that of his legates met with little response. In Cologne the Pope's preacher was driven from the pulpit by an angry mob, and all attempts to interest Francesco Sforza, the new Duke of Milan and Italy's leading soldier, in personal participation in the crusade failed. Only the Spanish cardinal Carvajal, legate to Hungary, the country most affected by the Turkish advance, could claim any real success in his mission. He together with the fiery Franciscan preacher, Giovanni Capestrano, and the Hungarian leader John Hunyadi managed to overcome the factional strife which rent Hungary and produce the strength and enthusiasm necessary to gain the great victory of Belgrade over the Turks. Calixtus was overjoyed although he had been able to make little contribution to the victory, and he tried to follow it up by sending money and encouragement to the Albanian leader Skanderbeg.[11]

However Calixtus' personal endeavours met with more success nearer to home where he succeeded in creating a papal crusading fleet and dispatching it to the eastern Mediterranean.[12] Within a month of the election arrangements were going ahead for the hiring and building of galleys. In May 1455 Antonio Olzina was given a *condotta*, initially for six months, to serve with his two galleys in the papal fleet against the Turks or any other enemies of the Pope. At the same time Antonio Frescobaldi was authorised to fit out four galleys in Porto Pisano for the fleet. But more dramatic still, Rome itself was turned into a shipyard. The banks of the Tiber on the

Vatican side were soon seething with carpenters summoned from Spoleto, with shipwrights, and with sailmakers. A palisade was built round the area and Pietro Torres was brought from Barcelona to take charge of the new arsenal. Overall supervision of these preparations was in the hands of the Chamberlain, Cardinal Scarampo, who was subsequently to take command of the fleet. Calixtus gave 200,000 ducats from the secret treasury to help pay the expenses of all this activity, and part of the estates confiscated from the Prefects of Vico by Eugenius IV, Vallerano, Carbognano and Vignanello, were sold to raise further funds.

A first squadron made up largely of Catalan galleys set sail in September 1455 under Pietro Urrea, Archbishop of Tarragona. Basing himself in southern Sicily, Urrea was presumably proposing to prevent Turkish infiltration into the Western Mediterranean. But he and his captains seem to have shown little discrimination in the ships which they seized and looted, and soon protests were pouring in to the Pope about the piratical activities of his squadron against Christian shipping.

By mid 1456 Cardinal Scarampo was preparing to leave the Tiber with a second squadron of sixteen galleys mostly built in Rome. His vice-admiral was a Portuguese sailor Valasca Farinha of Lisbon and, although most of the captains still seem to have been Catalans, there were amongst them Carlo di Campobasso, Count of Termoli, and also some of the powerful Roman Anguillara family. By this time Urrea had proceeded to the eastern Mediterranean but he was already in disgrace, and by the time the remnant of his squadron joined up with that of the Cardinal, he had quietly slipped from the scene.

The fleet remained in the eastern Mediterranean for eighteen months while Calixtus laboured to prepare and send out reinforcements. Notable among the captains who were entrusted with galleys and funds to take out to the Cardinal were Miguel and Juan Borja, and Juan Lanzol, all relatives of the Pope. Cardinal Scarampo with the limited fleet at his disposal, certainly no more than thirty galleys, could not hope to achieve very much. Calixtus in his enthusiasm called for an attack on Constantinople itself, but the real role of the fleet was to defend the remaining Christian held islands in the Aegean and to act as an example and a spur to the rest of Europe to send reinforcements. There were constant reports of activity in the shipyards of France, Genoa, and even Portugal. Alfonso of Naples took the cross and committed his fleet to the crusade, but no other galleys reached the Cardinal. In 1457 he succeeded in driving a Turkish fleet away from Lesbos, and in 1458 was even able to take the offensive and briefly occupy the Acropolis at Athens, and Corinth. But on the death of Calixtus all the enthusiasm generated by the ageing Pope melted away. Cardinal Scarampo sailed home, and his galleys were allowed to rot away in the Tiber so that by 1464 when Pius II desperately needed ships for his crusade, he could not even rely on this hard earned nucleus of papal galleys.

A crusading fleet would have been active in the eastern Mediterranean before 1457 if Alfonso V had been more co-operative. The Neapolitan fleet was promised for this purpose in the early months of the pontificate, but Alfonso chose to use it instead for an attack on Genoa. Calixtus was naturally furious at this betrayal of Christian interests, and his pontificate far from being a period of Aragonese domination of Rome as many Italians had feared, was marked by constant friction between the Pope and his ex-master. Calixtus even as chief minister of Alfonso had shown his spirit of independence, and as Pope he was not prepared to tolerate the traditional pattern of Neapolitan interference in the affairs of the Papal States, or Alfonso's lukewarm attitude towards the crusade.

It was not only Alfonso's misuse of his fleet and the crusading funds which had gone into fitting it out which stirred the Pope's indignation. There was also the question of the ex-Venetian *condottiere* Jacopo Piccinino. Piccinino, released from Venetian service after the peace of Lodi, had turned his restless gaze on central Italy as a suitable area in which to carve out a state for himself. Encouraged, and in fact paid, by Alfonso who was always interested in seeing the Papal States in confusion, Piccinino attacked Siena. Calixtus was enraged by this flagrant breach of the Italian League which had seemed at last to have brought peace to Italy and to have prepared the way for crusading unity. He mobilised the papal army against Piccinino and, with the aid of Francesco Sforza who was also concerned for the peace of Italy, succeeded in forcing Piccinino to withdraw into Neapolitan territory. In this campaign the treachery of the papal commander, the Count of Ventimiglia, provided Calixtus with a justification for replacing him with his own nephew Pedro Luis. However in the last resort the only way of satisfying the ambition of the frustrated *condottiere* and of preventing him from becoming a permanent threat to the security of the Papal States was to pay him an immense bribe to which Siena, Florence and the Papacy all had to contribute. Calixtus' energy on this occasion was of course as much motivated by concern for his own territories as it was by disinterested zeal for the peace of Italy and the crusade. But Siena was grateful to him, and Sano di Pietro painted his portrait as the protector of the city, one of the few portraits of the first Borgia Pope that have remained to us. It was on this occasion that Aeneas Silvius Piccolomini, the future Pius II, wrote to the Sienese about Calixtus: 'You have a Pope who is very attached to your republic; you should seek to profit from this, because his energy is as great as his generosity, and nothing is dearer to him than justice.'[13]

It was to Sienese envoys that Calixtus revealed one of his

rare recorded flashes of humour. When they asked him to grant a pardon to the whole city for their summary execution of the disloyal *condottiere*, Giberto da Correggio, the Pope replied jokingly that he could not do that 'because you Sienese would then be too strong in Paradise'.[14]

Alfonso continued to provoke Calixtus by his interference in the Papal States, by his support for the rebellious Orsini family, and by his demands that he be given the March of Ancona. By 1457 Calixtus was already threatening him with deposition on the traditional grounds that Naples was a fief of the Papacy; and on the same grounds, when Alfonso died in the next year, he prepared to resist the succession of his illegitimate son Ferrante. It has often been claimed that Calixtus was preparing to replace the Aragonese dynasty in Naples with Pedro Luis, and that this was an outrageous example of the lengths to which his nepotism could go. But the background of conflict between Naples and the Papacy and the immediate events of Calixtus' pontificate make his attempts to alter the Neapolitan succession more than understandable. The possibility of giving the crown to Pedro Luis was certainly in his mind, but so also were other solutions to the problem. He ordered a new investigation to be made into the claims of the Angevins in Naples thus preparing the ground for a reversion to the Angevin dynasty. By resisting the succession of the illegitimate branch of the Aragonese house, and thus the division of the Aragonese empire, he was acting in the true interests of Aragon and anticipating the policy of Ferdinand the Catholic.[15] Whatever his motives and plans, Calixtus' own death within a month of that of his enemy frustrated them and Ferrante was able to succeed peacefully to his father's throne.

If Italians were perhaps relieved that the election of a Spanish Pope had not resulted in the subjection of the Papacy to Aragonese interests, the Roman barons were very disappointed in their hopes that an aged foreign Pope would leave them as master of Rome. Calixtus, who had spent so much of his life striving for papal supremacy over Councils and anti-popes, was not prepared to sacrifice that supremacy in Rome itself. No Pope ever interfered more in the quarrels between Orsini and Colonna. When his coronation ceremony was disturbed by armed brawls in the Lateran itself between the Orsini, and the Anguillara and Colonna families, Calixtus sternly ordered Cardinal Orsini to control his family.[16] Because of their increasingly threatening position as masters of Tuscia and the Sabina, their control of the office of Prefect of Rome, and their alliance with Alfonso, Calixtus chose to concentrate his energies against the Orsini, and sought an understanding with the Colonna. But although Cardinal Colonna was entrusted with the task of reducing the Sabine fortress of Palombara to which the Orsini had retreated, it was to Pedro Luis Borja as Captain General of the Church that Calixtus entrusted the main work of subduing the Orsini. Pedro Luis attacked the Orsini castles and in 1458 on the death of the incumbent Orsini he was made Prefect of Rome and took over the great apanage of the Prefects which included Civitavecchia as well as the area round Lago di Vico. In this way the tightening pressure of the Orsini on the northern routes out of Rome was eased, but a legacy of bitterness was created between Orsini and Borgia which was to colour the remainder of Borgia history.

Calixtus had quickly learnt from experience the isolated position in which a foreign Pope stood in Rome. This as much as family feeling or national sentiment led him to turn more and more to his relatives and to Catalans to carry out his policies. He himself protested that his sisters and their relatives used to force themselves on him, but he scarcely needed such persuasion to choose a path of nepotism already traditional and soon to become all-pervading at the Vatican. The

Roman nobility, the traditional secular advisers of the Papacy, found themselves gradually excluded from the main work of papal administration; not unnaturally this soon led to jealous exaggeration of the Pope's motives and greed.

The two members of his family on whom Calixtus principally relied were the two young sons of his sister Isabella, Rodrigo and Pedro Luis. Rodrigo, destined from childhood for a life in the Church, was sent to study canon law at the University of Bologna, and then in 1456 made a cardinal at the age of twenty-five. Elevated at the same time was his older cousin, Luis Juan de Mila, already Bishop of Segorbe and papal legate in Bologna.[17] The promotion to the ranks of the Sacred College of two men so young and so untried aroused bitter opposition amongst the cardinals. But so for that matter did subsequent nominations by Calixtus of men more obviously worthy. One cannot escape from the conclusion that the cardinals were resolved to oppose any appointments by a Spanish Pope which were seen as a threat to the independence of the College.

After his elevation to the cardinalate Rodrigo was dispatched as Legate to the March of Ancona where he quickly restored order in an area much coveted by Alfonso V. He recaptured the papal city of Ascoli which had revolted, and earned wide respect both for his determination and administrative ability. On his return to Rome Calixtus made him Vice-Chancellor of the Church, an office which had been vacant since the death of Cardinal Gondulmer, a nephew of Eugenius IV, in 1453.

Although Rodrigo had thus served his uncle faithfully as an administrator in the Papal States, Calixtus' principal temporal lieutenant was his other nephew Pedro Luis. He was made Captain General of the Church by his uncle at the same moment as Rodrigo became a cardinal. As we have seen he was principally employed against the Orsini, but he was also commandant of the fortress of S. Angelo, the key to the security of Rome and of the Pope himself, Duke of Spoleto, Foligno and Orvieto, Governor of the Patrimony, and in 1458 Prefect of the city of Rome. Pedro Luis was a handsome and high spirited young man whose arrogance and whose rapid rise to supreme military authority in the Papal States earned him almost universal hatred and jealousy. When on his deathbed Calixtus invested his nephew with the papal cities of Terracina and Benevento which had reverted to the Papacy on the death of Alfonso, this jealousy knew no bounds.

Apart from these main figures, there were other members of the Pope's family employed in a military capacity to assist in the work of controlling the Papal States. The key fortress of Ostia was in the hands of Juan Borja who also served as a galley captain. Miguel Borja, another galley commander, held the important papal fortresses of Orte and Soriano. Galceran Borja was Governor of Spoleto and continued to serve Pius II in the administration of the Papal States.[18]

While Calixtus used his relatives largely to counterbalance the military threats of the Orsini and Colonna, he used his fellow countrymen not only for this purpose, but also to staff his domestic household. That there should have been widespread jealousy and dislike of the Catalans surrounding Calixtus III was inevitable. Indeed from the very moment of his election we are told that the French and German chancellery employees were leaving Rome as they could not bear to be ruled by Catalans.[19] Everyone expected an invasion of grasping Catalans and they were not to be disappointed; but inevitably the extent of the invasion was exaggerated. 'The Catalans are in command,' wrote Leonardo Vernacci to Piero di Cosimo de' Medici two days after the end of the conclave in 1455;[20] but even taking the pontificate as a whole one cannot help noticing that relatively few official Vatican posts fell into the hands of Catalans. Amongst the Chancellery and Camera officials the proportion of known Catalans was about one in five.[21] In the papal household they predominated; Cosimo de Montserrat, the papal confessor and controller of the household; Bartolome Regas, papal secretary; Jaime Quintana and Fernando Lopez de Jativa, the papal doctors; Bernardo Agullana, the papal cook, and Pietro Daltell, the treasurer of the household, were all Catalans. In addition many important military and administrative posts in the Papal States were given to Catalans as men whom the Pope could trust in the turmoil of Italian rivalries.[22] Many of the nuncios sent out to foster the crusade were inevitably Catalans. But at the same time most of the benefices conferred on Spanish clergy in the Pope's entourage were Spanish benefices not Italian ones. There is little evidence of Calixtus enriching his Spanish followers with the wealth of Italy or the Church. Even the papal jewels, which according to Vespasiano da Bisticci were to be seen adorning the stockings of Pedro Luis, were jealously guarded by Cosimo de Montserrat.[23] Their disposal, according to the detailed inventories of Cosimo, was dictated almost entirely by the exigencies of the crusade. Some were given to Cardinals Estouteville and Barbo to dispose of for crusading purposes, some were given to the ambassadors of the King of Hungary. Rodrigo Borgia received four manuscripts and four items of jewelry from his uncle; Pedro Luis received nine items in all from the papal treasure. Of the latter none could have conceivably been hung on his stockings as they consisted of silver and gold cups and a decorated bed cover.[24]

When one remembers the known parsimony of Calixtus and his allocation of all his wealth to the crusade, one is scarcely surprised to find that the stories of his dispoliation of the Church for the sake of his nephews seems to be exaggerated. 'Take them away for the crusade; earthenware is enough for me,' he is reported to have cried on seeing the silver salt cellars accumulated by Nicholas V.[25] Again under the watchful eye of Cosimo de Montserrat lead candlesticks replaced the silver ones in the papal chapel; plain wood and iron furniture filled the papal apartments. The Vatican of Calixtus was never a social centre; there were no parties or orgies to delight the chroniclers of the period. Household expenses fell from about 2,500 ducats a month under Nicholas to about 1500 ducats a month in 1456. However a large part of this saving was achieved by reductions in major expenditure on the Vatican palace itself.[26]

Parsimony and thrift are also the clue to the Pope's relationships with the humanists and his attitude to patronage. Unlike his predecessor Calixtus had neither the artistic inclination, nor the breadth of humanistic learning to continue the passionate work of converting Rome into a Renaissance capital. But what was more important he was not prepared to divert funds badly needed for the crusade to patronage. In Spain he had devoted a part of his income as Bishop of Valencia to endowing a chapel dedicated to St. Anne in the collegiate church at Jativa. In Rome he pressed on with the restoration of many of the ruined churches and completed the fortification of the Ponte Milvio started by Nicholas V. He also repaved St. Peter's Square.[27] But by and large the humanists and artists of the Vatican received little sympathy from him in their pleas for emoluments and commissions, although he did give encouragement to Lorenzo Valla and Flavio Biondo. Naturally the articulate humanists felt this neglect and did much to contribute to the growing hostility to the Borgia Pope. To the humanist Filelfo and also to Vespasiano da Bisticci, we owe the legend of Calixtus' disposal of Nicholas V's library. The legend is abundantly disproved both by catalogues of the time and by surviving relics of Nicholas' collection today. But Calixtus does seem to have ordered that the precious bindings should be in part stripped off the manuscripts and sold to help pay for the crusade.[28] However in recompense he left his own not inconsiderable collection of legal works to the growing Vatican library.

Throughout his papacy Calixtus was a sick man and rarely left his bed. But there seems to be no doubt that his endless labours for the crusade and his refusal to leave Rome at the height of the unhealthy summer months of 1458 hastened his death. By early August 1458 it was known that the Pope was dying. The Catalans began to melt away into hiding; the Orsini were riding armed through the streets of Rome. They were after the blood of Pedro Luis who had to be smuggled out of Rome by Rodrigo and Cardinal Barbo only to die of fever at Civitavecchia. Rodrigo returned to the bedside of his uncle and remained with him until the end. That end came on 6 August and in the midst of the confusion and rivalries rife in Rome. Alonso Borja was hastily laid to rest in Santa Maria delle Febbri. In later years his body was removed to the church of the Spaniards, Santa Maria di Monserrato.

CHAPTER FIVE

CARDINAL RODRIGO BORGIA

The death of his uncle left Rodrigo Borgia isolated in Rome at the mercy of anti-Catalan feeling. Pedro Luis had fled to a lonely and feverous death at Civitavecchia; Cardinal de Mila returned to his bishopric of Segorbe; other members of the family were with the fleet in the eastern Mediterranean. Rodrigo's survival in these circumstances says much both for his ability and for his capacity for attracting people and making himself popular.

Rodrigo was at this moment twenty-seven years old; heavily handsome with great personal charm and a splendid physique. He was described by Jacopo Gherardi da Volterra as 'a man of versatile intellect, and great sense and imagination; an eloquent speaker and well read in a rather general way; he has a warm nature but above all is brilliantly skilled in conducting affairs. He is immensely wealthy and in great favour with many kings and princes.'[1] He was already showing that enormous zest for life which was one of his most striking characteristics, and yet combined with this was a seriousness of purpose, a pride and self-sufficiency which were peculiarly Spanish. Those who deplored his ostentatious hedonism could not help but admire his intellectual gifts and his administrative capacity. Those who were repelled by his showmanship and his self esteem were often reconciled by his friendliness and boisterous good humour. His upbringing contributed much to his strange many-sidedness which was such an enigma to his contemporaries.

Rodrigo Borgia was born in 1431 the son of Jofrè de Borja of the senior line of the family and Isabella, sister of Calixtus III.[2] The first ten years of his life were spent in the Borja palace in Jativa and they were years which he always remembered with affection. He had four sisters and a brother, Pedro Luis. From very early years Rodrigo was destined for the Church, presumably with the anticipation that his uncle, already well placed as Bishop of Valencia and councillor to the King, would be able to help him in his career. When he was ten his father died and his mother moved with the family to Valencia where she took up residence in the bishop's empty palace. Even in the absence of the bishop, life was frugal for his relations in the palace and Rodrigo acquired here that taste for abstemiousness in his diet which was to astonish the Italians when compared to the extravagance of his public life. However, outside the walls of the bishop's palace, Valencia had the reputation of being one of the most pleasure loving cities in Europe and it was here that Rodrigo pursued his studies, perhaps at the university, for at least eight years.

The date at which he was summoned to Rome by his uncle and sent to undertake more serious study at Bologna has been the subject of much dispute. It is often said that it was not until he became Pope in 1455 that Calixtus called his nephews to his side and then sent Rodrigo for an abbreviated course of study in canon law at the University of Bologna. Certainly the records of the University only refer to him in 1455 and 1456.[3] The fact that the future Borgia Pope was apparently able to obtain a degree in canon law after little more than a year of study has often been regarded as an example of the way in which the Borgias were able to twist and bribe their way through life, and implicitly as an indication of an extremely cursory and insufficient education. However this explanation poses a number of problems; why should Cardinal Alonso Borja, installed in his palace at Quattro Coronati for eleven years before he became Pope, wait until 1455 before bringing the young members of his family to Rome? Rodrigo in particular, destined for the priesthood, could only profit from coming to the capital of the Church at the earliest possible opportunity. Furthermore what education was he undergoing before the age of twenty-four when he is supposed to have gone to the University of Bologna? There is an illogicality about this very late move which does not fit in with Borgia family pride and dynastic ambitions.

In fact in 1449 Nicholas V granted young Rodrigo leave to enjoy the fruits of his benefices (he was already canon of the collegiate church of Jativa and sacristan of the cathedral of Valencia) *in absentia* 'whether living in Rome or studying at university'. This of course is not proof that he took advantage of the permission but the wording is significant, and it would seem logical to suppose that at the age of eighteen his uncle would decide to take Rodrigo's education in hand, not at the age of twenty-four. Furthermore there is clear indication in 1453 in another grant from Nicholas V that he was by this time a student at Bologna.[4]

Thus we find Rodrigo probably coming to Rome in 1449 or soon after and being placed under the tutorship of the humanist Gaspare da Verona, who at this time kept a school for the young relatives of the higher prelates at the Vatican. Gaspare described Rodrigo thus: 'He is handsome; with a most cheerful countenance and genial bearing. He is gifted with a honeyed and choice eloquence. Beautiful women are attracted to love him and are excited by him in a quite remarkable way, more powerfully than iron is attracted by a magnet.'[5] Subsequently, probably in 1452 or 1453, for he certainly did not complete a full five year course at Bologna, Rodrigo went to Bologna where, as the nephew of a relatively obscure cardinal, his presence did not arouse very much interest. Once however Calixtus was elected Pope and Rodrigo and his cousin Luis Juan de Mila returned to Bologna in state having attended the ceremonies in Rome, then Bologna really took an interest and we find plenty of information about the final year of their studies at the University. Rodrigo was housed in the ex-Collegio Gregoriano which at this time belonged to the Dominicans, while his cousin, already bishop of Segorbe, had been nominated Governor of Bologna by Calixtus and lived in state in the bishop's palace. Both cousins followed the course in canon law and sat at the feet of Andrea Barbazza, the famous Sicilian canonist, who spoke well of Rodrigo's abilities as a student.

In March 1456 both Rodrigo and Luis Mila, together with Don Jaime of Portugal, were created cardinals by Calixtus in secret conclave. With the end of the academic year in the autumn, the two cousins took their degrees and set off for Rome to receive their cardinals' hats. The opposition to these nominations in the College of Cardinals has already been discussed, and that opposition becomes even more understandable when it is realised that Don Jaime was also only twenty-two and his nomination smacked very much of political manoeuvring at a time when Portuguese assistance was needed for the crusade.[6]

While Cardinal Mila returned to his post at Bologna, Rodrigo was now dispatched to another part of the Papal States, the March of Ancona, as legate. Here his mission was short and successful; the papal fortress of Ascoli was reduced to obedience after a short siege, and Rodrigo by a judicious use of force and generosity restored order in the troubled area. On his return to Rome in triumph he was made a commander of the papal army and Vice-Chancellor of the Church. He had convincingly proved his worth to his uncle who gave him rapid promotion and began to heap benefices on him, while Cardinal Mila languished in probably deserved obscurity. Nepotism was not always blind.

As Vice-Chancellor Rodrigo now occupied a position of great importance second only in the hierarchy of the government of the Church to the Pope himself. He was directly responsible for the day to day operations of papal government and in addition he was president of the Sacred Rota. These were posts which he occupied with a good deal of distinction for thirty-five years. During this period it is said that he never missed a consistory except when ill or away from Rome, and certainly he was able to build up a unique experience of the workings of papal administration. He was also in a splendid position to increase his own wealth; as Vice-Chancellor he was the first to know of any rich benefices which had fallen vacant, and each of the five Popes whom he served contributed to the steady growth of his income. As Vice-Chancellor his income was reckoned at 8000 ducats which was a relatively modest sum considering the importance of the position. But as cardinal he was first Bishop of Albano and then after 1476 Bishop of Porto. In 1458 he was given the bishopric of Valencia by Calixtus, in 1462 he also became Bishop of Cartagena, and in 1489 Bishop of Majorca. It was reported in 1492 that he held sixteen Spanish bishoprics but this was a gross exaggeration. As one of the few Spanish cardinals in the College it was natural that he should tend to accumulate Spanish benefices, but what was more significant was his tightening grip on important Italian abbeys and benefices around Rome. By 1492 he was in control of Nepi, Civita Castellana and Soriano, the three vital fortresses controlling the Via Cassia and Via Flaminia to the north of Rome. In 1471 after the election of Sixtus IV he received the *commenda* of the abbey of Subiaco which included the lordship of twenty-two villages controlling the routes into the Abruzzi. While to the south he held the *commenda* of the abbey of Fossanova astride the Via Appia and the route to Naples. That he was able to build up this very significant strategic grip on the routes in and out of Rome at a time when a series of nepotistic Popes were attempting to concentrate wealth and power in the hands of their own families is an indication of two important facts. First that Rodrigo Borgia commanded a pre-eminent position at the papal court and in the confidence of the Popes throughout this period. Secondly it reveals the importance which he attached to the control of the Campagna from a very early moment. At the time of his election in 1492 the position which he had established was largely broken because he was forced to distribute the vital strongpoints to other cardinals. But we shall see that throughout his pontificate he sought to recover this strategic stranglehold on Rome by gifts to his family; a policy which brought him face to face with the traditional controllers of the Roman Campagna, the Orsini and the Colonna, and which by 1503 was largely successful.

It has been argued that despite this considerable concentration of wealth in the hands of Rodrigo, his expenses were such that he can have had little in reserve by 1492.[7] The implications of this will be considered in their proper place, but it is certainly clear from the start that Rodrigo Borgia was a great spender. His first major expense as cardinal was the building of his palace. While the Popes of the Renaissance were busy creating a more sumptuous and suitable palace for themselves in the Vatican, the cardinals were devoting similar energies to the building of palaces more appropriate to their new role as princes of the Church. While Cardinal Barbo started the construction of the Palazzo Venezia, and Cardinal Nardini the Palazzo del Governo Vecchio, Cardinal Borgia also began work on what was considered the finest palace in Italy. The site, together with the old mint which stood on it, was bought by Rodrigo from Calixtus in 1458 for 2000 ducats. The palace was probably not finished for several years and in the meantime Rodrigo lived close by in far more humble surroundings and in the shadow of the Orsini fortress of Monte Giordano.

The palace built by Rodrigo forms the nucleus of the present Palazzo Sforza-Cesarini on the Corso Vittorio Emmanuele. Pius II on the occasion of the great procession which took place in 1462 for the reception of the precious relic of St. Andrew's head, likened the palace to the Golden House of Nero because Rodrigo had outstripped all the other cardinals in the sumptuousness of the decorations which he had put up for the occasion.[8] Jacopo Gherardi described it as 'no less ornate than it was comfortable'.[9] But the most complete description was that of Ascanio Sforza in 1484: 'The palace is splendidly decorated; the walls of the great entrance hall are hung with tapestries depicting various historical scenes. A small drawing room leads off this, which was also decorated with fine tapestries; the carpets on the floor harmonised with the furnishings which included a sumptuous day bed upholstered in red satin with a canopy over it, and a chest on which was laid out a vast and beautiful collection of gold and silver plate. Beyond this there were two more rooms, one hung with fine satin, carpeted, and with another canopied bed covered with Alexandrine velvet; the other even more ornate with a couch covered in cloth of gold. In this room the central table was covered with a cloth of Alexandrine velvet and surrounded by finely carved chairs.'[10] The palace was built round a rectangular courtyard with three-storied loggias on at least two sides. Parts of these loggias are the only visible remains of the fifteenth century palace today, and the slender octagonal columns reflect the Tuscan influences in mid-fifteenth century Roman architecture. However, in the tradition of Roman palaces, a tower was incorporated into the façade, and the palace was certainly the tallest building in the whole neighbourhood.[11]

If Rodrigo's love of display and penchant for sumptuous

6 Cesare Borgia; woodcut from Paolo Giovio, *Gli Elogi* (Basle, 1577). The portrait was in Giovio's own collection and is one of the more authentic of the many, mostly posthumous, representations of Cesare, who was at one time said to be the handsomest man of his day.

7 Lucrezia Borgia; a portrait medal struck soon after her marriage to Alfonso d'Este showing her at about the age of twenty-four. On the reverse a blindfolded Cupid tied to a laurel tree.

8 Nepi Castle; Lucrezia's residence as governor of the city in 1499–1500.

entertaining was held in check during the early years of his career as Vice-Chancellor by the delay in the building of his palace, the other notorious characteristic of his private life, his pleasure in feminine company, was clearly established from an early date. Gaspare da Verona remarked on his immense physical attraction for women, and his sensuality was a feature of his character noted in many descriptions of him. But at the same time he did not make an ostentatious display of his disregard for ecclesiastical conventions, of his mistresses or of his children, at any time while he was a cardinal. The mystery which shrouds the dates of birth of his first three children and even the name of their mother is an indication of a considerable degree of discretion which he exercised at this stage. But
[illegible] moral shortcomings of Rodrigo Borgia
[illegible] culous failure, a failure which has cast
[illegible] justifiable attempts to rewrite other
[illegible] egend.[12]
[illegible] Borgia's eldest son, was probably born
[illegible] his eldest daughter, in 1467. These are
[illegible] moral implication of which are in no
[illegible] e probability that Rodrigo did not take
[illegible] 468. As a cardinal he was just as much
[illegible] f chastity as was a priest. But Rodrigo's
private life as a cardinal was not marked by an outrageous public display of immorality, and attempts to prove otherwise by emphasis on the well-known Siena letter of Pius II need to be reconsidered.

Among Rodrigo's close associates in the Sacred College during the pontificate of his uncle had been Cardinal Piccolomini, whose success in the conclave of 1458 and election as Pius II was in part due to Rodrigo's decisive intervention. It was Pius who had noted earlier: 'Rodrigo Borgia is now in charge of the Chancellery; he is young in age assuredly, but he is old in judgement',[13] and it was he who confirmed Rodrigo's position and benefices immediately after his election; it was his support which protected Rodrigo in that difficult period. Soon after the election Pius II went north to attend the Diet of Mantua and Rodrigo accompanied him. It was while they were returning and while Pius was taking the waters at Petriolo in his native Tuscany that he received reports of an apparently outrageous affair which had taken place in Siena. Cardinals Rodrigo and d'Estouteville, the ageing and extremely wealthy French cardinal, were reported to have led the revels at a scandalous orgy in a Sienese garden. It was reported that after a baptism ceremony, to which the two cardinals had been invited as honoured guests, the party had adjourned to a walled garden to which only the cardinals, their followers, and the ladies of the party were admitted. There from morning until six in the evening they were shut in while 'there was dancing without restraint, and no allurements to love were spared, and you (Rodrigo) yourself behaved as if you were one of a group of young laymen.' It was further reported that all Siena was laughing at this incident.

Pius was not unnaturally extremely perturbed at these reports and wrote off immediately to Rodrigo reproving him in no uncertain terms for his behaviour which was bringing scandal on himself and the Church.[14] This letter has often been regarded as a general indictment of Rodrigo's behaviour throughout his career as cardinal and even the reasonably judicious but frankly hostile Von Pastor by quoting the letter and the incident four times not only grossly exaggerates the incident itself but succeeds in spreading its influence over thirty-five years of Rodrigo's life.

In fact Pius' first letter cannot be taken in isolation; for a proper review of the significance of the incident it must be examined along with the second letter which Pius wrote to Borgia three days later in which he admits that he may have reacted over hastily to rumours and that the affair does not seem to have been as serious as he at first thought.[15] There is also a report of the Mantuan ambassador which brings out that the party was exclusive in a social sense rather than in any strict division of the sexes. He himself was not able to get invited and it was only the cardinals and their clerical followers who were admitted from outside Sienese high society.[16] Certainly there was a gay and protracted party in Siena that day at which the deportment of the two cardinals made all Siena smile; but Siena would scarcely have smiled if the leading citizens had been forcibly excluded from an orgy at which two cardinals dishonoured their wives and daughters. The fact that Pius did not feel that it was necessary to reprove d'Estouteville shows his particular affection for Rodrigo and the relative insignificance of the affair. Finally Pius II, a man who had certainly erred in his youth, but who was by now exceptional for the sanctity and austerity of his private life, would scarcely have continued to heap benefices on a cardinal whose usual behaviour was that attributed to Rodrigo by the hostile interpreters of the famous letter.

I have devoted some space to this incident because it has bulked so large in the estimation of those who have sought to see Rodrigo Borgia as a monster of ostentatious immorality. Of his immorality there can be no doubt, but we shall never understand his great influence as a cardinal, or his election as Pope, if we regard the traditional picture of this incident as the epitome of his private life. But for the discretion with which he habitually veiled his family in these early years, we should not be confronted with the acute problems of learning and writing about them.

The later years of Pius II's pontificate were devoted to preparations for the long awaited crusade. To raise the money for the expedition, Pius proposed to create and sell additional posts in the Papal Chancellery. Such venality was to become increasingly common in the papal administration and

Rodrigo was to resort to it himself on an even greater scale when he was Pope, but on this occasion he opposed the plan vigorously on the grounds of its damage to the efficiency of the Chancellery, and the fact that the new college of abbreviators was to be taken out of his control. The humanists to whom the posts were to go bitterly resented his attitude and one can perhaps date from this moment the beginning of that antagonism of the more articulate propagandists which was to do him so much damage.

If he opposed Pius over this, Rodrigo made amends by being the only cardinal to fit out a galley at his own expense for the crusade. He accompanied the declining Pope on his last pathetic journey to Ancona in 1464. There, in the appalling conditions of the overcrowded city filled with reluctant and ill-equipped crusaders, Rodrigo himself fell very seriously ill, probably with the plague.[17] When Pius died just as the Venetian fleet appeared to join his crusade, the whole venture collapsed and the cardinals hurried back to Rome to take part in the new conclave. Rodrigo, still severely ill, just got back in time but seems to have played little part in the election of his old ally Cardinal Barbo. A Venetian Pope was an obvious choice in view of the importance of Venetian participation in any crusade, and Barbo commanded wide respect both for his learning and for his wealth.

We know little of Rodrigo's activities during the pontificate of Paul II. The building of his palace was by now probably complete and we can imagine that he felt fully at ease in the heightened splendour of the Vatican controlled by the luxury loving Venetian aristocrat. There are some indications that during the period the antagonism of both the Orsini and the humanists relaxed towards Rodrigo, as Paul II became the object of their joint hatred for his active policies in the Roman Campagna and his failure to live up to the high hopes of humanist patronage which his election had created. Among other reforms he abolished Pius' college of abbreviators and restored the powers of his Chancellor, Rodrigo.

By 1471 when Paul II died, Rodrigo, already a cardinal for fifteen years, was amongst the more eminent figures in the conclave. He can hardly have considered his own chances very high at this stage, but his intervention on the side of Francesco della Rovere seems to have been a decisive factor in the election. Della Rovere was general of the Franciscans and a monk of apparently unsullied reputation. His election was generally regarded as a reaction against the worldliness of Paul II and a step towards a new impetus for a crusade. Rodrigo as a reward for his support received the *commenda* of the abbey of Subiaco, and in the following summers he spent a good deal of his time there with his family to escape the heat of Rome. Both the town and its monasteries owe much to Borgia patronage. He rebuilt the castle with the massive Torre Borgiana and restored the buildings of the monasteries. He also extended the jurisdiction of the town over a number of neighbouring castles and granted privileges for weekly markets and periodic sporting festivals.[18]

But this was all somewhat in the future because in 1472, as part of the new Pope Sixtus IV's programme for propagating a crusade, Rodrigo Borgia was sent as papal legate to the Spanish kingdoms. In Spain the permanent crusade against the Moors was still in progress, so there was little hope that Rodrigo could succeed in winning active Spanish support for a new venture in the eastern Mediterranean. But an essential first step towards any possible Spanish participation in a crusade was pacification of the internal civil wars which were raging and the final achievement of the unity of the Castilian and Aragonese crowns. In both these directions the legation of Rodrigo Borgia was to be crowned with success.

Rodrigo made elaborate preparations for his journey. He was returning to his native land as a cardinal and Vice-

Chancellor of the Church and he naturally wanted to put on a display suitable to the occasion. He pledged his income for years to come and assembled an imposing following. On his departure from Rome in May 1472 he was accompanied, as tradition demanded, by all the cardinals to the Porta San Paolo. From there he proceeded to Ostia where two Neapolitan ships were waiting to take him to Valencia. The voyage was uneventful and after a brief call at Bonifacio in Corsica, the ships arrived off Valencia on 17 June. In Valencia there was consternation as the great preparations which were going forward for the reception of her bishop were not yet complete. Rodrigo with characteristic good humour and in no way willing to mar the impact of his arrival had the ships sail up the coast to Puig where he went ashore on 20 June. There in the parish church he spent the night in vigil before the image of the Virgin, and on the 21st his procession set out on the short journey into Valencia. Accompanying Rodrigo were the bishops of Assisi, Orte and Fano, and the painters Paolo di San Leocadio da Reggio and Francesco Pagano. On the way he was met by a great procession of Valencian notables including the auxiliary bishop, chosen by Rodrigo himself, Jaime Perez, an Augustinian monk of noted sanctity.[19] The scene was described in a contemporary letter: 'At the junction of the road to Murviedro (ancient Sagunto) all the councilmen, the governor general, and other prominent noblemen and gentlemen, to the number of twelve, waited for him with a magnificent canopy, under which the cardinal entered, mounted on his steed; and the porters of the canopy were all on foot. And when they arrived at the city walls, where the gates were overhung with crimson draperies, he entered the city to the various sounds of trumpets and kettledrums.'[20]

All Valencia turned out that Sunday afternoon to meet her bishop who was accompanied in state to the cathedral. There he celebrated mass, and three days later he gave a great banquet to all the officials of the city. There was certainly a style about Rodrigo's entertaining and bearing which did not please some of his more ascetic fellow cardinals, and also no doubt made others jealous. But it was what was by now expected of a prince of the Church, and particularly by the Valencians. Furthermore Rodrigo's stay in Valencia was by no means all spent in feasting and pleasure. Throughout July he remained carrying out a series of diocesan visits and making himself familiar with the problems of the diocese. He addressed a speech to the assembled clergy of the diocese which, if it has been reported correctly, was a model of pastoral sincerity and rectitude.[21]

But Rodrigo had not come to Spain to attend to the affairs of his diocese, welcome and surprising though his concern was, but to serve the politico-religious interests of the Pope. On 31 July he set out northwards to meet King John of Aragon and his son Ferdinand. Having weighed up the character of Ferdinand he decided that his marriage with Isabella of Castile, which had already taken place but still required a valid papal dispensation because of consanguinity, and the inevitable subsequent union of Aragon and Castile, were in the best interests of the Church.[22] He therefore presented the necessary dispensation which Sixtus had entrusted to him to use at his discretion. He then journeyed to Castile in the autumn and with the promise of a cardinal's hat persuaded the influential Archbishop Gonzalez de Mendoza to support the match. He spent Christmas at the court of King Henry of Castile and did a good deal to win over the Castilian nobility to the political volte-face which the marriage involved. He also added the weight of the Church's authority to Henry's programme of currency reform which was designed to put the Castilian economy to rights.[23] Finally he travelled back to Catalonia and worked to bring about the end of the civil war there which had been plaguing King John for years. He had made a lasting impression on the future King Ferdinand which was not only to result in considerable advancement for the Borgia family in Spain, but was to have a significant impact on Papal-Spanish relations for the remainder of the century. He had played no small part in the cementing of that marriage alliance which was to mean so much in the history of united Spain.

In July 1473 Rodrigo returned to his diocese for a final two months before departing for Italy. During this period he visited Jativa, his birth place, and pointed out with pride the palace where he had been born to his companions. At last in September he and his suite, together with many young Valencian nobles who had chosen to accompany him to Italy in search of their fortunes, embarked on two Venetian galleys for the return voyage.

The voyage was a disastrous one. The galleys ran into a violent storm off the Tuscan coast. One sank outright and the other, badly damaged, managed to limp ashore and beach itself near the mouth of the Arno. The cardinal and a few followers were taken to safety, but most of his suite including the three bishops and the majority of the hopeful Valencian courtiers were drowned. 30,000 ducats worth of property and all the valuable cargo of the galleys were lost to the sea or to Tuscan wreckers. Rodrigo and the few survivors spent some days in Pisa recovering from the disastrous experience, while emissaries from Lorenzo de' Medici did their utmost to recover some of their lost possessions and make the cardinal welcome.[24] Finally in mid October the depleted party made its way down to Rome by land.

The Rome to which Rodrigo returned in late 1473 was very different from that which he had left eighteen months earlier. The Franciscan Della Rovere Pope had proved to have a large and rapacious family, and the conversion of the Holy City into a luxurious capital and a centre of diplomatic intrigue was going ahead fast. Rodrigo must have felt quite at home, if somewhat eclipsed, in the new atmosphere, and he quietly resumed his position as one of the principal figures in the papal court. It was he rather than one of the papal nephews who was chosen at the express wish of Ferdinand of Aragon to preside over the wedding and coronation of Queen Juana of Naples, Ferdinand's sister.

Rodrigo's policy throughout this period was to assist the Papacy to maintain good relations with her immediate neighbours Florence and Naples. He was a persistent adherent of the policy of an Italian balance of power and deplored the extent to which Sixtus IV, in the interests of his family, was bent on destroying the peace of Italy and embroiling the Papacy in war with Florence. In maintaining good relations with Naples, Rodrigo was in line with the policy of the Pope; but his continued friendship with the Medici during the Pazzi War must have damaged his influence in the Vatican. Thus although he seems to have remained on fairly good terms with the Della Rovere and Riario families during the lifetime of Sixtus IV, the stage was being set for the bitter antagonism between Rodrigo and Giuliano della Rovere which was to some extent to dominate the rest of his life. One of the essential elements of this antagonism was a completely different approach to the position of the Papacy in international affairs. Rodrigo Borgia was essentially a diplomat, a politician, a believer in balance of power and temporisation; Giuliano della Rovere was a more martial and impatient figure, a man who believed in force to create unity in Italy, a unity to be led by a militant Pope.

The first round of this struggle was the conclave of 1484, after the death of Sixtus IV. By this time at the age of fifty-three with nearly thirty years in the Curia behind him, Rodrigo was poised to make his great effort to win the papal throne. He could command Spanish support, but the Spanish Cardinals Mendoza and his own cousin Luis Juan Mila did not attend the conclave. He also had the enthusiastic support of Cardinal Ascanio Sforza, uncle of the Duke of Milan, and had cultivated an alliance with the Colonna family. But France, the group of Sistine nephews and the Orsini were against him, and it was reported by the Florentine envoy that 'Borgia has the reputation of being so false and proud that there is no danger of him being elected.'[25] There was a considerable danger that out of this deadlock the Venetian Marco Barbo, widely respected personally, would emerge as Pope. Indeed he received the most votes in the first scrutiny. But this was a moment when Venetian ambitions had aroused the suspicion of all the other states of Italy, and the danger of a Venetian Pope brought Rodrigo and Giuliano della Rovere together in a compromise. A compromise, however, which resulted in the election of Giovanni Battista Cibo, an amiable enough figure, but one who was a good deal more under the influence of Giuliano than Rodrigo probably realised. On the other hand the pontificate of Innocent VIII and this extended period of Della Rovere domination in the Vatican, probably made it easier for Rodrigo to collect votes in the next round of the struggle when Giuliano was generally more feared than he was.

For the eight years of the pontificate of Innocent VIII was to be a period of intense preparation for Rodrigo, preparation for the conclave which could well prove to be his last chance. He clung tenaciously to his Neapolitan policy while Innocent VIII, belying his reputation as a man of peace, encouraged the Neapolitan barons in their revolt against King Ferrante. It was largely owing to the efforts of Rodrigo and Ferdinand of Aragon that peace between Naples and the Papacy was finally patched up in 1486. He maintained his alliance with Ascanio Sforza and the Colonna but at the same time did his best to stifle the traditional feud between his family and that of the Orsini. Virginio Orsini was a witness at the marriage of Girolama Borgia to Gianandrea Cesarini in 1483, and Rodrigo's cousin Adriana de Mila was married to an Orsini. It was in Rodrigo's palace that the famous wedding between Orsino Orsini and Giulia Farnese took place in 1489.

When in 1490 Innocent VIII fell seriously ill, Rodrigo and Ascanio were seen to be hard at work canvassing for votes.[26] Rodrigo through his friendship with the Pope's doctor, Ludovico Podocatharo, was able to get first hand information about the Pope's health. Marco Barbo and his followers who had a deep rooted contempt for the worldly Borgia were seriously alarmed at the way things seemed to be going.[27] But already the growing political split between Naples and Milan was endangering Rodrigo's position. Had Innocent VIII died in 1490 it would probably have been an easy conclave for Rodrigo. In 1488 the Florentine ambassador Lanfredini had remarked that Rodrigo could easily become the next Pope if he wanted to.[28] But by 1492 the possibility of support from both Naples and Milan was irretrievably lost and Rodrigo's chances therefore seemed slim when the long awaited moment finally came.

Although the salient features of Rodrigo Borgia's public life as a cardinal are reasonably well established, it is always somewhat surprising, after the immense amount of true and apocryphal detail which has come down to us about Rodrigo's private life as Pope, how little we know about this before his election. Even the sumptuous entertainments in the Palazzo Borgia have only been noted on two or three occasions. During the pontificate of Paul II Rodrigo seems to have occupied a position as official papal entertainer. He welcomed Don Federigo, son of King Ferrante, when he passed through Rome on his way to Milan to escort Ippolita Sforza back to Naples to marry his brother. It was also he who welcomed the Emperor Frederick III on his visit to Rome in 1468. In 1484 Alfonso, Duke of Calabria, was entertained by Rodrigo and it was after this occasion that Ascanio Sforza wrote the description of Rodrigo's palace which has already been quoted.

To keep up this state Rodrigo was surrounded by a considerable entourage most of whom were Spaniards.[29] Rodrigo's first language was of course Catalan and he wrote much of his correspondence in this or in Castilian.[30] All his children were more at home in Spanish dialects than they were in Italian, being educated by Spanish tutors. But two non-Spaniards stand out in Rodrigo's court, Ludovico Podocatharo his secretary, and Lorenz Behaim, the master of the household. Podocatharo was a Greek, a scholar and a doctor who probably took a part in the education of Rodrigo's children. Lorenz Behaim on the other hand was German, a member of the Roman Academy of Pomponius Laetus, and a noted figure in Roman humanist circles.

Another aspect of this style of living was artistic and architectural patronage. We already know something about the Borgia palace in Rome and its magnificence, but to get a fuller view of Rodrigo's participation in Vatican patronage at this time we must also consider the palace built for him in Pienza by Rosellino. The conversion of the little Tuscan village of Corsignano, the birth place of Pius II, into a papal summer resort resulted in the creation of a triumph of Renaissance architecture and town planning that was renamed Pienza. Many of the cardinals were invited to participate in the project and Rodrigo Borgia was among the first to build a palace there, a palace which is now the Palazzo Vescovile. The style of both this building and the palace in Rome with their tiered loggias represents a blend of medieval and Renaissance, of Tuscan and Roman, of monastic and secular which is very much in keeping with the spirit of the papal court of this time.[31]

Most of the remainder of Rodrigo's building activities were devoted to fortifications, particularly at Subiaco and Nepi. The importance of the control of these and other key points to Borgia policy has already been stressed, and an essential feature of that control rested on improved fortifications. The castle at Nepi which was to be a favourite Borgia residence in later years was considerably strengthened, with a new *enceinte*, designed by Antonio da San Gallo, the elder, built round the earlier nucleus.[32]

Of other Borgia artistic projects at this stage we know less. It is interesting to note the two painters who accompanied Rodrigo to Spain in 1472, and it was perhaps on this visit that Rodrigo arranged for the completion of the chapel in Valencia which had been started by Calixtus III. In Santa Maria del Popolo in Rome the carved high altar by Andrea Bregno was commissioned by Rodrigo during this period, while frescoes in one of the side chapels by Pinturicchio were ordered by Vanozza, his mistress for many years and the mother of four of his children.[33]

When we turn to consider Rodrigo's rapidly growing family we are plunged into a world of uncertainty tinged with acrimonious and often libidinous hypothesis. However as an understanding of much of Borgia dynastic policy depends on a clear picture of Rodrigo's family, on the order of seniority of his children, and on his changing hopes and plans for their future, it is essential to consider the problem.

Rodrigo's children, of whom there were certainly eight, and possibly nine, can be divided into three groups: those born before the Spanish legation in 1472, those born to Vanozza de' Cataneis between 1475 and 1481, and those born after Rodrigo became Pope. There have been some who have felt that Vanozza was also the mother of the earlier children, partly on the grounds that it would seem more likely that Rodrigo was attracted by her as a girl of eighteen than as a mature woman of thirty-one, partly in an attempt to give a greater air of respectability to Rodrigo's private life. However there is no concrete evidence to support this theory and Vanozza's epitaph cites her as the mother of only the four children born between 1475 and 1481.[34] That the earlier three children should have been forgotten by the composer of the epitaph seems impossible in view of the fact that one, Isabella, was still alive and well known in Rome when Vanozza died in 1518, and another, Pedro Luis, as first Duke of Gandia, created for himself a position of some importance.

Pedro Luis was born in 1462 and named after his uncle, Calixtus's Captain General, who had died at Civitavecchia in 1458.[35] He seems to have lived most of his life in Spain and, as a result of the relationship established between Rodrigo and Ferdinand of Aragon in 1472, was quickly brought to the attention of the King. Although Rodrigo was generally on very good terms with Ferdinand during this period and was in 1478 invited to be godfather to Ferdinand and Isabella's son, there was a moment in 1484 when relations were very strained. Rodrigo had at that moment acquired the bishopric of Seville which Ferdinand had wanted for his bastard son, Alfonso. This, combined with Rodrigo's diligent policy of accumulating honours and wealth for himself and Pedro Luis in Spain, infuriated Ferdinand and led to the imprisonment of Pedro Luis who was serving in the Aragonese army in Granada, and the confiscation of all Borgia estates. However the breach was temporary as Rodrigo and Ferdinand once more came together in opposition to Innocent VIII's anti-Neapolitan policy, and in 1485 Pedro Luis was released and restored to favour. He acquitted himself well at the siege of Ronda and was permitted to purchase the estates of Gandia and given the title of Duke, an honour normally reserved for members of the royal house. As an additional mark of favour he was betrothed to Maria Enriquez, a cousin of Ferdinand. As Maria was not yet of marriageable age, Rodrigo quickly summoned Pedro Luis to Italy lest he should fall into disfavour before this match could be completed. However in 1488 Pedro Luis died in Rome having made a will bequeathing his duchy to his younger brother Juan, and 10,000 ducats as a dowry to Lucrezia.

Rodrigo's next two children were girls; Isabella born in 1467 and Girolama born in about 1471. Both of these spent all their lives in Italy, and both were married to Roman noblemen. Girolama was married in 1483 in great style to Gianandrea Cesarini, but both bride and bridegroom died shortly after the wedding. Isabella was betrothed, also in 1483, to Pietro Matuzzi and married soon after.[36] The Matuzzi were a relatively minor Roman noble family and the couple lived in a house provided by Rodrigo in Via dei Leutari close to the Borgia palace. Pietro Matuzzi spent his life in the administration of the city of Rome, first as one of the *maestri delle strade* and then as head of the Capitoline chancery. A descendant of this match was to be Innocent X, through the marriage of a grand-daughter of Isabella into the Pamfili family. In 1501 Isabella and one of her daughters were seized by the Orsini family in reprisal for Cesare Borgia's capture of the wife of Fabio Orsini, but otherwise the Matuzzi household seems to have had little contact with the rest of the Borgia family. Isabella finally died in 1547, a respected Roman matron.

It was probably after his return from the Spanish legation in 1473 that Rodrigo commenced his protracted affair with Vanozza de' Cataneis. Vanozza was a Roman, born in 1442, and her father was a certain Jacopo Pinctoris. She seems to have been a woman of remarkable beauty and understanding, who brought a degree of order if not respectability into Rodrigo's tempestuous private life. She was married three times; first in 1474 to Domenico da Rignano, an elderly lawyer who died soon after the birth of Cesare in lawful wedlock. Vanozza's second husband was the Milanese Giorgio San Croce, an apostolic secretary to Sixtus IV, whom she married in 1480 or 1481. On the death of Giorgio in 1486, Vanozza, now no longer the mistress of Rodrigo and a widow with a reasonable patrimony inherited from her two husbands, married the Mantuan Carlo Canale. Canale was a man of letters who had been chamberlain to Cardinal Gonzaga. He relished the influence which marriage to Vanozza gave him in Rome and was proud of his indirect connection with the Borgias. Vanozza's life after this became increasingly devoted to good works and careful investment. She is reputed to have owned three inns, the Albergo del Sole in the Campo dei Fiori, the Biscione and the Vacca. She also endowed convents and hospices.[37] Her children by Rodrigo always seem to have regarded her with respect and affection, and Cesare Borgia remembered her in the disastrous days of 1503 and sent her to safety in Civita Castellana.

Cesare was the eldest of the sons of Vanozza, born in 1475.[38] As such he was Rodrigo's second son and in the traditional manner destined from youth for a career in the Church. Although born to Vanozza while she was the wife of Domenico da Rignano, Cesare, if he was to enjoy the advantages of his Borgia parenthood, had to be officially freed from the stigma of illegitimacy. Thus in 1480 Sistus IV dispensed Cesare from this slur for all ecclesiastical offices except that of the cardinalate, while in the following year Ferdinand of Aragon formally legitimised him for the enjoyment of Spanish estates. Cesare always lived in Italy but his earliest benefices were Spanish and all in his father's diocese of Valencia. At the age of seven he was made an apostolic protonotary, canon of the cathedral of Valencia, archdeacon of Jativa and rector of Gandia. All this was entirely in keeping with the practice of the day whereby the sons of important families, who were destined for the Church, began to receive benefices from a very early age. This not only reflected honour on the family but provided the financial means whereby the future ecclesiastic could receive the best possible education. Cesare's early tutors were Paolo Pompilio and Giovanni Vera, both

9 Alfonso d'Este, Duke of Ferrara; portrait by Dosso Dossi (1516) in the Galleria Estense, Modena. Alfonso bears the insignia of the Captain General of the Church, and his reputation as an artillery expert is indicated by the prominence given to the cannon in the picture.

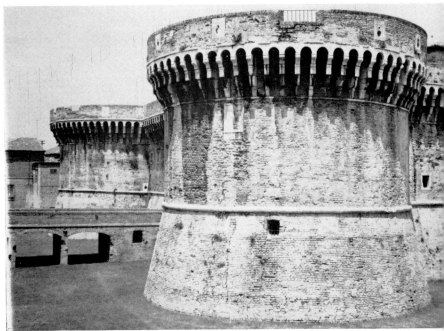

10 The Rocca at Imola; surrendered to Cesare Borgia after a short siege in December 1499.

11 The Rocca at Senigallia, refortified about 1480. It was surrendered to Cesare after the famous *coup* in January 1503.

Catalans, and at the age of fourteen he was sent to the University of Perugia to study law. From there he passed in 1491 to the University of Pisa to study under Filippo Decio, the famous jurist. It was at this stage that Innocent VIII made Cesare Bishop of Pamplona. His disputation in the following year which gained him a degree in canon and civil law was generally recognised to have been exceptionally brilliant. By this time he had been given by his father what appears to have been his first Italian estate, the lordship of the small but strategically important Etrurian town of Blera.

There can be no doubt that Cesare was the outstanding figure amongst Rodrigo's children. After the death of Pedro Luis, Rodrigo began to pin his hopes on his younger sons and increasingly, despite his paternal fondness for Juan, on the brilliant Cesare. Juan was born in 1476 and in 1483 received 25,000 ducats from his father to purchase Spanish estates. He seemed to be destined to follow in the steps of his elder half-brother Pedro Luis, and in 1488 inherited his title and became 2nd Duke of Gandia. He also inherited his brother's affianced bride as part of the continuation of the alliance between Ferdinand and Rodrigo Borgia. Juan seems to have been a man of limited abilities and considerable vices to whose subsequent tragic career we shall return later. But in 1492 he seemed to be poised on the threshold of an illustrious career as a Spanish grandee.

It was also towards Spain that Lucrezia, Vanozza's third child born in 1480, seemed to be turning by 1492. Lucrezia, after an initial period under the care of her mother, was entrusted to the care of Rodrigo's cousin Adriana de Mila who was married to Ludovico Orsini, Lord of Bassanello. With the rich dowry left her by Pedro Luis she was betrothed at the age of eleven to a young Spanish nobleman Juan de Centelles. In the next year arrangements were changed and a rather more noble bridegroom was chosen for her in the person of

Don Gasparo, Count of Aversa. After her father's election to the papal throne all ideas of a Spanish match were abandoned and she became increasingly a pawn in Rodrigo's Italian policies.

Finally amongst the children of this period came Jofrè, born in 1481 and like Cesare destined for the Church. He received his first benefices, all Spanish, from Innocent VIII and by 1492 was already archdeacon of the cathedral of Valencia.

While he was a cardinal, Rodrigo was not only concerned with the advancement of his own children. Since the death of his mother in 1466 he had taken increasing responsibility for the welfare of his sisters and their children. His four sisters were all married to Spaniards and themselves played no part in Italian affairs. But their children, and particularly those of Juana Borja married to Pedro Lanzol were always the object of concern to the head of the family. Juan Borgia-Lanzol, the elder, was made Archbishop of Monreale by Innocent VIII, and was a frequent visitor in the Borgia palace before 1492.

Finally perhaps no account of Rodrigo's family and private life would be complete without some mention of Giulia Farnese, Giulia la Bella as the Romans called her. Giulia at the age of nineteen in 1489 was married in the Borgia palace to Orsino Orsini, the son of Adriana de Mila. Whether this was the occasion of the first meeting between Rodrigo and Giulia, or whether the affair was already under way is not clear. But there seems to be no doubt that both before and immediately after his election Giulia was Rodrigo's mistress.[39] That the Pope should openly flaunt a mistress was certainly a novel situation, but it was perhaps the relationship between an old man and a beautiful young girl which enraged contemporaries more than anything else about the Borgias at that time. It offended the Renaissance sense of aesthetics and provided the subject for innumerable lewd epigrams. It also, needless to say, exacerbated the long-standing and thinly veiled breach between the Orsini and Borgia families.

It would seem therefore that Rodrigo Borgia as cardinal did not yet have great Italian dynastic ambitions for his family. They were Spaniards and by adroit utilisation of his position as one of the few Spanish cardinals, and by his notable successes during his Spanish legation, Rodrigo was able to attract towards his children both papal and royal favour. By 1492 with one of the premier Spanish dukedoms in the hands of one son, a good bishopric and innumerable benefices in those of the other two, and a satisfactory marriage into the Spanish nobility arranged for Lucrezia, Rodrigo could feel justly proud of the position of his family. The Roman marriages of his two elder daughters should be seen more as an attempt to protect his own personal position in Rome, and the natural desire of a father to have his daughters close at hand, than the beginning of a serious dynastic policy in Italy. The Cesarini match was a good one and valuable in protecting Rodrigo from isolation amongst the Roman families, but it is difficult to attach any deep significance to the marriage of Isabella to the relatively obscure Matuzzi.

It is also important to note that the very considerable dynastic successes were achieved not only before Rodrigo became Pope, but also very largely with significant help from outside the family. It was Ferdinand of Aragon, and the Popes Sixtus IV and Innocent VIII, who laid the foundations of the Borgia dynastic position. Certainly once Rodrigo became Pope the whole direction of the policy was changed, but the Spanish base was never completely abandoned.

Thus in 1492 Rodrigo Borgia was poised for what would probably be a final effort to win the Papacy. Whether or not his apparently growing interest in a Spanish base for his family can be taken to indicate a certain loss of confidence in his own chances, it certainly appeared that in terms of potential votes which he could command his position was deteriorating. But on the other hand Rodrigo was very much in the public eye in 1492; it was he and Cesare who had organised the famous bullfight to celebrate the fall of Granada early in the year. As Vice-Chancellor he also played a prominent part in the ceremonies which attended the arrival of the Holy Lance in Rome in May 1492. Despite his Spanish speech and his Spanish entourage, Rodrigo was popular in Rome, and despite his Spanish political connections he seemed to stand more clearly for an Italian papal policy than some of his colleagues. These factors were perhaps not to be without influence in the forthcoming conclave.

CHAPTER SIX

ALEXANDER VI: THE ELECTION AND EARLY YEARS, 1492–4

The significance of 1492, the year in which Columbus first sighted the golden beaches of Hispaniola, has been much disputed by students of European exploration. But for the Italian historian Francesco Guicciardini this significance had nothing to do with maritime adventures and discovery. 'It is indisputable that since the Roman Empire . . . Italy had never known such prosperity or such a desirable condition as that which it enjoyed in all tranquillity in the year of Our Lord 1490 and the years immediately before and after. For, all at peace and quietness, cultivated no less in the mountainous and sterile places than in the fertile regions and plains, knowing no other rule than that of its own people, Italy was not only rich in population, merchandise and wealth, but she was adorned to the highest degree by the magnificence of many princes, by the splendour of innumerable noble and beautiful cities, by the throne and majesty of religion; full of men most able in the administration of public affairs, and of noble minds learned in every branch of study and versed in every worthy art and skill. Nor did she lack military glory according to the standards of those times; and being so richly endowed, she deservedly enjoyed amongst all other nations a most brilliant reputation.'[1] For Guicciardini it was the golden sunset of the Italian state system; that system which had grown up protected from dark 'barbarian' influences by the Alps, and which had provided the forcing ground in which the economic and cultural predominance of Italy over the rest of Europe had been established.

Much as we may now wish to dispute the clear cut outline of Guicciardini's picture, we cannot escape the impression that Italians of the day themselves felt that they were living in momentous times; that they were witnessing the passing of an old order and the appearance of a new and infinitely alarming one. The precarious equilibrium, which had been established in Italy by the Italian League of 1454 and which had succeeded in reducing the perpetual state of warfare in Renaissance Italy to a series of isolated and relatively contained outbreaks, was rapidly disintegrating. For nearly forty years the constantly shifting pattern of alliances within the increasingly anachronistic framework of the League had served to contain serious aggression by any one of the major Italian powers. The preoccupation of France, Spain and the Empire with their own internal problems of unification and strengthening of central authority had allowed Italians to think themselves safer than they really were behind the Alps. But by 1492 the situation both within Italy and outside was changing.

Venice was being increasingly regarded by the other Italian states as the main threat to the peace of Italy. Her policies were denounced as expansionist by her main territorial neighbour, Milan, and her main economic rival, Florence, and there was a widespread belief, fostered by Florentine propaganda, that her aim was to rule all Italy. This fear more than anything else contributed to the growth of two blocs within the League: Milan, Florence and Naples on the one side, held together by the political genius of Lorenzo de' Medici; Venice, usually supported by the Papacy, on the other. But Venice, although her motives were often misunderstood and exaggerated by her enemies, was certainly increasingly attracted towards the Romagna, the crucial strategic triangle between the Adriatic, the Appenines and the river Po. This tendency of Venetian policy was inevitably creating a rift with her only ally, the Papacy, particularly when the politically inadequate Innocent VIII was about to be replaced by a Pope whose conception of papal temporal power was of a different order. At the same time all was far from well with the other side of the Italian balance. In Milan the young Duke Giangaleazzo Sforza, who was married to Isabella, the granddaughter of Ferrante of Naples, was being steadily pushed into the background by his uncle Ludovico. The complaints of the spirited Isabella to her father Alfonso and to her grandfather about her increasingly difficult situation at the Milanese court were rapidly creating a rift in the alliance. The rift was exacerbated by long-standing disputes about the overlordship of Genoa, and about an old claim to the Duchy of Milan possessed by the Aragonese dynasty in Naples. Each of the Italian states was feeling a growing sense of isolation, and when an Italian state felt isolated in fifteenth century politics the answer was always the same one, to turn to a foreign power for support. Early in 1492 Ludovico Sforza had already opened negotiations with France, and the French King was now no longer the canny Louis XI who regarded foreign adventures with suspicion, but Charles VIII, a young man just reaching maturity and fired with religious zeal and visions of personal grandeur.

Charles VIII had inherited the Angevin claims to Naples, and his cousin Louis of Orleans could boast claims to Milan. Although France was scarcely yet ready for extravagant expansionist policies, the rich prizes in Italy were an increasing lure for subjects, while a vision of a French-led crusade setting out from a newly occupied base in Naples was inspiring her King. In Spain also Ferdinand of Aragon had never accepted the division of the Aragonese empire, which had taken place at the death of Alfonso V, as permanent. The occupation of Naples by the junior and illegitimate branch of the Aragonese royal house was a situation which he regarded with mixed feelings of patronising tolerance and ultimate self interest. Above all he was not prepared to allow his kinsman's lands to fall into the hands of France.

It was against this deteriorating background that we must see the impact of the death of two of Italy's five main rulers. In April 1492 Lorenzo the Magnificent died prematurely at the age of forty-three. His successor, Piero, was not only to alienate Florentine support within two years by his personal arrogance and autocratic behaviour, and his unpopular foreign policy, but he also abandoned his father's efforts to hold the Milan–Florence–Naples axis together and threw in his lot decisively with Naples, thus accentuating Ludovico's sense of isolation. In July Innocent VIII died. This set the scene for one of the most dramatic and one of the most controversial of all papal elections.

The main divisions within the College of Cardinals, and the general lines which the contest would take, had already been clear for some time before the end of Innocent's pontificate. Furthermore there could be little doubt in the minds of contemporaries as to what sort of conclave it was going to be. The tense political situation and the examples of the two previous conclaves made it clear that worldly considerations were likely to predominate. Observers were soon hard at work assessing the political affiliations and the economic potential of each of the possible candidates. This in itself was an immediate indication of the kind of election which was generally expected.[2]

Since the year before, it had been recognised that the College of Cardinals was roughly split into two groups. On the one side there was Giuliano della Rovere, nephew of Sixtus IV and the predominant influence behind Innocent VIII, who was determined to maintain at least an indirect control over the Papacy. Although his natural affiliations were with France where he was papal legate, he was now more powerfully supported by Ferrante and the Kingdom of Naples. His techniques at papal elections were already well tried, and he now had considerable Neapolitan funds on which to draw.[3] It seems unlikely that he can have entertained any great hopes of ascending the papal throne himself on this occasion; the parties seemed to be too evenly balanced to allow any of the obvious leaders to triumph. But he had two very respectable candidates in his following: the Portuguese Cardinal Costa and the Venetian Cardinal Zeno. To support either of these he could count on the cardinal representatives of the Colonna and Savelli families whose armies were in the pay of Naples. He could also rely on the remaining members of his own family who had been elevated by Sixtus IV, Domenico della Rovere and Girolamo Basso della Rovere, and on the Venetian and Genoese Cardinals, Michiel, Fregoso and Cibo who could be expected to support a Genoese candidate against the Milanese.

Against this formidable group of nine or ten apparently safe votes were ranged Ascanio Sforza and the Milanese. With relations between Milan and Naples deteriorating, this purely political division of the College was inevitable, and Ascanio like Giuliano della Rovere could rely on heavy financial support from his political allies. Again like Giuliano he could not reckon much on his own chances of election and seemed at first to be pinning his hopes on the saintly Cardinal Carafa, although in conversation with Giuliano della Rovere before the conclave he had expressed a preference for Rodrigo Borgia.[4] For votes he could rely first of all on Rodrigo Borgia who had been his ally for some years and who was known to be violently opposed to Giuliano. Then there was Ardicino della Porta, a Milanese cardinal, Sanseverino, a member of the exiled Neapolitan family, the more senior Cardinals Riario and Piccolomini who shared the general distrust and dislike of Giuliano, and finally Cardinals Orsini and Conti who would automatically oppose the choice of the Colonna and Savelli.

Amongst the cardinals other than the candidates of these two main parties whose chances were discussed by contemporary observers was Rodrigo Borgia. In fact what evidence has come down to us seems to have largely discounted the possibility of Rodrigo's election at this time and there was general surprise when the result was finally declared. One observer did make a detailed and grossly exaggerated analysis of his possessions and benefices which it was felt could be discreetly used to swing votes in his favour.[5] But to set against this was his position close to the head of one of the main groups which was likely to make it as difficult for him to get the necessary two-thirds majority as it was for Ascanio Sforza or Giuliano della Rovere. At the same time he did not seem to have the direct support of any of the European or Italian powers, while his Spanish blood was generally considered to be a great handicap in an election which was already coming to be regarded as largely an Italian affair.

It has often been argued by Borgia's enemies that the reason why the prospect of his success in the election was generally discounted was because of his notoriously immoral way of life. But there was an element of hindsight in this judgment as the disorderly nature of his private affairs seems to have been fairly discreetly veiled up to 1492. There is no evidence of a widespread prejudice against him on these grounds, and indeed one suspects that even a more blatant flaunting of the irregularities of his private life would not have influenced the votes of his fellow cardinals, who were, some of them, no better monuments of celibate virtue.

The conclave started on 6 August 1492 and five days later at the fourth scrutiny or vote, and to the astonishment of most observers, Rodrigo Borgia was elected Pope and took the name of Alexander VI. How this result was achieved and what went on behind the closed doors of the Conclave have been the subjects of a vast amount of contemporary vituperation and historical conjecture. One of the principal charges levelled against Rodrigo Borgia both at the time and later has been that he bought the throne of St. Peter by simony. How else, contemporaries asked themselves, could the cardinals have brought themselves to vote for this iniquitous man? The answer in part to this question lies in the suggestion already made that Rodrigo was not in 1492 the horror figure which he later became; he was far better known at that time as a worldly but generally popular prelate and an exceedingly able administrator and politician. It seems hardly reasonable that the election of such a candidate should be regarded as implicit proof of simony.

However the charges of simony rest on rather more than emotional assumptions of this nature. The traditional picture of the conduct of the 1492 election was best presented by Pastor in his classic *Lives of the Popes*. It is from him that we learn of the stalemate which lasted through the first three scrutinies with the parties of Giuliano della Rovere and Ascanio Sforza evenly balanced and no prospect of victory for either. Then there was a sudden change; Ascanio, despairing of his own candidacy and that of Carafa, accepted the bribe of the Vice-Chancellorship and shifted his vote to Borgia; many of his party and some of Giuliano's were then induced to follow him by offers of lands, benefices or cash. Four mules loaded with silver were said to have been seen going from Rodrigo's palace to that of Ascanio.[6] There was soon a positively indecent rush to support Rodrigo and participate in the rewards, so that the fourth scrutiny became a formality. Only the more honest and upright of the cardinals, Carafa, Piccolomini and Costa, refused to be bribed. The distribution of the rewards came at the first consistory after the election and is clearly documented. For Pastor and for many others the proof of simony was irrefutable.

But even before Pastor's death and before the final, personally revised, editions of his great work came out, the full details of the first three scrutinies of this conclave had finally been found and published.[7] The implications of these scrutiny lists have been very fully discussed by several historians but have never been fully assimilated into the stream of popular Borgia historiography. These lists reveal that Rodrigo Borgia was one of the leading candidates from the first scrutiny onwards. Each cardinal was able to name three preferences in each scrutiny, and in the first three scrutinies Rodrigo at no time received less than seven votes, including those of Ascanio, Piccolomini and Carafa. This at one blow shatters two of the main arguments for the thesis of simony; two of the supposed incorruptibles had in fact voted for Rodrigo before the final and decisive scrutiny, and Ascanio did not suddenly switch his vote. What Ascanio did switch were the votes of some of his party, but there is every indication that this was deliberate policy and not the result of bribes. The third scrutiny had shown that if anything Giuliano's party was beginning to gain ground; Ascanio probably felt that he had to act quickly and change his plans if a landslide were to be averted. Borgia in fact was the obvious solution after the prolonged stalemate of the first three scrutinies; he already had eight votes in the third scrutiny and Carafa, with the full weight of the Sforza party behind him, could not gather more than ten. The alliance between Ascanio and Rodrigo had been a notable feature of the manoeuvrings in the years before 1492, and Rodrigo now appeared to be anti-Neapolitan. Furthermore although perhaps Ascanio would have preferred a less forceful personality as his candidate, Rodrigo did hold the highest and most lucrative office in the Church, after the Papacy itself, and this would inevitably be vacated on his election.

This last consideration is one of the keys to the whole issue of simony at papal elections. An elected Pope inevitably had all his offices and benefices to give away; that he should give these incidentally or as rewards to cardinals who voted for him is not surprising nor in itself any evidence of promises given beforehand. Is this therefore simony? Rodrigo had to give the Vice-Chancellorship to someone, to whom more likely than the man who for largely political reasons had given him the most help throughout the election. Rodrigo's palace already housed the offices of the Chancellery and therefore passed naturally with the post of Vice-Chancellor. Similarly the bishoprics of Cartagena, Majorca and Porto had to be reallocated as they were the new Pope's own sees. The great castles of Soriano, and Civita Castellana, and the abbey of Subiaco were also in Borgia's hands before 1492; these were given to the 'Roman' cardinals, Orsini, Savelli and Colonna, not so much as a reward for their votes as to placate the great Roman families and preserve the balance of power amongst them. Finally it seems poor evidence of simony to claim that the votes of such wealthy figures as Cardinals Sclafenati, Riario and Domenico della Rovere were swung over by the offers of minor abbeys and benefices as Pastor does. Indeed the full scrutiny lists reveal that all three of these cardinals voted for Borgia during the early stages of the election and simony played no part in their choice.

It is also perhaps not irrelevant to consider the problem of why Giuliano della Rovere with vast financial resources at his disposal was not able to outbid Rodrigo and stem the Borgia landslide. One cannot help feeling that if, in the words of Guicciardini, Borgia really 'in a manner unprecedented for the times, bought the votes of all the assembled cardinals',[8] Della Rovere, with a reputation for simony at least equal to Borgia's, would have been able to do something about it. The fact that he could not indicates not only that the seriousness of the political situation, and primarily fear of the French, outweighed all other considerations, but also that personal antipathies to Borgia were not strong.

What we appear to have in fact in the 1492 conclave is not an example of the depths to which the Renaissance Papacy could stoop when the papal throne was shamelessly bought and sold, but a final realisation that in the circumstances of the time political and purely worldly factors were bound to predominate in the election of a Pope. Both Carafa and Costa were eminently suitable candidates of a traditional type, support of whom would not have disgraced any fifteenth-century cardinal. But in 1492 a realisation both of the increasingly secular nature of the Papacy itself, and also of the seriousness of the political situation of the time, led the cardinals to abandon the more saintly candidates and choose a man who was noted for his administrative abilities and his political acumen rather than for his saintliness. Promises and simony there may have been, but it seems likely that they were not out of proportion to practices at previous conclaves, and that they did not greatly affect the outcome of the election. The conclave of 1492 acknowledged, perhaps not for the first time, but more decisively, more unequivocably than ever before, the changed nature of the Renaissance Papacy.

It was then about an hour before dawn on 11 August 1492 that the official announcement 'Papam habemus' was made. One can well imagine the excitement and understand the surprise which the news must have aroused. The evening before rumours of the outcome of the third scrutiny would have circulated through the streets of Rome. All night the Romans would have been discussing the reported deadlock between Carafa and Costa, between Milan and Naples, and between, in purely local terms, Orsini and Colonna. The deadlock was an expected and familiar one, and few of the uninformed spectators could have foreseen a speedy solution. And yet before many were even out of bed on the 11th, the news was being carried through the streets: Rodrigo Borgia the Vice-Chancellor was elected; the conclave was over.

For the populace of Rome the news was a welcome surprise. Borgia was one of the most familiar and open handed of the cardinals. But for the Roman nobility and for most of the foreign ambassadors present in the city the surprise was far from being a welcome one. To the Roman barons a strong Pope was a constant threat, and particularly was this true of a Pope with a large family and a known propensity towards nepotism. Whatever would be given to papal relations would be given largely at the expense of the Roman nobility. For the foreign envoys their vociferous sense of outrage was not perhaps uninfluenced by the fact that many of them had been proved bad forecasters. Those who had failed to consider Borgia's chances in their dispatches prior to the conclave were the first to point to simony as the explanation for their misjudgments. The Venetians were particularly alarmed as they feared that an alliance between the Papacy and the Sforza spelt trouble for them. The Venetian ambassador, Capello, was one of the most violent in denouncing as simoniacal an election which was so distasteful to his government. Similarly the Neapolitans were scarcely pleased by the outcome of their wasted efforts; King Ferrante is reputed to have wept when he heard the news, but he quickly covered up his chagrin with fulsome letters of congratulation. The small states of the north, Ferrara, Mantua and Modena, all feared the possible extension of Milanese power as a result of the new alliance. In Florence Piero de' Medici seems to have been ambivalent in his reactions. Valori, one of the Florentine envoys in Rome, wrote that his master should be well pleased with the result, and Michelozzi, who was the adviser of young Cardinal Giovanni de' Medici, reported that the election was honourable and just.[9] But both men also showed a certain reserve in committing their views to paper. Giovanni himself is reported to have remarked to a colleague as the election was announced, 'Flee, we are in the clutches of the wolf', and there was plenty of gossip about simony in Florence which Manfredi, the Ferrarese ambassador in the city, was able to pass on to his Duke.[10] The Sienese, who heard the news within ten hours of the proclamation, were delighted remembering their friendly relations with Rodrigo's uncle, Calixtus. Finally Ludovico Sforza was not unnaturally pleased that his brother should have had so great a hand in the election.

The gratification of the new Pope at the successful fulfilment of his ambitions was apparent to all. It was said that he put on the papal vestments with an almost childish enthusiasm, and this, combined with his genial good looks and his abounding zest, attracted many hearts. The coronation ceremony on 26 August was one of the most splendid ever seen; cardinals and foreign envoys vied with each other in the magnificence of their contributions. 'Anthony was not received with as much splendour by Cleopatra as Alexander by the Romans', wrote one observer. The Borgia panegyrists Michele Ferno and Hieronimus Porcius have described the scenes in glowing terms reminding one of the triumphal processions of ancient Rome. In the procession from St. Peter's to the Lateran first came thirteen squadrons of cavalry followed by the papal household, the foreign ambassadors, and the cardinals. All were mounted on richly caparisoned horses and each cardinal was attended by a retinue of twelve. Then riding before the Pope came the Count of Pitigliano, Captain General of the Church, with his sword drawn, a symbol of his role as defender of the Church. The Pope, himself riding under a canopy, was followed by the Captain of the papal guard with his men, and the rear was brought up by the protonotaries and senior officials of the Curia.[11] But although the Borgia arms, a bull grazing on a gold field, were to be seen everywhere, this magnificence was a good deal more than a Borgia pageant. It was a symbol of the Renaissance Papacy; a splendid and co-operative display for an essentially worldly occasion.

All reports emphasise the physical strength and energy of the new Pope, but the long procession from the Vatican to the Lateran and the subsequent ceremonies were too much even for Alexander's strength and he fainted twice. However, the splendour and ceremonies by no means ended with the coronation itself. For the next few weeks embassies bearing homage and congratulation from the Italian states continued to arrive in Rome. The Florentines were the first to arrive with Piero de' Medici himself leading the embassy and Puccio Pucci, the brother-in-law of Giulia Farnese, and Poliziano, the poet, amongst his following. Don Federigo, the younger son of Ferrante, led the Neapolitan embassy, and Hermes Sforza, brother of Ludovico and Ascanio, that of Milan. From Caterina Sforza came lawyers to ask for a renewal of her vicariate over Forlì and Imola, and from the Duke of Ferrara his eldest son Alfonso subsequently to be Lucrezia's third husband. Rome was for a time a greater diplomatic and social centre than ever.

Alexander's first Consistory was held on 31 August and it was on this occasion that many of the new appointments and donations, which provoked the accusations of electoral simony, were announced. This was a pattern which every first consistory of a new pontificate during the second half of the fifteenth century had followed. The newly elected Pope publicly divested himself of all his benefices and distributed them amongst his cardinals; there was nothing unduly novel or sinister about this occasion. What was perhaps a good deal more sinister than the distribution of rewards was the Papal announcement of the appointment of Juan Borgia-Lanzol, Archbishop of Monreale, to be a cardinal, and the nomination of Cesare Borgia to be Archbishop of Valencia. Valencia had been Alexander's own see, so it was vacant, and Cesare's see of Pamplona had already been given to Cardinal Pallavicini. However the signs of nepotism cannot but have been disturbing and ominous to contemporaries.

In the days immediately following his election Alexander seemed to be making a genuine effort to keep his numerous family at a distance. Although Lucrezia and Jofrè were living in the Palazzo Orsini under the care of Adriana de Mila, Cesare was not permitted to come to Rome immediately. He was at the time still at the University of Pisa, and in October he went to Spoleto.[12] But by March of the following year he had arrived in Rome to be joyfully greeted by his father. By this time great matches were being planned for Alexander's other three children by Vanozza, and the programme for the establishment of the Borgia family in the ranks of the highest Italian aristocracy had begun. The Ferrarese ambassador, Boccaccio, remarked with typical Italian exaggeration that 'ten Papacies would not be sufficient to satisfy this swarm of relatives'.[13]

The situation which the new Pope inherited was an unenviable one by any standards. The circumstances of the election had placed him clearly on the side of Milan in the approaching political crisis, with the prospect of Neapolitan hostility and pressure on the southern frontiers of the Papal States. They also placed him in an ambiguous position towards the approaching French intervention in Italy, a position not only alien to his natural Spanish affiliations, but also contrary to his often declared and probably genuine desire to keep foreign powers out of Italy. Because if we can discern any clear principles in Alexander's policies they were essentially conservative, to preserve the balance of power in Italy thus protecting the Papal States from invasion and molestation, and to keep out the foreign powers whose appearance would offer the greatest threat to the traditional pattern of Italian politics.

Thus in an increasingly inflammable political situation he was already to some extent committed to alignments and policies which he disliked.

In the Papal States the central authority of the Popes, which some of Alexander's immediate predecessors had tried courageously if intermittently to re-establish, was being undermined by growing external interference in the Romagna and by frequent disorders in the papal cities. Assisi was in an uproar as rival factions fought for control; Perugia seemed to be slipping under the unofficial lordship of the Baglioni family; in Cesena the Tiberti and the Martinelli were struggling for supremacy. Brigandage and piracy were rife; the Roman barons with their increasing stranglehold on the Roman Campagna seemed to be threatening the communications and the food supplies of the city itself. In Rome the *sede vacante* had seen more than its usual spasms of disorder and violence.

Finally the College of Cardinals remained more than usually divided. With its predominantly Italian membership the divisions in Italian politics were quickly reflected within its ranks, and immediately there was strong opposition to the new Pope led by his disappointed rival, Giuliano della Rovere.

The reaction of Alexander to this variety of problems was characteristic. On the domestic issues he acted vigorously; immediate steps were taken to restore order in Rome. Murderers were hunted down and punished; their families proscribed and their houses often pulled down. A commission was set up to inspect the prisons and Alexander set aside Tuesdays for personally hearing complaints and petitions. The papal guard was strengthened and placed under the command of Rodrigo Borgia-Lanzol, a great nephew.[14] Roman armourers were forbidden to sell armour or arms without the consent of papal officials.[15] The Count of Pitigliano, Captain General of the papal armies, was dispatched to restore order in Perugia.

On the diplomatic issues Alexander acted with greater caution and increasing duplicity. But domestic and foreign affairs were fused in the problems created by the sale, within a few days of the conclave, of his castles by Franceschetto Cibo, the son of Innocent VIII, to Virginio Orsini. Cibo had been given by his father as papal fiefs some of the castles taken from the Anguillara family by Paul II. These included Anguillara itself which was situated to command the Via Cassia and the Via Clodia, and Cerveteri which dominated the Via Aurelia. These castles were now sold for 40,000 ducats to Virginio Orsini with the active support of Giuliano della Rovere in whose palace the transaction took place. Furthermore the deal was approved by both Piero de' Medici, who was related to both Virginio Orsini and Franceschetto Cibo, and Ferrante of Naples whose army Virginio commanded. Thus the sale of the castles raised a number of far-reaching issues.[16] In the first place it considerably strengthened the position of the Orsini in the Roman Campagna north of Rome. This not only threatened the authority of the Pope but endangered the precarious balance between Orsini and Colonna. Secondly Alexander justifiably maintained that the sale of papal fiefs without papal consent was illegal and a direct defiance of papal authority. Thirdly it reflected the interference by Florence and particularly Naples in the affairs of the Papal States. Finally it presented further evidence of the understanding between Florence and Naples which seriously alarmed Milan and drove Ludovico further along his path towards a French alliance.

Alexander was extremely disturbed by this affair. He dispatched briefs to all the European powers denouncing the Orsini and their backers and calling for assistance and support against them. Among the powers approached was France and this was the first move in what was to be a complex formulation of attitudes towards the impending French invasion.

Alexander has often been accused of deliberately encouraging the French and sometimes indeed of being the prime instigator of the invasion. There is no justification for this latter view and it is clear that in the long run his attitude was one of opposition. But at least for the first year of the pontificate he maintained an equivocal position, leaving, as was his wont, his ultimate decision obscure until the last possible moment.

However if Alexander's attitude towards France remained ambiguous, his hostility towards Ferrante for the part he had played in the affair was clear cut. With the encouragement of Ludovico and Ascanio Sforza papal diplomacy played its part in creating a new diplomatic line-up in April 1493 when Venice, the Pope and Milan signed the League of St. Mark for mutual protection. This League seemed to mark an end to Ludovico's temporary isolation and might, had it lasted, have avoided the French invasion. But it was a league founded on mutual distrust and self interest. Venice was basically anti-Florentine rather than anti-Neapolitan, and the Pope was only concerned with gaining military assistance for the recovery of the Cibo castles. This was promised by Milan and Venice, and in the spring months of 1493 papal forces were assembling north of Rome for a trial of strength with the Orsini. The need for outside help was apparent as so many of the papal commanders were *condottieri* of the Orsini family.[17] Even the Captain General, the Count of Pitigliano, was an Orsini, although Alexander had already promised that post to Prospero Colonna in an attempt to win Colonna support.

Papal adherence to the League of St. Mark seemed to be sealed by the marriage of Lucrezia to Giovanni Sforza, Lord of Pesaro. Giovanni was a cousin of Ludovico and one of the papal vicars of the Romagna; he was also a soldier whose services were badly needed by Alexander. He was the illegitimate son of Costanzo Sforza and in 1493 was twenty-six years old and already a widower. The marriage is a clear example of how Alexander's dynastic policies were interwoven with papal diplomatic and political needs. Giovanni Sforza was socially not a better match than Lucrezia's Aragonese betrothed, the Count of Aversa; but the opportunity to keep his daughter closer to him and to use her as a pawn in papal policy made it convenient to abandon the Aragonese betrothal. Alexander at one stroke not only added a dynastic element to the League of St. Mark, but brought under his control one of the more independent and militant of his vicars.

The marriage ceremony took place on 12 June 1493 and was a splendid affair. It was not the first time that a daughter of the Pope had been married in the Vatican, but it was the first of a number of occasions when Alexander was able to give full rein to his love of display and festive entertainment by turning a domestic occasion into an ecclesiastical festival. Lucrezia was accompanied in great state by Battistina, granddaughter of Innocent VIII, and 150 girls from the greater Roman families, from her temporary residence in the palace of Cardinal Zeno at Santa Maria in Portico to the Vatican. There the ceremony took place and was followed by an official reception at which a pastoral eclogue was recited by Serafino d'Aquila, and Plautus' *Menaechmi* was performed which bored Alexander to distraction.[18] In the evening there was a wedding feast in the papal apartments for a select party of relatives and friends. This feast seems to have been a typical Renaissance princely occasion with ladies present, dancing (reliable reports suggest that the ladies danced among themselves as was common at this period), music, and the performance of a 'worthy comedy'.

For the next year Lucrezia lived with her husband in Rome while he served periodically in the papal army. It was not until mid-1494 that she paid her first visit to Pesaro.

Meanwhile King Ferrante, alarmed by the formation of the

League against him, had thought from an early stage of appealing to Alexander's dynastic ambitions and recovering papal friendship by suggesting two Aragonese-Borgia marriages. It was suggested that both Cesare and Jofrè should abandon their ecclesiastical careers and marry Neapolitan princesses. These first suggestions were made before the League of St. Mark was signed, but attractive as they must have been to Alexander, he turned them down as they left the problem of the Cibo castles unsolved. Alexander was not prepared to accept suggestions for the advancement of his family while his authority as Pope and his control over the Papal States was left in question. However when in mid summer Ferrante finally offered to bring pressure to bear on Virginio Orsini for a compromise over the castles, then a settlement was quickly reached. As cardinal Alexander had always been a supporter of good relations between Naples and the Papacy. He appreciated that as long as Naples was strong she constituted the greatest military threat to the Papal States and therefore peaceful relations were important. Thus an alliance with Naples was for him always the desirable cornerstone of papal policy; when this could be linked to a solution of his immediate internal problem and to the advancement of his own family, he did not hesitate. In July 1493 agreement was reached. Jofrè was to be rescued from his ecclesiastical commitments and married to Sancia, illegitimate daughter of Alfonso of Calabria. He was to become Prince of Squillace and a Neapolitan grandee. Ferrante brought pressure to bear on a reluctant Virginio Orsini to compound his fault in buying the castles without papal consent for 35,000 ducats. This left the castles in his hands, but the principle of papal consent in the transfer of papal fiefs was recognised. Alexander was not entirely happy with the compromise and promised himself that at the first opportunity he would renew his efforts to recover the castles. However for the time being Ferrante had withdrawn his support from the Orsini and from the dissident cardinals led by Giuliano della Rovere.

This new understanding with Naples was closely linked to parallel negotiations with Spain. During the early summer Ferrante had been protesting vigorously to his kinsman Ferdinand of Aragon about what he described as the war-mongering attitudes of the Spanish Pope. His letter of 7 June, when he was isolated and under great pressure from the Pope, is one of the first complete diatribes against the Borgias which has survived.[19] Following this in June Ferdinand's ambassador Don Diego de Haro arrived in Rome *incognito*, ostensibly to protest on his master's behalf about Alexander's attitude towards Naples, and his Church policy. However there were other more far-reaching matters to be discussed and Ferdinand wanted the help of his old Borgia ally. Spanish interests in the New World were seriously threatened by parallel Portuguese expansion and there were clear precedents for bringing the matter to the Pope for arbitration. Alexander's famous division of the world in his Bull *Inter Caetera* was not an empty gesture nor yet was it just arbitration; it reflected to some extent a recovery of politico-religious prestige by the Renaissance Papacy and gave the Pope a stake in the religious aspects of the Age of Discovery.[20] His intervention was at the request of Spain and very much in favour of Spain; it gained for Alexander implicit Spanish support, and hastened the progress of Juan Borgia, Duke of Gandia, into his destined place amongst the Spanish nobility. The promised betrothal to Maria Enriquez was pushed ahead and in August Gandia left Italy for Spain to claim his royal bride.

As befitted a young man of seventeen he took with him some stern letters of advice from his father who was concerned not only for his personal welfare but also for the impression that he was going to make in Spain. Gandia was advised to be pious and God-fearing, to serve the King faithfully, to honour his wife, and to avoid gambling and games of chance. His father also stressed the need to choose good advisers and administrators, to conserve his resources and not to covet other people's wealth. Jaime Serra, Archbishop of Oristano in Sardinia, who accompanied the young Duke as tutor and adviser, was also given strict instructions, instructions which went as far as detailing the clothes which Gandia should wear for his official entry into Barcelona.[21]

Unfortunately Gandia seemed unable to live up to the good advice given him. The Mantuan ambassador remarked that he left loaded with jewels and rich furnishings which no doubt he would leave in Spain and soon return for another load.[22] Certainly the surviving inventory of the effects which he loaded into the four galleys in which he sailed to Spain give an astonishing impression of wealth and extravagance.[23] But the ducal palace in Gandia was enormous and the young Duke no doubt wished to emulate the growing luxury of Italian Renaissance styles rather than the more ascetic ideals of fifteenth-century Spain. Nevertheless he caused great offence in Spain by his ostentatious display and his arrogance, and soon angry reports were coming back to Alexander accusing Gandia of disrespect towards his wife's family and failure to consummate his marriage while he spent all his time in brothels. Jaime Serra wrote that the last charge was not true and that the marriage had been consummated, but both Alexander and Cesare wrote stern letters of rebuke to Gandia in November 1493.[24]

These letters were written from Viterbo while Cesare and his father were on an extended tour north of Rome. Alexander enjoyed travelling and inspecting the fortresses and towns of the Campagna the strategic importance of which he fully appreciated. He also enjoyed the opportunities for display which his travels offered and liked to supervise the details of these progresses himself.[25] On this occasion Alexander had left Rome on 26 October to avoid a plague epidemic. Having visited his old castle of Nepi he spent a few days in Viterbo before passing on to the coast and Corneto (Tarquinia) and Civitavecchia. From there he moved inland to Pitigliano where he visited his Captain General. Then, passing through Viterbo again on the way, he travelled to Orvieto where Cesare was installed as Governor and considerable tax concessions made to the city.[26] Alexander also took this opportunity to spend a few days at Capodimonte, the country home of the Farnese family, before returning to Rome in early December. Cesare had been out of Rome even longer than his father as he was in Caprarola in August. While there he heard that his horse had won the Palio in Siena, although the victory was disputed by the other contestants on the grounds that Cesare's jockey had resorted to the time-honoured and usually acceptable trick of throwing himself off his horse at a crucial moment to allow it to gain added speed in the final stages of the race. Cesare wrote a sharp and imperious letter of protest that his victory should be disputed, but we do not know the outcome of this particular incident.[27]

However, to return to the main stream of events, one of the factors which had accelerated the joint Aragonese-papal rapprochement was the approach of a French embassy to Rome led by Peron de Baschi to claim investiture of Naples for Charles VIII. The French arrived two days after the league with Ferrante had been concluded and consequently received a rebuff to their demands from Alexander. But the rebuff was not framed in sufficiently categorical terms to dismay Peron de Baschi entirely, and nor indeed was it meant to be. It was always Alexander's policy to avoid final breaches until the last possible moment. He had no wish to drive France to extreme steps, nor to provoke an already growing anti-papal sentiment in that country. Similarly he assured Milan that his treaty with

Ferrante was merely a marriage treaty and had no diplomatic significance.

Furthermore in the following months relations between Naples and Alexander seemed to cool. In September 1493 Alexander appointed his first large group of cardinals and the aims of his policy towards the College were clear in these appointments. He had already met with heavy opposition in a small, largely Italian College where every move which he made in Italy was opposed by a clique amongst the cardinals. His answer was to flood the College with non-Italian members, and increasingly with Spaniards. But this group had an international character, and was made up for the most part of men of considerable standing. It included two Frenchmen, La Grolaye and Perauld, the latter being recommended by the Emperor; the Spaniard Carvajal who had preached a fierce sermon calling for reform at the conclave in the previous year; the English Morton, and the Polish Archbishop of Cracow, Frederick Casimir. Amongst the Italians appointed were two eminent theologians, Grimani and Sangiorgio, the former being a Venetian; the Milanese Lunati; two representatives of the Roman nobility Farnese and Cesarini, the former, Alessandro, being the brother of Giulia Farnese; and Ippolito d'Este, the fifteen-year-old son of the Duke of Ferrara. Finally Cesare Borgia was now elevated to join his cousin Juan Borgia-Lanzol in the Sacred College. With the exception of the two Romans and Ippolito and Cesare, these were good appointments. They were all men of considerable repute, representing all the major states with the exception of Naples. This omission was no doubt deliberate; concessions to Ferrante could be kept for future more profitable use, and on this occasion Alexander was anxious not to give the impression of being too close to Naples. The two Romans were chosen from the smaller noble families to balance the influence of the Orsini, Colonna, Savelli and Conti cardinals. In this context the elevation of Alessandro Farnese, and Alexander's whole connection with the Farnese family, was particularly important as they possessed lands north of Rome on the southern shores of Lake Bolsena and could be used to squeeze the power of the Orsini to the south. Alessandro was not just the 'petticoat' cardinal, as the Romans loved to describe this brother of Giulia Farnese; he was the representative of an important Roman family and was also the future Paul III.

Giuliano della Rovere and the opposition cardinals were furious and the new appointments were resisted bitterly, but the resistance reflected traditional motives and the reaction to the large non-Italian group, rather than opposition to the nomination of Cesare to which it has normally been imputed. Now the cardinal opponents of Alexander began to leave Rome and establish themselves round Charles VIII. This gave the intentions of the French King in Italy an increasingly ecclesiastical flavour as Alexander's enemies called for a General Council, reform of the Church and the deposition of the Pope on the grounds of a simoniacal election. This opposition movement reached its height when early in 1494 Giuliano della Rovere fled to France and added his personal hatred of his rival to the more genuine complaints of some of his fellow cardinals.

The growing threat to Alexander's personal position alarmed him even more than the French political threat to Naples, and for the remaining months of 1493 he continued to conceal the extent of his commitment to Naples. Ferrante for his part accused him of ill faith and made no efforts to complete the arrangements for the marriage of Jofrè and Sancia. However the death of Ferrante in January 1494 in a sense brought matters to a head. Alexander was now forced to declare himself completely as he had either to recognise Alfonso and invest him formally with Naples, or refuse the investiture and abandon the Aragonese. Alfonso also realised that the French threat was closing in and that he had at all costs to get complete papal support. He offered further concessions and advantages to the Pope's family, and Alexander moved decisively on to his side with recognition of Alfonso's title, formal investiture, and a strongly worded brief to Charles VIII denouncing the forthcoming invasion.

It would be wrong to see this sequence of events as Alexander finally making up his mind. His mind had been made up long before, indeed he probably never seriously considered supporting the French invasion. French control of Naples could not fail to be a disastrous situation for an independent Papacy. The death of Ferrante forced Alexander to declare his position clearly, a step he never liked taking, and although there were superficially stronger reasons than ever for propitiating the French whose threats were now ecclesiastical as well as political, he did not hesitate. A Pope concerned only to advance his family would have naturally gravitated to the side of Charles VIII, but with Alexander, important as his family was to him, there were other considerations and he was now determined to resist.

From the early spring onwards the situation in Rome became increasingly clear. In April Giuliano della Rovere fled to France leaving his fortress of Ostia in the hands of Giovanni della Rovere, the Prefect, and the Colonna. This family had been won over to the Milanese-French side by the blandishments of Ascanio Sforza, and the papal reconciliation with the Orsini. On 8 May Cardinal Juan Borgia-Lanzol crowned Alfonso in Naples and on the Pope's behalf received his oath of loyalty. In this magnificent ceremony, carefully organised by Burchard, the papal master of ceremonies, not only was the position of Naples as a fief of the Papacy stressed, but also the Borgia family played a prominent part. Juan Borgia-Lanzol as papal legate presided; Jofrè in his new capacity as prince of the kingdom and Protonotary assisted by carrying the crown; Gandia, who was absent in Spain, was created Prince of

Tricaria, and Cesare received rich Neapolitan benefices. A brother of the cardinal, Galceran Borgia-Lanzol, was also present as a standard bearer for Jofrè. Never had a Pope established such a grip on Naples by both politico-religious and dynastic means. Three days later the marriage between Jofrè and Sancia was celebrated. Jofrè in addition to his estates as Prince of Squillace received a *condotta* for 10,000 ducats from Alfonso.[28]

This marriage was never a great success; Jofrè, although he made a good impression on the ambassadors in Rome when presented to them a few months earlier, was several years younger than Sancia and seems to have been a weak and superficial character.[29] Sancia on the other hand was a headstrong, extravagant girl whose name was soon being associated with those of men other than her husband. Within a few weeks of the marriage Alexander was furious to hear embarrassing reports about the extravagance and dubious moral tone of his youngest son's household. Although an indulgent father, he disliked unnecessary extravagance, and asked Alfonso to send a commission to investigate the stories. The Count of Marigliano was accordingly dispatched and the servants of the Prince and Princess of Squillace were closely questioned. As a result Sancia's name was temporarily cleared when it was reported that the only man, apart from her husband, who entered her apartments was sixty years old, but the extravagance of the household was manifest. Jofrè alone had seventy-three personal retainers, while Sancia had a further thirty-two.[30]

However, questions of greater moment were occupying more of Alexander's attention. By the end of May combined Neapolitan, Orsini and papal pressure had forced the Colonna to surrender Ostia, and in July Alexander and Alfonso met at Vicovaro to coordinate military plans to resist the French. The invasion was now imminent and Alexander was fully committed to resist it.

CHAPTER SEVEN

THE BORGIAS UNDER PRESSURE, 1494–8

In September 1494 Charles crossed the Alps into Italy. Although his passage was largely uncontested, progress southwards was relatively slow. Charles himself fell ill with smallpox at Asti and it was to be nearly four months before he finally entered Rome. This period was one of extreme difficulty for Alexander. The army of Charles VIII represented not only a military and political threat to the security of the Papal States and the Italian balance of power, but also a threat to the position of the Pope himself accompanied as it was by Giuliano della Rovere and the dissident cardinals clamouring for reform and the deposition of Alexander. After the meeting with Alfonso at Vicovaro Alexander continued to think only of resistance. Military preparations went ahead fast and the Pope himself took a close interest in the disposition of troops and the strengthening of the castles of the Roman Campagna.[1] With the Colonna already allied to Giuliano della Rovere and committed to the French, the defence of Rome was largely in the hands of the Orsini. Naples promised 3000 infantry but the bulk of Neapolitan forces were committed to a naval demonstration off Genoa and to opposing a French march southwards through the Romagna. Thus Alexander was relying for the defence of Rome on a traditional pattern of an alliance with an Italian power and a papal army commanded by Roman barons. In the circumstances he could find no better defence, but it was a defence which was far from adequate. The Neapolitan fleet was defeated at Rapallo and driven off the coast of Liguria; the Neapolitan army was outmanoeuvred in the Romagna as Charles chose the westerly route through Italy;[2] Florentine resistance buckled as the first shots were fired at her frontier fortress of Sarzana. On 18 September the Colonna with French support again seized Ostia and the defences of Rome itself were turned and her food supplies threatened.

Alexander was now forced to think of negotiation and Cardinal Piccolomini was dispatched to meet Charles VIII. The choice was an unfortunate one as Piccolomini was related, by the marriage of his brother, to the Neapolitan royal house, and Giuliano della Rovere was able to persuade Charles to refuse to see him. Alexander thus found himself increasingly helpless as his attempts to negotiate were rejected, his allies crumbled and his own barons deserted. Pandolfo Collenuccio, the Ferrarese ambassador, found him vainly protesting at the weakness of the Italians, and declaring that he would never be a chaplain of the King of France. 'But', said Collenuccio, 'the Pope is one who talks more than he acts'; a judgment which perhaps did not take sufficient account of Alexander's continued efforts to strengthen his defences, or of his impossible political situation.[3]

As the French army approached in December, the Neapolitan army under Alfonso's son Ferrantino moved across to protect Rome and Alexander was encouraged to make one last forceful bid. Cardinal Ascanio Sforza and others of the pro-French party were arrested, and Cardinal Perauld's palace in Rome was sacked by the Neapolitan soldiers and the Roman populace. The French ambassadors were informed that free passage through the city would not be granted, and the Pope made a personal appeal to the German colony, one of the largest of the foreign groups in Rome, to assist in the defence of the city. But the full weakness of Alexander's

12 Cardinal Francesco Borgia (?); detail from the *Assumption* by Pinturicchio in the Borgia Apartments. The identification as Francesco is often disputed on the grounds that this cannot be a portrayal of a man of over sixty.

13 The Torre Borgia, added by Alexander VI to the Vatican, contains on the first floor two of the rooms of the Borgia Apartments, and above these the room in which Alfonso, Duke of Bisceglie, was murdered.

position was revealed when the Orsini deserted to the side of the French and Charles VIII was invited to make use of the Orsini fortress of Bracciano. French troops moving south past Viterbo surprised and captured Giulia Farnese and Adriana de Mila as they were returning to Rome from a visit to the Farnese castle at Capodimonte. Alexander acted hurriedly to ransom his womenfolk and prepare for the now inevitable French arrival. On Christmas Day Ferrantino was asked to leave Rome with his troops. The Pope, having toyed with the idea of fleeing from Rome to Naples, decided rightly that his best policy was to stay and face his enemies and accusers in person. There were good grounds for believing that the immature and impressionable Charles would not be up to the task which Giuliano della Rovere was expecting of him, that of deposing a Pope and reforming the Church. The *Conservatori* of Rome with the Pope's approval advised Charles at Bracciano of the submission of the city, and on 31 December the French army marched in through the Porta del Popolo.

For the next month the experience and political sagacity of Alexander stood him in good stead. Protected in Castel Sant' Angelo he maintained an air of polite detachment while Charles in the Palazzo Venezia became increasingly aware of the political realities of the situation. While Giuliano della Rovere and the French cardinals pressed for the deposition of an immoral and simoniacal Pope and the calling of a General Council to elect a successor, the cardinal emissaries of Alexander pointed out that Charles' own aims, the investiture of Naples and the furtherance of the crusade, might be best pursued by an accommodation with the reigning Pope whose authority was still largely undisputed. In the circumstances Charles' ultimate decision was easily foreseeable; on 15 January terms were agreed. The French army was to have continued free passage through the Papal States on its march towards Naples; Cardinal Cesare Borgia was to accompany the King as legate and hostage. Some key fortresses were to be handed over to the French, but Alexander was to keep control of Castel Sant'Angelo. To further the cause of the crusade Prince Djem, the brother of the Sultan Bayezid II, was handed over to Charles VIII.

Djem had been a prisoner in the West since his brother's accession, and Bayezid had happily paid 40,000 ducats a year to keep him so. In 1489 Djem had been transferred to the custody of Innocent VIII and since then had lived in considerable if solitary state in the Vatican. The Borgia family had rather taken to him and he was often to be seen riding through the streets with one or other of the Pope's sons. This brother of the Sultan now represented a considerable factor in the proposed French crusade. Alexander with an implied threat to hand over Djem to the French had sought Turkish help against the French invaders. The capture of his emissary, Bocciardo, with letters revealing the negotiations gave the Pope's enemies a considerable propaganda weapon with which to beat him and diminished the value of Djem to Alexander as a diplomatic pawn. But in fact the reality of Turkish power since the fall of Constantinople made alliance with the Turks an increasingly popular and effective feature of European diplomacy, and the French who pretended such horror at the Pope's manoeuvres at this time were the first to pursue the same line when in difficulties themselves. But for the moment Djem's usefulness to Alexander was minimal, and to hand him over to Charles was a small price to pay for the relaxation of French pressure on him. When Djem died a month after leaving Rome in French custody, Alexander was inevitably accused of having had him poisoned. But there is no evidence of how this might have been done, nor indeed of why Alexander should have wished to do it, apart from the bribe supposedly offered by Bayezid which certainly does not seem to have been collected.[4] All the indications are that the unhappy Turkish prince died of natural causes.

Nothing is more indicative of the way in which the young and impressionable French King was outmanoeuvred by the infinitely more astute and experienced Alexander than the account of their first meeting. On 16 January while Alexander was still in Castel Sant'Angelo Charles was received in the Vatican and entertained to lunch. After lunch Alexander was carried back in his litter through the gardens towards the Vatican, and Charles came out to meet him. As the Pope descended from his litter Charles began to make the traditional obeisances as he approached. Alexander to avoid appearing to accept the elaborate genuflections as his natural right and thus running the risk of offending the French, and yet at the same time appreciating the importance of establishing a clear personal superiority over the French King, pretended not to observe Charles' approach. At the last moment with an air of friendly condescension Alexander brought the ritual to a close and, refusing to allow Charles to kiss either his foot or his hand, treated him as an equal. This air of informal friendliness adopted by Alexander in all his meetings with Charles in the next few days, created an unmistakable impression of superiority without giving any grounds for offence. At the same time all the attempts by Charles and his advisers to press the Pope in the matter of the investiture of the Kingdom of Naples were adroitly turned aside, and the question of reform of the Church was never even mentioned. Finally on 27 January Charles took his leave with no progress made on either of these two main points. Rome breathed a sigh of relief as the French troops moved out southwards, and within a few days Cesare had, after careful preparations, fled from the French camp, and Charles had lost even his Borgia hostage.

One of the hidden sources of strength of Alexander's position at this time was that Spain, however hesitant she might be to show her hand, could not allow permanent French control of the Papacy or Naples. Even as the final shreds of Neapolitan resistance crumbled and Alfonso II abdicated the throne in favour of his son Ferrantino, Spanish diplomats were assisting in the work of creating an anti-French league, and Spanish troops and ships were collecting in Sicily. While the French occupied Naples and Ferrantino fled to Sicily with the last remnants of his faithful baronage, including Jofrè and Sancia, round him, the ambassadors of Milan, Venice, Spain, the Pope and the Emperor were arranging the Holy League. All were concerned now to put an end to the French enterprise in Italy although that was as far as their common interest went. The League was announced on 31 March 1495 as Charles, still unable to win the papal investiture although he had offered Alexander 150,000 ducats down and an annual tribute of 40,000, was rapidly losing the support of those Neapolitans who a few weeks before had welcomed him joyfully. With his ephemeral crusading visions shattered, his rule in Naples increasingly unpopular, and his communications and escape route threatened, Charles was faced with no alternative but to withdraw at least his own person and a part of his army.

Alexander was now faced with the return of the French military threat to the Papal States. Despite the formation of the Holy League he was still unable to do anything to resist. Milan and Venice had both promised troops to protect Rome but only isolated contingents had materialised; the papal army was leaderless with both the Orsini and the Colonna still committed to the French cause. Alexander's only sensible course of action lay in ensuring that the French army passed through the Papal States as quickly as possible. This time there was no advantage to be gained by the Pope remaining himself in Rome to meet Charles VIII. The threat to the Pope's own position, which had not materialised in January when Charles had the concerted support of a strong group of cardinals and leisure with which to act, was not likely to materialise now that he was in a hurry and his cardinal allies were disillusioned with his performance as a reformer of the Church. So as the French troops approached Rome from the south, Alexander with most of the cardinals and a strong covering force of troops, retired northwards to Orvieto. Cardinal Pallavicini was left behind to welcome Charles and to protect Rome as far as he could from the depredations of the French troops. Charles, desperately anxious to meet the Pope not only to press for the Neapolitan investiture, but now also to draw him away from the Holy League, passed through Rome hurriedly hoping to catch up with Alexander at Orvieto. But Alexander had already made arrangements to move further off the French line of march to Perugia, and he now did this placing himself beyond the reach of the hurrying French. According to the Perugian chronicler, Matarazzo, Alexander took this opportunity to attempt the overthrow of the Baglioni and re-establish direct papal government in the city; an attempt which failed and indeed provoked a good deal of local resentment against the Borgia.[5] Meanwhile with the army of the League assembling in the north and further pursuit of the Pope impossible, Charles passed on once more frustrated. The French army succeeded in breaking past that of the League at Fornovo, but it hurried on its way to the frontier. Alexander returned to Rome in something like triumph and had indeed contributed considerably to the discomfiture of the French. In this crisis the interests of the Papal States, and indirectly of Italy as a whole, and a concern for his own position seem to have dictated Alexander's policies, not the advancement of specific Borgia interests. He seems to have regarded this first French invasion as a storm to be weathered rather than an opportunity to further Borgia dynasticism.

In the months following the withdrawal of Charles VIII,

Alexander continued to work for Italian unity to prevent the possibility of a repetition of the disastrous experiences of 1494. With Ludovico Sforza already cooling in his attitude towards the Holy League and making his own arrangements with the French, and with the reconquest of Naples by Ferrantino and the Spanish still in progress, Venice seemed to be the most reliable Italian ally for the Papacy. Alexander therefore endeavoured to court the friendship of Venice and at the same time sought to break the dangerous link between Florence and France. The advance of the French in 1494 had brought about the fall of Piero de' Medici, partly because his policies had brought Florence into collision with the French, and partly because having done this he surrendered so weakly. The advance also encouraged Pisa to revolt against Florence and added economic disruption to national humiliation. Since this moment traditional pro-French sympathies had been uppermost in Florentine policies. To the natural desire of Florentine merchants to protect their valuable interests in France was linked the powerful influence of Savonarola, the fierce Dominican preacher, who had foretold the coming of Charles VIII as a necessary scourge for the sins of Italy. Florentines thought that it was Savonarola's influence over Charles VIII which had saved the city from the French army, and his moral and political authority was inextricably linked with that of the pro-French party. It was probably true to say that it was Savonarola's association with a strong Francophile feeling in Florence and his position as spokesman of a group which saw in the French the best hope of recovering Pisa and resisting a Medici restoration, which strengthened his authority in the city, rather than his personal authority which kept Florence in the French camp despite all Italian pressure on her. But Alexander and the members of the Holy League saw it the other way round and regarded the overthrow of the influence of Savonarola as a necessary preliminary to destroying the Franco-Florentine connection. It was thus primarily for political reasons, and not because of his personal attacks on the Pope or the religious disorders which he was causing, that Alexander gradually increased the pressure on Savonarola. When attempts to silence him by persuasion and threats failed, it became necessary to discredit him and destroy his political influence before proceeding to ultimate measures against him.

The crux of all Florentine policy in this period was the recovery of Pisa. The revolt of this city at the moment of the French invasion had been not just a blow to Florentine prestige, but a crippling commercial and economic loss. The patient attempts to build up a commercial empire based on Pisa and a clear route to the sea lay in ruins; the costs of commodities soared; grain prices with the loss of much of the fertile land of the Pisan *contado* rocketed; the wealthy Florentines who, encouraged by the Medici, had developed Pisan estates saw their efforts wasted.[6] As a result any power wishing for the alliance of Florence had only to offer to help recover Pisa; any power desiring to damage Florence had only to lend assistance to Pisa. The French, whose arrival had fired the Pisan revolt, were seen by the Florentines as the most likely source of help in the recovery of the lost city. But in 1496 both Milan and Alexander sought to woo the Florentines and win them away from the French alliance by offering assistance and mediation. Maximilian, the Holy Roman Emperor, was encouraged to play a part in the reduction of the obstinate Pisans by the offer of a papal coronation. But all failed; both Milan and Venice began to see greater advantage in helping Pisa and thus incapacitating Florence, and Alexander, encouraged by the extent to which Savonarola's own lack of moderation was undermining his influence, relied on destroying the great preacher as a means to the political end. The way in which Savonarola was allowed to discredit and destroy himself was consummate papal policy. No one could complain of persecution and few, at the time, saw the Dominican's fate as martyrdom. The Florentines, weary of the severity of the moral regime to which they were being subjected, disillusioned by the visionary extravagances of their preacher, frankly horrified by the implications of the famous ordeal by fire into which Savonarola allowed himself to be manoeuvred, wearied of their hero and allowed him to go to his death and to perpetual silence. His personal attacks on Alexander certainly played a part in the creation of the Borgia legend, but the extent to which he was discredited makes one wonder how great a part this was.[7]

But the final chapter in the drama of Savanarola was still eighteen months ahead when, in the late summer of 1496, Alexander felt able to turn his attention once more to the strengthening of his temporal position and the advancement of his family. With the French threat averted, the Italian powers largely friendly, and the opposition within the College of Cardinals further diluted by the addition of another batch of friendly or uncommitted cardinals, the moment had come to deal with the most immediately pressing of all the problems which beset the Renaissance Papacy, the Roman barons. Both the Colonna and the Orsini had deserted the Pope in 1494, but it was the betrayal of the Orsini which Alexander felt particularly keenly, coming as it did at the last moment in 1494. Furthermore the Orsini were still in the service of the French whereas the Colonna had been reconciled. The Orsini were the oldest enemies of the Borgias, and by their retention of the Cibo castles had made themselves the more dangerous of the two families. Finally the moment for an attack on the Orsini was particularly opportune as Virginio was a prisoner of the Neapolitans after the surrender of the last French forces in the Kingdom, and the League was prepared to lend its general Guidobaldo da Montefeltro, Duke of Urbino, one of the most noted *condottieri* in Italy, for the enterprise. On 1 June the Orsini were formally excommunicated for disobedience and treason.

But Alexander was not prepared to trust the destruction of the Orsini either to their rivals, as some of his predecessors would have done, or to a mercenary general whose services might be withdrawn at any moment. So it was that Juan Borgia, Duke of Gandia, was summoned back from Spain to be Captain General of the Church and to lead the attack on the Orsini. This appointment served a double purpose as not only could Juan be trusted to be completely loyal to his father, but also what more suitable heir to the confiscated Orsini estates could be found? Papal policy and Borgia dynasticism could thus be advanced at the same time as was so often the case with Alexander's actions.

On 10 August 1496 Juan Borgia entered Rome in state to take up his role as papal and Borgia champion. Juan was now a young man of twenty. He had been away from Italy for three years living the life of a Spanish grandee; he was therefore less known and even more distrusted than the rest of his family. As one of the premier dukes of Spain he betrayed a natural arrogance and pride which infuriated the Roman nobility who regarded him as an upstart, the incompetent son of a doting Pope. He was without doubt his father's favourite, a gentler, more open character than Cesare, but without his brother's consuming ambition and unscrupulous decisiveness. His relative failure as a general and a man of action together with his flamboyant style of dress and his loose morals have led him to being dismissed by most of his contemporaries and later historians as a rather unpleasant nonentity. Certainly he had made a bad impression in Spain and was described in one near contemporary account as 'a very mean young man, full of false ideas of grandeur and bad thoughts, haughty, cruel and unreasonable'.[8] He had little significant military experience and was no more fitted to be Captain General of the Church than any number of young Italian princes who were given titular command of the armies of the time. Successful generalship in the Renaissance was largely a matter of trial and error, with a fair proportion of luck as an essential ingredient. Most young Italian nobles aspired to military success, few achieved it in any lasting manner. Gandia had only one chance, and then the hatred and distrust which surrounded him destroyed him. In fact we know little of the real character of the man except that it seemed to lack strength.

By October all was ready for the campaign against the Orsini. A powerful army had been assembled and with it a reasonable train of artillery. The Colonna could be counted on to play their part in the destruction of their rivals, and young Fabrizio Colonna, later to be one of the most famous Italian commanders of his day, was available as second in command to the Duke of Urbino. Guidobaldo da Montefeltro himself, who arrived in Rome to take over the military control, although not the supreme command, of the expedition, was a *condottiere* by tradition rather than by successful experience. The Montefeltri had always been soldiers; they had gained the Duchy of Urbino as a reward for military services, and the finances of their Duchy depended very largely on the income of the Duke as a mercenary. But Guidobaldo was not really cut out for the life. He was a typical example of the second generation *condottiere*; the courtly son of a martial father, he preferred the life of a Renaissance prince to that of a soldier. He was a famous patron of literature and the arts, he was a beloved and successful Duke in Urbino, he was also in a sense a professional soldier. But his reputation had been easily made and was scarcely deserved.

Thus when on 26 October Gandia and Guidobaldo knelt before the Pope in St. Peter's to receive the banners of the

Church, and the former the staff of the Captain General, the chances of their success were not as bright as they appeared. The Milanese Cardinal Lunati was appointed legate to accompany the expedition and receive in the name of the Pope the submission of the Orsini castles. This choice was no doubt intended to indicate the participation of the League in the campaign.

The following day the army marched out of Rome and began the investment of the Orsini castles. The opening weeks of the campaign were attended by considerable success. Castle after castle opened their gates as the papal army approached. Sacrofano, Galeria, Formello and Campagnano, all considerable natural fortresses as even their appearance today suggests, offered little resistance; Anguillara, one of the vaunted Cibo castles, welcomed the papal troops joyfully. To the north and west of Lake Bracciano, Veiano, Bieda and Bassano di Sutri were taken. By early December Gandia and Guidobaldo were encamped before Isola Farnese, the key Orsini fortress sited amidst the ruins of Etruscan Veii and commanding the Via Cassia. This too quickly surrendered once the papal artillery, recently arrived from Naples, was turned on it. Thus with the campaign only two months old the Orsini were left with only the two lakeside castles of Bracciano and Trevignano.

The castle at Bracciano had been refortified and greatly enlarged by Napoleone Orsini in the 1480s, and it was therefore a considerably more sophisticated fortress than any of those which had fallen so swiftly to the papal troops. Trevignano on the other hand was a castle of traditional design little altered since the Middle Ages despite the developments of siege artillery. It was however strongly sited on a natural pinnacle towering over the little walled town which jutted out into Lake Bracciano. The two castles were able to communicate and send supplies and reinforcements to each other across the lake. To cut this link Gandia and Guidobaldo attempted to bring a small ship overland from the Tiber, but the convoy was intercepted by Bartolomeo d'Alviano, the Orsini commander in Bracciano, and the ship was burnt.

However early in the New Year, although Guidobaldo had been wounded and was temporarily out of action, Gandia's troops stormed Trevignano and the town was sacked. This left only Bracciano; but two successive assaults on this fortress in January 1497 failed. Meanwhile help was on the way. Carlo Orsini and Vitellozzo Vitelli with French money had been raising troops in Umbria and southern Tuscany. They were joined by the Baglioni from Perugia and Giovanni della Rovere, and now moved southwards taking advantage of the possession by Cardinal Orsini of the key fortress of Soriano. The papal army was forced to raise the siege of Bracciano and moved out northwards to face the new threat. The two armies met on 24 January on the slopes of the Monti Cimini between Bassano di Sutri and Soriano. The battle of Soriano which ensued has often been described as an ignominious defeat for the papal army and a monument to Gandia's military incompetence. But as most of the chroniclers of the event were highly delighted at the result and the opportunity to celebrate a Borgia defeat this is hardly surprising. However both Sansovino, the Orsini historian, and Sigismondo de' Conti, a chronicler who took a keen interest in military affairs, regarded the battle as closely fought.[9] The papal forces got the better of the early exchanges and began to drive the Orsini back. Then an over-ambitious attempt at a flanking move by Fabrizio Colonna left a part of the papal army exposed to a determined counterattack by Vitellozzo. The Duke of Urbino was captured and Gandia slightly wounded as the papal troops broke leaving 500 dead on the field.

The set-back was a severe, although not perhaps a disastrous one. The papal forces had lost their principal general and Bracciano was relieved; however the papal army quickly re-

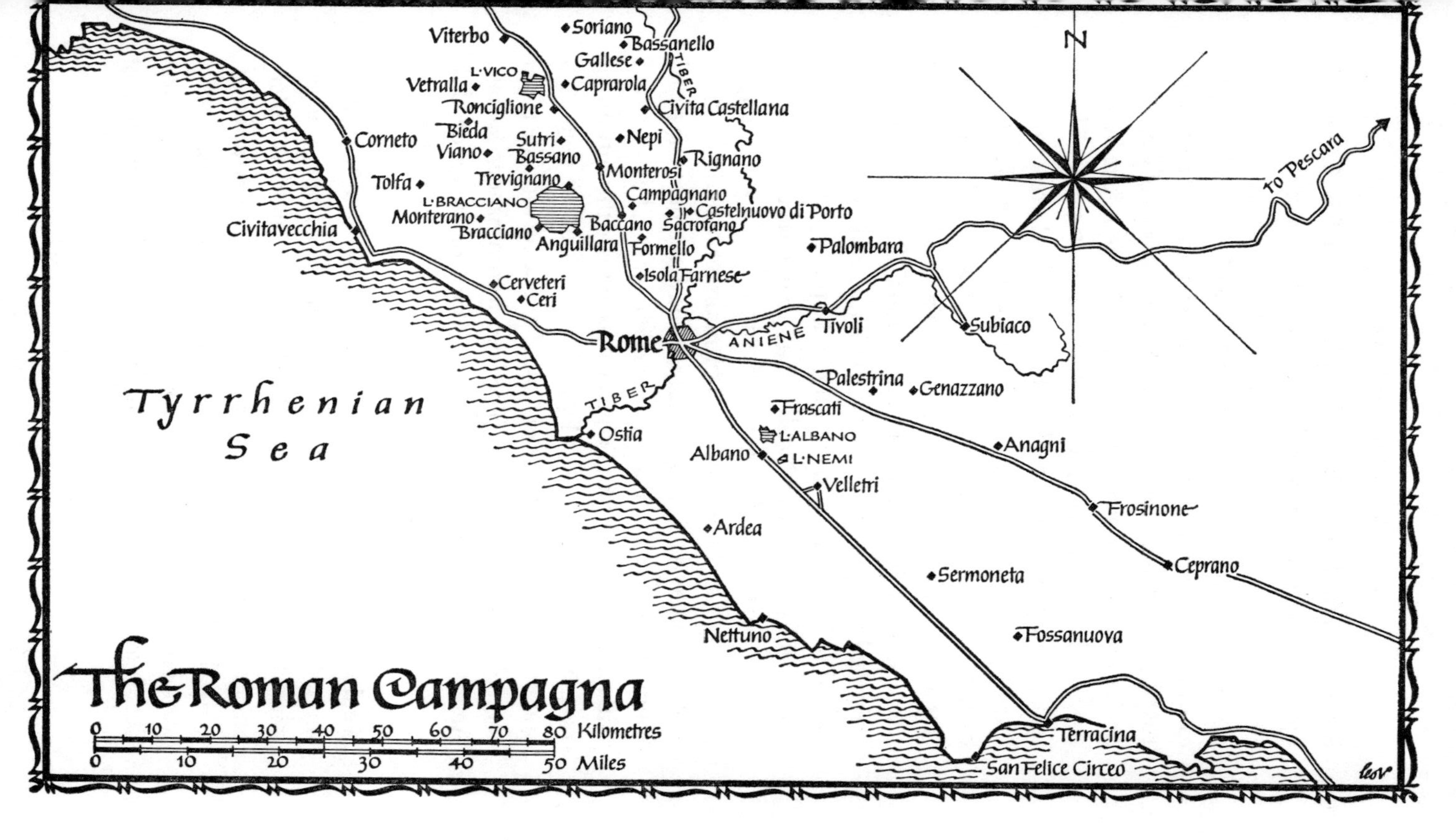

The Roman Campagna
Tyrrhenian Sea
N
to Pescara
Viterbo
Soriano
Bassanello
Gallese
TIBER
L·VICO
Vetralla
Caprarola
Ronciglione
Civita Castellana
Corneto
Bieda
Sutri
Nepi
Viano
Bassano
Rignano
Monterosi
Tolfa
Trevignano
Campagnano
L·BRACCIANO
Castelnuovo di Porto
Monterano
Baccano
Sacrofano
Civitavecchia
Bracciano
Anguillara
Formello
Palombara
Isola Farnese
Cerveteri
Ceri
Tivoli
Subiaco
Rome
ANIENE
Palestrina
Genazzano
TIBER
Frascati
Ostia
L·ALBANO
Albano
L·NEMI
Anagni
Velletri
Frosinone
Ardea
Ceprano
Sermoneta
Nettuno
Fossanuova
Terracina
San Felice Circeo
0 10 20 30 40 50 60 70 80 Kilometres
0 10 20 30 40 50 Miles

formed and the bulk of the artillery had been left in Anguillara for safety. But diplomatic factors were beginning to play a part. The support of the French for the Orsini had been clearly affirmed, and now both Spain and Venice began to exert pressure on Alexander to come to terms with his unruly vassals. The Orsini, fearful lest the Spanish troops of Gonsalvo de Cordoba which were moving up to Rome might be used against them, were also anxious for an early peace. Thus a further chapter in the conflict between the Borgia and the Orsini was brought to a close with a compromise. The Orsini castles were restored by the Pope with the exception of Anguillara and Cerveteri which he retained as hostages for the payment of an indemnity of 50,000 ducats. The Orsini further promised not to make war on the Pope, and he in his turn agreed to intercede with the King of Naples for the release of the Orsini prisoners in Naples. The major share of the indemnity paid by the Orsini was given to Gandia whose hopes of winning the Orsini lands had been disappointed.

Within a few days of the signing of the agreement the papal army, still under Gandia, was in action again. The fortress of Ostia had been held by a French garrison since the autumn of 1494. It represented the last French foothold in the peninsula and now the Spanish army of Gonsalvo united with the papal forces for its final reduction. The French commander Menaut Aguerre was later to accuse the Pope of using devilish weapons against the fortress including some form of poison gas produced by throwing chemicals on to bonfires to the windward of the walls.[10] However what seems to have been more influential in the fall of Ostia in March 1497 was the joint effect of an artillery bombardment by Gandia's artillery on one side and an assault by the Spanish infantry on the other.

At the Easter celebrations in 1497 the two commanders were both present, and Burchard reported that Gonsalvo was deeply resentful at the precedence accorded to the Duke of

Gandia at his expense.[11] Gonsalvo was by no means the only man of influence in Rome who was by this time both angry and apprehensive at the growing power of the Borgia family. Since the late summer of the previous year Alexander had had all his children round him. At that time Jofrè and Sancia had returned after two years' absence, and Sancia established herself alongside Lucrezia as one of the official hostesses of Vatican society. During the winter rumour was rife about the indiscretions of Jofrè's Aragonese princess. It was suggested that Cesare and Juan were rivals for their sister-in-law's favours, which if true tells us much about the moral tone of the Neapolitan royal house as well as that of the Borgias.

Meanwhile all was not well at the palace of Santa Maria in Portico where Lucrezia and Giovanni Sforza were residing. Their marriage had been one of political convenience, the significance of which had been outdated almost as soon as it was completed. For nearly three years now papal policy had rested on an alliance with Naples and only while the Holy League was active could this be reconciled with alliance with the Sforza. By 1496 Milanese adherence to the League had distinctly cooled. Furthermore Giovanni's usefulness both as a soldier and a Romagna princeling was distinctly suspect. He had been suspected of passing information to Milan about Neapolitan troop movements in the Romagna in 1494, and had on several occasions been extremely dilatory in answering papal calls to arms. He also was present in the papal army during the Orsini war but does not seem to have made any greater contribution on this occasion than he had done in his previous campaigns. Lucrezia seems to have been profoundly bored with the provincial life of Giovanni's capital, Pesaro, and plans were probably already developing in Borgia minds for the annihilation of the Romagna vicars rather than alliance with them. Therefore as a dynastic or a political move the marriage had been a failure and it was clear late in 1496 when

Lucrezia refused to return to Pesaro after the summer in Rome that it was near to foundering.

Lucrezia was far from being the lurid and shameless courtesan which she has been painted and the extravagant legends about her relations with her father and brothers are quite unfounded. But she was a gay and pleasure loving girl who enjoyed presiding over the court of the Renaissance Papacy a good deal more than being married to a middle-aged soldier and being the hostess in an unimportant social backwater. Giovanni returned to Rome after Christmas and was also present at the Easter festivities. But he can have drawn no comfort from the dark looks cast at him by the Borgia brothers, and soon after fled in disguise to Pesaro. The evidence for explicit threats against Giovanni's life are untrustworthy, but immediately after his departure proceedings for a divorce were opened against him.

Another of Italy's soldiers who was nursing a grievance against the Borgias was the Duke of Urbino. Alexander had refused to ransom him from the Orsini prison in Soriano and he had been compelled to find the money himself. As he does not seem to have been employed by the Pope, and as it was not customary for an employer to be responsible for his unlucky *condottiere*'s ransom anyway, Alexander's refusal is hardly surprising. But it rankled with Guidobaldo particularly when it came on top of the blows to his pride which had no doubt been inflicted during the campaign by the arrogant Gandia.

But above all it was the Roman barons who were by this time feeling the full weight of the Borgia presence in Rome. The Colonna had received no reward for their assistance in the Orsini war, and the Orsini themselves were far from reconciled to the heavy indemnity which they had been called upon to pay. Early in June 1497 the atmosphere of resentment and alarm in Rome was considerably exacerbated by two

14 The *Sala dei Santi* in the Borgia Apartments.

15 The castle at Civita Castellana, refortified on the orders of Alexander VI by Antonio da San Gallo, the elder.

16 Cardinal Gaspare Borja; this version of the disputed portrait by Velasquez of Philip IV's Borja adviser is in the Städelsches Kunstinstitut, Frankfurt. The original was painted about 1643 just before the Cardinal's death.

papal appointments. In Naples King Federigo had recently succeeded his nephew Ferrantino on the throne and the time had come for his formal investiture and coronation by the Pope. Cesare Borgia was now nominated as legate for this ceremony, an honour to which his youth and lack of seniority in the College of Cardinals by no means entitled him. Almost at the same time the Duke of Gandia was given Benevento and Terracina as hereditary fiefs. These two important cities, the one in the heart of the Neapolitan kingdom and the other on its frontier, had been the objects of much rivalry between Naples and the Papacy. They ranked amongst the most precious possessions of the Papacy, and their alienation to the Borgia Dukes of Gandia aroused great feeling. In the College of Cardinals only Piccolomini dared to protest; King Federigo needed his investiture too much to react strongly, but Spain registered immediate resentment.

With feelings so thoroughly inflamed it seems likely that Alexander would have been forced to withdraw this last concession. But the issue was to be resolved in another way. On 14 June the Duke of Gandia was attacked, stabbed nine times in the neck and body, and his corpse thrown into the Tiber.

On that evening Cesare, Juan and Cardinal Juan Borgia-Lanzol, the elder, had gone to dine with Vanozza in her vineyard near San Martino ai Monti. The occasion of the dinner was to bid farewell to Cesare about to depart on his Neapolitan legation. The three Borgias with their entourage rode back towards the Vatican at dusk and were about to cross Ponte Sant'Angelo when Juan Borgia excused himself, pleaded an urgent engagement, and rode off with a groom, and a masked man, who had been in attendance all evening, mounted behind him. The groom was subsequently ordered to return to the Vatican to collect the Duke's light armour and meet him with it at the Piazza Giudea. The Duke never kept this appointment although he was, according to one report, seen in this area about midnight having spent the intervening hours with Madonna Damiata, a well known Roman courtesan.[13]

When next morning the Duke was still missing, no one in the Vatican was seriously alarmed as he was noted for his nocturnal adventures. However by late afternoon Alexander began to be concerned and ordered a search to be made. Early next morning a Slav boatman, who was accustomed to sleep in his barge moored at the Ripetta, reported that on the night in question, about midnight, he had seen a man on a white horse accompanied by four men on foot approach the river bank. Across the horse's back was thrown a body which was rolled off into the river. Acting on this information the search was concentrated on the northerly stretch of the Tiber as it flowed through the city, and there later in the day the body of the Duke was found. The corpse was laid out in state in Castel Sant'Angelo, and Alexander in an agony of grief himself directed the search for the killers.

From what has gone before it can be seen that there was no shortage of potential suspects. In addition to Giovanni Sforza, the Duke of Urbino, the Orsini, and Gonsalvo de Cordoba whose possible motives have already been considered, other names were linked to the crime. Ascanio Sforza, who had had a terrible row with Gandia only a few days before over the killing of one of Gandia's servants and the subsequent execution of some of Ascanio's men, absented himself from the Vatican on the grounds that suspicion was falling on him. Alexander, who announced that he had a good idea who was responsible, disclaimed any suspicion of Ascanio. He also in consistory absolved from blame Giovanni Sforza, the Duke of Urbino and his own son Jofrè who had fallen under suspicion on the grounds that he might be a vengeful cuckold. Another name mentioned was that of Count Antonio Maria della Mirandola whose daughter was said to have been seduced by

Gandia, and whose house was near the point on the river where the body had been thrown in.

One name which was not mentioned at the time was that of Cesare. With all the powerful enemies that Gandia had, the thought that his own brother, preoccupied as he was with preparations for the important Neapolitan legation, might have been responsible for the murder does not seem to have crossed anybody's mind. It was not until nine months later that the first suggestion of Cesare's complicity appeared in a Ferrarese report, and the story gained strength in Venice and Ferrara where Giovanni Sforza and the Orsini exiles were gathered. After the murder by Cesare of Lucrezia's second husband, Alfonso, in 1500 it became widely held that a man who could kill his brother-in-law must have killed his brother. His motives were taken to be jealousy of Gandia's position in their father's affections and the desire to supplant him as a secular prince. The whole subsequent course of Cesare's career starting from his abandonment of his ecclesiastical career fourteen months later are seen to stem from this event, and indeed the direction of this career must have been already mapped out in Cesare's mind if determination to supplant his brother is to be seen as a viable motive for the crime. Cesare was already poised on the threshold of a great ecclesiastical career which could not inconceivably have led to the Papacy itself. Nor need his innate martial character have been necessarily proscribed by such a future, as Cardinals Vitelleschi and Scarampo had shown before him and as Julius II was to show later. Nor indeed was it necessary for Cesare, already determined to abandon the Sacred College and capable of the sort of domination over his father which his accusers have postulated, to go to the extravagant lengths of murdering his brother to achieve his ends.

The case against Cesare in fact depends on the subsequent uncovering of a possible motive in the apparent advantages which he gained at a considerably later date from the death of his brother, and on a growing awareness of his ruthless qualities. He was capable of doing it; he eventually appeared to have profited from it; therefore he must have done it, runs the argument. But there is absolutely no evidence that he did do it. In their search for contemporary indications of Cesare's guilt historians have suggested that the sudden abandonment of the search for the murderers by Alexander indicated that he had discovered Cesare's responsibility and could not bring himself to do anything about it. From this moment therefore Cesare had a hold over his father and all subsequent Borgia history is presented as depicting this growing subordination of father to son. But it seems to me that this idea is also unfounded, that subsequent Borgia successes were achieved by close cooperation between Alexander and Cesare, with the Pope always the planner and director of operations. So why must we believe in this dramatic moment of a father confronted with the realisation of a son's fratricide? An awareness that the murderer was any one of Gandia's influential enemies would have been sufficient to cause Alexander to call off the hunt and turn instead to planning a future revenge. Because one thing that contemporaries seemed to be agreed on was that the murderers had 'denti lunghi'; despite the attractive possibilities that the killing was the result of one of Gandia's squalid adventures, it was generally felt that someone with great influence was behind it. Although we cannot attach much importance to the fact that most of the potential suspects were publicly cleared by Alexander, those who were left out of the Pope's exculpations, the Orsini, do seem the most likely objects of suspicion. Even if Gandia was not a great threat to them personally, he was the man to whom the Pope had promised their estates. He was the object of affection of the hated Borgia who in addition to everything else was now held responsible for the death of the head of the clan, Virginio, in his Neapolitan prison. He was the man who had sacked Trevignano and directed his guns against the walls of Bracciano.

But all this is in the realms of speculation and there is little likelihood now that we shall ever know the whole truth. We must instead turn to the events following the murder and the more apparent consequences of it.

Alexander's paternal feelings for Gandia and deep sense of personal loss were apparent to all. It was said that his cries of anguish could be clearly heard as the Duke's body was borne out of Castel Sant'Angelo for burial. In consistory the Pope bewailed that he would have given seven papacies to have his son restored to him and publicly proclaimed that this was God's judgment on him for his sins.[14] The immediate result of this personal tragedy was to impel Alexander towards reform of the Church, as well as of his own life. He set up a reform commission of six of the more spiritually minded cardinals and gave them a very full brief to set in motion reform from the top, not excluding the Pope himself. The outcome of the work of the commission during the second half of 1497, work in which Alexander himself seems to have played a full part, was a series of proposals for reform embodied in a Bull which for a number of reasons was never promulgated.[15]

The reform constitutions of 1497 take their place amongst a number of similar reform programmes which emerged within the Catholic Church during the century before the Council of Trent. On the whole the programme failed to gain acceptance for the same reasons. Reform of the Church, and particularly reform of the upper echelons of Church administration, was always blocked by the deep-rooted vested interests against which it was aimed. It was for this reason that the Catholic Reform movement of the early decades of the sixteenth century stressed reform of the individual, reform from the bottom, as the most effective path to a reformed

Catholic Church. The constitutions of 1497 with their restrictions on the sale of curial offices and with their proposals for the reform of the College of Cardinals were unlikely to receive much support in the Vatican itself. Suggestions that cardinals should be more abstemious in their daily lives; that they should be served with only one boiled and one roast meat at table; that the Holy Scriptures should be read during meals, rather than the performance of music or the recitation of historical tales; that no cardinal should have more than one diocese, nor an income of more than 6000 ducats; that cardinals should be drawn proportionately from all nations—such suggestions were not likely to appeal to either the Italian or the worldly majority of late fifteenth-century cardinals. At the same time it was admitted that an essential precursor, and indeed generator, of reform must be a General Council. It was because the reform commission considered that the detailed proposals of reform should come from a General Council that the constitutions of 1497 themselves were in no sense intended to be a complete programme of reform. But a General Council was regarded with deep suspicion by Renaissance Popes, and the dangerous political situation of the last decade of the fifteenth century seemed an inopportune moment both to Alexander and to the Italian cardinals to call such a Council.

Finally what of the attitude of the Pope himself? It is usually said that it was the lukewarm and transitory nature of Alexander's desire for reform which brought the work of the commission to a halt, that within a few months his thoughts had turned once more to the advancement of his family and the consolidation of papal temporal power. This is to some extent true and the Pope's attitude was no doubt affected by the extent to which the proposed reforms aimed at restraining the secularisation of the Papacy. It is also true that the constitutions contained a strong element of the election capitulations which had become a feature of the relations between Renaissance Popes and their cardinals. The number of cardinals was to be limited to twenty-four; the advisory and consultative powers of the College were to be considerably increased particularly with regard to the appointment and removal of bishops and the alienation of Church lands. It was perhaps as much these attempts to use the reforms as a weapon in the confrontation between Pope and cardinals, as any personal considerations, which led to Alexander's reluctance to press the reforms. That it was not just a question of lack of concern for the Church in its spiritual aspects is indicated by Alexander's real spiritual involvement manifested in his concern for the reform of the monastic orders, for the purity of doctrine, for the suppression of heresy and for the protection of the liberties of the Church against secular rulers.[16]

During the summer months while the reform commission was at work, Alexander seemed anxious to keep his children at a distance. Jofrè and Sancia were packed off to Squillace, and Cesare was absent in Naples on his legation. It was remarked that on Cesare's return in September his father's attitude towards him seemed to be markedly cold. But these observations were based on their official meeting the day after Cesare's return, by which time Cesare had already reported privately to his father.[17] Any coldness observed after this was probably a continuation of Alexander's attempt to restrain his feelings for his family, rather than a particular animosity towards Cesare.

However Alexander was not entirely forgetful of his family during this period, and within a few days of the murder of Gandia plans were going ahead again for the divorce of Lucrezia from Giovanni Sforza. During the summer while Lucrezia sheltered in the cloisters of San Sisto on the Appian Way, another commission of cardinals was considering this question. Although the reasons for obtaining this divorce seem to have been primarily political and dynastic, Alexander was anxious to avoid achieving his aim by arbitrary papal decree. The idea that an incomplete revocation of Lucrezia's original betrothal to the Count of Aversa might provide grounds for the nullity of the marriage was squashed by Cardinal Pallavicini, a member of the divorce commission and one of the leading canonists in the College. So Alexander was forced back on the plea of non-consummation of the marriage, the implications of which were indignantly denied by Giovanni Sforza. For nearly six months the struggle went on; Giovanni's counterclaims of incestuous relations within the Borgia family, although almost certainly untrue, were probably genuinely believed by himself. A naturally rather cold man he was astonished and shocked by the ostentatious affection of the links which bound the Borgias. But his resistance was not just a matter of protecting his honour; there was a dowry of 31,000 ducats to protect, and he was also probably aware that his one hope of retaining his vicariate lay in preserving a link with the Borgia family. However in the last resort it was political pressure which produced the political divorce. Ludovico Sforza, anxious that Milanese relations with the Papacy should not be damaged by what he considered a trivial and rather amusing dispute, brought pressure to bear on his cousin and threatened to withdraw Milanese protection from Pesaro. In November Giovanni capitulated and signed the necessary statement which enabled the divorce commission to pronounce in favour of a divorce. By the end of December Lucrezia was once more free to play her part in Borgia dynastic plans, and indeed if the story of her affair with the young Spaniard Pedro Calderon during this period is to be believed, there was no time to be lost. There were reports that Lucrezia gave birth to a child in the spring of 1498 and certainly Calderon was mysteriously murdered about the same time. Gossip connected his name with that of

Lucrezia for whom he had acted as messenger during her retreat in San Sisto, but defamatory rumours were often in themselves sufficient to provoke the Borgias to violent action.[18]

The motives behind the determination to free Lucrezia from her first husband are by no means clearly established. That they should have been primarily dynastic and political has been generally assumed. The marriage with Giovanni Sforza represented the Milanese connection of 1492–3, a connection which by 1497 was something of an anachronism when Milan and Naples seemed to be no longer opposed to each other and when the preservation of a balance between the two was no longer necessary. Naples was always the natural object of papal diplomacy and the extension of papal influence, and the substitution of a close link with the Neapolitan royal house for a rather tenuous connection with the Sforzas was a logical progression in papal policy. At the same time of course such a substitution represented a remarkable increase in Borgia social prestige. But if these motives were at the root of Borgia policy they were kept well-hidden as Alexander considered a number of alternative suitors for Lucrezia's hand after the divorce. As the Duke of Gravina, Ottaviano Riario and Antonello Sanseverino were each in their turn considered as possible successors to Giovanni Sforza, the impression was given that the divorce itself had been primarily a domestic issue and that there were no social or political implications in the choice of a successor. But such a lack of policy does not ring true in the context of the Borgias, nor yet is there any real evidence of a significant domestic breach between Lucrezia and Giovanni. Lucrezia was too weak a character to have transformed her undoubted discontent with her husband and his court into a determined demand to be released from him, and Giovanni was obviously very anxious to preserve his marriage. One is left therefore with the impression of a steadily mounting pressure for extension of the Borgia connection with Naples.

This pressure is indicated not only by the conclusion of arrangements for the marriage of Lucrezia to Alfonso, Duke of Bisceglie, the illegitimate son of Alfonso II and the brother of Sancia, but also by the emergence of a Borgia plan for the marriage of Cesare to Carlotta, the daughter of the new King Federigo. Throughout the second half of 1497 rumours had been circulating in Rome about Cesare's desire to abandon his ecclesiastical career and succeed to the temporal position which his murdered brother had been establishing. In the early months of 1498 more clear cut plans for basing this position on a Neapolitan marriage became apparent. It was at this moment that the premature death of Charles VIII and the succession of his cousin Louis with his Orleanist claims to Milan necessitated a reorientation of Italian politics. Alexander quickly began to adapt his policies to meet the new situation.

CHAPTER EIGHT

THE BORGIA ADVANCE, 1498–1502

It was during the summer of 1498 that the new direction of Borgia policy began to emerge. It was a policy essentially shaped to the realities of the Italian political situation. At his accession the new French King Louis XII had clearly declared his claims to the Duchy of Milan and the Kingdom of Naples, and with a growing entente with Venice a new French invasion seemed imminent. In the face of such a threat the Holy League lay in ruins. All attempts both of coercion and blandishment had failed to win Florence away from her reliance on France, although the discrediting and death of Savonarola made it unlikely that Louis could expect much active help from her. Venice was now pursuing an anti-Milanese policy and quickly sought an alliance with France. Naples, bankrupt and devastated, now had a pacific king dependent on a Spanish army. Spain and France, increasingly aware of their conflicting interests in Italy, were for the present content to compromise and negotiate on the division of the potential spoils.

In the circumstances it was becoming increasingly unrealistic for the Pope to concentrate his energies on protecting the liberty of Italy from the 'barbarians'. The defence of the Papal States and Borgia interests demanded acceptance of the impending reality of a foreign presence in Italy and the hope for the Pope lay in maintaining a balance of foreign powers, in playing them off against each other, in always keeping the

Papacy on the winning side in any conflict between these powers, and above all in avoiding isolation. With the Orsini and the Colonna temporarily united against him and intriguing with King Federigo, and with even the Farnese in opposition, the danger of isolation at this juncture was a very real one. However for the moment, before invasion finally engulfed Italy, there seemed to be a good chance of exploiting the weakness of Naples and tying it closely to the Church. At the same time the imminent threat of a French invasion supported by Venice demanded the attention of papal diplomacy. There seemed to be little chance of opposing it without throwing Italy, and Naples in particular, into the arms of Spain. From this situation sprang the Neapolitan marriage projects and the negotiations with France in 1498/9.

In June Lucrezia was married to the Duke of Bisceglie with a dowry of 41,000 ducats and the stipulation that she should not be compelled to go to Naples during her father's lifetime. The ceremonies once again took place in the Vatican but without the public display of Lucrezia's first wedding and therefore with less public comment.[1] At the same time the possibility of a marriage of Cesare to Carlotta, the daughter of Federigo himself, had been suggested, a project which both father and daughter resisted strongly. The implications of this Borgia infiltration were all too clear and probably weighed more with Federigo than his expressed disgust about marrying his daughter to an unfrocked cardinal. Carlotta herself, living in France, was in love with a Breton nobleman and had no intention of sacrificing her love for Borgia dynastic considerations.

The value of Louis XII's possible influence over Carlotta, resident at the court of Anne of Brittany, was therefore an added reason for the negotiations which now opened between Alexander and the French King. At the same time, if the Neapolitan project for Cesare's future finally foundered, as seemed likely, his interest would inevitably be turned to the

Romagna or Tuscany. In this area the French as future participants in north Italian politics could well be useful. Thus all considerations pointed in the same direction and in July the papal ambassadors set out for France. Their overt instructions were to encourage French support for a crusade, and to seek to confine French interference in Italy to assistance in the restoration of Pisa to Florence. It was in these terms that the dispatch of the embassy was defended by Alexander's nuncio to the Emperor Maximilian. But the true nature of papal policy soon became apparent particularly as other negotiators were busy discussing the Pope's side of the potential bargain with France, Louis XII's divorce.

Charles VIII had finally succeeded in bringing the almost independent apanage of Brittany under the control of the French crown by his marriage with Anne of Brittany. But Charles' premature death left Anne an eminently marriageable widow, and Brittany the prey of likely suitors. In the circumstances Louis proposed the logical if somewhat unconventional solution of marrying his predecessor's widow himself. The only stumbling block to this dynastic programme was Louis' wife Jeanne to whom he was not closely attached and from whom he now sought a divorce. This was a situation from which Alexander was determined to extract maximum profit, and his bargaining position was made stronger by the fact that Georges d'Amboise, the chief counsellor of Louis XII, wanted to be a cardinal; a whim for which France could be made to pay dearly.

A commission of two bishops was set up to examine the grounds put forward by Louis for his divorce, and Cesare Borgia also took an interest in the affair in the hope of winning for himself the gratitude of the French King. Thus it was Cesare, having in August 1498 finally renounced his cardinalate on the grounds that he was unsuited to the cloth and that a continuance of his present way of life under ecclesiastical vows would endanger his soul, who set out for France with the papal dispensation for Louis' new marriage and Amboise's red hat in his baggage. Louis XII had already honoured him with the title of Duke of Valence, a title which provided a curiously apt continuity with his previous one of Cardinal of Valencia, and led to his Italian nickname, 'Il Valentino'.

Cesare at this moment was twenty-three. He had been a cardinal for five years and was said to have collected benefices worth 35,000 ducats a year. This was by no means an astonishing figure; Pietro Riario, the favourite nephew of Sixtus IV, had an income twice this size at the time of his premature death in 1474. Nevertheless Cesare was surrendering a secure, lucrative and steadily improving position in the Church for the chance of secular and military power. His father on whom he depended more than he cared to admit was still in unusually good health, but he was sixty-seven and no one could predict how long Cesare had to establish himself, to win a princely position which he would be able to maintain after his father's death. He was therefore from this moment on always a man in a hurry. He had many advantages of physique and intellect; he was reputed to have been a brilliant student at Perugia and Pisa universities and was described by many as the handsomest man of his day. 'His head is most beautiful,' reported the Venetian ambassador. 'He is tall and well built, and more handsome than King Ferdinand,' a comparison which was perhaps more flattering to the forty-eight year old Spanish King than it was to Cesare.[2] Even as a cardinal he tended to dress flamboyantly and in the height of lay fashion. He excelled in all forms of martial exercise from wrestling with country folk to fighting bulls. All who knew him could see that he was ambitious, arrogant and loose-living; but of his more sinister qualities there was little evidence as yet.

Cesare sailed from Civitavecchia in two French galleys on 4

October. He landed at Marseilles and was well received on his long progress through France to the court of Louis XII at Chinon. French observers were astonished and horrified at the splendour and haughty demeanour of a Pope's son and his entourage. But they had been isolated from the changes which had taken place in the Papacy since the Popes had left Avignon, nor were they accustomed to the ostentatious display of the Italian courts. They had never seen Pietro or Girolamo Riario, or Franceschetto Cibo. If they had, their reaction to Cesare might have been less unflattering.

There ensued a long drawn out diplomatic game at which Cesare in his impatience to get on with his career was not yet adept. As outward signs of the alliance between France and the Pope, Cesare needed not only his French duchy, but also a good marriage to either Carlotta under French protection or to a French princess, and French military assistance in the Romagna. Louis needed his divorce, Amboise's cardinalate and appointment as resident papal legate in France, and if possible papal support in his Italian campaigns. Throughout the winter of 1498/9 the inducements were bartered. Cesare had his duchy, Amboise got his hat but not immediately the legateship. Cesare reluctantly handed over the papal dispensation for Louis' new marriage at the same moment as the divorce commission pronounced the previous marriage dissolved. But the point was clearly made that the Pope could rescind the dispensation on the grounds of having been misinformed. For three months the negotiations hung fire at this point as Cesare fretted in France, and Alexander tried to keep Milan and Naples guessing in Italy. He postponed their inevitable realisation that he had deserted them by first maintaining that the negotiations with France were purely personal ones and did not indicate a political realignment, and then by appearing to consider abandoning the negotiations altogether. Neither Ludovico Sforza nor Federigo were really deceived by these manoeuvres, but they could not be sure that all hope had gone of winning the Pope back to their side. They made extravagant offers themselves; Alexander, the great temporiser, pretended to consider them; but he was playing his favourite diplomatic game of keeping in with both sides as long as possible to gain the maximum advantage from the final alliance, and to reduce to a minimum the danger from the corresponding final breach.[3]

At last in May 1499 Louis committed himself. The Carlotta marriage project was finally abandoned, and Cesare was married to Charlotte d'Albret, the sister of the King of Navarre. Louis promised a military force to assist in the Romagna after Cesare himself had served in the impending French campaign against Milan. This was all the military assistance that Louis was able to get from the Pope who was able to claim that he had to protect himself against possible attack from Naples. Such an attack in fact did not materialise; Federigo was too bankrupt, and the Milanese collapse in the face of the combined French and Venetian invasion too rapid, for there to be any serious cooperation between the last two united Italian states.

Even more dangerous to Alexander than the enmity of Naples and Milan provoked by his French alliance, was the inevitable suspicion of Spain. The Spanish ambassador Garcilasse de la Vega left Rome in fury when he heard of the completion of the Franco-Papal alliance. He warned Alexander that he was becoming the chaplain of the King of France and would soon himself be seeking asylum in Spain. But the emergence of the Franco-Spanish entente for the partition of Naples made it impossible for Ferdinand and Isabella to remain hostile to the Pope, and he in his turn mollified them with the concession of wide control over the Spanish Church. Thus within a month of the departure of Garcilasse a new ambassador arrived in Rome not only to announce the resumption of diplomatic relations, but also to offer on behalf of

Ferdinand and Isabella the archbishopric of Valencia to a Borgia. The offer was promptly accepted on behalf of Juan Borgia-Lanzol, the younger, who had been made a cardinal in 1496.

By early October, after a campaign of barely a month in Lombardy which concluded with Ludovico's flight over the Alps, Cesare was free of his commitment to Louis and could count on Louis' commitment to him. A French army of 1800 cavalry and over 4000 Swiss and Gascon infantry under Yves d'Alègre were placed at his disposal, and the overthrow of the semi-independent vicars of the Romagna could begin.

It would be idle to pretend as some have tried to do that Borgia dynasticism played no part in the creation of the Romagna duchy for Cesare; that he was merely acting as the instrument of the Church, as another and to some extent more successful Cardinal Albornoz. At the same time one cannot close one's eyes to the clear precedents for this aspect of Borgia policy, to the obvious advantages which the Church could derive from the overthrow of the vicars and the establishment of unified government in the Romagna, to the fact that this was completely in line with what the Renaissance Papacy was trying to do. Alexander had perhaps additional justification for his plans, in that Venetian influence and interest in the Romagna had been steadily increasing during his pontificate and the vicars were becoming more than ever dependent on external powers rather than on their true sovereign, the Pope.[4] There had been rumours in Venice in 1497 of a conspiracy of the vicars against the Pope, perhaps particularly inspired by Giovanni Sforza who had personal reasons for hating the Borgias.[5] Thus when in July 1499 Alexander excommunicated the vicars and declared their vicariates forfeit, it was not just on the grounds of non-payment of the annual census; his action would have been considered justified by any fifteenth-century monarch.

On 20 November Cesare entered the Papal States with an

army consisting largely of French troops. He was received with watchful respect by Giovanni Bentivoglio in Bologna, while Venice as the ally of France remained docile but suspicious.

The first objective of the campaign was the vicariate of the Riario, the cities of Imola and Forlì, ruled by Caterina Sforza as regent for her son Ottaviano. Caterina was the one Romagna ruler who had resisted Venetian infiltration and whose downfall therefore was unlikely to cause any great concern in Venice. She was also an obvious target after the fall of her uncle Ludovico. She had been aware of her danger for some months and had made desperate efforts to prepare her fortresses to resist the attack. But there was strong opposition to her in both the main cities and she could only personally conduct the defence of one of them. While she herself therefore commanded the garrison of Forlì, that of Imola was entrusted to two Romagnol *condottieri*, Dionigi Naldi in the fortress and Giovanni Sassatelli in the town itself. These two men were professional soldiers, mercenary captains, who as a group were not noted, in the Italy of their day, for their loyalty to lost causes. Nor were the citizens of either Imola or Forlì prepared to risk the consequences of resistance to the dreaded French troops for the sake of a lady whom many of them feared and hated. The previous appearance of French troops in the Romagna in 1494 had proved disastrous for the citizens of some of the smaller towns, Mordano in particular, and memories of this did not encourage resistance now.

So it was that when Achille Tiberti, himself another Romagnol captain, arrived with Cesare's standard and an Italian advance guard before the gates of Imola, the town surrendered immediately. Naldi, however, in the fortress was not subject to the same pressures from the townspeople as Sassatelli had been and prepared to defend himself. But once Cesare had moved his artillery up and began to bombard the weakest point of the walls which had been revealed to him by a local carpenter, Naldi agreed to surrender on terms if help did not arrive within three days. This formality concluded, the fortress was surrendered and Naldi himself took service under Cesare. Dionigi Naldi was a good acquisition for Cesare for he was not only one of the more noted infantry captains of his day, but he also, owing to his local connections, could draw on the loyalty of the Val di Lamone, a famous recruiting ground for hardy Romagnol infantry. It was to be the frequent presence of these locally raised mercenaries in Cesare's armies which contributed to his rather mistaken reputation with Machiavelli of being an enlightened exponent of the use of a citizen militia.[6]

On 17 December Cardinal Juan Borgia-Lanzol, the younger, who accompanied Cesare as papal legate to the Romagna, received the oath of obedience to the Pope of the city of Imola. Two days later Forlì opened its gates, again to Achille Tiberti as spokesman of his master, and Caterina Sforza withdrew into the fortress to make her last stand. It had been part of the surrender terms agreed between Tiberti and the Forlivesi that the French troops should not be allowed to enter the city. This proved to be a promise impossible to maintain as the fortress itself lay within the walls, and the depredations of the Gascon infantry in Forlì did a good deal of damage to Cesare's reputation as a disciplinarian. The local chronicler Bernardi described the scenes in Forlì after the entry of Cesare's troops as a 'glimpse through the gates of hell'.[7] Although we may imagine that a local reporter might well exaggerate the sufferings of his own home town, we must accept that the apparently just and eminently politic clemency of the capitulation agreements drawn up between Cesare and the Romagna cities were not always honoured.[8] This was not necessarily owing to any breach of faith on the part of Borgia himself, but owing to his inability to control certain sections of his army.

For over three weeks Caterina Sforza held out in the fortress of Forlì. Her natural courage and determination were buoyed up by news that her uncle, Ludovico, was about to stage a counterattack in Milan, a move which would certainly lead to the withdrawal of Cesare's French troops. But Cesare's well directed artillery caused a breach in the walls a little too quickly. The Gascon infantry poured in and seem to have taken the garrison somewhat by surprise. Caterina's attempt to blow herself up with the powder magazine failed as the fuse misfired, and she was taken prisoner by a French soldier.

The fact that Caterina was a French prisoner was to have considerable repercussions. It caused trouble immediately as Cesare and his father naturally wanted to deal with her themselves. The French had chivalrous, and to Italian eyes unrealistic, views about the status of women, and in this case D'Alègre and his officers were much more impressed by Caterina's spirit and beauty than they were by the trouble she had caused and the dangers which she represented to papal authority if allowed to go free. Eventually a compromise was reached; Cesare paid a ransom for her and guaranteed that she would be treated properly, and the French reluctantly handed her over. There are reports that Cesare abused and assaulted Caterina while she was his prisoner in the Romagna but there is no reliable evidence of this. It would seem more likely, knowing Caterina's reputation, that she may have offered herself to Cesare in the hope of winning his support and consideration. But Cesare seems to have been a man whose actions were entirely unaffected by his relations with women; with the exception of Lucrezia for whom he had a genuine affection and concern.

With Imola and Forlì in his hands Cesare now turned his attentions to Pesaro, the home of his ex-brother-in-law Giovanni Sforza. Giovanni had already fled from the city, and

Venice, although officially recognised as his protector, was not prepared to commit herself against the French for the sake of a Sforza. The army marched southwards past Cesena, which was already a papal city and was to become the capital of Cesare's state, and set out on the road to Pesaro. But at this moment news of Ludovico's return to Milan at the head of a Swiss mercenary army reached the camp. Yves d'Alègre and his troops were recalled to defend the French conquests and Cesare was left with only his small force of Italians. With bitter reflections on the disadvantages of relying on French help, he abandoned his attack on Pesaro. Useful as the French had been not just as a military force, but also for the prestige and diplomatic strength which their presence gave him, Cesare resolved that in future he would not be dependent on them. Now he withdrew to Cesena, set up one of his Spanish captains, Don Ramiro de Lorqua, as governor of his new state, and prepared to return to Rome. Ahead of him had already gone his colleague and relative Cardinal Juan Borgia-Lanzol. But the cardinal had been taken ill on his journey and had died at Urbino a few days later. Inevitably the story went round that he had been poisoned by Cesare who was said to be jealous of his ability and growing prestige. Able and of growing value to the Borgias for his administrative and diplomatic skill he certainly was, but once again there is absolutely no evidence of this supposed jealousy. The death of Juan Borgia, the younger, was a considerable loss to the family. He had been a successful governor of Perugia and had been to some extent responsible for lessening Florentine and Venetian hostility to Borgia plans in the Romagna when he had visited the two cities as papal legate earlier in 1499. He and Cesare seem to have been on very good terms and worked well together in the Romagna. But for his untimely death he would probably have played an important part in administering the Romagna, a part which was now somewhat unfortunately dominated by Cesare's Spanish military aides.

On 25 February Cesare entered Rome in triumph. A procession of one hundred light carts covered in black cloth, 700 Swiss pikemen, and 125 mounted men-at-arms clothed in black, preceded Cesare and Vitellozzo Vitelli through the streets. Cesare was flanked by Cardinals Orsini and Alessandro Farnese, and the severe black of his costume was relieved only by the golden collar of the French Order of St. Michel conferred on him by Louis XII. It was reported that the black ordered for this occasion was a sign of mourning for Cardinal Juan, but Cesare's penchant for black showed itself on other occasions than this. The Pope had been overjoyed at his son's success and now welcomed him with unconcealed delight. Caterina Sforza whom Cesare had brought south with him was lodged in the Belvedere, recently built and lavishly decorated by Innocent VIII. But when she refused to sign away her rights and those of her children to Imola and Forlì, and made persistent attempts to escape, she was moved to a considerably less salubrious prison in Castel Sant' Angelo.

But awkward as the obstinate resistance of Caterina was there were many more pressing problems to occupy Alexander and his son during the summer of 1500. Rome had become a great centre of diplomatic intrigue as the attention of both France and Spain centred on Italy and on the Kingdom of Naples in particular. 1500 was also Jubilee Year. From the beginning of the year the pilgrims had been arriving in ever increasing numbers. By Easter Sunday there were 200,000 pilgrims present in St. Peter's Square for the Pope's traditional Easter blessing. To prepare for this occasion Alexander had been doing his utmost to improve the appearance and communications of the city. It was at this moment that the Via Alessandrina was opened up, cutting through the medieval slums which surrounded the Vatican from Ponte Sant'Angelo to the doors of St. Peter's. Buildings were torn down and streets widened throughout the city.

In the atmosphere of general enthusiasm created by the Jubilee, Alexander also tried to get support for a crusade. The Turks in the previous year had erupted once more against the Venetian empire in the eastern Mediterranean. Alexander invited all Christian states to send representatives to a conference to discuss the problems, but with little response. Then in the spring of 1500 the envoys of the foreign powers in Rome were invited to a secret consistory. Stefano Taleazzi, Bishop of Torcello, was asked to prepare a brief on the steps necessary for the launching of a crusade.[9] Arrangements were made for legates to be sent out over Europe to preach the crusade, and the collection of a crusading tenth was authorised. Crusading funds were already in a healthy state as the profits from the papal alum mines at Tolfa were devoted to this purpose. Now even the cardinals were called upon to contribute and it was not for lack of money that little was achieved. When the crusading Bull was launched on 1 July it made as little impact as had the efforts of Alexander's immediate predecessors. However the Venetians who were the most directly concerned felt that Alexander was doing his best, and indeed in the next year some results began to appear. A combined fleet was organised and gained some successes in the eastern Mediterranean; a league was formed between Venice, Hungary and the Pope and some of the crusading money was used for the activities of these allies. But there was always the suspicion that Turkish pressure on Venice was an advantage to Borgia plans in the Romagna, and also that not all the money collected for the crusade was used for the right purpose. However not even in contemporary scandal were there any implications that Alexander was deliberately encouraging the Turks. On the other hand one cannot help wondering if his crusading zeal did not stem to some extent from self interest.

One of the reasons why France and Spain were not much concerned with a crusade was because they were busy planning the joint occupation and division of Naples. An understanding, growing out of mutual suspicion and a realisation that unilateral action in Naples was unlikely to lead to a lasting result, led to the signing of the Treaty of Granada in November 1500. By this the kingdom of Naples was to be partitioned between France and Spain; France was to have Campania with Naples itself and Abruzzi and Basilicata; this left Spain Puglia and Calabria. The Pope as overlord seems to have given tacit consent at this stage and publicly announced and supported the dismemberment of his fief in the following year. The justification for the destruction of the Aragonese dynasty in Naples was Federigo's attempts to gain Turkish support for his doomed kingdom. Once again Alexander was to some extent presented with a *fait accompli*; any further protection of Naples was doomed in the face of such an attack and Alexander's only hope lay in encouraging the division and hoping, with some justification, that two powerful masters in Naples would prevent it being any threat to the dominions of the Pope.

The final abandonment of Naples to its fate by the Borgias is often seen to have been dramatically announced by the abrupt end of Lucrezia's second marriage. In August 1500 Alfonso, Duke of Bisceglie, was murdered on Cesare's orders after an earlier assassination attempt by unknown hands had failed.

The presence of Alfonso, and to a lesser extent Sancia, at the papal court had been an increasing embarrassment since the public announcement of the Pope's alliance with France. The trend of papal policy and the ultimate sacrifice of the Aragonese dynasty were clearly implied in this entente and in the summer of 1499 Alfonso fled from Rome fearing for his safety. At this time Lucrezia, angry with her father because his policies had deprived her of her husband, was sent off to be Governor of Spoleto. After some months of negotiations and blandishments Alfonso was persuaded to return to his wife but his situation was obviously a difficult one. Thus when he was attacked by a group of armed men on the steps of St. Peter's on the evening of 15 July, there were perhaps good reasons for imagining that the Borgias were behind it. Alfonso did however have other enemies, and the identity of the attackers was by no means apparent to the Romans at this stage. The hand of the Orsini was seen by many, and the fact that Lucrezia had recently acquired the Gaetani estates and was steadily encroaching on Orsini lands as the Governor of Nepi, might have made her husband a target for baronial anger. Furthermore Alfonso himself was an ally of the Colonna and it was to their castle of Genazzano that he had fled in the previous year.

For the moment however Alfonso was saved; he was carried more dead than alive into the Vatican and zealously tended by Lucrezia and Sancia, his sister. Cesare gave orders for a stricter policing of the area, but at the same time muttered ambiguously that what had been started at noon could be finished by nightfall. He is also reported to have said, 'I did not wound the Duke, but if I had it would have been no more than he deserved.'[10] If Cesare was responsible for the first attack some curious anomalies have to be considered. In the first place although a Borgia motive for getting rid of Alfonso is clear, it is not clear why it had to be done in such an ostentatious way. Nor yet is the bungled affair on the steps of St. Peter's typical of Cesare's better known efficiency in disposing of enemies. Finally if it had become a matter of policy to get rid of Alfonso, why was a month allowed to elapse before the *coup de grace* was administered? Because it was not until 18 August that Cesare's lieutenant Michele

Corella, better known as Don Michelotto, forced his way into Alfonso's sick room in the Vatican and strangled him. This was an act of such outrageous effrontery that one cannot help but think that Cesare may have been telling the truth when he claimed that he had done it because his life was threatened and as a spontaneous act of revenge. The Venetian ambassador, Capello, fills in this motive for us by recounting how Alfonso, already convalescent and walking in the Vatican gardens, had seen Cesare walking unarmed below him and, believing him to be the author of the previous attack, had attempted to kill him with a cross bow.[11] It was this which may have provoked Cesare into the controlled fury of that brutal strangling scene.

The common belief that Cesare was a murderer did him untold damage, and it is hard to believe that he deliberately chose so cumbersome and unnecessarily dramatic a method of pursuing a purely diplomatic and dynastic policy. It has been argued that Cesare, the predominant partner in the Borgia family and fully committed to a French alliance, was deliberately shattering his father's chances of a rapprochement with Spain. But this sort of dichotomy in Borgia interests does not seem to exist at this point, and the murder of Alfonso scarcely affected Spain who had already abandoned the Neapolitan Aragonese to their fate. Everything therefore seems to point to a crime of passion rather than a subtle political assassination; in which case the probabilities are that Cesare was not responsible for the first attack. Lucrezia was obviously deeply attached to Alfonso and after his death retired to Nepi for some months to mourn her loss.

It has been suggested that the attempt to cut down Alfonso may have been the work of the Roman barons, and the main families were indeed becoming increasingly apprehensive under steadily mounting pressure. In the previous year it had been the turn of the Gaetani to lose their stranglehold on the

Via Appia and the communications between Rome and Naples. The Gaetani estates stretched from the coast at San Felice Circeo and Nettuno across to Ninfa and Sermoneta. With this position on the frontiers of the Papal States and Naples, their alliance was sought actively by the Neapolitans and at this time they were attached to the Neapolitan cause. It was this infidelity to their papal overlord which was the justification for the attack on them. Giacomo Gaetani was arrested and imprisoned in Castel Sant'Angelo; his brother fled to France. The Gaetani castles surrendered with scarcely a struggle in November 1499, and were promptly sold for 80,000 ducats to Lucrezia. Lucrezia by this time was already Governor of Nepi and seemed to be playing an increasing role in Alexander's dynastic programme. She and her children, of whom the first, Rodrigo, was born in this year, were available for this purpose until her father's death under the terms of her marriage agreement. At the same time one cannot help but wonder if the extent to which she was being used at this time does not reflect some genuine administrative flair which distinguished her from Jofrè. The latter seems to have been justifiably excluded from any significant part in the Borgia dynastic programmes in the Papal States. Alexander was a good judge of men even where his own family was concerned and Jofrè's talents seemed to have been exhausted with the command of a hundred soldiers. Lucrezia also had a son which was something that Jofrè and Sancia had failed to produce, and this opened up clearer dynastic possibilities. But the fact remains that whatever Lucrezia's talents may have been, the real burden of the administration of the new Borgia estates, and the same of course applied to Cesare Borgia's duchy of the Romagna, fell on trained papal civil servants. Borgia expansion implied professional and improved administration regardless of the individual talents of the Borgias themselves.

Following the collapse of the Gaetani, of whom the head of the house, Giacomo, died in Castel Sant' Angelo under suspected but not necessarily suspicious circumstances, it was the turn of the Colonna. Once again it was their Neapolitan affiliations which served to damn them, and in this case even more justifiably as the Colonna in close alliance with Federigo fought against the French and papal armies invading Naples in 1501. The collapse of the Neapolitan resistance left the Colonna defenceless and their excommunication and dispossession followed rapidly. The inevitable isolation of the Colonna may have contributed to Alexander's acceptance of the partition of Naples and certainly the Papacy gained greatly from it. Subiaco and its surrounding towns were given *in commenda* to Cesare. The great Colonna fortresses of Genazzano, Marino, and Rocca di Papa were surrendered to the Pope, and with his usual energy and interest he set out on a close personal inspection of the towns. It must have given him great satisfaction as he passed through the narrow streets of Genazzano to see the birthplace of his predecessor Martin V who had restarted the work of extending papal authority in the Papal States, and yet who had helped to create the Colonna power which had become one of the principal barriers to the extension of that authority. It was at Genazzano, among many other places, that Alexander ordered elaborate improvements to the castle and fortifications. While Alexander was away on this journey, Lucrezia was left in charge of the Vatican. This choice astonished and shocked contemporaries but is itself adequate testimony of Alexander's completely secular view of the papal administration.

While great progress was being made towards Borgia control at the expense of some of the Roman families, others had been temporarily reconciled by a judicious use of marriage alliances. As early as 1498 Girolama Borgia-Lanzol, the sister of Cardinal Juan Borgia-Lanzol, the younger, had been betrothed to Fabio Orsini, while in 1500 her sister Angela was betrothed to Francesco Maria della Rovere, the heir to the Duke of Urbino. This last was a brilliant dynastic manoeuvre which was never completed as the fall of Urbino to Cesare in 1502 put an end to the need for this connection.

At this moment also two young Borgia children began to play a part in Borgia plans. Besides Rodrigo, the son of Lucrezia and Alfonso who had been christened with great ceremony in the Vatican in November 1499, and who had inherited his father's Bisceglie estates, there was the mysterious *Infans Romanus*, Giovanni Borgia, born in 1498. Giovanni was the subject of two successive Bulls in 1501 recognizing him first as a son of Cesare born before his marriage, and secondly as a son of the Pope himself.[12] The second Bull was kept secret and for some years the young boy was generally accepted as the son of Cesare; as such he became in 1502 Duke of Camerino, Cesare's most recent conquest in the Marches, with the implication that this title should be that of the eldest son of the Duke of the Romagna.[13] There had been speculation as to whether Giovanni was in fact an illegitimate son of Lucrezia, born as a result of an indiscretion in 1497–8, and the timing of the Bulls may have been designed to scotch such rumours on the eve of Lucrezia's third marriage.[14] However a few years after Alexander's death when Giovanni was under Lucrezia's care in Ferrara, he was always described as Lucrezia's half brother and the papal paternity recognised in the second Bull has been usually accepted ever since. The fact that the Este family took no great exception to Giovanni's presence in Ferrara seems convincing proof that they at least had no doubts about the impossibility of Lucrezia being his mother. In 1501 these two young Borgia children were elevated simultaneously to dukedoms with estates carved out of the confiscated lands in the Roman Campagna. It was the impending departure of

Lucrezia to Ferrara for her third marriage that created the occasion for a reshuffle of Borgia estates. Lucrezia's son Rodrigo, who by tradition was not able to remain with his mother when she married again, was entrusted to the guardianship of Francesco Borgia and created Duke of Sermoneta with estates including the Gaetani lands purchased by Lucrezia and some of the recently confiscated Colonna estates. The territory of this Borgia duchy stretched from Nettuno and Ardea on the coast across the Via Appia and into the Appenines, including Sermoneta and Genazzano. Meanwhile Lucrezia's position in Nepi was transferred to Giovanni Borgia who became Duke of that city and whose estates also included Palestrina and Frascati to the southeast of Rome. The estates of the Duchy of Nepi north of Rome were steadily expanded in the next two years to include the old papal stronghold of Gallese to the north and Castelnuovo di Porto to the south. With these two large areas north and south of Rome in the hands of Borgia dukes and papal administrators, the work of consolidation and pacification of the Roman Campagna was largely complete.

However in describing this process of the gradual extension of Borgia and papal authority over the Roman Campagna, we have left behind Cesare and his schemes as they were maturing in Rome in the summer of 1500. Plans were going ahead rapidly for a second campaign in the Romagna. This time Cesare was determined to be less dependent on French troops and this meant raising a powerful mercenary army of his own. With the resources of the Papacy behind him this did not prove difficult. The income from the Jubilee and the crusading taxes was to hand and in addition twelve new cardinals were appointed who, with the unofficial application of the principle of first fruits, contributed large sums to the papal coffers. As with all Alexander's cardinal creations there was a strong international and particularly Spanish flavour to this group of new entrants to the Sacred College. Luis Borgia-Lanzol took the place of his brother Juan who had died earlier in the year, and the mysterious Francesco, often reputed to have been the son of Calixtus III, who had been Alexander's treasurer since 1492, also entered the College. Jaime Serra, a relative and close associate, and Giovanni Vera, the one-time tutor and administrative adviser of Cesare, were also amongst the new appointments. Two other Spaniards completed the representation from that kingdom, and to mollify French feeling Aimery d'Albret, the brother of Charlotte, and Trivulzio, the brother of one of Louis XII's leading Italian generals, were also elevated. Other Italians included were Podocatharo, Alexander's secretary and doctor and a man widely respected in intellectual circles, Ferrari, the Datary and hated papal financial administrator, and Cornaro, the Venetian. Finally the forthcoming crusading alliance between Venice, Hungary and the Pope was heralded by the appointment of the Hungarian Bakocs.

These gestures towards Venice, and her preoccupation with the Turks prepared the way for the next stage of Borgia conquest in the Romagna. In the autumn Cesare Borgia was voted a *gentiluomo* of Venice by a majority of 850 to 50 in the Great Council and Venetian protection for the lords of Rimini, Faenza and Pesaro was implicitly withdrawn. Capello's reports of the justifications for the murder of Bisceglie were obviously believed in Venice for there to be so overwhelming a majority in favour of honouring the murderer. Meanwhile Cesare with an army of nearly 10,000 made up largely of Spanish mercenaries was now ready to set out. French support in the form of d'Alègre with 300 lances was again on its way as Louis XII needed reciprocal help from Cesare for his forthcoming invasion of Naples.

On 2 October Cesare marched out of Rome with his army.

Among his corps commanders were Gianpaolo Baglione, the *condottiere* lord of Perugia, Paolo Orsini, and Vitellozzo Vitelli. The last, one of Italy's foremost artillery experts, was in charge of a train of twenty-one cannon. Many of the infantry were Spanish and Ugo Cardone and Michele Corella figured amongst the Spanish captains who had joined Cesare's army. Finally in close attendance beside a group of young Roman nobles were the papal administrators the Bishops of Elna, Santa Sista and Trani, Cesare's secretary Agapito Gheraldini, and his treasurer the Sienese banker Alessandro Spannochi.[15]

The first objective of the campaign was Pesaro. Giovanni Sforza had already been excommunicated on the grounds that he had been privy to negotiations with the Turks to which his cousin Ludovico had resorted in a desperate attempt to save his position in Milan. He had received a token reinforcement in the form of one hundred men from his brother-in-law through his first wife, the Marquis of Mantua. He also had a well-provisioned and fortified castle; but the people of Pesaro were no more prepared to lay down their lives or jeopardise their possessions for the sake of their lord than had been the subjects of Caterina Sforza. Although there seems to be little evidence of tyrannical rule in Pesaro by Sforza, his position in popular esteem had been considerably damaged by the part he was made to play in the divorce proceedings in 1497, and by his dealings with the Turks.[16] As a result the gates of the city were opened to Cesare without a shot being fired, and the conqueror made an impressive entry on 27 October. Pandolfo Collenuccio, who was sent by the Duke of Ferrara to congratulate Cesare, spoke highly of the discipline and order in Cesare's army, and he could see no evidence of any appreciable damage done to the city or its inhabitants.[17] Giovanni Sforza, realising the hopelessness of resistance, fled to Bologna and ultimately to Venice where he attempted to sell his state to the Republic. Venice, already committed to accepting Cesare's presence in the Romagna, politely declined the offer. The castle of Pesaro quickly surrendered as Cesare's troops took up positions round it, and seventy pieces of artillery were taken out and added to the papal artillery train.

Within a few days Cesare was on the move again, this time in the direction of Rimini where the hated Malatesta had already been abandoned by his subjects. How different to the days when the Malatesta had held the papal army at bay for years on end, and allied themselves with the leading princes of Italy! Now Rimini had been surrendered peacefully to Cesare's commissary, the Bishop of Isernia, earlier in October, and Pandolfo had departed to Venice. Cesare therefore wasted little time here and after reaching agreement with the citizens over the return of exiles and the maintenance of civic rights, he returned to Cesena and his army. This army was now about to see action for the first time in the campaign, for Faenza, the next object of attack, was not to be acquired so easily.

Astorre Manfredi, the young Lord of Faenza, was an old client of Venice, having been educated under Venetian protection; he was also a grandson of Giovanni Bentivoglio, and in addition it was felt that Florence could not be completely blind to what was happening just over her frontier. But none of these powers were now in a position to help Manfredi and it was on the loyalty of his subjects that he relied, and with the aid of which he was able to resist Cesare for nearly six months. As Cesare's army moved up to advance headquarters at Forlì and began to encircle Faenza, the defenders of that city refused to allow Astorre Manfredi to capitulate and prepared to defend themselves. The Manfredi were feudal lords in the Val di Lamone as well as vicars of Faenza, and it was on the personal loyalty of Val di Lamone infantry that Astorre depended rather than on the dubious adherence of the citizens of Faenza.[18]

When an initial assault on the walls was repulsed bad weather and approaching winter began to have their effect on the morale of Cesare's army. Baglione withdrew with his troops to Perugia after bitter quarrels with the Spanish captains, and supplies for so large an army encamped round the city were running short. Cesare therefore decided to withdraw the bulk of his forces into winter quarters spread along the Via Emilia from Forlì down to Rimini. Leaving a token force to maintain the blockade on Faenza, he himself withdrew to Cesena where he spent Christmas and the winter months. During this whole period Cesare placed great emphasis on the discipline of his troops and on just payment for the food supplies which his army consumed. As long as his army was quartered in the Romagna everything possible had to be done to protect those cities which were now loyal to him from it. From the accounts of Bernardi who had been so bitter about the depredations of the French in the previous year, it seems that Cesare was now more successful in imposing discipline.[19]

The winter months were spent at Cesena organising the government of the Duchy and getting to know the people of the Romagna and their problems. This was almost the only moment in which Cesare was able to concentrate on these internal problems, and how much progress he made towards their solution will be discussed in a later chapter.[20]

With the approach of spring the army moved out again, now reinforced by the arrival of the French contingent, and the siege of Faenza was resumed. In April after a long bombardment the city surrendered on terms. The terms were generous and included a safe conduct for Astorre Manfredi and his immediate followers. However Astorre remained in Cesare's camp, whether as a prisoner from the outset, in breach of the capitulation conditions, or whether of his own free will as a member of Cesare's staff is a matter of dispute. Papal policy certainly required that the deposed Romagna vicars, particularly popular ones like Astorre, should not be allowed to go free to act as focal points of opposition and resistance, and one must suspect that Astorre was held under duress. Certainly by July he was a prisoner in Castel Sant' Angelo and in June 1502 his strangled corpse was found floating in the Tiber. This was political assassination of a standard pattern from which few contemporary rulers were entirely free. But the youth and popularity of the victim on this occasion attracted widespread sympathy and horror at his fate, and significantly increased the opprobrium in which the Borgia name was held. Caterina Sforza, still a prisoner in Castel Sant'Angelo when Astorre arrived, escaped a similar fate owing to the intercessions of the French. She was eventually prevailed upon to sign away her rights and retire to Florence.

With the fall of Faenza the subjugation of the Romagna was almost complete. The only town which remained outside Cesare's control was Castel Bolognese lying on the Via Emilia between Faenza and Imola, and an obvious bone of contention with Bologna. No sooner had Faenza fallen than Cesare began to exert diplomatic and military pressure on Bologna for the cession of the outlying fortress. He can scarcely have hoped to occupy Bologna itself which was under French protection, but the possession of Castel Bolognese and a favourable alliance with the Bentivoglio were essential steps towards the unification and the security of the Romagna.

A swift demonstration against Bologna in which Cesare's troops advanced to within fourteen miles of the gates of the city was sufficient to bring Giovanni Bentivoglio to terms. An agreement was signed ceding Castel Bolognese to Cesare and binding Bentivoglio to provide troops and assistance to Cesare when called upon. On the other hand the security of Bologna was guaranteed. At the request of Bentivoglio some of Cesare's captains including members of the Orsini family and Vitellozzo Vitelli were named as parties to the treaty. This was probably intended as a device to stop them attacking Bologna independently of Cesare, but it served in fact as a check on Cesare and a link between Bentivoglio and the *condottieri* when in the next year Cesare was planning once again to attack Bologna.

Thus by the end of April Cesare had reached the limits of possible expansion sanctioned by his position as Captain General of the Church and by Alexander's instructions. The Pope, fearful lest he might offend Louis XII by any further aggression, ordered him to return to Rome by the routes through the Romagna and Umbria. But Cesare, flushed with success, with a powerful army at his disposal, and surrounded by a group of restless and aggressive captains, resolved to try and draw further benefit from the situation. Vitellozzo Vitelli, whose brother had been executed by the Florentines for treachery, and the Orsini who were partisans of the Medici urged him to attack Florence. Florentine interests in the Romagna and a suspicion that they had been sending help to Faenza also attracted Cesare towards some sort of demonstration against Florence. It is unlikely that Cesare was considering any serious attack on the Tuscan city at this juncture, as French protection for Florence was likely to be both swift and effective. But there were more rewarding possibilities of intervention in Pisa, Siena or Piombino, and the march southwards could well be turned to effect to wring concessions out of the Florentines. He therefore moved swiftly down into the Arno valley, and at Campi, some ten miles from the gates of Florence, he met the Florentine commissioners sent out to treat with him. The Florentines, terrified by the possibility of an attack on the city before French help could arrive and with their government in total confusion, were only too happy to buy off Cesare with a treaty of alliance and the offer of a *condotta* of 36,000 ducats annually. Cesare tried to insist on a down payment, but time was against him and he was constrained to move on with nothing more than promises gained; promises which were never fulfilled.

The final stage of the campaign was however more successful. Although the Pisans had offered their city to Cesare early in 1500, French concern with the Pisan problem was too immediate to make a move in that direction feasible. Therefore moving quickly through southern Tuscany, Cesare's army arrived before Piombino where Jacopo d'Appiano ruled a small state dependent on the good will of Siena and Genoa. Both these states were now indifferent to his fate, as was France, and indeed Siena gave active support in trying to bring about the quick surrender of D'Appiano. Eight Genoese galleys also assisted in the occupation of the island of Elba where the rich iron mines were an added attraction. Piombino with its good harbour and its control of the Via Aurelia was a useful acquisition for the Papacy, and although Cesare himself was not there for the conclusion of the campaign, Vitellozzo accepted the surrender of the city in July 1501 after a two month siege.

Cesare, now officially described as Duke of the Romagna, had returned to Rome early with a part of his army including a force of Romagnol infantry arrayed in his livery of scarlet and yellow, because the French campaign in Naples was about to begin and he was committed to giving his assistance. The French army was already assembling outside the walls of the city to the north of the Ponte Milvio, and the French commanders d'Aubigny and Yves d'Alègre entered Rome a few days after Cesare.

The campaign in Naples was brief. Capua, defended by the Colonna, alone barred the route to the French army and this was assaulted and brutally sacked, with Cesare and his Romagnol infantry in the vanguard of the French attack. Cesare has attracted extraordinary notoriety for his part in this event, and the story of the forty Capuan beauties led away for his later enjoyment has helped to place the principal blame for the carnage on his shoulders. However it must be remembered that Cesare had only 400 men under his direct command and, although the French commanders tended to push their Italian subordinates forward in the hope of lessening the hostility of the defenders to a basically French invading army, it was d'Aubigny who commanded the operation and German and Gascon troops who did most of the damage.[21]

The assault on Capua was the only display of force required of the French before Federigo surrendered and went into permanent exile in France. By mid-September Cesare was back in Rome and negotiations were going forward for Lucrezia's third marriage. Rumours about the possibility of a match with Alfonso d'Este, the heir to the Duchy of Ferrara, had been circulating in Rome throughout the year, but it was not until mid-summer that serious negotiations started. The advantages of such a marriage for the Borgias are obvious; the Duke of Ferrara was the most secure and respected of all the papal vicars and the house of Este had established themselves as leading Italian princes. The marriage of Lucrezia to the heir to the Duchy was a dynastic coup beyond the dreams of any of Alexander's predecessors. At the same time Ferrara, traditionally anti-Venetian, was a valuable ally and protection against Venetian hostility in the Romagna. It was not only Lucrezia but also Cesare who was likely to profit from this alignment. On the other hand Ercole d'Este, the Duke of Ferrara, although wary of the possible damage to his prestige and his son's reputation that might result from the link with the Borgias, and determined to drive the hardest bargain possible, was genuinely concerned about the growing strength of Cesare to his south and was anxious to secure his state from Borgia aggression. Furthermore Louis XII was anxious to preserve good relations with the Pope at least until Neapolitan affairs were satisfactorily arranged, and added his pressure to that of the Borgias for a quick conclusion of the marriage negotiations.

Ercole d'Este held out for 100,000 ducats as Lucrezia's dowry and for the permanent remission of the annual census which he owed for his vicariate. Both these demands were serious financial blows to the Camera Apostolica and, despite the political and diplomatic advantages which the Ferrarese alliance brought, it would seem that at this moment Alexander was more concerned with the advancement of his family than with the economic stability of the Church. Furthermore the festivities which attended the proxy wedding ceremony on 30 December were spectacular and costly, as Alexander turned the occasion into a triumphant display of Borgia power. All Rome was in carnival as public pageants succeeded the more private celebrations in the Vatican. Finally on 6 January 1503 Lucrezia set out on her journey to her third husband accompanied by Cardinal Francesco Borgia and by a large retinue of Roman nobles. Her progress through the Papal States added a further dimension to the Borgia achievement. As the gorgeously arrayed following of over 700 courtiers and servants moved northwards, all the cities on the route vied with each other to do honour to the daughter of the Pope. At Spoleto, where she was already well known as governor, and throughout her brother's Romagna cities the festivities in honour of Lucrezia were particularly splendid. The Duke of Urbino complained that the passage of the company through his duchy cost him a month's revenue. It was nearly a month before Lucrezia finally arrived in Ferrara at the end of her exhausting but spectacular journey.

After her departure Alexander and Cesare also spent the next few weeks exhibiting the extent of Borgia power by carrying out tours of inspection of the various fortresses which had fallen into their hands. First the lands of the young Duke of Sermoneta were inspected, and then in February and March father and son moved northwards to Civitavecchia, Corneto, Piombino, and finally Elba. On the return voyage from Elba the Pope's galley ran into a serious storm and while his suite and the crew were in deadly fear for their safety, Alexander showed that strange philosophical calm in the face of physical danger which was characteristic of him. It was the second time that his life had been in danger at sea, and he now sat quietly praying in the bows and long before the danger had passed called for food to be brought to him.[22] The galley was unable to put into Piombino and finally reached safety in Civitavecchia. Alexander at the age of seventy still seemed to have plenty of life left in him, and Cesare was already planning the campaigns for the coming summer which would add further strength to the family position.

CHAPTER NINE

THE BORGIA ZENITH, 1502–3

Pandolfo Collenuccio once said of Cesare Borgia that he was more interested in winning states than in administering them, and certainly as the spring of 1502 advanced Cesare was itching to be on the move.[1] With Ferrara's friendship now secured and with France still anxious for papal support in Naples, the moment was propitious for further military action against the remaining vicars. The Romagna was now all Cesare's, but to the south there remained Camerino where Giulio Cesare Varano had established for his family an unofficial vicariate, and Senigallia where Francesco Maria della Rovere and his mother represented one of the last strongholds of Sistine nepotism. There was also the Duchy of Urbino, but few thought that Cesare would dare to attack so well established a prince as Guidobaldo da Montefeltro, papal vicar though he was.

On 5 June the excommunication of Varano was republished; he was accused of the murder of his brother years before and of harbouring rebels of the Church. These were both legitimate charges although perhaps action about the first was rather overdue. Camerino was obviously the declared objective of the expedition which was about to set out; but the day after the excommunication was published news reached Rome of a revolt in Arezzo against the Florentines, and of the occupation of Arezzo by Vitellozzo Vitelli, one of Cesare's captains. There seems little doubt that this was a planned move by the Borgias against Florence, although they swiftly denied any complicity. Vitelli, although he had his reasons for hating Florence because of the execution of his brother, was unlikely to have acted on his own initiative in this way. The Duke of Urbino was in fact ordered by the Pope to send assistance to Vitelli, and Vitelli himself felt disillusioned and angry when subsequently ordered to withdraw by Cesare. However as Cesare's army moved out of Rome a few days later both Cesare and Alexander were protesting that Vitelli had acted without instructions. But a crisis was obviously brewing up in the much disputed frontier area between Florence and the Papal States, and Cesare with a powerful army of 6000 infantry and over 2000 cavalry was moving to the scene. This army was largely made up of Spanish and Italian mercenaries; the commanders were by now familiar figures: Paolo Orsini and his cousin the Duke of Gravina; Oliverotto Euffreducci, Lord of Fermo; Gianpaolo Baglione and Vitelli, who were already on the spot, and the Spaniards Ugo de Moncada and Michele Corella.

For a week after the army left Rome Cesare's intentions were carefully concealed. Permission was asked for his artillery to pass through the Duchy of Urbino along an easier road than the direct one to Camerino; troops were massing in the Romagna under Ramiro de Lorqua. Guidobaldo da Montefeltro, irritated that he had been called upon to assist Vitelli against Florence, with whom he was on friendly terms, was pondering whether he dared to disobey the papal commands.[2] Although he had long distrusted the Borgias and felt a certain insecurity whenever Cesare's armies moved his way, he did not really believe that the blow was likely to fall on him. It was thus that Cesare, by pushing 2000 men of his main army up the Via Flaminia by a forced march, with his artillery already entering the Duchy peacefully, and by calling in the Romagnol troops from the east, achieved complete tactical surprise. Guidobaldo had scarcely time to escape, as indeed he was not intended to, and his fortresses and the city of Urbino itself surrendered without firing a shot.

This was Cesare's greatest coup to date and it certainly made both Italian and foreign politicians sit up and take notice. The steady erosion of the power of the Romagna vicars had not created much stir; the predominance of French troops in the campaigns had seemed sufficient explanation for the Pope's successes against his own troublesome subjects. But Guidobaldo da Montefeltro, although legally in a similar position to the other vicars, was a *condottiere* of international if undeserved repute and his family had links with all the princes of Italy. His complete defeat by an army generalled by Italians put Cesare's operations in an entirely different light. There was widespread shock and horror at the duplicity and treachery of the attack and yet at the same time a certain sneaking admiration for the skill shown by Cesare. The first sentiment was perhaps not entirely justified as Guidobaldo had disobeyed papal instructions and was also preparing to help Camerino; the second was clearly expressed by Machiavelli who was hurriedly sent by Florence with the Bishop of Volterra to discover what Cesare's next moves would be. Machiavelli's report on arrival in Urbino cannot have given much satisfaction in Florence: 'This Lord is truly splendid and magnificent, and in war there is no enterprise so great that it does not appear small to him; in the pursuit of glory and lands he never rests nor recognises fatigue or danger. He arrives in one place before it is known that he has left another; he is popular with his soldiers and he has collected the best men in Italy; these things make him victorious and formidable particularly when added to perpetual good fortune.'[3] This original judgment was to colour all Machiavelli's thinking about Cesare and he was never able to rid himself of the initial impression which the new Prince made on him.

For the moment Florence was desperately anxious to discover what Cesare was going to do about Vitelli in Arezzo. But with the French reacting energetically to the threat to their satellite and moving troops into Tuscany, Cesare had no choice but to call off this gamble. Vitelli was ordered to withdraw and attention was turned to Camerino which at first resisted gallantly. But here, as in so many other cities attacked by Cesare, internal factions played their part; the Varani were not universally popular and the gates were opened by a section of the population anxious to avoid a sack by the Spanish troops. The arrival of the news of the fall of Camerino caused great enthusiasm in Rome where Alexander, slightly reluctant to show too much pleasure over the blow at Urbino, now gave full rein to his satisfaction at his son's achievements. Although the final decision to attack Urbino seems to have been taken at the last minute by Cesare, there is no doubt that the possibility had been discussed beforehand in the Vatican. It was just a question of waiting to see if Guidobaldo would offer a reasonable pretext for the attack on him.

With the twin successes at Urbino and Camerino Cesare's position seemed to be immeasurably strengthened. But at the same time the list of Borgia enemies had also been significantly lengthened. Guidobaldo da Montefeltro and Florence now added their voices to the chorus of complaint against the Borgia activities, and when Louis XII suddenly arrived in Milan a number of the dispossessed vicars hurried to his court. Louis was already angry about the attack on Arezzo and there seemed to be a serious danger of a breach between the French and the Borgias. At the same time Cesare was suspicious of his Italian commanders who were not unmoved by the lesson of what had happened to Urbino and sensed that their own states might well become the next targets of Borgia attack. It was in this situation at the beginning of August that Cesare decided to visit Louis and seek to re-establish the personal friendship that had grown up between them in 1499. Travelling fast and in disguise Cesare appeared in Milan before any of his enemies had realised what he was planning, and the bold move achieved everything that he wanted. Alexander was very alarmed when he heard of Cesare's journey and feared that his son was placing himself in the power of the French King. But Louis was flattered by the personal visit and by Cesare's respectful apologies for the activities of Vitelli. He was also already aware that a clash with Spain in Naples was inevitable and he was anxious to have Cesare's powerful army on his side. So he received Cesare with great honour and even promised him military assistance against Bologna, a city which had formerly enjoyed French protection. In addition he gave his approval to a proposal for the marriage of Cesare's infant daughter Louise to Federigo Gonzaga, heir to the Duke of Mantua. This proposal was one more step in the process of building up a ring of small allied states to protect the Romagna. After nearly a month at the French court Cesare returned as quickly as he had come, only stopping to visit Lucrezia in Ferrara and cheer her up at a moment when she was dangerously ill.

Early in September Alexander was in Camerino to install the young Giovanni as Duke of the newly regained city, and it is extremely likely that he and Cesare met to discuss the next moves. With the promised French aid Bologna now seemed the obvious target, but the unrest of the Orsini and the other *condottieri* was a growing problem. The proposal to attack Bologna proved to be the turning point in the new situation. Giovanni Bentivoglio, now himself threatened, became one of the leading spirits in the conspiracy which was building up against Cesare. At the same time the *condottieri* who had given their guarantees not to attack Bologna in the previous year now felt that they had solid grounds for a revolt. At a series of meetings in September and early October, first at Todi and then at Magione, a sort of alliance against the Borgias began to take shape. The participants in the so called Diet of Magione were an ill-assorted group united only in their fear of the Borgias but each seeking to protect his own interests. Of the dispossessed vicars only Guidobaldo da Montefeltro was represented, but Baglione from Perugia, Oliverotto da Fermo, Vitelli from Città di Castello, and Bentivoglio from Bologna all felt that their states were threatened. They were joined by Pandolfo Petrucci, lord of Siena, who was thought to have been the brains behind the conspiracy. Then of course there were the Orsini; the crafty, diplomatic cardinal who had already approached Louis XII for assistance and felt that there was a chance of French support; the unstable and credulous Paolo Orsini, nicknamed even by his own men 'Madonna Paolo'; and young Francesco, Duke of Gravina, a past aspirant for the hand of Lucrezia and a brave but unlucky soldier.

These were by now desperate men but they acted in a strangely uncoordinated and indecisive way. A large part of Cesare's army was under their command and had they shown anything like the urgency and tactical skill which Cesare himself had displayed three months earlier they must have overwhelmed him. But their delays and their indecisiveness disillusioned their potential supporters. Florence was scarcely less afraid of Vitelli and the Orsini, supporters of the Medici, than she was of Cesare himself, and she was certainly not prepared to commit herself until the conspirators had achieved some considerable success. Louis XII, although not averse to seeing the Papal States in confusion and the Pope embarrassed, was not going to lift a finger to help and in fact was already committed to send troops to Cesare. Venice was still too preoccupied with the Turkish war to support a movement for which she had undoubted sympathy.

So the conspirators were dependent on their own resources,

resources which were already being equalled by Cesare as, forewarned, he strove to build up his depleted army. The *condottieri* revealed their disunity as, while Baglione and Vitelli moved forward to assist a revolt in Urbino and succeeded in defeating a force of Spaniards at Calmazzo, the Orsini were already negotiating with Alexander in Rome. Cesare, once again observed by Machiavelli who had arrived in Imola as Florentine envoy, quickly drew his reduced army back from Urbino and Camerino and concentrated on the defence of the Romagna. New *condottieri* were employed, emissaries were dispatched to Lombardy to hire Gascon and Swiss mercenaries, the local Romagnol militia was called out. Within days of his arrival at Imola on 7 October Machiavelli was convinced that Cesare would survive the storm: 'As regards the situation here, the state of this lord, since I arrived here, has been held together by good fortune; of which the chief cause has been the firm conviction held here that the King of France will help him with men, and the Pope with money; and another thing which has been helpful to him is the delay of his enemies in closing in on him. Now I judge that it is too late to do him much harm because he has provided all the important cities with garrisons, and has provisioned all the fortresses.'[4]

Cesare pressed for a Florentine alliance but Machiavelli's reports had already done all that was needed by convincing the Florentines that it would be madness to support the *condottieri*. French troops were approaching, and the conspirators began one by one to sue for terms. Each hoped to win Cesare's gratitude and gain personal security by being the first to come to an agreement with him. Before the end of October Paolo Orsini, Bentivoglio and Petrucci had all made approaches to Cesare, while Cardinal Orsini was negotiating in Rome. Justifiably could Cesare refer to the conspirators as the '*dieta di falliti*', and, apart from strengthening his army, wait in active until like over-ripe plums his enemies dropped into his hands.

The final terms of the agreement which Paolo Orsini carried to his colleagues, and which all accepted except Baglione, who realised that they were playing straight into Cesare's hands, were generous but at the same time scarcely reassuring. Camerino and Urbino were to be restored to the Borgias; the *condottieri* were to be forgiven and have their *condotte* restored to them, but only one was to serve at a time; each of the *condottieri* was to hand over one of his sons to Cesare as a hostage. A separate agreement was signed with Bentivoglio confirming his position in Bologna and binding him to Cesare as a *condottiere*; thus the most powerful of the conspirators was isolated from the rest. It seems scarcely credible that the *condottieri* could believe that all was forgiven. Cesare was now as strong without them as he had ever been; his vengeful character was well known and both Machiavelli in Imola and Giustinian in Rome sensed that the solution could scarcely be a lasting one. 'I fail to understand how such injury can be expected to find forgiveness,' remarked the Florentine secretary,[5] and Giustinian in his dispatch of 1 January 1503 expressed himself even more clearly: 'The nature of the Duke is not to pardon those who have injured him nor leave the vendetta to others; he has threatened those who have offended him and in particular Oliverotto whom the Duke has sworn to hang with his own hands, if he can get him into his clutches.'[6] But for six weeks harmony seemed to be restored as Cesare reoccupied Urbino and Camerino, and laid his plans for capturing Senigallia, plans which included a final reckoning with his now redundant allies.

While Cesare was engaged in this tense struggle with his own generals, Alexander, although watching with deep concern, sending increasing sums of money to pay for the new army and carrying on his end of the negotiations with Cardinal

Orsini, was engaged on a wider diplomatic front. The issue of the moment in Italy was the confrontation between France and Spain in Naples; the old rivalries between the Italian states, the festering problem of Pisa, had disappeared into the background as diplomatic issues. Italy was now about to become the battleground for the two major military powers in Europe. No one regretted this more than Alexander. Although he could gain certain advantages from allying the Papacy with one power or the other, the authority of the Pope in Italy and the security of the Papal States were severely threatened by the ultramontane invasions.

In 1502 Alexander was still largely committed to the French cause and, particularly at the moment of the conspiracy of the *condottieri*, still needed French help. But he was seriously concerned about having the French in both Milan and Naples and the inevitable constant military traffic across the Papal States which this involved. He was determined both by natural inclination and for reasons of policy to avoid a breach with Spain. In the autumn of 1502 both sides were seeking his support in the coming conflict and in purely diplomatic terms the papal position seemed to be very strong. Alexander was determined not to surrender that position by committing himself until the last possible moment. He knew that 1503 would be a decisive year when the Neapolitan issue would be finally resolved, and he was determined to pick the right side. As he said to Giustinian, 'We shall temporise until the spring and then see who is the stronger of these two'.[7]

But to be on the winning side was not the only aim of Alexander's policy. He still hoped that some sort of Italian league could be created which would contain or even evict the foreign powers. Over and over again during the winter he pleaded with Giustinian for an alliance with Venice: 'See, ambassador, how each of these two Kings, of France and Spain, is striving to drive the other out of Naples. . . . It would be an evil affair for us and for you if the Spaniards possessed this Kingdom, but it would be still worse if it fell totally into the hands of France, because they would have us bottled up here and would have us acting like their chaplains. Nor would it be any better for you. For the love of God let us have an end to our differences. Let us understand each other a little and busy ourselves with the welfare of Italy.'[8] Alexander wanted the Venetian alliance not just to prevent Venetian interference in the Romagna; the Turks were already doing that quite satisfactorily. Nor yet did he want it just to protect Cesare after his death; he was realist enough to know that no treaties were then likely to guarantee the course of events. He wanted it as a possible solution to the political difficulties of the Papacy and of Italy. For, as he said, 'Although Spaniards by birth, and temporarily allied with France, we are Italians and it is in Italy that our fortune lies'.[9] This was not just idle rhetoric. Giustinian, who had an almost pathological distrust of the Pope, admitted that these sentiments seemed to be genuine and to come from the heart. But Venice, harassed by the Turks and having little fear of Spain in Naples, could not see the Pope's point of view and consistently refused his advances. Roberto Cessi, the Venetian historian, has remarked that 'in refusing to direct Italian policy according to the clear vision of Alexander VI, Venice prepared her own ruin', thus linking the diplomacy of 1502–3 with the disaster of Agnadello.[10] This is perhaps looking too far ahead because there is no saying that an alliance with Alexander would have saved Venice from the wrath of Julius. But it is hard to escape from the conclusion that Alexander's policies were concerned with wider issues than just self interest and Borgia dynasticism.

One thing that seems clear is that Alexander's pursuit of a Venetian alliance did not fluctuate with Cesare's fortunes. For while the Pope was pressing Giustinian most urgently, Cesare was riding on the crest of a wave. All through December 1502 his strength grew and his enemies became increasingly apprehensive. The attack on Senigallia remained the only immediate project and an army of 12,000 was scarcely needed for that. As Cesare moved down to Cesena and Machiavelli followed him, desperately trying to pick up some crumb of information as to his intentions, never were the contrasts in the character of this strange man more clear. Open and approachable towards his Romagnol subjects and on social occasions, he remained frequently withdrawn and impenetrable on matters of policy. Ambassadors waited for months to see him, while he moved freely amongst the people of the Romagna, joining in their wrestling matches and listening to their complaints. His office was a hive of activity at night as messengers hurried to and fro, and Cesare worked and talked through the small hours. But all through the morning until long after noon the Duke slept and everyone waited with bated breath. His spasms of fierce energy were followed by long spells of indolence, and frustration for all around him. Even Alexander became impatient as the days passed and the expenses mounted. He was certainly aware that a blow against the *condottieri* was imminent and he played his part by lulling the suspicions of Cardinal Orsini in Rome. But the details and the long term plans were obscured even from him.

On 20 December the contingent of French cavalry which had arrived only a few weeks before were sent back northwards. They were expensive and too independent of his control for Cesare's immediate purposes; perhaps also their departure was intended to lull the *condottieri* into a false sense of security. Cesare then announced his plans for the assault on Senigallia and summoned his captains to meet him there. Here was action at last and the *condottieri* moved to obey the orders. Baglione who had refused to be a party to the reconciliation with Cesare remained in Perugia, and Vitellozzo moved his troops down towards the sea with the greatest reluctance. Perhaps as the best soldier amongst them he realised better than his colleagues that there was something odd about assembling so large a force for so small a target. By 30 December the contingents of the *condottieri* lay around the little Adriatic port. The town itself had surrendered without a blow to Oliverotto but Andrea Doria in the citadel refused to surrender except to Cesare in person. Cesare was approaching from the north with his army moving in widely dispersed contingents to conceal its real strength.

In mid-afternoon on 31 December Cesare met his commanders outside the walls of Senigallia. After a few moments friendly conversation they moved together towards the gates of the city accompanied by large bodies of Cesare's personal troops. Each of the *condottieri* had a small following with him but they were now effectively cut off from their main contingents which were camped some distance away. As the column entered the city the gates were quietly closed behind it. Seven of Cesare's closest assistants had received their instructions the night before and now everything went smoothly. The doomed *condottieri* followed Cesare to a palace prepared for his occupation and there tried to take their leave of him. Cesare effusively invited them in as there were matters to discuss about the surrender of the fortress on the next day. Once inside they were quietly arrested by Cesare's guards. Their immediate followers were quickly dispatched. Their leaderless contingents laid down their arms in the face of Cesare's overwhelming strength. By the morning Vitelli and Oliverotto had been strangled; the fate of the Orsini remained in the balance. Couriers sped to Rome to carry the news to Alexander and he immediately arrested Cardinal Orsini and the other heads of the family who were in the city.

Cesare immediately justified himself to Machiavelli and to the world on the grounds that the *condottieri* were once more plotting against him and he was merely acting first. But for Italians the coup at Senigallia needed no justification; for them it was a logical and brilliantly executed revenge, a classic and perfect vendetta. It was also an incredibly lucky stroke; the *condottieri* had played straight into his hands and in reality the amount of long range planning involved was minimal. But flushed with his success Cesare once again showed that resolution which marked him out from most of his contemporaries.[11]

Within twenty-four hours of entering Senigallia his army was on the move marching inland to exploit the successes gained. Vitelli's state of Città di Castello was quickly occupied. Gianpaolo Baglione who had refused the reconciliation was not strong enough to resist the revenge. His defences in Perugia crumbled and he was forced to flee. Perugia was brought once more under the direct government of the Church and Cesare turned on Siena where Pandolfo Petrucci, the last of the conspirators at Magione, prepared to defend himself. Guidobaldo da Montefeltro had also taken refuge in Sienese territory, in the Orsini fortress of Pitigliano, and Alexander was particularly anxious to get his hands on him. As the army crossed into Tuscany the Duke of Gravina and Paolo Orsini were quietly executed; but no more of Cesare's enemies were to fall into his hands. The Sienese, terrified for their safety, expelled Petrucci. Cesare, not yet confident enough to challenge French protection of the Tuscan cities, at last hesitated. Alexander was clamouring for his return to Rome and reluctantly he turned his army southwards.

In Rome the rounding up of the Orsini had gone almost according to plan. The cardinal had been imprisoned in Castel Sant'Angelo where he quickly succumbed to the rigours of his new way of life. Giulio Orsini had however escaped and now from his fortress at Ceri, ten miles west of Rome, was carrying out a vigorous series of counterattacks. He attacked and wrecked the Tolfa alum mines, and succeeded in stirring up the remnants of the baronial families to a last combined offensive against the Borgias. Alexander had only Jofrè to help him, and Jofrè, although he was sent out to occupy the Savelli fortress of Palombara, was something of a broken reed. As a result Rome was in confusion; the guards on the walls and in the Vatican had been strengthened, but Alexander felt his insecurity deeply. For him the final destruction of the Orsini and their allies was of more importance than Cesare's ambitions in Tuscany or the final elimination of the Magione conspirators. Instructions were dispatched to Cesare to return immediately, and it was said that the Pope had even threatened to excommunicate his son if he did not obey him.

This moment, when the interests of Alexander and Cesare seemed to have diverged, gives us interesting evidence as to the real relationship between them. It has often been suggested that Cesare gained a complete moral ascendancy over his father and became the controller of Borgia policy; that this was the explanation for the Borgia alliance with France against the Spanish inclinations of Alexander; that Alexander's occasional angry outbursts against his son were the result of fretful impotence in the face of a superior will. But the evidence of close cooperation between the two, the control which Alexander always exercised over the wider aspects of Borgia diplomacy, the permanent links with Spain and the clear indications that by 1503 the Borgia were moving back towards a Spanish alliance, and above all the events of this spring when Cesare reluctantly turned to obey his father, all seem to belie this interpretation. At this moment Cesare was straining towards new horizons of power, towards the ultimate aim of an independent state in central Italy. But Alexander, more realistic, more concerned with security at the centre, held him in check and forced him to return to finish off the destruction of the barons. This done they could turn together back to the wider ambitions and with Alexander's diplomacy united to Cesare's force prepare for the culminating blow.

Even once his army had re-entered the Papal States, Cesare moved with considerable reluctance. The remaining heads of the Orsini family had powerful friends. Both the Count of Pitigliano and Bartolomeo d'Alviano, the defender of Bracciano in the first Orsini War, were employed by Venice as *condottieri*. But, although members of the family, these two formidable soldiers were rarely seen in Rome and their estates were too far away to be a strategic threat. Alexander therefore did not feel obliged to attempt a final reckoning with them.

Giangiordano Orsini however, who had inherited Bracciano from his father Virginio, was an obvious target. But he was a protégé of Louis XII and was a member of the French Order of St. Michel, a chivalric order to which Cesare also belonged and which bound its members not to fight each other. For this reason, and perhaps also because the towering walls of Bracciano had proved too great an obstacle in 1497, Cesare refused to attack Giangiordano and indeed came to an agreement with him. Bracciano was left unchallenged and the army passed on to deal with the impetuous Giulio whose operations had caused so much dismay.

But Cesare could not concentrate on the siege of Ceri with his usual determination. His thoughts were in Tuscany and the Romagna, where indeed Petrucci had been welcomed back to Siena as soon as Cesare's army had withdrawn, and he left the siege to his subordinates while he fretted moodily in Rome. Eventually in April after intense artillery bombardment Giulio Orsini surrendered. He was allowed to retire to France and his fortress was rendered indefensible by having its cisterns destroyed and by steps cut up the unscalable cliffs on which it was perched. Alexander himself supervised this work. The problem of Giangiordano was eventually solved by negotiation. Louis XII, desperately anxious for Cesare's assistance in the coming Neapolitan campaign, persuaded Giangiordano to surrender Bracciano into his hands as arbitrator and also to retire to France. Alexander could claim that the Campagna was at last freed from the stranglehold of the barons although perhaps the final outcome was not as decisive as he would have wished.

But events were moving towards a swift climax. The Spaniards after a prolonged stalemate in Apulia seemed to be on the verge of a spectacular triumph in Naples. Gonsalvo de Cordoba's victory at Cerignola had forced the French into a general withdrawal, and Louis XII was now gathering his forces for a counter blow. He hoped that he could still rely on the support of the papal army, but Alexander was becoming increasingly disillusioned with his French alignment. With the Romagna and Umbria now subdued, every possible step forward by Cesare was barred by French influence. Bologna, Florence, Siena, the Orsini had all in their turn appealed to Louis XII for protection against the Borgias, and all had received it. The realisation of French military weakness in Naples, and the growth of Cesare's independent strength made the French alliance both redundant and positively dangerous. For the next stage of Borgia expansion which was to be inevitably northwards, Spain, hitherto uncommitted in the north and more powerful in the south, was likely to be the more useful partner.

A strong ally was more needed than ever as the hostility of Venice to the Borgias was becoming increasingly apparent in the spring of 1503. A truce had at last been signed with the Turks, and Venice, by strengthening her forces in Ravenna and encouraging her *condottieri* Pitigliano and d'Alviano in their resistance to Cesare, was beginning to show her true colours. Giustinian in Rome seemed to be becoming the focal point of anti-Borgia diplomacy, and Alexander's continued pleas for an alliance with Venice were now at last decisively rejected.

But despite this growing opposition the preparations for some new Borgia enterprise were apparent to all. The Orsini campaign concluded, Cesare's army was quartered in Umbria and southern Tuscany. Negotiations were being conducted with the Imperial ambassador for the investiture of various Tuscan cities for Cesare, and in early August Pisan ambassadors left Rome carrying Cesare's acceptance of the lordship of their city.[12] Money from the sale of offices and the creation of nine new cardinals was pouring in. The cardinal appointments of 1503 included five more Spaniards, bringing the total of Spanish cardinals created by Alexander to sixteen. Everything pointed to a campaign in Tuscany either as a part of a general Spanish offensive against French influence in Italy, or conceivably with France blackmailed into acceptance by the promise of continued Borgia support in Naples. The aim seemed clearly to be to create a permanent hereditary state for Cesare which would free him from the ambiguous position of being a papal vicar to a potentially hostile Pope. Giustinian also suspected plans to confer Ascoli on Jofrè and Fermo on one of the younger Borgias to round out the dynastic supremacy of the family in Central Italy.[13]

This was the situation in the summer of 1503 which can with some justification be described as the zenith of Borgia power.

CHAPTER TEN

BORGIA GOVERNMENT

To some extent our estimate of the Borgias as either an entirely evil and self-seeking family whose intervention in history was wholly unfortunate and best forgotten, or as a phenomenon in keeping with the historical trends of the moment, a family whose contribution to the development of the Papacy was both real and significant, hinges on the question of Cesare Borgia's government of the Romagna. Here there is a chance to see what the extension of papal authority over the Papal States might have meant. The overthrow of the vicars and the reduction of the whole of the Romagna to a single state ruled by a papal nominee was already a considerable achievement. Alexander and Cesare had gone much further towards asserting papal authority than any of their predecessors, and, as Julius II was the first to admit, the ground for his better known work of subduing the Papal States was to a large extent prepared by the Borgias. They had achieved so much partly because of the favourable political situation, in which the interference of the great powers in Italy placed valuable allies at the disposal of the Pope, and left the vicars isolated, as their former supporters amongst the Italian states struggled for their own survival. Furthermore the Romagna was unusually disaffected largely owing to a difficult economic situation. But at the same time no explanation of the Borgia success in the Romagna would be complete without recognition of the determination, unscrupulousness and intelligence with which the campaigns were carried out. The entire financial resources of the Papacy were deployed, financial resources which were at last beginning to improve; armies, on a scale hitherto undreamed of by the Popes, were raised; and the whole expertise of papal diplomacy was thrown into the campaign to isolate the vicars and protect the newly won states. All this is undeniable, but did it in fact represent any real improvement in the government of the area and in the living conditions of its inhabitants? It certainly strengthened the temporal position of the Pope as long as the unified vicariate remained in the hands of a vicar loyal to papal interests, but can one perceive any wider justification for Borgia policy, and Renaissance papal policy as a whole, in Cesare's handling of the Romagna?[1]

Contemporary or almost contemporary observers and later historians have differed widely in their assessment of the government of Cesare Borgia. Machiavelli in the *Prince* claimed that the popularity and effectiveness of Cesare's rule was borne out by the way in which the Romagna cities remained faithful to him after his father's death.[2] Guicciardini in the *Storie Fiorentine* remarked, 'Only the states of the Romagna stood firm. . . . because he had placed in the government of those peoples men who had governed with so much justice and integrity that he was greatly loved by them.'[3] This is the well known '*buon governo*', good government, of Cesare Borgia which has, in the minds of many of his biographers, rescued him from the general ignominy of his family.[4] But on the other hand it has been argued that the positive achievements of Borgia rule in the Romagna were almost non-existent and that the population was terrified and discontented under ruthless and arbitrary rule. Matarazzo stated that 'the people remained quiet and silent from fear rather than contentment', and the Venetian Priuli remarked that 'his subjects were full of discontent for the tyranny and violence used against them by the Duke Valentino'.[5]

There are in fact two points at issue; the actual government, and the effects of that government on the popular mind, the popularity or not of Cesare's government. Strict and in a certain sense good government is not necessarily popular, certainly not with all sections of the community. But most of the reports which we have about the government of the Romagna are concerned with the attitude of the people towards that government and it is hard to find details of the government itself.

The great problem with the administration of the Romagna both in practice and in historical interpretation was that there were two completely opposed conceptions of what constituted good government. To the bulk of the population of the Romagna good government consisted of the guarantee of local and group privileges, fair administration of a traditional justice, relief from taxes, the establishment of order so that the old pattern of Romagnol society could live on undisturbed. Such a conception of *buon governo* was essentially conservative, and Cesare fully recognised its importance. All the negotiations, which his representatives conducted with the individual towns of the Romagna, concentrated on the protection of local privileges and autonomies and the preservation of traditional rights. Here was the key to general popularity and a quick restoration of a certain stability and order. But in such a programme there was no room for innovations, for new and particularly for centralised organs of administration, for the evidence, which historians have sought, of an entirely different conception of *buon governo*. This conception, which was that implied by Machiavelli, involved the creation of a new type of government for the Romagna, the breakdown of local jurisdictions and the establishment of a unified state. Such a policy was obviously inherent in the whole temporal conception of the Renaissance Papacy; it was lauded by Machiavelli and to some extent executed by Cesare, but it was not likely to be popular with a majority of the local population.

Cesare's government of the Romagna was essentially a shifting compromise between these two ideas. For each city, as it surrendered to him, the terms were generous and concentrated on the rapid restoration of order and traditional government.[6] As far as possible local officials were confirmed in their positions and local privileges guaranteed. Small towns were offered protection against and independence from their larger neighbours. The country population was protected against exploitation from the towns. Offences against the old regimes were pardoned, taxes reduced, and building subsidies offered. All this Cesare could afford to do as he had the resources of the Papacy behind him. Inevitably there was military occupation at first, but there were attempts to protect the civilian population, to preserve discipline in the army, and to ensure that the army's supplies were bought at fair prices. Discipline was never a strong point in fifteenth century armies, and the normal policy amongst mercenary armies in Italy had been to sacrifice the civilian population to the needs of the army. Cesare obviously was not entirely successful in reversing this trend, and he had particular difficulty controlling his French troops in the first campaign. There is however some indication that within the boundaries of the Romagna a stricter, more effective discipline than usual was imposed on Cesare's troops. Outside the Romagna they were allowed to behave in the accepted manner, and it was from outside the Romagna that most of the reports about the licence allowed to Cesare's troops came.

Together with military occupation as an obvious first stage in the pacification of the Romagna came the installation of Spanish officers as governors and administrators. Ramiro de

Lorqua became the first Governor and the popularity gained by administrative conservatism was to some extent dissipated by the harshness of these alien rulers. But as order was restored and the whole of the Romagna was brought under control, so the policy began to change. Civilian and Italian administrators began to take over. Ramiro de Lorqua was gradually excluded from civil government, and eventually dramatically executed. The work of administration increasingly fell on trusted papal administrators like Giovanni Olivieri, Bishop of Isernia, who received the surrender of Rimini and organised the administration of Pesaro; Francesco Loriz, Bishop of Elna, who was lieutenant in Forlì; Giovanni Vera, Cesare's life-long companion and adviser, who is said to have urged clemency towards Faenza; Cardinal Francesco Borgia, who brought his experience as papal treasurer and administrator of the Borgia duchies of Nepi and Sermoneta to the service of Cesare; Cardinal Serra, who had been Governor of Rome and was now made Governor of Cesena. These were men of a calibre and experience hitherto unknown in the government of the Romagna, and one must assume that their activities began to be effective.

Parallel with this trend towards civil government was the selection of Cesena as the capital of the new state. Plans were laid for the building of lawcourts, a university, and government offices. Leonardo da Vinci, who was Cesare's chief engineer in the summer and autumn of 1502, was instructed to prepare plans for the improvement of the declining Porto Cesenatico and for digging a canal linking it to the new capital.[7]

The only centralised institution which emerged in the time available was the Rota, a circuit court of appeal which was to sit for one month at a time in each of the six major cities of the Romagna. The President of the court was Antonio da Monte, a lawyer of unsullied reputation, the choice of whom is generally felt to throw credit on Cesare's government. Although instituted in mid-1502, the Rota did not hold its first session until July 1503 only a month before Alexander's death, so the extent of its importance is hard to estimate. But even within that month and following the first full session of the Rota, Antonio da Monte, accompanied by at least one of his fellow auditors, set off on a tour of the Duchy of Urbino hearing cases and administering justice.[8] It can certainly be argued that, although this was an attempt to provide a uniform justice for the whole of the Romagna, it was also an infringement of the jurisdiction of the Roman Rota, which aroused opposition at the time amongst the cardinals, and was to that extent a denial of complete centralisation within the Papal States. It has been seen in fact as a move towards the independence of Cesare from Rome and the setting up of an autonomous state in preparation for the death of his father and the emergence of a potentially hostile Pope. At the same time it would seem clear that any genuine good government of the Papal States had to be based on some compromises of this nature. Judicial appeal to Rome over the head of an emerging ducal government in Cesena was obviously an impossible situation, and if any sort of unity in the Romagna was to be created it had to be extended into the judicial sphere.

On the other hand the creation of a Romagnol militia, a sort of citizen standing army, which has been seen as both an instrument of unification and an indication of Cesare's popularity and the support which he received from the local population, is a more obscure question. Machiavelli, who had strong views about the value of citizen militias fighting to protect home and family, as opposed to the unreliable and expensive mercenary armies which had been Italy's shield for so long, seems to have been impressed by Cesare's example in this area. Both he and other observers report on the raising of a militia based on the conscription of one man per household in the Romagna during the crisis of the revolt of the *condottieri*.[9] But to argue from this that Cesare was finally converted to the use of militia and that thereafter his army was a national conscript army in the modern sense of the word, is pressing the facts too far. It seems clear from an examination of the components of Cesare's army, particularly in 1503, that, although he relied to some extent on Romagnol *condottieri* and Romagnol mercenaries, he never to any extent relied on a conscripted militia.[10] Such a force was raised in emergency, placed under Spanish commanders, and used briefly at the taking of Urbino. But it was quickly disbanded, and the army which Cesare led out of the Romagna after Senigallia was entirely a mercenary army. The famous Romagnol infantry, who marched into Rome in Cesare's livery, were mercenaries from the Val di Lamone, a traditional recruiting ground for tough infantry. Furthermore the practice of raising a conscript militia was a customary one with the Romagna vicars, as indeed it had remained in many of the city states of Italy. Thus, although the parade of militia from all over the Romagna, which Machiavelli saw in Imola in October 1502, was no doubt an impressive sight for one of his views, it was an entirely temporary phenomenon and of no lasting significance. Cesare was a *condottiere* of a traditional type and used mercenary troops in a traditional manner.

A final point which needs to be considered in connection with Cesare's government of the Romagna was the formation of a court and to some extent a literary and artistic circle round thc Duke. Such a development was almost essential for a Renaissance prince for reasons of prestige, and because the secretaries and chancellery staff, needed to conduct diplomacy and administration, tended to be humanists and literary figures in their own right. At the same time there are indications that Cesare himself, although not apparently greatly interested in the visual arts, had genuine literary and scientific interests. When he entered Pesaro in the autumn of 1500 he had with him, besides his military commanders, three bishops—all professional administrators, Don Ramiro his principal assistant, Alessandro Spannochi of the Sienese banking family, who was his treasurer, and Agapito Gheraldini his humanist secretary.[11] Gheraldini was a pupil of Pomponius Laetus and a frequenter of the Roman Academy, but he was also a diplomat and administrator of great experience, who had served not only Popes but also Ferrante of Aragon.[12]

The essentially practical nature of this group was greatly augmented during the periods of residence in Cesena. A considerable following of young Roman nobles attended on Cesare and formed the nucleus of his personal cavalry. At the same time a number of literary figures of some eminence in their day attached themselves to this new source of patronage. Carlo Valgulio, the teacher of Poliziano and friend of Copernicus, was amongst this group, as also were Fausto Evangelista, a historian and member of the Roman Academy who later enjoyed the favour of Leo X, Francesco Sperulo and Piero Justolo, two Latin poets, whose reputations fortunately did not depend on their Borgia panegyrics, and Francesco Uberti, a local humanist whose epigrams reflected the degree of adulation which Romagnol men of letters could lavish on this new Mycaenas. But above all there was Serafino Cimino, 'L'Aquilano' as he was known, who was described as the Petrarch of his age and who commanded a wider national reputation than any of his colleagues. This circle has been described rather brutally as 'this crowd of mediocrities and nullities, of adulatory poetasters and adventurers',[13] but the literary and artistic entourage of a Renaissance prince reflected not only his own tastes but also the state of the market and the attraction of conditions at the court in question. Cesare was known to be reasonably generous towards his entourage, but the turn of the century was not a great moment for Italian letters, and some of the figures whom he did succeed in attracting were better known to their contemporaries than they are to us. Furthermore there was an impermanent, vagrant quality to Cesare's court which did not appeal to all. Leonardo da Vinci, whose work greatly interested Cesare and who was given the crucial task of supervising the fortifications of the Romagna, soon tired of his employment when called upon to follow Cesare on his campaigns through southern Tuscany. On the other hand for a man like Piero Torrigiani, who was employed primarily as a soldier rather than a sculptor, the life could have been congenial. Torrigiani apart, the only other artist of note who seems to have been patronised by Cesare was his father's favourite, Pinturicchio, who received a pension from the Duke but does not seem to have completed any work in the Romagna.

What conclusions can we draw then either about the effectiveness or possible permanency of Cesare's government of the Romagna? The whole problem is of course vitiated by the time factor, and historians have been forced back on hypotheses as to what he might have achieved if given longer. Machiavelli maintained in the *Prince* that Cesare had prepared for everything except his own illness at the time of his father's death, but it is quite clear that the reorganisation of the Romagna was not complete and that a further period of assistance from papal administrators and papal finances was needed. Without the assistance of a friendly Pope, Cesare would have been at best a struggling papal vicar, forced to reimpose taxes on his subjects and increasingly driven into a traditional framework of Romagnol government. On the other hand there are clear indications of a pattern emerging in the government of the Romagna, a pattern of centralised authority and diminishing military control, which was popular with certain sections of the population. As I have suggested, it was a programme which was unlikely to be generally popular and one has to regard with some suspicion reports of the popularity of Cesare's government. Similarly the extent to which the Romagna cities remained faithful after the death of Alexander cannot be used as a gauge of popularity. It was not a particularly impressive fidelity anyway, although presumably Renaissance politicians like Machiavelli and Guicciardini expected unhappy populations to revolt the moment their ruler was in difficulties. But the issues were much more complex than just good or popular government; on the one side there were Cesare's Spanish garrisons holding out in the fortresses, on the other the advancing Venetian and Florentine interests supporting the return of the old vicars.[14] The ultimate victory of the latter was inevitable, appealing as they did both to the conservative elements in the population and to those who saw possible advantages in a link with the rich and powerful neighbouring states. Self interest is the key to all Italian politics of the period and no less to those of the Romagna. There were too many 'Vicars of Bray' in the Romagna for the new administration to stand on its own against the returning tide of vested interests and foreign armies.

The effects of Borgia rule in the remainder of the Papal States is even harder to assess. The authority of the Pope in each city and district varied considerably, and the situation seemed to change little during the pontificate of Alexander. One of his first concerns was always defence. He devoted large amounts of money to his own castles and regarded control of the fortresses throughout the Papal States as an essential step towards extending papal authority. In the Marches, where there had been four castles maintained by the provincial treasurer in 1455, there were fifteen by 1500.[15]

The more important of these were in the hands of Spanish castellans, although the majority of the commanders were still Italians. However, it was on the whole true that it was important to Alexander, not only that as many fortresses as possible should be in the hands of papal appointees, but also that the key fortresses should be in the hands of Borgias or at least Spaniards. Viterbo, where first Juan Marrades, the papal chamberlain, and then Francesco Troche, confidential secretary, were in charge; Orvieto, where Cesare Borgia was governor and commander of the fortress for life; Spoleto, in the hands first of Lucrezia then of Cardinal Pedro Luis Borgia, were all examples of the way in which the key strategic points were controlled. Furthermore, in the tradition of his uncle, Calixtus III, Alexander maintained a small fleet of galleys, under the command of Ludovico Mosca, to protect the coasts of the Papal States from attacks by corsairs.

The aim of these defensive measures was as much internal control as defence against external attack. Problems of internal disorder, struggles between local factions, and open brigandage were the principal ones which faced papal authority. The period of the French invasions was a disastrous one from the point of view of the preservation of order. Deserters from the armies and thousands of homeless countryfolk swelled the numbers of brigands; the factions fought each other more fiercely for local control, as communications and food supplies were hampered. Alexander, faced with a rising population in Rome, was particularly sensitive to the problems of keeping the roads open and maintaining the food supplies of the city. As bands of Corsican brigands landed on the coast and raided far inland, even attacking travellers on the Via Flaminia, Alexander countered by dispatching commissioners with companies of troops to keep the roads open. Domenico da Capranica and Piero Jacopo degli Ermanni were principal figures in this work; the former was Governor of

Civitavecchia for a time, but he was more usually to be found attempting to purge whole areas of brigands.

The Jubilee in 1500 imposed particular problems of public order, as thousands of pilgrims streamed along the roads leading to Rome. Alexander stepped up his efforts to keep the roads secure and even proposed a police militia system similar to the Spanish Holy Brotherhood as a possible answer. The idea of a conscripted citizen police force with powers of summary justice was anathema to the feudal nobility who firmly vetoed the scheme. Alexander replied with a Bull of 1500 ordering that 'if a pilgrim is robbed, the lord of the territory on which the crime is committed must restore the stolen goods'.[16] In the autumn of 1500 a full-scale campaign was waged against the rebellious nobility of Umbria. Altobello da Canale, the Lord of Acquasparta, who had for months terrorised the area, was captured and executed.[17]

Perugia was one of the most faction-ridden of all the papal cities and here we are told by the local chronicler, Matarazzo, that Alexander, when taking refuge in the city during the invasion of Charles VIII, tried to overthrow the rising dominance of the Baglione family and re-establish papal control.[18] He later sent Cardinal Juan Borgia-Lanzol, the younger, as legate to the tormented city, but he sent him without troops hoping that order could be restored by peaceful persuasion. Cardinal Juan left him in no doubt as to the hopelessness of his task when he wrote that 'armed force is the only way to deal with these demons who have no respect for holy water'. The cardinal managed to execute one murderer in Perugia, a display of firmness which had some impact, but the task was an almost impossible one.[19] In the circumstances it was forcible discipline rather than abstract justice which was required from the papal governors, and as many of these were Spaniards and soldiers this was often the line they took, for which they were naturally feared and hated.

It was an earlier legate in Perugia who had brought out another feature of Borgia administration. Juan Castellar, Archbishop of Trani and a relative of Alexander, was described by Matarazzo as 'testy, harebrained and given over to a vicious life'. Apparently for a fortnight in 1495 he administered justice well but then began to give way to bribes.[20] To accept the favours of one party in order to destroy the other was a natural temptation for a legate without the necessary force of his own, but at the same time the constant need for money by the Borgia administration tended to turn justice into a matter of payments.

Fines, compositions and confiscations were a key feature in the finances of the Papal States, but they were not the whole picture. Alexander was a parsimonious man at heart and with the great papal and dynastic projects which he had in hand he fully appreciated the value of money. As we shall see, he succeeded in balancing the budget of the Church for the first time for half a century, and there is evidence that the provincial treasuries of the Papal States were more efficiently run under his supervision than they had been for a long time. There was no question of increasing the tithe rates or imposing new taxes, although there was a tendency to extract more from the special taxes on the Jews; but there was pressure on the tax farmers and the treasurers to improve their methods of collection and particularly to extract debts from those cities and villages which had fallen behind with their payments. In 1501 Antonio Spannochi had to pay 21,500 ducats for the farm of the treasury of the Marches instead of the 15,000 which he had paid before. This was no reflection of rising revenues but rather of a considerable backlog of debts owed by the cities of Ascoli, Fermo, Camerino and others which it was hoped that he would collect.[21]

But the overall impression which one gets of Borgia administration of the Papal States outside the Romagna, which was a special case, is one of growing intensity of government rather than any administrative innovations. The establishment of the Borgia duchies and isolated examples of small towns being withdrawn from the jurisdiction of large provincial centres and administered directly by the Apostolic Camera, reflect a tendency towards centralisation, but it is hard to read into this a clear policy. It has been argued that Alexander introduced considerable reforms into the municipal government of Rome but on closer investigation there seems to be little in the way of innovation in the *Reformationes Alexandri* of 1493.[22] There was here, as in the Papal States as a whole, a concern for order and to some extent justice, but little administrative change. Borgia administrative policy was largely opportunist, a matter of maintaining order and raising money, but it was not wholly dynastic. Members of the Borgia family figured prominently amongst the papal governors and castellans, but they figured as papal servants as much as Borgia dependents. The grants of estates and duchies were in a sense permanent, but they also involved an extension of central control; the allocation of administrative and military posts conferred large salaries but implied responsibility and service to the Pope, and considerable impermanence.

Reference has already been made to the state of the finances of the Papal States, but there was little indication there of how the vast sums needed for Borgia schemes was raised. It was above all Cesare who was the great spender after 1498. Extravagant by nature and encouraged to put on a good display by his father, he spent 200,000 ducats on his journey to France. Half of this was spent on fitting out his suite, and it was said that all the shops of Rome were stripped of fine cloth, silk and jewelry. After his return it was reckoned that the maintenance of his household alone, with the hundred gentlemen who attended him and the 300 horses in his stables, cost 40,000 ducats a year.[23] The campaigns in the Romagna were an enormous drain on the papal resources. The first campaign cost 130,000 ducats, part of which was borrowed in Milan.[24] This was already about half the normal income of the Papacy spent on a two month campaign. During the third campaign Alexander began to get worried about the expense; he claimed that Cesare was spending 1000 ducats a day on his army; but Machiavelli put the cost at closer to 2000 ducats a day.[25] Some records of the payments to Cesare can be found in the Vatican cameral accounts and in Giustinian's reports, but they are obviously incomplete, and so the total cost of the Romagna campaigns cannot be known.[26] But we know enough to be able to say that it was totally beyond the normal resources of the Papacy.

At the same time Cesare's expenses were by no means the only additional burdens on the papal purse which Borgia rule implied. Alexander, although in many ways a parsimonious man, and although he achieved considerable savings in the domestic expenses of the Vatican, was always generous to his children and dependents. Lucrezia was able to find 80,000 ducats to buy the Gaetani estates in 1499 and one suspects that this sum must have partly originated from papal funds. Her dowry of 100,000 ducats which she took to Ferrara was certainly paid by the Apostolic Camera. Alexander also spent heavily on display and ceremonies; not only did he love to make a good show in public but the prestige of the Renaissance Papacy demanded it. His coronation cost 3000 ducats, but this was in fact relatively little compared to the 15,000 spent on the funeral of Innocent VIII.[27] Most of the ceremonial expenses of the coronation, and indeed of many papal ceremonies, were borne by the cardinals and the nobility of Rome who all put on individual displays for the occasion.

Although, as we shall see, Alexander did not spend great amounts on artistic patronage, he did not spare money on fortifications and defence. He spent 63,000 on artillery alone in the spring of 1502, and even in 1493 the major portion of Camera expenses was devoted to the payment of *condottieri* and troops.[28] Finally, although it is often said that crusading funds were diverted to Borgia purposes, there is good evidence that Alexander spent a lot on genuine crusading purposes. After 1500 Ladislas, King of Hungary, received 40,000 ducats from the funds, and in that year 15,000 were sent to Venice to assist in preparing a fleet against the Turks. Furthermore the crusading tenths, collected all over Europe at this time, by no means all reached Rome; in the case of both Venice and the Empire the proceeds of the crusade tax were allocated to local crusading expenses. It is probably true however that as far as the Emperor was concerned this was in the nature of a bribe to win the imperial investiture of Pisa, Lucca and Siena for Cesare.

How were these vast additional expenses met? By what means did Alexander 'make the papal income what he wanted it to be' as Giustinian put it in 1503?[29] In the first place there were the crusading funds which were always an additional source of income over and above the normal receipts of the Apostolic Camera. The permanent source of income for the crusade fund were the Tolfa alum mines where production was steadily rising in this period. In 1500 a long-term contract for the exploitation of the mines was given to Agostino Chigi and a period of more rapid development of these resources followed.[30] In 1503 the mines were sacked by Giulio Orsini, an event which further increased Alexander's fury against the Orsini and was a blow to one of the most important sources of papal income.

The crusade Bull of 1500 imposed a tax of one-tenth on all Christendom and even the cardinals were expected to contribute. The levy on the cardinals produced 35,000 ducats a year for three years.[31] The surviving records of cardinals' incomes and crusade payments are probably not accurate as indeed the tax returns of wealthy men very rarely were. The wealthiest cardinal was reported to be Ascanio Sforza with an income of 30,000 ducats which seems very low by previous standards of cardinals' wealth. But it is interesting to note from these records that the four Borgia cardinals in late 1500, and what one might call the Borgia associates like Jaime Serra, Giovanni Vera, Ferrari, Podocatharo, etc., were by no means the wealthiest of the cardinals at this stage.

But the crusading tenth was not the only means by which Alexander tapped the wealth of the cardinals. Cardinals appointed by Alexander were expected to pay for the honour. An informal first-fruits system was imposed on the new cardinals from the beginning of the pontificate when Cardinal Cesarini paid 22,000 ducats for his red hat.[32] In 1503 the nine new cardinals appointed in the summer were said to have contributed 120,000 ducats to the papal treasury. Furthermore Alexander insisted on his right to take possession of the wealth of cardinals who died, particularly those who died in Rome. It was traditional that the accumulated wealth of a cardinal returned to the Church on his death, unless he had been given special permission to make a will. In the case of Cardinal Zeno who died in Padua in 1501 such permission had been given by Sixtus IV, but Zeno by leaving Rome at the beginning of Alexander's pontificate had seriously offended the Pope and the permission had been withdrawn.[33] On Zeno's death both Alexander and the Venetians claimed the cardinal's considerable wealth and in the end settled for a compromise division of the spoils. When cardinals died in Rome, as did the other wealthy Venetian cardinal Michiel in 1503, Alexander had a better chance to get their moveable wealth before other claims were advanced. But he had to act with unseemly haste if papal rights in these matters were to be protected.[34]

It has often been claimed that Alexander and Cesare in their anxiety for money were unable to wait until cardinals died natural deaths and resorted to poison to hasten the end of the wealthier prelates. But indiscriminate accusations of poisoning against the Borgias, even in cases where the supposed victim died well out of reach of the family, seriously weaken the charges where the possibility seems more likely. Suspicion of poison emerges as a factor in nearly all the sudden deaths of important figures at this time. Medical knowledge was incapable of accurate diagnosis or careful autopsy, and even the descriptions of the symptoms in many cases are sufficient to convince us of causes of death far less exotic than poison. Attempts by historians to discover the nature of the famous *cantarella* which the Borgias are supposed to have used have ended in ridiculous failure. Poisoning was itself a very inexact science and the use of such concoctions as the more imaginative writers have proposed, like the saliva of a mad pig hung upside down and beaten to death, could scarcely have been fatal.[35] There is no evidence, apart from confessions extracted by torture by Julius II from servants of dead cardinals, that the Borgias resorted to poison; had they been such experts it seems unlikely that ostentatious strangling would have been their normal method of disposing of enemies. Twenty-seven cardinals died during the eleven years of Alexander's pontificate; thirty-six, during the nine years which Julius II reigned. These figures are a reflection of the increased numbers of cardinals rather than the increasing unscrupulousness of Popes.

The Jubilee and the sale of indulgences connected with it was a further source of additional income for Alexander. Exactly how much was raised during the Jubilee is not known, but it is likely that this was the source of the funds for the second Romagna campaign. The sale of offices also continued to be a lucrative source of additional wealth for the Church.

Alexander had opposed such methods as Vice-Chancellor, but like most other Popes of the period he resorted to it once in supreme authority. There was a certain need for an increasing number of papal secretaries and curial officials as the temporal interests of the Papacy increased. In 1500 Alexander created a new secretariat for the handling of diplomatic correspondence, so extensive had this business become.[36] In 1503 eighty new offices were created and sold for 760 ducats each.[37] Like all sales of offices in this period, these transactions were regarded as being a type of loan in which the lender was repaid both interest and capital in the form of his salary. The man responsible for this side of the fund raising was Ferrari, the Datary from 1496 to 1500, a man who was widely hated for his grasping ways and whose death in 1503, another case of suspected poisoning, caused widespread satisfaction.

Then of course there were the confiscations. Ascanio Sforza, when arrested and imprisoned by Louis XII, lost all his benefices and art treasures to the Pope. The estates of the victims of the coup of Senigallia brought in 100,000 ducats, and the frequent confiscations from the Roman barons were even more lucrative.

Therefore, although there was a tendency to raise a little more from the normal income of the Church in this period by more careful accounting and by greater pressure on the tax farmers, it was by extraordinary means that Borgia funds were raised. When Alexander became Pope the treasury was empty and the Papacy was in debt to the extent of at least 120,000 ducats. By the terms of the League of 1493 with Venice and Milan, the papal armies were to be paid by the allies, as the Pope could not afford the expense. But gradually this picture changed. Debts were written off at reduced rates, and after a long period of almost continuous debit financing Alexander by 1496 had succeeded in balancing the papal budget and producing occasional surpluses.[38] After 1498 both expenses and extraordinary income increased greatly and we have no indication of the balance in these years, but on his death Alexander left large sums in cash which were seized by Cesare. The papal treasury was once again empty, but one gets the impression that during the pontificate the secret treasury or privy purse had been an increasingly important vehicle for the extraordinary funds raised and needed, and it was this which was full at Alexander's death.

Extravagant though Alexander was in the pursuit of the temporal aims of the Church and the dynastic advancement of his family, a very different picture is revealed by a study of the household accounts of his pontificate. The Ferrarese ambassador, Boccaccio, reported that usually only one course was served at the papal table and that cardinals used to avoid eating with the Pope because they fared so poorly in his company.[39] This frugality is amply borne out by the household expenses. Alexander spent approximately 20,000 ducats a year on his household which was very similar to the expenses of his uncle, Calixtus III, whose frugality and parsimony were notorious.[40] This was at a time when the size of the papal household was steadily rising; only a few years later Leo X was able to spend up to 100,000 a year. These expenses covered the salaries of his immediate household which numbered about sixty and the living costs of a rather larger group who lived and worked in the Vatican; in addition there were incidental expenses connected with the Vatican and almsgiving. There were few days when more than twenty ducats were spent on the needs of the household, but this did not include the stocks of grain and wine which were bought in bulk. Indeed so large were the purchases of these commodities that it is clear that the Pope was providing food for a much larger number than his immediate household. The grain was on the whole brought in from the papal estates in the Campagna, but the wine came from much wider sources. Particularly popular at the Borgia court was Corsican wine of which nearly 300 butts were bought in 1501. In addition large quantities of wine were obtained from Frascati and the Alban Hills, and Fiano. In 1502 a quarter of the papal purchases consisted of Greek wine.

The itemised daily accounts of the papal *expenditori* complete the picture of a limited and frugal diet for the Pope and his household. Friday and Lenten abstinence from meat was rigorously observed and at these times sardines figured prominently on the papal menus. At other times of the year mutton was the principal meat eaten, although during the summer veal, beef, pork and chicken appeared more often to reduce the monotony of the diet. Salads were common but other vegetables rare; bread and pasta presumably played a major part in the diet, but cheese and eggs appeared rarely. However the Pope employed a chicken keeper amongst his household, so presumably eggs were provided from domestic sources.

The feast days of the Church were occasions for greater indulgence, at least for the household if not for the Pope himself. Epiphany, Shrove Tuesday, Easter Day, Corpus Christi, All Saints Eve, St. Martin's Day, Christmas, and New Year's Eve, were all celebrated by slightly increased expenditure and improved menus. Shrove Tuesday 1502 saw the purchase of fourteen goats and six lambs as well as the inevitable 673 lb. of mutton; while on 5 March 1502 the Lenten sardine diet was varied by the purchase of tuna, mullet and cod.[41] 11 August, the anniversary of Alexander's election, was also treated as an occasion for some celebration. But in all this there is little evidence of what might be described as an orgy.

However, Alexander and his children delighted in visual entertainment. Music, dancing and dramatic performances, essential ingredients of Renaissance festivities, were also commonplace in the Vatican. The Ferrarese ambassadors negotiating Lucrezia's third marriage reported how the round of gaiety was exhausting them, and also Cesare and Lucrezia who led the revels. It was only, they said, when the Pope went to Nepi that anybody got any rest.[42] But the same ambassadors, watching carefully the behaviour of the future wife of their Duke's son and heir, made no mention of the famous feast of the courtesans which figures so largely in most accounts of life at the Borgia court.

This party was given by Cesare in his apartments in the Vatican on or about All Saints Eve, 1501, presumably as a part of the celebrations of Lucrezia's approaching wedding. The fact that the party was given by Cesare can explain why no trace of it is to be found in the papal household accounts; indeed the Pope's household was fasting on fish that night. The occasion has been described not only by the hostile, and usually distant, Borgia observers like Matarazzo, Sanuto and the writer of the Savelli letter, but also by the staid master of ceremonies, Burchard.[43] For this reason the account has to be taken more seriously than might otherwise be the case. Burchard describes the scene when fifty Roman courtesans were invited to the private supper party, danced naked with the servants, competed to pick up chestnuts off the floor, and were then competed for themselves by the men present. All this in the presence of the Pope, Lucrezia and Cesare. The fact that this is the only such occasion which Burchard describes in all his account of Alexander's pontificate leads one to imagine that it may have been exceptional. On the other hand the fact that he describes it with no comment or apparent surprise suggests that it was a common event, or that the description is an interpolation. Another theory recently advanced is that Burchard himself became increasingly hostile to the Borgias in the later years and in this section of his work was copying from the Savelli letter which he quotes extensively in the following pages.[44] Whatever the truth of this particular incident, there is no evidence that it was typical of the nightly entertainments in the Vatican. Giustinian, who arrived in Rome later, referred on several occasions to the 'usual pleasures' of the Pope, but these seem to have been evening entertainments of a relatively restrained type at which women were certainly present but at which there is no hint of undue licence or debauchery.[45]

One of the indications of the increasingly secular nature of life within the Vatican is the rapidly expanding papal household. Here we see not only a growing number of laymen attached to the papal court but also the growing number of servants, cooks and provisioners needed to cater for them. In the accounts of the papal household which have remained, a distinction is made between an inner group directly attached to the Pope and paid out of the palace expenses, and the household in a wider sense which consisted of all the residents of the palace. The composition and size of the two groups changed considerably during the second half of the fifteenth century.[46] At the time of Eugenius IV the immediate entourage of the Pope consisted of 34 people including three doctors, five cooks, five servants and two chamberlains. At the same time the complete household, numbering a further 120, included the staff of the Apostolic Camera, the Datary office, and many of the officials of the city. By the later years of Alexander's pontificate the size of the following paid directly from palace expenses had almost doubled, and this group no longer included the doctors, who by now numbered eight, or the chamberlains. There were now six cooks and twelve household servants, and a number of menial staff such as muleteers and water carriers had come onto the Pope's payroll. The wider group on the other hand no longer included any Curia or city officials but was largely made up of honorary courtiers, the staff of the papal chapel, and nineteen couriers (only six had been needed fifty years earlier). Thus, whereas in the 1440s the Pope's entourage or 'family' was a complete group consisting of close assistants, clerks, and domestic staff paid directly by the Pope, by 1500 numbers had increased to such an extent that the components of the 'family' filled the whole Vatican to the exclusion of the Curia officials, and only the domestic staff were still paid directly out of palace expenses.

There was inevitably a strong Catalan element in the household under Alexander VI. The Master of the Sacred Palace was first Pedro d'Aranda, Bishop of Calahorra, who was tried and imprisoned for heresy and harbouring Jews in 1498, and then Diego Melendez de Valdes, Bishop of Zamorra, whose monumental tomb designed by Andrea Bregno is in Santa Maria di Monserrato.[47] Amongst the chamberlains were Juan Marrades, Francesco Troche, Jacopo de Casanova, Francesco Cabaynes, and Pedro Caranza. Two out of Alexander's three Dataries were Catalans, Juan Lopez and Juan Ortega da Gomiel; Bartolomeo Flores, the secretary who was imprisoned for life in 1497 for forging papal briefs, was a Catalan. Amongst the doctors Pedro Pintor and Gaspare Torella were both Catalans, as was Alexander's fool Gabrielletto. Torella was also Vatican Librarian and his two predecessors under Alexander VI, Pedro Garsias and Juan de Fuensalida, were Catalans.[48] The commander of the papal guard was always a Borgia, and Francesco Borgia was for a long time treasurer of the household. In fact the only Italians who figured prominently in the papal household were Giovanbattista Ferrari, the Datary from 1496 to 1500, Adriano Castellesi, confidential secretary in the later years, and Bernardino di Bonioanne, Bishop of Venusa, Alexander's favourite doctor.

In contrast to this picture, the artists and men of letters who enjoyed Alexander's favour were nearly all Italians. Alexander has often been compared somewhat unfavourably with other Renaissance Popes as a patron; he has been described as parsimonious and lacking cultural appreciation, as being more a man of the Middle Ages than of the Renaissance. He was certainly a man of spontaneous emotions to whom visual pleasure meant more than intellectual content.[49] His favourite painter was the Umbrian, Pinturicchio, whose narrative and highly decorative compositions cover the walls of the Borgia apartments in the Vatican and also originally filled the main rooms of Castel Sant'Angelo. There has been a long tradition of disregard for Pinturicchio from Vasari down to Berenson which has tended to reflect on the taste of his Borgia patrons. This is based on the idea that he was an anachronism, a Gothic courtly painter born out of his time and fighting against the mainstream of Florentine Renaissance painting. But to see Pinturicchio in this light is to neglect the strong continuing stream of courtly painting in the Renaissance from Pisanello and Gozzoli through to Veronese, which was not just a survival but a live and progressive style. It was a style which under the influence of Pinturicchio derived much from classical precepts, and the Borgia apartment frescoes are by no means the naive and unoriginal decorations which they are sometimes thought to be.

The suite of rooms called the Borgia apartments were built by Nicholas V but had remained bare and gloomy until the election of Alexander. His decision to have them sumptuously decorated and to occupy them himself was an immediate one, and Pinturicchio's work was completed between 1492 and 1494. Pinturicchio, although the coordinator of the whole work, left a good deal of the execution to his assistants, and the Room of the Saints is the only one in which he painted all the main frescoes himself. The programme of the frescoes in the seven rooms is an elaborate if largely traditional one reflecting northern European as well as Italian influences. Although the prominence of the Borgia bull in the iconography reflects a personal pride and a sense of power, it also perhaps indicates how much Alexander's own ideas and inclinations had to do with the work. Similarly the space allotted to the Seven Joys of the Virgin, and astronomy amongst the Seven Liberal Arts, in the iconographical programme reflect Alexander's veneration for the Virgin Mary and his interest in astronomy. Equally clearly some of the most contemporary humanist ideas of Marsilio Ficino are reflected in the synthesis of Christian, Jewish and pagan symbols and in the interest in and respect for Egyptian traditions which are implied in Pinturicchio's work. Pinturicchio's position as a leader in the revival of illusionist decoration based on the classical examples of 2nd Pompeian style wall painting and the ceiling decorations of the Golden House of Nero, discovered at this time, must also condition Vasari's judgment on him and the implied judgment on his patron.[50]

From what we know of the vanished Castel Sant'Angelo frescoes painted a year or two later, they appear to have been a narrative cycle of the life of Alexander. As such they would have been invaluable to us as portraits of the Borgia family, particularly as the portraiture often perceived in the Borgia apartment frescoes is rather suspect. But such a cycle would probably have told us little more either about Pinturicchio as a painter or about Alexander as a patron.

Apart from these two main fresco commissions most of the rest of the work sponsored by Alexander was architectural. He built the Torre Borgia onto the Borgia apartments and this at the time served as part of the outer defensive works of the Vatican. When built, it projected well above the rest of the Vatican, as the building to which it was attached was two storeys lower than it is today, and with its crenellated battlements it had all the appearance of a medieval fortification.[51] Alexander was also responsible for the completion of Pius II's benediction loggia in front of St. Peter's and for the fountain in St. Peter's Square. He was in fact an embellisher and finisher of other people's projects and had none of the monumental ideas which had characterised the patronage of Nicholas V or Sixtus IV.

In the city of Rome the work of restoring the churches went on, and Sant'Agostino and San Niccolò in Carcere in particular were restored under Alexander's initiative. Antonazzo Romano, the leading local painter who had contributed to the decorations for the coronation, as had Perugino and Pietro Turini, worked on Sant'Agostino, while San Niccolò was Alexander's cardinalate church, and as such particularly dear to him. The restored ceiling of Santa Maria Maggiore, on which the Borgia emblem is still to be seen, and on which the first gold to arrive from America was used, also dates from this period. Bramante's first commission when he came to Rome in 1499 is said to have been a painting above the Porta Santa of the Lateran of the Borgia emblem supported by angels, but otherwise the great architect did not enjoy papal patronage during this period. In fact Alexander's best known work in the city was concerned with pulling buildings down rather than putting them up. He widened streets, and cleared away slums round the Vatican to make way for the Via Alessandrina linking the Ponte Sant'Angelo with St. Peter's. But at the same time he showed no more respect for the classical monuments of the city than some of his predecessors, and continued the practice of despoiling them of stone for new buildings.

Alexander's major building projects were concerned with fortifications, and the fortress in which he took the greatest interest was Castel Sant'Angelo.[52] It was there that he took refuge when the army of Charles VIII entered Rome and already by that time much had been done to strengthen its defences. In 1492 the fortress was in a woeful condition of disrepair and little had been done to adapt it to meet improving siege methods. Alexander commissioned Antonio da San Gallo, the elder, to strengthen and improve the outer walls; houses were torn down to make more space and there was even a project for diverting the Tiber so that the defences could be expanded. The other main concern of the early years was to prepare the castle for a long siege by improving its provisioning facilities. Large granaries and oil deposits were prepared so that 185 tons of grain and 22,000 litres of oil could be stored, and it was reckoned that with these reserves the castle could withstand a three-year siege. At the same time the lower dungeons were cut out of the rock; the dungeons which were described so vividly by Benvenuto Cellini, and which were quickly put to use for Bartolomeo Flores, the Pope's erring secretary. In 1497 lightning struck the tip of the sword of the angel which surmounted the castle and all the upper buildings were destroyed. 30,000 ducats worth of damage was done and it was as a part of the rebuilding after this that some of Pinturicchio's later work took its place.

Besides this main defensive work Alexander ordered a massive reconstruction of the defences of the castle of Civita Castellana. This was the key to the approach to Rome along the Via Flaminia, and Antonio da San Gallo worked between 1494 and 1497 on preparing an outer enceinte which could withstand artillery assault. The living accommodation and the inner courtyard were also rebuilt and decorated with frescoes by Pier Matteo d'Amelia, so that this fortress could serve as a Borgia summer resort and refuge, as it did for Cesare after Alexander's death.[53] The castles at Tivoli, Civitella and Sermoneta were among others restored and strengthened by Alexander during his papacy, and these together with Nepi and Subiaco, on which he had already expended considerable sums as cardinal, represented not only a heavy outlay in cash but also a strong defensive ring of modern castles protecting the routes into Rome.

We cannot leave Alexander's building programmes without mentioning his patronage of the university in Rome. He rebuilt the Sapienza and gave great encouragement to the teaching of theology. Argyropoulos and Copernicus were among the teachers at the university during his pontificate, and it gained considerable prestige as a result.

Alexander in fact, although manifestly not an intellectual and somewhat out of touch with the intellectual currents of his day, nevertheless found himself inevitably at the centre of a considerable literary circle.[54] Among those who expressed great hopes at his election were Pico della Mirandola who had been excommunicated for his *Disputationes* and now sought, successfully, to have the excommunication withdrawn,[55] and the Venetian humanist Ermalao Barbaro in exile in Rome who, in his *Castigationes Plinianae*, wrote flatteringly of the new Pope. Others who wrote flatteringly but with less significance as they are less well known to us were Hieronimus Porcius and Michele Ferno. Porcius came from the talented Porcari family who were devoted Borgia adherents; he wrote a panegyric on the occasion of Alexander's coronation and continued to be one of the principal propagandists for Borgia rule, although Gregorovius described him a little unkindly as 'an affected pedant and empty-headed braggart'. Ferno was one of the leading students of the Roman humanist Pomponius Laetus; a man of considerable talents whose reputation has undoubtedly suffered from his connection with the Borgias. Pomponius himself was encouraged by Alexander; he was sent on a mission to Germany to collect manuscripts for the Pope, and on his death in 1498 Alexander ordered that all his court should attend the magnificent funeral given to Rome's leading man of letters.

Aldo Manuzio, the Venetian printer, was released from his ecclesiastical vows and given licence to print by Alexander, and Aegidius of Viterbo, the passionate Franciscan reformer, was invited to preach in the Vatican. Among those whose presence was more or less frequent at Alexander's court was Aurelio Brandolini, the poet and musician, Josquin de Prés, the Flemish composer and musician, Tommaso Inghirami, the student of Cicero much admired by Erasmus who was making a reputation for himself as an actor and probably took part in the dramatic performances which Alexander loved, Giovanni Lascaris, the most famed hellenist of his day, the young Sadoleto, Adriano Castellesi, Alexander's humanist secretary, and Lorenz Behaim, the former master of his household. Behaim's presence was part of the attraction which brought to Rome his more famous brother Martin, Copernicus, and finally Reuchlin.

In all this intellectual activity it is not always easy to see how much can be directly attributed to Borgia patronage, and how much was the natural intellectual life of a great city. The Roman Academy which met in the home of the latinist, Paolo Cortesi, was attended by a number of close Borgia associates, Giovanni Vera, Agapito Gheraldini, Castellesi and Ferno; but it is easy to exaggerate the extent of Borgia influence. Similarly the changes in the visual appearance of Rome during the period 1492–1503 were by no means all dependent on the Pope and his family. The cardinals, and increasingly the resident groups of foreigners, were contributing to the growth of Rome as a capital city. Cardinals Riario, Cesarini and Farnese were building their palaces; Cardinal La Grolaye commissioned the Pietà from Michelangelo in 1498; Cardinal Grimani was building up his famous collection of marbles; Pollaiuolo was engaged on finishing the tombs of Sixtus IV and Innocent VIII. The French church of Santa Trinità dei Monti began to rise on the Pincio in honour of Charles VIII's visit to Rome; the Spaniards founded Santa Maria di Monserrato; Bramante completed San Pietro in Montorio in 1502 for Ferdinand and Isabella; in 1500 the

German ambassador laid the foundation stone of Santa Maria dell'Anima. Renaissance Rome was emerging from the miasma of the cattle pastures which marked the Roman forum, and the stinking pollution of the huddled medieval city crowded amongst the ancient ruins. It was emerging at an accelerating pace to which Alexander made some contribution even if he was not taking the lead in the manner of some of his predecessors.

Finally, what of Alexander's government of the Church in a more spiritual sense? Here he was essentially a conservative as were all the Renaissance Popes; no radical innovations in doctrine or in ecclesiastical organisation marked his pontificate. Although basically a tolerant man and particularly so towards the Jews, until in 1498 the need to mollify Spain led him to initiate some persecution, Alexander was severe on heretics and made great efforts to settle the Hussite problem. He was assiduous in his care for and interest in the ceremonies of the Church, and insisted on regular attendance by the cardinals at services. He was very strict about the observance of Lenten fasts, but disliked long sermons. Although a great talker, he was not himself a great speech maker or preacher. On the other hand the pungent style of preaching of some of the hermit orders did appeal to him, and it was men like Aegidius of Viterbo and the Augustinian hermits who were the usual preachers in the papal chapel.

Alexander took a great interest in the monastic orders and in their reform. In fact he seemed to distinguish very clearly between the secular and the religious clergy in a way which was more characteristic of the Orthodox than of the Catholic Church. He approved the foundation of the hermit order of St. Francis of Paola, and reconstituted the Order of the Holy Sepulchre; he instigated a reform of the Franciscans in 1501, and always favoured the Augustinians. He advanced the cult of the Virgin Mary to which he was particularly attached, granting Bulls of indulgence to Marian shrines and participating in the patronage of Santa Maria del Popolo. He confirmed Sixtus IV's Bull forbidding discussion and dogmatic pronouncements about the doctrine of the Immaculate Conception.

His concern for the purity of Catholic doctrine showed itself in his authorisation of the first censorship of the press. In 1501 German printers were ordered to seek episcopal approval for all new books printed, and archbishops were authorised to inspect printers' catalogues to see that books already printed were sound in doctrine. Ecclesiastical censorship was an inevitable corollary to the development of printing, but the fact that it was Alexander who initiated it is an indication that his mind was not entirely on worldly matters. But at the same time the Church at the end of the fifteenth century was in need of much more positive and whole-hearted spiritual leadership than Alexander was either capable of or considered necessary.

CHAPTER ELEVEN

THE DEATH OF ALEXANDER

Rome in August 1503 was hot and sultry. In normal circumstances the papal court would have retired to the country and the hills to seek some relief. But the circumstances were not normal; great decisions had to be taken as the French army moved southwards for the final trial of strength in Naples. With Cesare's army spread out in camps between Rome and Perugia, the Pope and his son watched the political situation anxiously. There were rumours that Cesare was about to leave for the Romagna; thus he would have avoided by his absence the obligation to join the French as they passed southwards.

It was therefore perhaps a farewell supper party for Cesare which Adriano Castellesi gave in his vineyard on Monte Mario on 5 August. On the same day Cardinal Juan Borgia-Lanzol, the elder, had died suddenly of malarial fever which was rampant in Rome. He had been an invaluable administrative assistant to Alexander, but he had grown excessively corpulent in the last few years and Alexander was moved to remark gloomily that 'it was a bad month for fat people'.[1] The Pope's preoccupation and depression in these days was noted by many observers but it was not until the 12th, a week after the famous supper party at which fanciful enemies liked to imagine that the Borgias poisoned themselves, that Alexander and Cesare were both struck down by the fever.[2] The day before had been the anniversary of the election and once again the Pope's gloom, on a day which he normally celebrated with great enthusiasm, was noted. Now with the two Borgias lying dangerously ill the Vatican was in a turmoil. For six days the doctors fought to save them with all the crude methods at their command. Bleeding seemed to bring temporary relief to Alexander and one day he was even able to sit up and watch his attendants playing cards at his bedside. But his seventy-two years were telling against him and by the 17th all hope had been abandoned. The tension in Rome was rising as the Borgia enemies gathered, and the Borgia courtiers and prelates looked for shelter. Cesare, his own crisis surmounted, lay exhausted in his rooms above the papal apartments. On the morning of the 18th Alexander made his confession and received the Last Unction; by the evening his strength was ebbing fast and about vespers he died.

As was customary only twenty-four hours were allowed to lapse before the dead Pope was buried, in Santa Maria delle Febbri alongside St. Peter's. Only four cardinals took part in the funeral procession; but in fact few of the cardinals were in Rome and these were anxiously debating what steps should be taken to preserve order in the city.

The situation was certainly an exceptionally inflammable one, and there was every reason to expect something more than the usual disorder which attended a *sede vacante*. The French army was camped at Viterbo some forty miles north of the city, while Gonsalvo de Cordoba with his Spanish army was hurrying northwards from Naples. A good part of Cesare's troops were even closer at hand, but vital time had been lost in the few days before the Pope's death when he himself lay helpless. It was this period which could have been crucial. Cesare, possessing all his faculties, could have had six days to bring in his troops, establish firm control in the city and prevent the Orsini and the Colonna from gathering strength. As master of the city he might have achieved genuine control over the situation. Even as it was even with those precious days lost he was a force that had to be reckoned with.

On the news of his father's death, Cesare was already sufficiently recovered to send Michele Corella to seize the private treasure of 100,000 ducats and attempt to occupy Castel Sant'Angelo. His troops filled the Borgo, but Roccamura, the castellan of Sant'Angelo, refused to take sides at this juncture and shut the gates to all comers.[3] The Spanish cardinals provisionally agreed to support Giovanni Vera as a suitable successor to Alexander. Steps were taken to prevent Giuliano della Rovere reaching Rome. Agapito Gheraldini, in the name of his master, concluded an alliance with the Colonna promising restoration of their estates and a marriage alliance if they would now support Cesare. But that confidence and resolution which Machiavelli had admired so much in Cesare in the Romagna had depended largely on advance planning and a realisation of the weakness of the enemy. Now the planning had been disrupted and the enemies had been allowed to gather strength. The anti-Borgia tumult across the river gave the Italian cardinals the initiative and convinced the Spaniards that it was hopeless to expect the election of another of their countrymen.

Cesare now changed his tactics and sought to negotiate with the cardinals already assembled in Rome. He swore loyalty to the College and was confirmed as Captain General. But the cardinals, led by Carafa and rapidly gaining confidence, refused to entertain the idea of the Conclave taking place until all armies, including that of Cesare, had withdrawn a safe distance from Rome. The Spanish and French ambassadors, anxious to break the predominance of Cesare and secure the election of a Pope directly dependent on their individual kings, encouraged this determination and guaranteed that their own armies would respect the security of the city.

A stalemate thus ensued until Cesare, perhaps alarmed by

the confused and to some extent unfavourable reports coming in about the situation in the Romagna, agreed to withdraw northwards. On 2 September his troops began to move out and he camped them round Nepi and Civita Castellana. At the same time he concluded a new agreement with Louis XII offering to support a French candidate to the Papacy in return for protection and guarantees of his position in the Romagna.

The situation in the Romagna was certainly very delicately poised. Guidobaldo da Montefeltro and the Varani had re-entered Urbino and Camerino; Venice was providing assisttance to Giovanni Sforza and the Malatesta, who reappeared in Pesaro and Rimini in the first week of September. On the other hand Cesena had declared its loyalty to Antonio da Monte and stoutly resisted Venetian infiltration, while Forlì, Imola and Faenza were showing little enthusiasm for the return of the Riario or the Manfredi. Venice was obviously determined to profit from any Borgia or papal weakness, while Florence, deeply suspicious of her Venetian rival, was anxious not to be left out in any grab for spoils. In September Cesare's renewed alliance with France and the continued loyalty of his Spanish garrisons, helped to stabilise the situation briefly. Both Venice and Florence were reluctant to commit themselves against France and all now depended on whether Cesare would enjoy the support of the new Pope.

The prospects for the conclave, plans for which were now going ahead, were no less confused than the situation as a whole. Cardinal d'Amboise was making a determined play for the tiara. With the French votes supported by those of Ascanio Sforza, released from custody for the occasion, and the two Florentine cardinals, Medici and Soderini, and in addition Cesare's influence over the Spanish cardinals, there seemed to be some prospect of his success. But Cesare, if he really intended his support for a French candidate to be meaningful, was overestimating his influence over the

Spanish cardinals. For there was really little prospect of Spanish support for a French cardinal and thus d'Amboise, feared by most of the Italians, was unlikely to be successful. Giuliano della Rovere, although he enjoyed considerable support amongst the Italian cardinals, and they numbered twenty-two out of the thirty-seven who had assembled for the conclave, was decisively rejected by the Spaniards and had himself renounced his previous French affiliations. Any prospect of a Spanish success had already been ruled out. Thus when the conclave opened on 16 September the probability of a compromise candidate emerging was already great. The names of several Italian cardinals had been mentioned in such a context before the conclave started, but the one who emerged as the unanimous choice of all parties was Cardinal Piccolomini, who took the title of Pius III.

Although Piccolomini had been one of the few cardinals who had stood up to Alexander and yet at the same time had not fled from Rome, Cesare must have been well satisfied with the election. The new Pope was an old man, plagued by gout as had been his uncle Pius II, and he was unlikely to have the determination to dispossess Cesare either of his command of the papal forces or of his fiefs in the Romagna. Indeed one of the first acts of the new Pope was to order the people of the Romagna to maintain their allegiance to their Duke. He then, under pressure from the Spanish cardinals, allowed Cesare to return to Rome.

However, although these were favourable signs, Cesare's position was still extremely uncertain. Despite his illness, he had demonstrated the effectiveness of Alexander's dynastic policies by exerting much more influence over papal affairs after his father's death than had either Girolamo Riario or Franceschetto Cibo in similar situations. But his presence was now urgently needed in the Romagna where, although his captains had reoccupied Rimini, there was a danger of the unity of the Duchy breaking up. He would probably have done better at this moment to have re-established his base there rather than risked his fortunes in Rome. Already his army was dwindling rapidly; part of his cavalry had been attached to the French army which had now resumed its march southwards; cash was running short and the Romagnol infantry were anxious to return home. Thus when Cesare returned to Rome in October his army numbered little over 1000 men, although Michele Corella was camped near Orvieto with a force of infantry. The Orsini on the other hand were gathering strength. They had been joined by Bartolomeo d'Alviano and succeeded in detaching the Colonna from Cesare, thus uniting all Rome against him. Added to this, the Pope was dying; the strain of the coronation ceremony and the labours of his short pontificate had proved too much for the ageing Piccolomini.

Cesare tried to escape from the false position into which he had got himself. He attempted to force his way out of the city but was turned back by the overwhelming strength of the Orsini. He now took refuge in Castel Sant'Angelo with the two infant Borgia dukes and recalled his troops from Orvieto and the French army. Three days later, on 18 October, Pius III died and Cesare's position was more isolated than ever.

The situation on the death of Pius III was now substantially different to that at the death of Alexander two months earlier. The French army had departed from the scene and with it any hope of a serious French candidate in the forthcoming election. Giuliano della Rovere, by his vociferous denials of French affiliations during the previous conclave, had not only reassured many Italian cardinals but had also convinced the Spanish cardinals that his election need not be regarded as a political defeat for their king. Already the most powerful candidate the month before, Giuliano now appeared unbeatable, and there was scarcely any discussion of possible rivals. In these circumstances Cesare's decision to support his old enemy was hardly surprising. Machiavelli who had once more arrived at the scene as Florentine observer commented both at the time, and later in the *Prince*, that Cesare was deluded and blind to trust a man whom his family had so sorely offended.[4] But in reality he had no alternative; it had already been proved in the previous conclave that the Spanish cardinals were not under his control to the extent that was sometimes thought. It is extremely unlikely that he could have taken these votes away from Giuliano, nor did there seem to be any likely alternative candidate to whom he could have shifted them. He therefore came to an agreement with Giuliano, an agreement in which his position was strengthened by his possession of Castel Sant'Angelo and his supposed influence over the Spanish cardinals. With these weapons he was able to extract from Giuliano a promise of confirmation in all his offices and his vicariates in return for his support in the election. He hoped, and with some justification, that the promise, publicly given and guaranteed by the Spanish cardinals, could not be lightly set aside.

With this support assured the result of the conclave was a foregone conclusion. For once the old Roman adage that 'he who enters a conclave as Pope leaves it a cardinal' was to be confounded, and also once again, the ostentatious bribery to which Giuliano resorted to round off his voting strength, probably made no difference to the election. After the shortest conclave in the history of the Papacy, Giuliano was declared Pope Julius II on 1 November. On the same day Cesare surrendered Castel Sant'Angelo and took up residence in the Vatican. It was reported in Rome that his influence and that of the Spanish cardinals seemed to be fully restored.[5]

It was a few days after this that Machiavelli had his first interview with Cesare on 5 November and found him completely changed from the decisive and resolute figure whom he had so admired in the Romagna. Machiavelli's observations were confirmed by others including the Bishop of Elna, Cesare's old confidant, who remarked 'he has lost his head and does not know himself what he wants to do. He is fretful and irresolute'.[6] Cesare in fact was beginning to realise that his decision to support Giuliano, inevitable though it seemed, was not going to pay off. Julius, although never anything less than a bitter enemy of the Borgias, was still uncertain what to do about Cesare. He was very aware of the dangers of Venetian infiltration in the Romagna and realised that the overthrow of Cesare would leave a vacuum into which he, as Pope, had not for the moment any real strength that he could insert. He toyed with the idea of confirming Cesare's position in the Romagna as a counter to Venice until such time as he was strong enough to take over himself. But at the same time he had the greatest fear that once Cesare was re-established he would become too powerful and independent. Being essentially a blunt and outspoken man, he soon let it be known that his ultimate aim was direct Church control of the Romagna regardless of both Cesare and the Venetians. He also withheld confirmation of Cesare's post as Captain General and in every way made it clear that Cesare could expect little long-term support from him. It was the realisation of the total insecurity, and indeed hopelessness of his position, that was beginning to destroy Cesare's confidence and resolution. He had continued to play his cards with some skill for ten weeks after his father's death and had maintained a considerable influence on events in Rome and the Romagna. But Machiavelli now found him at a very low ebb and was not surprisingly disillusioned by what he saw.

Cesare, however, still had two factors in his favour; the friendship and support of the Spanish cardinals, and the loyalty of his Spanish commanders in the Romagna fortresses. Borgia confidence in the effectiveness of good fortifications was more than justified by the total inability of either the

Venetians or Julius to do anything about Cesare's control of the castles of Forlì, Cesena and Bertinoro. He also sought to strengthen the dynastic position of the family by proposing marriages between his daughter Louise and Francesco Maria della Rovere, the heir to the Duchy of Urbino, and young Giovanni Borgia and a niece of Venanzio Varano. By the middle of November with Julius still undecided about his next move, Cesare was negotiating with Florence for a *condotta* or at least for a safe conduct through Florentine territory to the Romagna. He still had a small force of troops and hoped that Florentine hostility to Venice would lead to the Tuscan republic welcoming his assistance. But Florence, warned by Machiavelli that Cesare was unlikely to get any long-term support from the Pope, refused his requests. Nevertheless on 18 November Cesare left Rome for Ostia from where he planned to take his troops by sea to Leghorn and then march across to the Romagna.

At the same moment news arrived in Rome that Faenza had surrendered to the Venetians. Julius was furious and when the Venetian ambassador protested that his government was not fighting the Church but the Borgias, the Pope felt that the moment had come to demand from Cesare the surrender of the remaining strongholds lest they also should fall into the hands of the Venetians. Messengers were sent after Cesare at Ostia to demand the surrender which was promptly refused. Cesare was then arrested and brought to Rome.

The negotiations which occupied the next five months were concerned with the surrender of the Romagna castles on the one side and guarantees of Cesare's liberty and moveable possessions on the other. Cesare was threatened with imprisonment in Castel Sant'Angelo but was allowed to spend December and January confined in the Torre Borgia. At an early stage he agreed to hand over the castles and gave the necessary passwords to the papal envoys. Machiavelli once again felt that Cesare was playing into the hands of his enemies and that his life would be worth little once the fortresses were handed over. 'It seems to me that this Duke of ours, little by little, is slipping down to his grave'.[7] Don Michele and the Borgia cavalry who had been sent overland to the Romagna were captured by Baglione, and in Rome Guidobaldo da Montefeltro was pressing for the return of his library, while Florence sought an indemnity out of Cesare's personal fortune which was banked in Genoa for the damage she had suffered during the 1501 invasion. But whether acting purely out of loyalty to their master, or whether on secret instructions, the castellans refused to surrender until Cesare was freed. Bearing in mind Cesare's persistent belief in his ability to recover his position in the Romagna, it seems likely that the castellans were acting on instructions. Julius was so angry when he heard of this refusal of the Spanish castellans, that the Spanish and Borgia factions remaining in the Vatican were seriously alarmed for their safety. Cardinals Luis Borgia and Remolino fled to Naples. But the final victory of the Spanish in Naples at the battle of Garigliano at the turn of the year seemed to strengthen the hands of Cesare and the Spanish cardinals in Rome. On 29 January a formal agreement was signed by which Cesare guaranteed that he would force the castellans to surrender within forty days in return for his liberty as soon as the surrender was complete. To protect him against any duplicity on the part of the Pope, he was transferred to the care of Cardinal Carvajal in Ostia.

In April the fortresses of Cesena and Bertinoro were finally surrendered and Cesare had ostensibly offered Gonsalvo de Mirafonte, the commander in Forlì, a compensation of 15,000 ducats if he would surrender; an offer which had been apparently accepted. At this stage Carvajal felt that Cesare's side of the bargain was now completed and allowed him to leave. A galley was waiting to take him to Naples where he was greeted with reserve by Gonsalvo de Cordoba, and with enthusiasm by the Borgia cardinals and by his brother Jofrè.

Cesare's escape from the clutches of the Pope seems to have restored his confidence to some extent. The castle at Forlì had not yet surrendered, and he still felt that he had a chance, if he could get to the Romagna with a small force, of establishing himself there and surviving against all attacks. He started collecting troops and tried to persuade Gonsalvo to give him some assistance. But Gonsalvo de Cordoba and his masters, Ferdinand and Isabella, were not prepared to assist Cesare in his adventures. The Spanish monarchs, now masters of Naples, wanted to be on good terms with the Pope, and Ferdinand when he heard that Cesare had arrived in Naples wrote apologising to Julius for unintentionally sheltering the Borgia and ordered Gonsalvo to arrest him.

So it was that when Cesare went to take leave of Gonsalvo on the eve of his departure with his small group of followers on a last, desperate enterprise, he was placed under arrest and imprisoned in Castel Nuovo. For three months Gonsalvo de Mirafonte in the castle at Forlì persisted in his resistance in the belief that Cesare might still have some use for the castle. But finally in August 1504 word seems to have reached him that his master had given up hope and that he genuinely no longer wished the castle to hold out. On 10 August Gonsalvo de Mirafonte marched out with the Borgia standard defiantly flying and 200 archers behind him. The last of Cesare's guarantees had gone and within days he was on board a Spanish galley and on his way to prison in Spain. There was much debate both at the time and later as to whether Gonsalvo de Cordoba, the Great Captain, had broken his word to Cesare and revoked his own safe conduct. An original personal safe conduct may have been granted to Cesare, but it was clear from the start that Gonsalvo and Spain would not help him against the Pope, and indeed his activities in Naples preparing an expedition against a friendly power provided adequate justification for revoking any safe conduct there may have been. It has also been suggested that Cesare was offered his freedom in return for the surrender of Forlì and that this promise was again broken, but it seems unlikely that Cesare would have been convinced by such a promise.[8]

He was sent at first to the castle at Chinchilla, two miles outside Valencia, and it was thus that the one-time archbishop visited his diocese for the first time.[9] However after an attempt to kill the governor he was moved to the royal fortress at Medina del Campo, far from the sea and any chance of escape. But escape he did in 1506 with the help of the Castilian nobles opposed to Ferdinand, and he sought refuge with his brother-in-law, the King of Navarre. When the news of his escape reached Italy there was a tremor of excitement. Julius was seriously alarmed at the thought of what might happen if he reappeared in the Romagna, where there was still at least an element in the population which looked back with nostalgia to his rule. Lucrezia was highly excited; the Venetians surprisingly alarmed. But there was little that Cesare could now do without influential support. His Valence estates and revenues had been confiscated by Louis XII; his supporters were scattered. In the next year, 1507, he was killed in a skirmish at Viana fighting for his brother-in-law in a civil war. It was an obscure death after the excitement of the preceding years, but one that was noted with satisfaction and relief in many quarters, and with regret and nostalgia in a few. The magnificent memorial raised to him in the church of Santa Maria in Viana was destroyed at the end of the seventeenth century by a fanatical bishop who thought that the church was profaned by the presence of the ashes of Cesare Borgia.

With the death of Alexander VI and the passing from the Italian scene of Cesare, the story of the Borgias is often seen to end—in failure. Everything which they had striven for, whether it was dynastic control of Central Italy or the strengthening of the Renaissance Papacy, seemed to have fallen in ruins. Within hours of Alexander's death the Orsini and the Colonna were riding hard for Rome; within days the standards of the exiled vicars were beginning to appear in the Romagna cities. The duchies of the infant Borgia dukes disintegrated; on every side the name of Borgia was reviled and cursed. But had the story ended? Was nothing permanent achieved?

Alexander himself was not easily forgotten. He was a man who dominated his surroundings both by his personality and by his activities. Sensual and yet in many respects austere; worldly and yet exhibiting an almost naive spiritual faith; frank in his appearance and yet often almost unbelievably devious in his actions; his character presented a maze of contradictions which bewildered his contemporaries. He brought scandal on the Church by ostentatiously flouting normal conventions of papal behaviour, and yet as Pope his alliance was sought by the great powers of Europe, his army was the strongest in Italy, his capital a centre of European diplomacy. As a result, on his death the prestige of the Papacy as a force in European politics had probably rarely been higher, but the prestige of the Pope as a spiritual leader can scarcely have been lower.

When Pietro Dolfini, the general of Camaldolese monks, wrote to Pius III on his election that he felt as if he had come out of the shadows into the light, he was thinking of the wars and violence which Borgia rule had produced.[10] It was true that, although Alexander had done as much as anyone to avoid the foreign invasions and the international wars which were beginning to destroy Italy, his internal policies were violent and destructive of the old order in Central Italy. The aim of these policies is the great problem of the Borgia story.

Where did the pursuance of the temporal power of the Renaissance Papacy end and Borgia dynasticism begin? Was it true that 'this Pope has no care for aught but of exalting his children by hook or by crook',[11] or was the legacy which Alexander wished to hand over to his successors a unified, well-governed Papal State which could play a part in the future of Italy? The answer seems to be that the two were so closely intertwined that they became inseparable; inseparable to such an extent that it might well be argued that the ultimate Borgia aim was permanent Borgia control of a strong Papacy. It seems clear that the intention was that Cesare should be able to control the papal election after his father's death. This was papal dynasticism carried to a logical extreme and the events of the months after Alexander's death showed how close it came to achievement.

Cesare, despite his illness, despite the incomplete nature of his control of the Romagna, and despite the unfavourable political circumstances which placed two major armies within reach of Rome at the time of the conclave, was still a force to be reckoned with. His alliance appeared to be necessary to both the two succeeding Popes. His troops and his supporters were decisive factors in the Romagna for a year after his own departure from the scene.

Neither Julius nor Ferdinand were prepared to put an end to him as they realised his potential value; but at the same time they guarded him with great care because they still feared what he might do if he escaped.

But nevertheless this central aim of Borgia dynasticism did fail. No Borgias were able to maintain their position in Central Italy and the efforts to create that position had irrevocably damaged Alexander's reputation. 'This Pope,' as Sigismondo de' Conti remarked, 'if he had not had children and so much affection for them would have left a better memory of himself.'[12] For despite the apparent failure of his policies the task of establishing papal authority in the Pope's own state was basically done. The Roman barons and the Romagna vicars were never to be the same problem again and the successes of Julius II owed a great deal to the foundations laid by the Borgias.

Similarly despite the apparent failure of dynastic policies in Central Italy, despite the disappearance of Cesare and the Dukes of Camerino and Sermoneta, Borgia dynastic influence was to live on. In Spain, in France, in Ferrara and in Naples heirs of the hated Borgias were established in impregnable positions. It is in these directions that we must now turn for our concluding chapters.

CHAPTER TWELVE

THE BORGIA DYNASTY

A few years after the death of Alexander VI Marcantonio Altieri remarked that 'all the Borgia had been uprooted from the soil and cast out as poisonous plants, hated by God and noxious to man'.[1] Certainly in the Rome of Julius II there was little hope of advancement for the Borgia family. All their territorial possessions were stripped from the young Borgia dukes; the Borgia cardinals, of whom six remained, went in fear of their lives. But the cardinals were able to survive as they were Spaniards and useful instruments of Spanish policy in a time of Spanish military predominance in the peninsula. Only Cardinal Francesco Borgia fell seriously foul of Julius II. He rashly expressed bitter feelings about the Della Rovere Pope in letters to Lucrezia at Ferrara which fell into the Pope's hands. He was arrested and imprisoned, and only released on the demand of the whole Sacred College. However he then joined Carvajal and the French cardinals in their abortive attempt to depose Julius at the Council of Pisa in 1511; he was stripped of his cardinalate and died of apoplexy in Pisa.

But even in Rome the purge was not complete. Isabella Borgia-Matuzzi lived on comfortably in her house in the Via dei Leutari until 1547. In 1519 she wrote to the Este family condoling with them on the death of Lucrezia. Her daughter Giulia married Ciriaco Mattei of a Roman noble family of some substance, and a daughter of this marriage married into the Pamfili family and was the grandmother of Pope Innocent X. Vanozza the mother of four of Alexander's children, died in 1518 much respected by the Augustinian monks of Santa Maria del Popolo to whom she left considerable endowments in her will. Masses were still being said for her soul in Santa Maria del Popolo 150 years later.[2]

The young Borgias on whom so much care had been lavished during the final years of Alexander's pontificate were particularly vulnerable after his death. A good deal of mystery still surrounds the children whom Alexander fathered as Pope. Rumours that he was the father of Laura Orsini, the daughter of Giulia Farnese, were inevitable but are now generally discredited. Alexander showed no interest in the child during his lifetime, and after his death Laura was married in 1505 to Niccolò della Rovere. That such an alliance was permitted by Julius II to his own family and with the ceremonies taking place in the Vatican, makes it extremely unlikely that Laura was a Borgia. She inherited from her father the lordship of Bassanello, and the possession of this Campagna fortress made her a significant acquisition for the ambitious Della Rovere family.

Giovanni, the *Infans Romanus*, derived little benefit from his Borgia parenthood whether it was Alexander or Cesare who was his father. Together with Rodrigo, the son of Lucrezia, he was in Castel Sant' Angelo with Cesare in October 1503, but soon afterwards was taken to Naples for safety and placed in the care of Sancia. In 1505 he was brought northwards and under the supervision of Lucrezia was placed in the household of Alberto Pio, the humanist lord of Carpi. For the next few years he was frequently resident in Ferrara and recognised as Lucrezia's half-brother. He accompanied Alfonso d'Este on a journey to France in 1518, but the Ferrarese courtiers despaired of making anything of him; he was indolent and capricious, and was only tolerated for Lucrezia's sake.[3] After her death in 1519 he disappeared, briefly to re-appear in 1527 when, on the death of Giovanni Maria Varano, he made a vain attempt to recover the duchy of Camerino by litigation. Although enjoying the titles of Roman patrician and papal envoy, in 1546 he was again litigating with a certain Margherita Bosia to whom he owed a few ducats. He died in 1548 in Genoa leaving considerable estates in Valencia.[4]

The third of the children often attributed to Alexander while he was Pope was Rodrigo, born in 1503. Nothing was known of this boy until a Bull of Leo X recognised his existence and his paternity. He entered a monastery at that time and subsequently became abbot of Cicciano di Nola. There are no reasons for rejecting the claim that Alexander was the father of this Rodrigo apart from the Pope's advanced age, but at the same time there is no evidence for the story that he was also the son of Giulia Farnese.[5] It seems clear that the relationship between Alexander and Giulia had ended long before 1503.

The other Rodrigo, Lucrezia's eldest son, Duke of Bisceglie and Sermoneta, was also in Sancia's care in Naples by the end of 1503. On Sancia's death in 1506 he was transferred to the household of Isabella d'Aragona, the widow of Giangaleazzo Sforza, at Bari. There he died in 1512. Lucrezia, who never saw her son after her departure for Ferrara, was deeply upset by his death. Her love for Alfonso was widely commented on and the separation from her son by him was yet another sacrifice which she was forced to make for the sake of her family.

Obscurity was also the fate of Cesare's two illegitimate children, Camilla and Girolamo. Camilla, probably born in Ferrara after Cesare's visit there in September 1502, was brought up by her aunt Lucrezia and, on entering the convent of San Bernardino in Ferrara, took the name of Lucrezia. She became abbess of the convent and died in 1573 widely respected for her piety and intelligence. Girolamo was also brought up in Ferrara, and he remained there after Lucrezia's death as Alfonso d'Este had taken a liking to him.[6] He married twice in the lower ranks of the Italian nobility, on the second occasion to the daughter of Alberto Pio da Carpi, who may also have acted as his guardian in his youth. After a violent career in which he was reputedly responsible for at least one murder, he died leaving two daughters whose subsequent careers are unknown.

However, when we turn our attention to the legitimate descendants of the four children of Vanozza, the central figures of Borgia dynasticism, the obscurity, and indeed notoriety, surrounding the family after 1503 disappears. Charlotte d'Albret had spent only two or three months with Cesare in the summer of 1499 and after his departure for Italy in the suite of Louis XII she never saw him again. In May 1500 she gave birth to her only child, Louise, who in the next three years was to play a part in Borgia dynastic arrangements. In August 1502 she was betrothed to Federigo Gonzaga as part of Cesare's plans for the protection of the frontiers of the Romagna. Then in the autumn of 1503 there was talk of a betrothal to Francesco Maria della Rovere as Cesare sought vainly for a reconciliation with Julius II. But throughout this period Louise remained with her mother in France. Alexander seemed anxious to bring Charlotte and her daughter to Italy, but Cesare made no move to do so. Charlotte, after an initial resistance to the marriage which was forced on her by Louis XII, became morbidly obsessed with the memory of her husband. She seems to have made little effort to join him in Italy, but she managed the French estates with great ability and after Cesare's imprisonment in Spain tried hard to raise support for him at the French court.[7]

When she heard of the death of Cesare, Charlotte and Louise went into deep mourning. From that day until her death in

1514 the widowed Duchess of Valence surrounded herself in black. The walls of her chateau of La Motte-Feuilly were hung with black crepe; she and her daughter slept between black sheets and they ate off black decorated plates; the mules which they rode had saddles and bridles edged with black velvet.[8] Louise was rescued from this macabre environment by the death of her mother, when she was transferred to the care of Louise d'Angoulême, the mother of Francis I. In 1517 she was married as a considerable heiress to the elderly and distinguished soldier Louis de la Tremouille. The French chronicler, Hilarion de Coste, described Louise as 'a very noble and virtuous lady, heiress to the perfections as well as the riches of her mother . . . a lady as chaste, virtuous and gentle as her father was possessed, cruel and wicked'.[9] However she was by repute not an attractive girl, short and ugly with a pock-marked forehead.

Tremouille was killed at the battle of Pavia in 1525 leaving Louise still childless and once more under the protection of the royal family. In 1530 she was married to Philippe de Bourbon-Busset, the head of a younger and illegitimate branch of the Bourbon family. Philippe was also a soldier, but before his death at the battle of St. Quentin in 1557 Louise bore him six children, six grandchildren of Cesare Borgia. Of these two died young but the remainder grew up to positions of consequence in the French nobility.[10] Claude de Bourbon, the eldest son, was a soldier like his father and lieutenant general in Limousin; he married Marguerite, daughter of Antoine de la Rochefoucauld, admiral of the galleys. He recovered a considerable indemnity from the French crown for the Borgia French estates which had been seized by Louis XII. Jean, born in 1537, married Euchariste de la Brosse, daughter of the French ambassador in Scotland.

One of the titles which Louise took to her second husband was that of Dame de Chalus, and the Bourbon counts of

Busset and Chalus survive to this day as direct descendants of Cesare Borgia. The family has never played an important part in French history. It produced a steady stream of competent soldiers; Louis de Bourbon-Busset was lieutenant general of artillery and killed at the siege of Fribourg in 1677; François Louis Antoine commanded a cavalry regiment at Dettingen and Hastenbeck in the War of the Austrian Succession, and became a marshal in 1761; François Louis Joseph was imprisoned in the Luxembourg at the age of twelve in 1794, and subsequently fought in Napoleon's armies in Poland and in Spain. He was captured at Albufera and after imprisonment in England joined the emigré forces on the allied side at Waterloo. He died a lieutenant general in 1856.

On turning to consider the life of Lucrezia after her departure from Rome in January 1502, we are confronted with the picture frequently painted by Borgia historians of a girl almost completely transformed. From being the arch-enchantress, the Messalina of the Vatican, she becomes the Duchess of Ferrara, honoured by poets and courtiers, the mother of a happy family and the founder of monasteries. This is the picture which contemporary reports and opinions encourage us to create, but it is both implausible and unhistorical.[11] Nowhere are the dangers of basing a history of the Borgias solely on the opinions of their contemporaries more fully revealed than in the story of Lucrezia. Lucrezia in Rome was a pleasure-loving adolescent caught in the toils of her father's diplomatic and dynastic policies. She loved dancing, fine clothes and parties, but she was already showing signs of a flair for administration. She may have had an illegitimate child in 1498 but if she did he was conceived in the convent of San Sisto to which she had retired to avoid the humiliations to which her divorce from Giovanni Sforza subjected her. Suitors from all over Italy competed for her hand when the ambitions or the violence of her family made her free to marry again. But the choice either of ending one marriage or in arranging another was never hers.

When Lucrezia went to Ferrara one significant change did take place. She escaped from the shadow of her formidable father and brother and came out into the limelight on her own. Although the Ferrarese envoy, Castellini, had reported from Rome that the sinister stories about her were not to be believed, the Este family watched her like hawks, noting every indiscretion and commenting on every action.[12] At the same time, although much of the praise and admiration lavished on her by the poets and humanists of Ferrara was courtly convention, there was not a complete absence of shrewd observation from this quarter. But while Lucrezia was judged more carefully and more on her own merits in Ferrara than she had been in Rome, the overall picture which emerges is not one of any dramatic change in her character or her behaviour.

Lucrezia in 1502 at the age of twenty-one was 'of medium height, delicate in appearance, her face rather long as also is her finely cut nose; her hair golden, her eyes greyish, the mouth rather large with brilliantly white teeth; the throat smooth and white, yet becomingly full. Her whole being breathes laughing good humour and gaiety.'[13] Probably none of the painted portraits attributed to Lucrezia are authentic, particularly not the famous St. Catherine of Pinturicchio in the Borgia apartments which was painted when she was thirteen, and so we are forced to rely on the medals and on verbal descriptions. The latter vary somewhat in the assessment of her physical beauty, but all convey the impression of gaiety, charm and gentleness. These qualities in themselves would have made her an attraction at the court of Ferrara noted for its entertainments and its brilliant attendants, yet presided over by a family which seemed to be singularly devoid of spontaneity. Ercole d'Este, the old duke, was avaricious and sombrely religious. He delighted in the company of ascetic monks and nuns, and had at one time been a friend of Savonarola. He was also a dedicated politician and devoted to the calculated advancement of his family. His patronage was particularly directed towards architecture and the theatre, but it was an unbroken succession of the plays of Plautus which he had considered suitable for the festivities to welcome his new daughter-in-law. The *Menaechmi* which had caused Alexander to erupt with frustrated boredom in 1493 on the occasion of Lucrezia's marriage to Giovanni Sforza, was once again the centrepiece of the celebrations for her marriage to Alfonso d'Este. Alfonso himself, apart from a notorious interest in women, was best known for his rather uncourtly pursuits. He was a passionate student of military theory and particularly of the potential of artillery. His interest in cannon involved him in the actual practical side of casting them as well as in the study of their use in war, and the workshop, rather than the ballroom or even the council chamber, was his natural ambience. His practical bent also showed itself in his proficiency as a potter and a decorator of ceramics, and in his skill as a musician. Even his famous sister Isabella, wife of Francesco Gonzaga Duke of Mantua, although a famous patroness and a great Renaissance beauty, inspired in her courtiers as much awe and restrained respect as spontaneous admiration and courtly enthusiasm.

It was Isabella who subjected Lucrezia to the most searching scrutiny on her arrival in Ferrara. She regarded her as a rival and was determined to outdo her at everything. Ercole, outwardly friendly and genuinely surprised and pleased by his new daughter-in-law, was mean over her settlement and suspicious of her extravagant Spanish and Roman attendants whom he gradually drove away from the court. Alfonso, at first non-committal and persistently inattentive towards his wife, gradually warmed to her to some extent, but remained always suspicious of her and solicitous only when she was pregnant. In this atmosphere of supicion and distrust, Lucrezia's first reaction was to withdraw into herself. She clung desperately to those non-Ferrarese attendants who were left to her; she protested bitterly about Ercole's meanness and maintained close contact with her father and Cesare. In the autumn of 1502 she was desperately ill and lost her first child by Alfonso d'Este. To convalesce she retired to the convent of Corpus Domini and this was to set a pattern of periodic retreats which became a feature of her life in Ferrara.

The death of Alexander and the collapse of Borgia fortunes in 1503 left Lucrezia dangerously isolated. Ercole did not hide his satisfaction at the death of the Pope, and Louis XII suggested that Alfonso's marriage should now be dissolved. But Lucrezia survived, not so much because she had already won her way into the heart of Alfonso and the Ferrarese, as because divorce was a humiliating business even for the side demanding it and the dowry would have had to be repaid, and because Cesare's influence and possible threat in the Romagna continued for some months after Alexander's death. Lucrezia even managed to raise some money for troops to help protect her brother's fortresses, and Ercole was not averse to seeing a continuance of Cesare's authority in the Romagna if it meant holding back the Venetians.

The one consolation for Lucrezia during this difficult period was the admiration and sympathy of the Ferrarese humanists, Pietro Bembo, and particularly Ercole Strozzi, whose influence both in literary and political circles was considerable. Strozzi, the lame poet-courtier, was a great consolation both through his personal friendship and through the stream of adulatory poems which he produced to soothe Lucrezia's bruised spirits. He also acted as go-between in Lucrezia's correspondence first with Bembo and later with

Francesco Gonzaga. The exact relationship between Lucrezia and Bembo in the period 1503–5 has provoked considerable discussion.[14] The passionate nature of the poems and letters which passed between them have led some to see the relationship as more than platonic; on the other hand Bembo was a humanist steeped in the romantic tradition of Petrarchan courtly love, and even the more extravagant of his passionate letters should not necessarily be taken at their face value. Lucrezia craved admiration and Bembo was the perfect foil to the uninspiring solidness of Alfonso, but it seems unlikely that Lucrezia would have run the terrifying risks of allowing him to be any more than an admirer.

Early in 1505 Ercole died. Alfonso, hurrying back from a journey to France and England, only just reached Ferrara in time and it was fortunate that he did so as there were bitter and longstanding rivalries amongst the sons of Ercole. The most prominent of these were Ippolito, a cardinal and yet the most worldly and naturally talented of the family, and Giulio, an illegitimate son of Ercole, a handsome, headstrong young man who was by no means reconciled to his junior position. Within a year of Alfonso's succession trouble had broken out in the family partly as a result of the activities of the flirtatious Angela Borgia-Lanzol, who had accompanied Lucrezia to Ferrara and remained with her as lady-in-waiting. Both Ippolito and Giulio were suitors for Angela's favours. In a fit of jealous fury Ippolito ordered his men to attack Giulio and they succeeded in half blinding him. Alfonso, anxious to keep the peace and loath to lose the services and support of the able cardinal, failed to take strong measures against him, and Giulio planned his revenge against both his rival and the Duke. His conspiracy, in league with Alfonso's legitimate younger brother Fernando, was betrayed and both Giulio and Fernando were imprisoned for life.

Lucrezia was now Duchess, and this, together with the fact

that suspicious attention was to some extent diverted from her by the family dissensions, made her position much more secure. Her natural gaiety and vivacity began to assert themselves and she began to play an increasing part in the government of the Duchy. Alfonso continued his custom of making long journeys abroad inspecting fortifications and talking to artillery experts, and in his absences Lucrezia and Cardinal Ippolito acted as joint regents. Lucrezia took on herself the task of dealing with the complaints and petitions of the Ferrarese, and in this role and by her assumption of the role of leader of the court she began to gain that popularity in Ferrara which historians have noted. She also directed the redecoration of the ducal apartments bringing Giovanni Bellini and Bartolomeo Veneto from Venice to work with the Ferrarese painter, Garofalo.[15]

Meanwhile Bembo had returned to Venice and, although his letters continued, his ardour gradually cooled. Soon only the dedicatory letter of the *Asolani* was left as public affirmation of his great love. Lucrezia had turned to an even more dangerous flirtation with Francesco Gonzaga. She had met Gonzaga many years before when he came to Rome as the hero of Fornovo and had attended her court in the palace of Santa Maria in Portico. He was an ugly but fascinating man and the husband of Lucrezia's great rival Isabella d'Este. This may have tempted her to gain some malicious pleasure from a secret liaison with Francesco. But certainly one of the original motives of seeking his friendship was to gain an influential ally for Cesare. Lucrezia never ceased her efforts to bring about her brother's release and Francesco Gonzaga was prepared to help her. Cesare's death in 1507 was a great blow to Lucrezia. Alfonso was away from Ferrara when the news came and Ippolito hesitated to tell her, knowing her great love for her brother. When she knew she retired to the convent for two days of seclusion and prayer, but otherwise was not as severely affected as Ippolito had feared. The correspondence with Francesco Gonzaga continued with Ercole Strozzi as the intermediary; but once again we do not know how much the affair meant. Even in 1509 when Gonzaga was a prisoner of the Venetians and even his wife could not get word to him, Lucrezia succeeded in getting a letter of comfort through. But by this time Ercole Strozzi was no longer the carrier of Lucrezia's letters. A year before he had been murdered in the streets of Ferrara a few months after he had married Barbara Torelli, the beautiful ex-wife of Giovanni Bentivoglio. It is probable that the Bentivoglio were responsible for the murder, but there were not lacking those who connected Lucrezia with the crime either in the role of avenger of a faithless lover, or as a party to the elimination of her messenger who knew too much.

How much Alfonso knew or suspected of Lucrezia's clandestine affairs we cannot tell, but by 1509 her position had been made much more secure by the birth and survival of an heir. Her first son, named Alessandro after his grandfather, had lived only a month, but in 1508 Ercole II was born and with his survival the future of the house of Este was for the time being assured. It was as well because the last years of the pontificate of Julius II were full of danger for Alfonso. In 1509 with the League of Cambrai formed against Venice he was named Captain General of the Church. But when in the next year Julius changed his policy and came to terms with Venice in order to drive the French out of Italy, Alfonso, always the friend of France, was left in a difficult position. With French encouragement and believing that there was still a chance of taking some territory off Venice, he persisted in the anti-Venetian alliance. Julius was secretly delighted at having the chance to attack one of his more powerful vicars and placed Ferrara under an Interdict. He prepared to lead an army in person against the city.

But as long as the French remained in Italy Alfonso was safe. He fought with his artillery on their side at the battle of Ravenna, and after the battle the French victors were welcomed with great honour in Ferrara. Amongst the French leaders was the Chevalier Bayard, and his contemporary biographer wrote of Lucrezia: 'the good duchess received the French before all the others with every mark of favour. She is a pearl in this world. She daily gave the most wonderful festivals and banquets in the Italian fashion. I venture to say that neither in her time nor for many years before has there been such a glorious princess, for she is beautiful and good, gentle and amiable to everyone, and nothing is more certain than this, that, although her husband is a skilful and brave prince, the above-named lady, by her graciousness, has been of great service to him.'[16] But Ravenna, although a victory for the French, had caused them such severe losses that they were now forced to retreat and abandon Ferrara to the mercy of the Pope. Alfonso hurried to Rome to make his submission and Lucrezia was once again left in charge in Ferrara. Alfonso's absence was longer than he had expected as he found a very hostile reception awaiting him in Rome and he was forced to seek refuge with the Colonna at Marino. It was some months before he succeeded in making his way back to Ferrara in disguise.

Those anxious days for Lucrezia and Alfonso ended with the death of Julius in 1513, and the last six years of her life passed in relative tranquillity. She still retained her passion for dancing and singing although frequent difficult pregnancies sapped her strength. Her increasing spiritual preoccupations showed themselves in her patronage of the Ferrarese convents and monasteries. In 1510 she founded the convent of San Bernardino, and at some stage she herself became a Franciscan tertiary. But to the end she also remained a Borgia; she corresponded with her mother Vanozza and welcomed at her court both Giovanni, the *Infans Romanus*, and the illegitimate children of Cesare. In 1519 she died after giving birth to a still-born child, and Alfonso, whatever his failings as a husband may have been, showed genuine sorrow at his loss.

Lucrezia left four surviving children. Ercole, who in 1534 succeeded his father as Duke, married Renée, the daughter of Louis XII of France. Ippolito, like his uncle and namesake, became a cardinal, and in 1550 when Governor of Tivoli he commissioned Pirro Ligorio to transform a Benedictine convent into the sumptuous Villa d'Este. Francesco became Marquis of Massalombarda, while his sister Eleanora was abbess of Lucrezia's favourite convent, Corpus Domini.

Lucrezia's descendants did not survive long as Dukes of Ferrara. Alfonso, her grandson, succeeded his father Ercole II in 1559, but he died childless in 1597 and the Duchy passed back under the direct control of the Pope. However, Lucrezia's other grandchildren, with their share of Borgia blood, held positions of international importance in the second half of the sixteenth century. Anna married Francis, Duke of Guise, and was the mother of the ill-fated Duke murdered in 1580 during the French Wars of Religion; Luigi became a cardinal; Lucrezia married the last Della Rovere Duke of Urbino, on whose death in the early seventeenth century Urbino like Ferrara fell under the direct control of the Church.

Meanwhile to the south in Calabria, the junior line of the Borgias also remained well entrenched. Jofrè had stood by Cesare in the first days after the death of Alexander, but he soon retired to Naples and was there to welcome his brother when he arrived in the spring of 1504. By this time there was an open breach between Jofrè and Sancia. Sancia, who had been rescued from Castel Sant'Angelo by Prospero Colonna in the previous autumn, was now his mistress and refused to allow Jofrè into her house. She however welcomed Cesare warmly and entertained him; she also became the guardian of Giovanni and Rodrigo Borgia.

Sancia died childless in 1506 and left Jofrè free to marry again. His estates had been somewhat curtailed in the general outburst against the Borgias, but he was still Prince of Squillace with large estates south of Catanzaro in Calabria. He now married Maria de Mila who is variously described as a niece of Ferdinand and as a niece of Adriana de Mila; in any event she was presumably a member of the family which was closely related to the Borgias. Maria bore Jofrè four children before his death in 1517, so the immediate future of the family was secured. His son Francesco succeeded to the title while his three daughters all made good marriages into the Neapolitan nobility. Antonia married the Marquis of Delicete, who was a descendant of the Piccolomini nephew of Pius II who had married into the Aragonese royal house; Lucrezia married a Carafa, and Maria, the Count of Simari, who was also a distant connection of the old Neapolitan royal family.[17]

The role of the Princes of Squillace during the next century was confined to that of landed nobility, and there is no evidence that they played any part in national or international affairs. Giovanni Battista Borgia, grandson of Jofrè and third Prince of Squillace, was responsible for the founding of the village of Borgia on his estates in 1547. The village, built in the hills south of Catanzaro, was founded as a refuge for the inhabitants of the two coastal villages of Palefrio and Magali which were being harassed by Turkish raids. Pietro Borgia, the fourth Prince, succeeded to the title in 1553, and, perhaps as a reflection of the declining economic vitality of southern Italy by the end of sixteenth century, spent the last years of his life gradually selling off his estates. He had only two daughters, Anna and Francesca. Anna, the heiress to the Squillace title, was married in 1602 to Francesco de Borja, Count of Mayalde, a descendant of Alexander's son Juan and one of the Spanish Borjas of Gandia.[18] The protracted negotiations for this marriage were directed by Philip II himself, and the union of the Italian and Spanish Borgia lines with the eventual union of the Gandia and Squillace titles was a dynastic alliance of some significance. Anna's sister, Francesca, married Michele Orsini, Duke of Gravina, a name and a title which echoed bitter memories of the events of a century earlier.

With the passing of the Squillace estates to the Spanish Borjas, the direct Italian descendants of Alexander VI died out. There remained, and still remain, Borgias in Italy, notably the Borgias of Velletri of whom Cardinal Stefano Borgia, the founder of the Museo Borgiano and a leading candidate in the conclave of 1799, was an outstanding descendant. But these Borgias, although perhaps distant offshoots of the Spanish family from an earlier emigration in the Middle Ages, were not connected with the Borgia Popes. For the most significant and lasting achievements of Alexander's dynastic policies we have now to turn our eyes to Spain, the natural home of the family, where the Dukes of Gandia carried the name of Borja into the middle of the eighteenth century.

CHAPTER THIRTEEN

ST. FRANCIS AND THE BORJAS OF GANDIA

The great ducal palace which dominates the little town of Gandia, south of Valencia, was the home of a long line of Borja descendants of Juan, the murdered son of Alexander VI. The palace was built in the fourteenth century and enlarged by both Pedro Luis and Juan. It was sacked during the revolt of the Germanias in 1520 and restored at the end of the seventeenth century and again in the late nineteenth century. As a result it is a strange blend of Gothic, Moorish, Italian Renaissance and Baroque styles. Although primarily Spanish in inspiration and partly Moorish in appearance, there are memories of Italy in the sunken gardens and in some of the decorative detail.[1] Here the Borgia bull, a symbol of violence and treachery for Italians, appears beside the relics of the life of St. Francis Borgia which make the palace to this day a place of pilgrimage.

Juan Borgia when he returned to Italy in the summer of 1496 to lead the papal army against the Orsini left behind him in this palace his young wife, Maria Enriquez, and a small son, Juan. Maria, who was a cousin of Ferdinand and daughter of the grand admiral of Castile, was also carrying a second child which was to be a daughter, Isabella. She was intensely religious and at the same time an extremely practical and determined woman. Widowed by the unknown Roman assassins of her husband in 1497, she devoted the next fifteen years of her life to the upbringing and material welfare of her children. Spanish to the core she had no time for the Italian adventures of her adopted family, particularly as she firmly believed the rumours that Cesare was the murderer of her husband. She sold all Juan's Neapolitan estates for 82,000 ducats to Ferdinand and used the proceeds to buy further Spanish lands for her son. These estates she managed so well that Juan, third Duke of Gandia, was an extremely wealthy man. Alexander no doubt resented this attitude of his daughter-in-law which cut him off from the children of his favourite son. He is said to have remarked bitterly that he did not care about the children of the Duke of Gandia, as they were closer to the King of Spain than to him.[2]

But it was for her religious zeal and her patronage of the churches of Gandia and of the Convent of the Poor Clares in the town that Maria Enriquez is best remembered. She enlarged the collegiate church of Gandia and commissioned the great altarpiece from the sculptor Damian Forment and the painter Paolo di San Leocadio.[3] This was the same painter who had first come to Valencia with Alexander in 1472 when he came on his Spanish legation. He had returned to Italy in the interval and absorbed some of the influences of late Quattrocento Italian styles, but was now given a permanent contract by the Borja family and came to reside in a house in Gandia built specially for him. The Convent of Santa Clara for which Pedro Luis had built a new church was the especial object of Maria's care. She longed to retire to its shady cloisters, and as soon as Juan had married and produced an heir she did so. She and her daughter Isabella, who also entered the convent about the same time, became the first of a long line of Borja nuns. Twenty-six other girls of the family joined the nuns of Santa Clara during the next two hundred years, providing an almost continuous succession of Borja abbesses. Each Borja duke in turn had aunts, sisters and daughters in the convent which became the natural object of their donations and the centre of the religious life of the family.[4]

Juan, third Duke of Gandia, brought up in this environment with both mother and sister destined for the monastic life, was himself a deeply religious man. While his sister is remembered for her devotional work *Holy Exercises and Spiritual Exhortations*, Juan had a special devotion for the Blessed Sacrament. Whenever he heard the bell which indicated that it was being carried to a sick or dying person, he would hurry from whatever he was doing to follow it and comfort the sufferer. But Juan was also Duke of Gandia, one of twenty Spanish noblemen recognised by Charles V as grandees, and it was to his family and to his estates that his first duty lay. His first wife was Juana de Aragon, grand-daughter of Ferdinand, daughter of the monarch's illegitimate son Alfonso, Archbishop of Saragossa. On her death in childbirth in 1520 he married Francesca de Castro, and his two wives together bore him seventeen children. He also had an illegitimate son at the age of fifteen, and within this extensive offspring was represented that strange combination of piety and worldly vice which characterised the Borgias and to some extent their age.

Of Juan's eighteen children the eldest Francesco was both a Spanish viceroy and a saint, two were cardinals, one an archbishop, and five were nuns. Of the remainder, four daughters married into the highest ranks of the Spanish nobility, and the sons were viceroys, soldiers and, in the case of Diego, a condemned and executed murderer. That a pious family tradition was not the only factor in leading so many Borja daughters into the Convent of Santa Clara was clear in the case of the children of Juan's first marriage. Only Luisa of the four daughters of Juana de Aragon spent her life outside the walls of the convent, and it was very much Juan's second marriage, the steady growth of a second group of Borja children, and the limitation of family funds for dowries, which created the situation in which Luisa's three sisters entered Santa Clara. There was something slightly incongruous in this as it was Luisa who was, of all the children of Juan, the most suited to conventual life. Instead she was married to Martin de Aragon, Duke of Villahermosa, and earned the title of 'The Holy Duchess' for her saintly life and good works.

However, the most famous of all the children of Juan was his eldest son Francesco, better known as St. Francis Borgia (or de Borja), third general of the Jesuits.[5] Born in 1510 he showed a precocious piety which was discouraged and to some extent suppressed by his father who, although devout himself, wished his eldest son to be a gentleman and true head of the family. In 1519 the revolt of the Germanias struck Gandia, and Juan evacuated his family to Peniscola while he took the field at the head of the royal army against the rebels. The ducal palace was sacked and the family permanently divided. Francis did not return to Gandia when his mother died and an unsympathetic step-mother took her place. He was, instead, sent to the household of his uncle, Juan de Aragon, Archbishop of Saragossa, to be brought up as a knight and a courtier. This was an upbringing which he could never have received at Gandia where his father was essentially the country gentleman, hating the court and suspicious of all foreign contacts.

The influence of the archbishop, himself the grandson of Ferdinand, was sufficient to get Francis appointed page to the Infanta Caterina, sister of Charles V, in 1522. Caterina lived with her mother, the mad queen Juana, in the castle of Tordesillas, and life in that household must have been a sore trial to the young Borja. On Caterina's marriage in Portugal, Francis returned to Saragossa and then in 1528 he was sent to the imperial court at Valladolid.

Francis made a great impact at the court of Charles V. He

was now a handsome young man of eighteen with thick dark hair, a long oval face, the high bridged Borja nose, and beautiful hands. Like so many of his family he had a remarkable fascination for women, but like few of them he fought hard to resist the temptations. He was modest and reserved in female company, and his chastity was regarded with some amusement at court. It was said that he put on a hair shirt when venturing into mixed society to remind himself of the dangers of the sins of the flesh. But at the same time he was widely respected as the epitome of the perfect knight: courteous, proud, a fine horseman and a talented administrator. He was welcomed by Charles V and the Empress Isabella as a relative rather than a subject and had unhindered access to the Emperor at all times. Charles also had a particular regard for the two Borja nuns in Santa Clara, Francis's grandmother and aunt, and is said to have remarked on one occasion: 'Ask your nuns to commend this business for me to God and see if they say anything about it; for I have never met persons more reliable than they are for knowing anything that is of importance to me.'[6]

In 1529 Francis married one of Isabella's Portuguese ladies in waiting, Eleanora de Castro, despite his father's objections to a foreign-born daughter-in-law. Francis is said to have got round his father's opposition by suggesting to Charles V that he invite the Duke to court to discuss the matter. When Charles sent the invitation, Juan hurriedly agreed to the marriage rather than be forced to leave his estates and attend at court. On his marriage Francis was created Marquis of Lombay, and he and his wife became even closer associates of the Emperor and Empress. When Charles left for Italy in 1530, it was Francis Borgia who became virtual controller of the household and chief adviser to Isabella. It has frequently been maintained, perhaps as an extension of the Borgia legend, that Francis's relations with the Empress were of an equivocal nature. But it is highly unlikely that there was anything more than the romantic devotion which female rulers of the time were accustomed to receive from their courtiers, added in this case to the genuine personal friendship with which both Francis and his wife were treated by the Imperial family. Francis, in addition to his other duties, was tutor and companion to Prince Philip.

In 1536 Francis accompanied Charles V on his campaign in Provence. It was his first experience of military life in the field and he found it something of a disillusionment. The sordid barbarity of much of the fighting and the wretched living conditions did not fit in with his rather romantic ideas. He saw one of his best friends, Garcilasse de la Vega, the poet, die a pain-racked death before the walls of Toulon. In the following year he fell very seriously ill and during a long convalescence occupied his mind with spiritual reading. Much has been written about the dual nature of Francis Borgia's life; some have seen his ultimate decision to join the Jesuits as the result of a sudden conversion, a moment of blinding inspiration; others have described him as the 'Jesuit in disguise', a brooding ascetic who was always unsuited to the life of the world but who was held to it by his family and by his sense of duty. The truth is that Francis's determination to change his life evolved very gradually. He was certainly always a religious man but at the same time not always an ascetic, and was for many years utterly involved in a secular career. But a long series of disillusionments and experiences gradually turned the Spanish grandee into a Jesuit priest. In fact the difference was not perhaps as great as it seems but this is a point to which we shall return.

One of the most significant of the experiences which affected Francis's career was the death of the Empress Isabella in 1539. Francis and Eleanora were responsible for all the funeral arrangements; Eleanora laid out the body and her husband accompanied the coffin on the long funeral journey to Granada. There, before the coffin was closed forever, tradition demanded that senior members of the court should inspect the remains so that they could swear that all was in order. After a long journey across Spain in high summer the corpse of his beloved Empress must have been a harrowing sight for Francis, but there is no evidence that the opening of the coffin in Granada was the decisive moment of conversion for him. There was no dramatic vow of chastity, no immediate renunciation of secular ties as older historians have maintained. Francis in later years did remember the anniversary of the death of Isabella, but not the anniversary of the last rites in Granada. It would be an exaggeration to say that the only impact of these events was that they left Francis and Eleanora without their jobs in the household of the Empress, but this was certainly one of the results. The vacuum was filled by Francis's nomination as Viceroy in Catalonia, a post which he took up in the same year.

Catalonia, and particularly its capital Barcelona, were serious trouble spots at this time. The union of the Spanish crowns brought about by the marriage of Ferdinand and Isabella had resulted in increasing Castilian predominance over the peninsula. Catalan commercial interests in the Mediterranean were neglected in favour of Castilian interests in the Atlantic and the New World. The Aragonese nobility, always accustomed to more independence and more political power than their Castilian counterparts, were now largely excluded from the court of the united monarchy. Francis Borgia arrived in Barcelona to find the countryside a prey to brigands, which viceroys had neither the money nor the strength to suppress, and the city a prey to the feuds and resentments of the nobility, who proudly denied royal authority. He wrestled with these problems as best he could and earned himself a reputation as a stern disciplinarian and a believer in strict justice, but he was not popular. His pride and his natural impatience did not help in dealing with the aristocracy of Barcelona; shortage of funds and troops impeded his attempts to preserve good order. His physical condition was also against him; since his illness in 1537 he had become enormously fat, a condition which did not make it easy for him to engage in arduous campaigns in the hinterland of Catalonia. It was said that his belt would go round three ordinary men, and his dining table had to have a special niche cut in it to accommodate his paunch.

This period of frustrations and tensions was brought to an end by the death of his father in 1543. It was now his duty as Duke of Gandia to take charge of the estates, and so he resigned his post in Barcelona and retired to Gandia. That this was not a conscious withdrawal from all public life is indicated by the fact that in the same year he was nominated by Charles V as master of the household to Prince Philip who was about to marry a Portuguese princess. Francis was quite prepared to take up this post and when his appointment was blocked by the Portuguese royal family for some unexplained reason, perhaps not unconnected with the memories which his name aroused, he regarded this opposition as a personal humiliation.

In his retirement, to some extent enforced, the spiritual side of Francis's life began to assume increased importance. There is a legend that as early as 1527 Francis, riding through the streets of Alcala, had come upon Ignatius Loyola being dragged off to the prison of the Inquisition, and the burning spiritual intensity of the glance which the future founder of the Jesuits had turned upon him had made an indelible impression.[7] Certainly by 1543 Francis had for some years been in correspondence with Loyola for whom he held a deep admiration, and in Barcelona his household had welcomed both Jesuits and noted preachers from other orders. Eleanora particularly delighted in the company of men like Texeda, the Franciscan mystic, and Pierre Favre, one of the original followers of Loyola who had come to Barcelona. Perhaps the greatest influence of all was the *Spiritual Exercises* of Loyola which he now had more leisure to study and which became the guide line of his spiritual life. Indeed in his increasing asceticism at this stage, in his long vigils in his chapel in the palace in Gandia, in the self-inflicted scourgings with which he sought to mortify his flesh, Francis was going beyond the demands and intentions of Loyola. On a more practical level he was at last beginning to lose weight by fasting. To cut down his consumption of wine, he used to melt a drop of wax each day into his glass thus gradually reducing its capacity. For the Jesuits he founded a college at Gandia in 1545, which became the first Jesuit university; and it was in the ducal palace, while the college was still being built, that the Jesuit Oviedo gave the first public lectures of the Jesuit educational programme. For it was at Gandia that for the first time the Jesuits accepted the role of educating laymen, as well as children and their own novices. Ignatius Loyola was reluctant that his Society should become involved in education to this extent, but Francis felt a responsibility to his ducal subjects, the majority of whom were of recently converted stock. He was determined that Gandia should have its own university, and equally determined that it should be in the care of the Jesuits.[8]

Despite all this Francis remained outwardly a great landowner and a Spanish grandee. The Gandia estates were doing particularly well at this moment as they were turned over to sugar production with the European demand for sugar rapidly increasing. The possibility of a position in Philip's household was still not finally discarded, and the problems of providing for his eight children, particularly the daughters, were pressing. It was the death of Eleanora in 1546 which provoked his final decision to abandon his secular life. Within a few weeks he had resolved to become a Jesuit, but the final implementation of his decision had to wait a further four years. With the consent of Loyola his decision was kept secret while he settled his family affairs. Meanwhile he began to follow a course in theology at the Jesuit college in Gandia and the tenor of his daily life became increasingly severe. He once referred to 'the two beasts of hot temper and lust' against which he had fought all his life; these were familiar beasts to the Borgias and his methods of subduing them gained him a lurid reputation as an ascetic.

By 1550 Francis felt that his worldly tasks were done. His eldest son, Carlos, was now twenty and married to Maddalena de Centelles, the daughter of the Count of Oliva. In 1548 on the death of Giovanni Borgia, the *Infans Romanus*, Francis had claimed his Valencian estates for his own children, and Paul III, who had already expressed his feelings towards the offspring of 'Alexander VI, of happy memory, to whom we owe all our fortune' in a letter of condolence on the death of Juan in 1543, now gladly granted Francis's request. Francis also persuaded Paul III to authorise the publication of the *Spiritual Exercises*, and had gained papal permission for the erection of a suitable funeral monument for the Borgia Popes in Santa Maria Maggiore.[9] This last project did not materialise as Francis's final renunciation of all his wealth intervened and the necessary funds were no longer available. This concern for the memory of his family, and for its social prestige, have to be weighed against the common but rather emotive conception of his asceticism as an expiation for the sins of the Borgias.

So at last Francis Borgia set out for Rome with his son Juan. He had already received special permission to take the vows of the Jesuits as a layman, and although his decision was kept secret, the news spread that the Duke of Gandia, one of the wealthiest and best known men in Spain, had joined the Jesuits. This was in many ways a decisive moment for the prestige of the Society. Officially recognised only ten years before and still regarded with great suspicion and hostility, particularly in Spain, the Jesuits were badly in need of influential patrons and converts. The adherence of Gandia gave the Jesuits that link with the traditional establishment which hitherto they had lacked; he was the confidant of the Emperor and did indeed seek to put the case for the Jesuits before his suspicious friend and master. That Francis Borgia should now be seen in this light and with this sort of influence, when less than a century before his family were little known provincial nobility, is some indication of the long term successes which Borgia policy had gained.

On his way to Rome Francis stayed with his cousin, the son of Lucrezia, Ercole II, Duke of Ferrara. He was received by the Jesuits in Rome with great excitement and honour and was embarrassed to find that a whole wing of the house of the Society in Rome had been set aside for his use. The Jesuits wanted to make as much as possible of their new recruit while Francis, about to renounce his title and estates in favour of his eldest son, wanted only to immerse himself in his new life and his new duties.

He did not stay long in Rome on this occasion and by the next year was established at the hermitage at Onate close to the Pyrenees. There he was ordained and began to preach. There his reputation and his oratory earned him the title of the 'Apostle of the Basques'. Thousands flocked to hear his sermons and receive his blessing, and his reputation as a healer soon equalled that of his great-grandfather as a poisoner. But Francis Borgia, much as he enjoyed his role as a simple preacher and hermit, could not entirely cut himself off from his past. Much of his value to the Jesuits lay in his influential connections, and at the same time it was said of him that 'it was impossible for him not to be first'. His influence, his administrative talents and his innate power of authority were wasted in the foothills of the Pyrenees, and he soon reappeared at the Spanish court. There he was enthusiastically welcomed by Juana, the daughter of Charles V, whose spiritual adviser he became, and when Philip went to England to marry Mary Tudor and Juana was left as regent in Spain, Francis found himself in a position of power equivalent to that which he had enjoyed in 1530 by the side of Isabella. He spent a good deal of time with Charles himself, both immediately before and after the Emperor's retirement to the monastery of Yuste. On his deathbed Charles asked for Francis to come to him, and it was Francis who preached the funeral sermon for the dead Emperor at Valladolid in 1559. Even at the Portuguese court he was a great sensation when he visited Lisbon in these years; the old suspicions of the name of Borgia which had impeded his appointment to the household of a Portuguese princess were washed away in the tide of popular admiration for his preaching and spiritual life.

But despite all this, things were not easy for Francis during the ten years which he spent in Spain as a Jesuit. His position in the Society was an ambiguous one; at first he had a sort of roving commission dependent only on the general in Rome. This aroused the bitter jealousy of Araoz, the severe and humourless Jesuit Provincial in Spain, and began to endanger the unity of the Society. At the same time public feeling was rising against the Borja family, as two of Francis's half-brothers, Felipe and Diego, became involved in a bitter feud with the Viceroy in Valencia. The son of the Viceroy, Diego de Aragon, was murdered by the Borja brothers, and public opinion and royal wrath forced them to flee into exile. Francis tried hard to protect his family, but after his final departure for Rome in 1561, Diego was executed by Philip II. Finally Philip himself never shared in his family's admiration for Francis; when he became King of Spain on his father's retirement, he quickly showed his resentment of the rising power of the Jesuits, an organisation which he saw as more closely attached to the Pope than to himself.

In an attempt to heal the rift within the Jesuits in Spain, Loyola divided the peninsula into four provinces and placed Francis over them all as commissary general. This gave him an established position and enabled him to participate in the organisation of the Society in Spain. He founded more than twenty houses for novitiates, thus creating a strong base on which the Jesuits could expand. But it also exacerbated the jealousies of Araoz and the other older Jesuits who felt that they had been passed over. By the late 1550s a combination of his enemies forced Francis to flee to Portugal. He was condemned by the Inquisition for heterodoxy and for undue tolerance towards suspected Lutherans, and finally, to avoid a complete breach within the Society, was summoned to Rome by Lainez, Loyola's successor, to be his assistant in 1561.

In Rome during the last years of his life it was once again Francis's contacts and his personal friendships with men of influence outside the Society as much as his own activity which made his contribution to the growth of the Jesuits so significant. The influential Milanese reforming cardinal, Carlo Borromeo, and Cardinal Ghisleri were both close friends of Francis, and when Ghisleri became Pope as Pius V, the Jesuits were for the first time admitted freely to the Vatican. Meanwhile Francis, having served as Vicar-General of the Society while Lainez was absent at the Council of Trent, was in 1565 elected General on the latter's death. Apart from the immense impact which his preaching and saintly life had made, and his wide influence, the choice was also a good one in that the Jesuits now needed more than anything a leader with a talent for organisation. The Society had expanded out of all recognition since the day in 1534 when Ignatius Loyola and his six companions had taken their first vows. Now with preachers in all parts of the world and with members of all classes clamouring for admission, organisation and consolidation were the first tasks of the new General and Francis Borgia spent the last seven years of his life on these tasks. By his immense correspondence he inspired and directed the Society's proselytisation programme; by his establishment of novitiates he staffed the future; by formalising the rules of the Society he gave it a permanent strength. He always wanted to spend his last years as a missionary in India, but instead, tied to his desk in Rome, he strove to answer the demands for missionaries from both the conquistadors in the New World and the Portuguese in the East.

On his first visit to Rome he had provided the funds for the restoration of the first Jesuit church of Santa Maria della Strada, and also for the founding of the Collegio Romano, the Jesuit college which was later to become the Gregorian university. In Spain he was constantly raising funds for the upkeep of the college in Rome, an activity which angered Araoz and his fellows who tended to be strongly nationalist. Now as General in 1568, it was Francis who purchased the site of the Gesù and laid the foundation stone of the great new Jesuit church, the decoration and whole artistic conception of which was to lead the way to a new phase in art, the Baroque.

In 1571 Pius V chose Francis to accompany Cardinal Alessandrino as legate to Spain and Portugal to promote a new coalition against the Turks. By this time the hostility against both himself and his family in Spain had died down and he was once more greeted with enthusiasm and respect. But Francis was no more successful than his great-grandfather had been, almost one hundred years earlier, in promoting enthusiasm for a crusade. He passed on to France with the cardinal legate and was again welcomed with great ceremony at the French court at Blois.

But by now his strength was failing. He was suffering from

incurable pulmonary disease and the journey back to Rome was a continual torment for him. Once again he broke his journey at Ferrara where, despite the insistence of Duke Alfonso, he refused to stay in the ducal palace and directed his litter towards the small Jesuit house on the outskirts of the town. While at Ferrara he heard the news of the death of Pius V and received indications that many wanted him to be the next Pope. But whether the reputation of St. Francis would have been sufficient to overcome the hostility to the possibility of another Borgia Pope was never put to the test. Francis was too weak and ill to consider the possibility even had he wanted to, but he did hurry to Rome with the intention of seeing the Holy City and his friends once more before he died. Outside the Porta del Popolo he ordered his bearers to stop while he prayed for half an hour before allowing his pain-racked body to be carried within the walls to the shelter and comparative comfort of the Jesuit house. There two days later on 30 September 1572 he died.

St. Francis was beatified in 1624 by Urban VIII and canonised in 1671 just under one hundred years after his death by Clement X. The relative haste of the process has been seen as an attempt by the Church to balance the reputation of Alexander VI and vindicate the name of Borgia. But the antithesis is not as clear cut as this pattern suggests. St. Francis owed his importance and in the last resort his sainthood to the fact that he was a Borja; but for the position of influence which he enjoyed as a grandee of Spain, a position entirely created by the dynastic policies of the Borgia Popes, his career would have been very different. At the same time the contrast often drawn between the saint who showed 'no sign of human weakness, little or no sign of human nature',[10] and the sensual, pleasure-loving Borgia Pope is an exaggerated one. The similarities between the two Borgias were almost as striking as the contrasts; Alexander would have appreciated the spiritual qualities of his descendant as well as being proud of his success; Francis honoured his family and the names of the Borgia Popes, and was far from unaware of the earthly temptations which had ruined the reputation of his great-grandfather.

Francis Borgia and Eleanora de Castro had eight children of whom inevitably one, Dorothea, became a nun in the convent of Santa Clara. However none of the remainder were drawn to the religious life by the example of their father. Even Juan, who had accompanied his father on his first visit to Rome and then to Onate, married the niece of Ignatius Loyola and renounced any intentions of becoming a Jesuit. Carlos, the fifth Duke, was a correspondent of Philip II who visited Gandia in 1586; he became Captain General in Portugal after the Spanish annexation in 1580, and later exercised the same authority in Genoa. Juan, with the title of Count of Mayalde, became a courtier and a diplomat. He was gentleman in waiting to Philip II, Spanish ambassador in Portugal (1569–75) and to the Empire (1576–81), and subsequently master of the household to Queen Margherita, wife of Philip III. It was his eldest son, Francesco, who married Anna Borgia, Princess of Squillace, and became Prince of Squillace. Francesco is remembered as a poet, the composer of a heroic poem *Napoles recuperada por el rey don Alonso* and the translator of the meditations of Thomas à Kempis, and also as Viceroy of Peru between 1615 and 1621. In Peru he founded the city of S. Francesco Borja and the University of San Marcos.[11]

It was also in the New World that the illegitimate offspring of Fernando, another son of St. Francis, made their names.[12] Juan, the eldest son, was President of New Granada which he governed for twenty-two years, and his descendants are still to be found in Peru and Colombia. In the nineteenth century the family produced Cesar de Borja, a doctor, writer and politician who was described as 'one of the most brilliant personalities in Peru'. Finally one of Fernando's sisters, the eldest daughter of St. Francis, married the Duke of Lerma and was therefore the mother of the all powerful cardinal and chief minister of Philip III.

In the reign of Philip IV Borja influence at court was particularly strong. Cardinal Gaspare de Borja was the first Spanish grandee to occupy a chair of theology, and he was also a close adviser of Philip IV. Immensely wealthy as Archbishop first of Seville and then of Toledo, he contributed 50,000 crowns from his personal fortune to the war chest for the war against France. He cherished an ambition to be the third Borgia Pope and spent some time in Rome as Spanish ambassador. But he was disappointed in this ambition and had to be content with his position as Primate of Spain in which capacity he baptised Philip's son, the future Carlos II. Two brothers of Gaspare, Melchior, Viceroy of Sicily, and Fernando, Viceroy of Aragon, were leaders of the noble opposition to the hated royal minister Olivares. Fernando was a friend and protector of Sor Maria of Agreda, the nun who had so great an influence over Philip IV in his final years.[13] The Duke of Gandia was at this time reported to have an income of 40,000 ducats, but the fortunes of the family were already undermined by the expulsion of the Moriscoes in 1609 which seriously damaged the economy of the Gandia estates. Only ten per cent of the inhabitants of the Duchy were of pure Spanish blood, and the purges of the early seventeenth century caused immense economic disruption in the whole area of Valencia.[14]

Gaspare was not the last of the Borja cardinals as two more members of the family were subsequently raised to the Sacred College. Francesco, son of the ninth Duke, was a man of singular piety and learning who was a councillor of Carlos II and Archbishop of Burgos. He became a cardinal in 1699 and, after his premature death three years later, his brother Carlos took up the role of chief ecclesiastic of the family. He was Patriarch of the Indies and chaplain to Philip V before also becoming a cardinal in 1720. But these two apart, the influence of the family was declining by the end of the seventeenth century. The last Borja Duke of Gandia, Luis Ignacio de Borja, the eleventh duke, died in 1740 without children, and the title passed to his nephew, Francesco de Pimentel, Duke of Benevente. His daughter Maria, heiress to the Gandia title, married Pedro de Tellez-Giron, Duke of Osuna, and thus the Dukes of Osuna moved into the ducal palace at Gandia until 1882 when the last of the indirect line, Don Mariano Tellez-Giron y Beaufort Spontin Pimentel, Prince of Squillace, Duke of Osuna and Gandia, died without heirs.

It was Don Mariano whom Disraeli met in Paris in 1838 and of whom he wrote, 'He is a great dandy and looks like Philip II...... When he was last in Paris he attended a representation of Victor Hugo's *Lucrezia Borgia*. She says in one of the scenes "great crimes are in our blood" and all his friends looked at him with an expression of fear. "But the blood has degenerated," he said, "for I have committed only weaknesses."'[15] Thus did the last of the Spanish Borgias in the middle of the nineteenth century still remember, perhaps with a certain complacence, the achievements of his distant ancestors in the fifteenth.

GENEALOGICAL TABLES

TABLE I THE BORJ

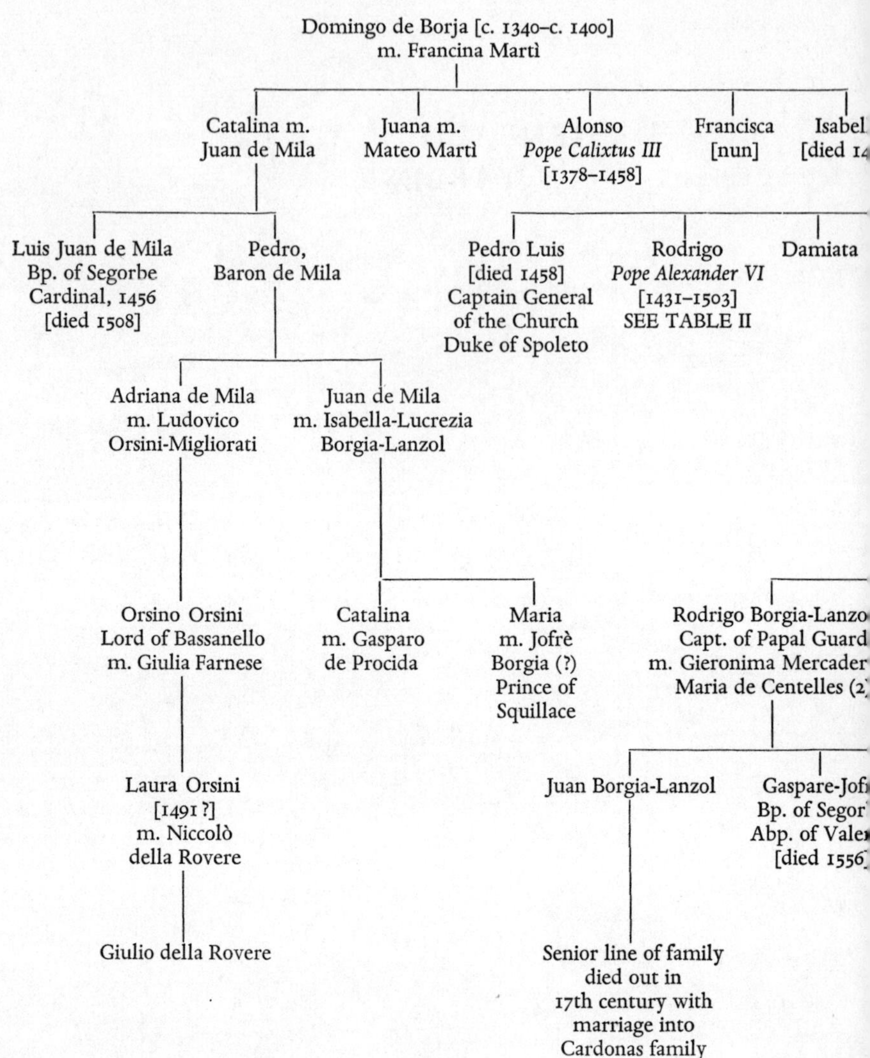
Domingo de Borja [c. 1340–c. 1400]
m. Francina Martì
Catalina m.
Juan de Mila
Juana m.
Mateo Martì
Alonso
Pope Calixtus III
[1378–1458]
Francisca
[nun]
Isabel
[died 14
Luis Juan de Mila
Bp. of Segorbe
Cardinal, 1456
[died 1508]
Pedro,
Baron de Mila
Pedro Luis
[died 1458]
Captain General
of the Church
Duke of Spoleto
Rodrigo
Pope Alexander VI
[1431–1503]
SEE TABLE II
Damiata
Adriana de Mila
m. Ludovico
Orsini-Migliorati
Juan de Mila
m. Isabella-Lucrezia
Borgia-Lanzol
Orsino Orsini
Lord of Bassanello
m. Giulia Farnese
Catalina
m. Gasparo
de Procida
Maria
m. Jofrè
Borgia (?)
Prince of
Squillace
Rodrigo Borgia-Lanzo
Capt. of Papal Guard
m. Gieronima Mercader
Maria de Centelles (2
Laura Orsini
[1491 ?]
m. Niccolò
della Rovere
Juan Borgia-Lanzol
Gaspare-Jof
Bp. of Segor
Abp. of Vale
[died 1556
Giulio della Rovere
Senior line of family
died out in
17th century with
marriage into
Cardonas family

AMILY OF JATIVA

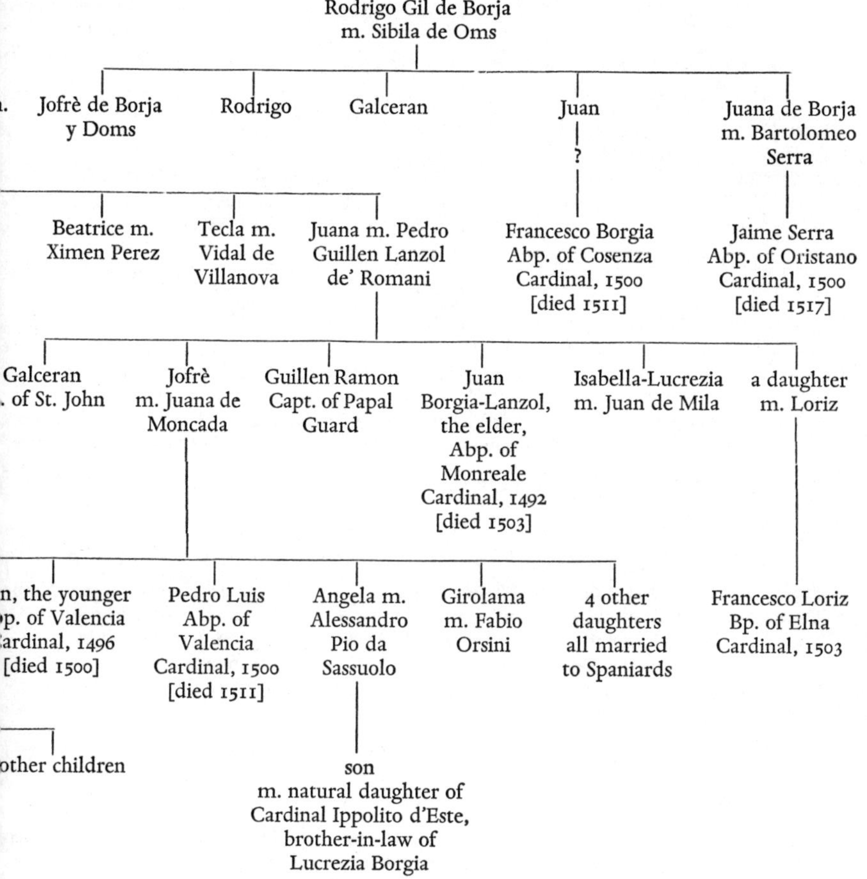

Rodrigo Gil de Borja
m. Sibila de Oms
Jofrè de Borja
y Doms
Rodrigo
Galceran
Juan
?
Juana de Borja
m. Bartolomeo
Serra
Beatrice m.
Ximen Perez
Tecla m.
Vidal de
Villanova
Juana m. Pedro
Guillen Lanzol
de' Romani
Francesco Borgia
Abp. of Cosenza
Cardinal, 1500
[died 1511]
Jaime Serra
Abp. of Oristano
Cardinal, 1500
[died 1517]
Galceran
. of St. John
Jofrè
m. Juana de
Moncada
Guillen Ramon
Capt. of Papal
Guard
Juan
Borgia-Lanzol,
the elder,
Abp. of
Monreale
Cardinal, 1492
[died 1503]
Isabella-Lucrezia
m. Juan de Mila
a daughter
m. Loriz
n, the younger
p. of Valencia
ardinal, 1496
[died 1500]
Pedro Luis
Abp. of
Valencia
Cardinal, 1500
[died 1511]
Angela m.
Alessandro
Pio da
Sassuolo
Girolama
m. Fabio
Orsini
4 other
daughters
all married
to Spaniards
Francesco Loriz
Bp. of Elna
Cardinal, 1503
other children
son
m. natural daughter of
Cardinal Ippolito d'Este,
brother-in-law of
Lucrezia Borgia

TABLE II THE FAMIL

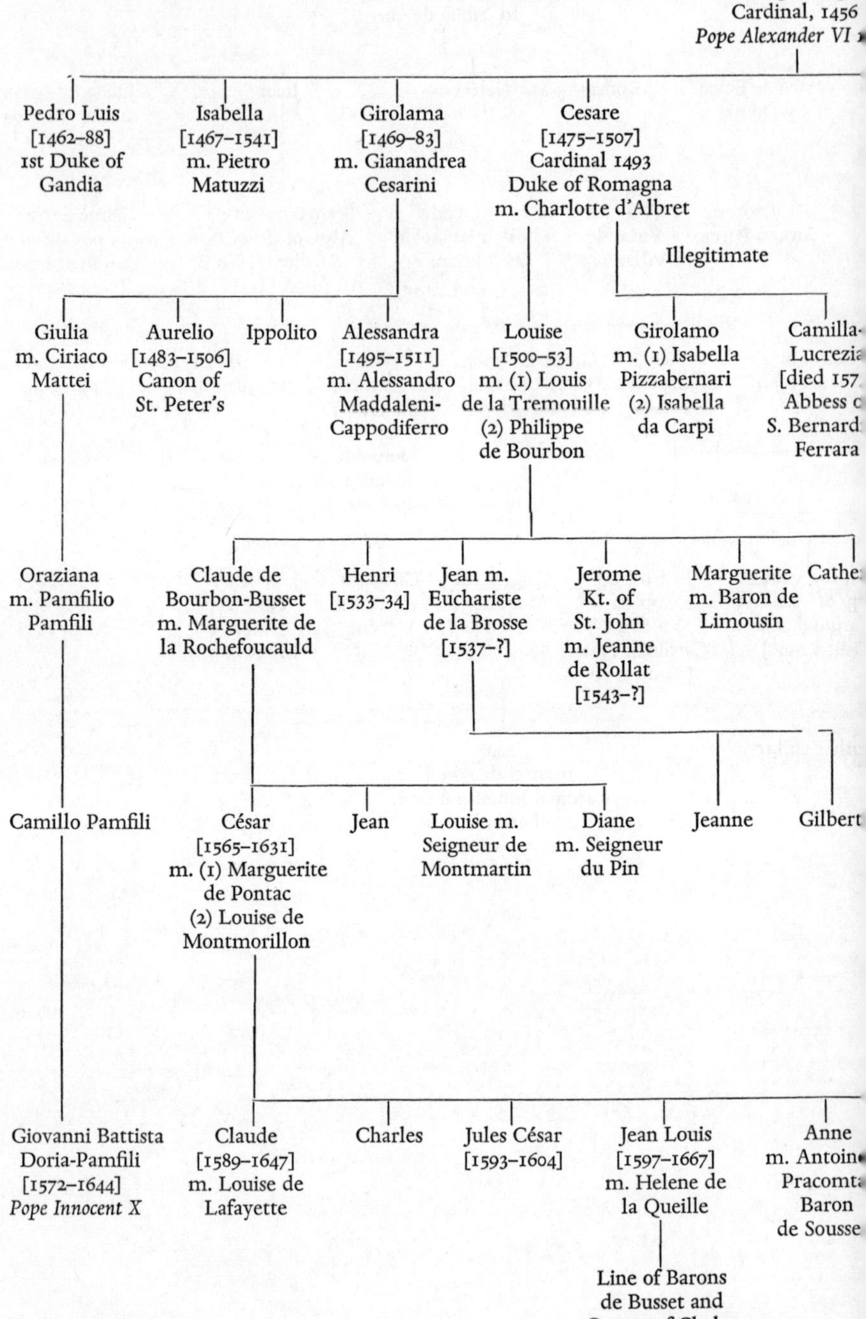

F ALEXANDER VI

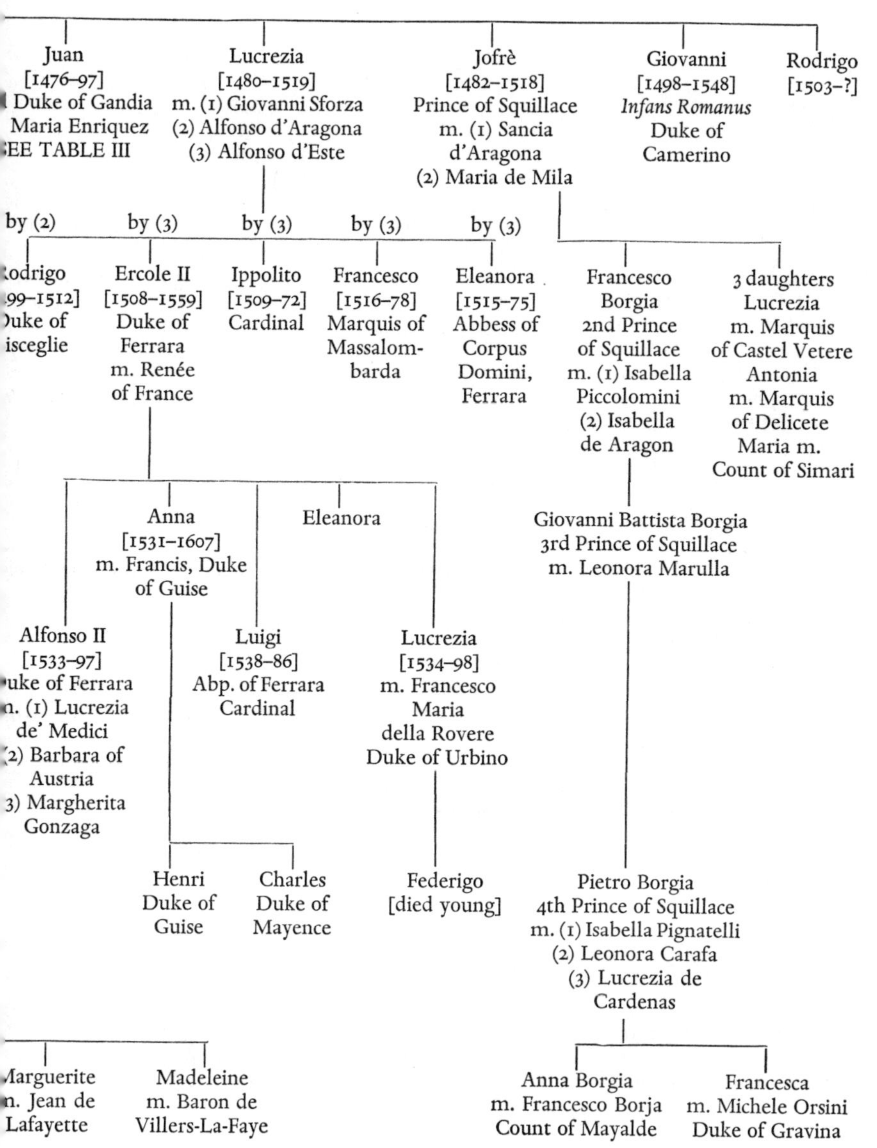

Juan
[1476–97]
Duke of Gandia
Maria Enriquez
EE TABLE III
Lucrezia
[1480–1519]
m. (1) Giovanni Sforza
(2) Alfonso d'Aragona
(3) Alfonso d'Este
Jofrè
[1482–1518]
Prince of Squillace
m. (1) Sancia
d'Aragona
(2) Maria de Mila
Giovanni
[1498–1548]
Infans Romanus
Duke of
Camerino
Rodrigo
[1503–?]
by (2)
by (3)
by (3)
by (3)
by (3)
odrigo
99–1512]
uke of
isceglie
Ercole II
[1508–1559]
Duke of
Ferrara
m. Renée
of France
Ippolito
[1509–72]
Cardinal
Francesco
[1516–78]
Marquis of
Massalom-
barda
Eleanora
[1515–75]
Abbess of
Corpus
Domini,
Ferrara
Francesco
Borgia
2nd Prince
of Squillace
m. (1) Isabella
Piccolomini
(2) Isabella
de Aragon
3 daughters
Lucrezia
m. Marquis
of Castel Vetere
Antonia
m. Marquis
of Delicete
Maria m.
Count of Simari
Anna
[1531–1607]
m. Francis, Duke
of Guise
Eleanora
Giovanni Battista Borgia
3rd Prince of Squillace
m. Leonora Marulla
Alfonso II
[1533–97]
uke of Ferrara
n. (1) Lucrezia
de' Medici
2) Barbara of
Austria
3) Margherita
Gonzaga
Luigi
[1538–86]
Abp. of Ferrara
Cardinal
Lucrezia
[1534–98]
m. Francesco
Maria
della Rovere
Duke of Urbino
Henri
Duke of
Guise
Charles
Duke of
Mayence
Federigo
[died young]
Pietro Borgia
4th Prince of Squillace
m. (1) Isabella Pignatelli
(2) Leonora Carafa
(3) Lucrezia de
Cardenas
Iarguerite
n. Jean de
Lafayette
Madeleine
m. Baron de
Villers-La-Faye
Anna Borgia
m. Francesco Borja
Count of Mayalde
Francesca
m. Michele Orsini
Duke of Gravina

TABLE III THE FAMILY O

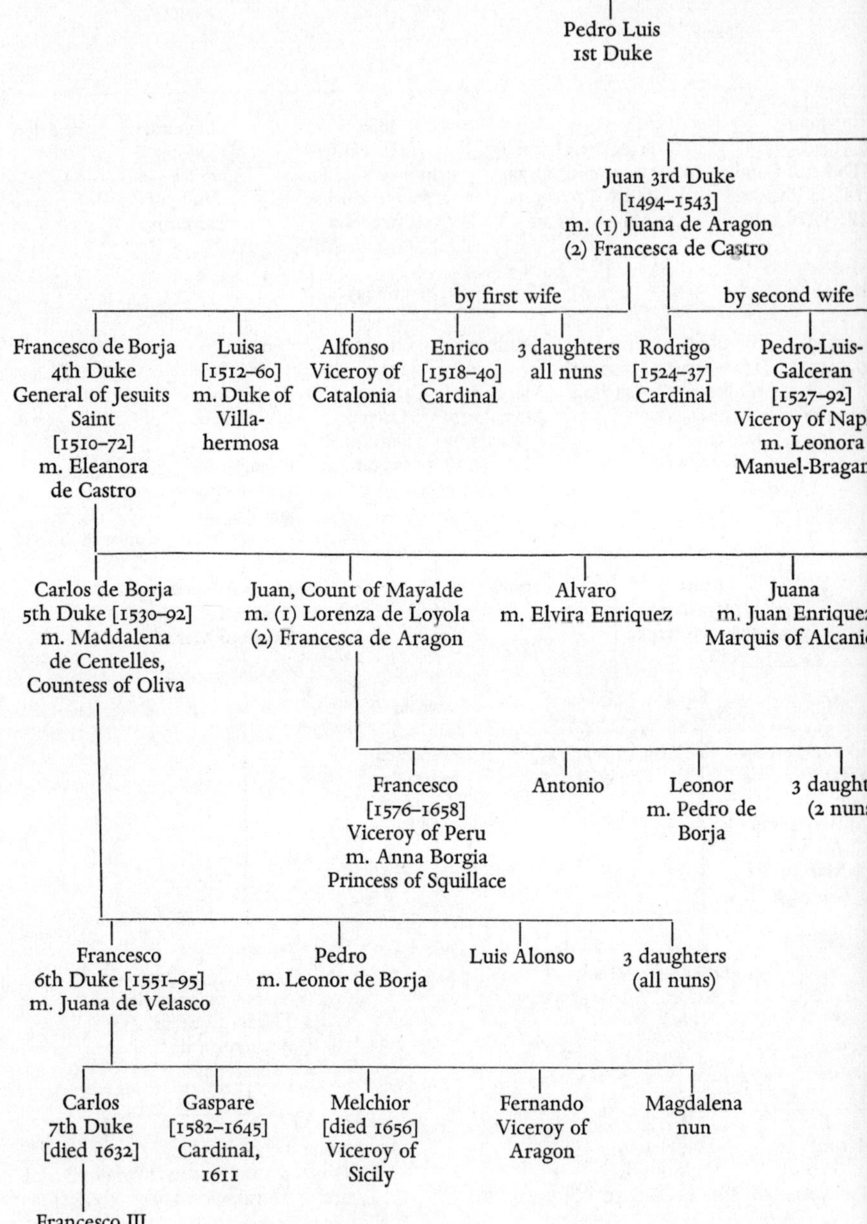

Pedro Luis
1st Duke
Juan 3rd Duke
[1494–1543]
m. (1) Juana de Aragon
(2) Francesca de Castro
by first wife
by second wife
Francesco de Borja
4th Duke
General of Jesuits
Saint
[1510–72]
m. Eleanora
de Castro
Luisa
[1512–60]
m. Duke of
Villa-
hermosa
Alfonso
Viceroy of
Catalonia
Enrico
[1518–40]
Cardinal
3 daughters
all nuns
Rodrigo
[1524–37]
Cardinal
Pedro-Luis-
Galceran
[1527–92]
Viceroy of Napl
m. Leonora
Manuel-Bragan
Carlos de Borja
5th Duke [1530–92]
m. Maddalena
de Centelles,
Countess of Oliva
Juan, Count of Mayalde
m. (1) Lorenza de Loyola
(2) Francesca de Aragon
Alvaro
m. Elvira Enriquez
Juana
m. Juan Enrique
Marquis of Alcani
Francesco
[1576–1658]
Viceroy of Peru
m. Anna Borgia
Princess of Squillace
Antonio
Leonor
m. Pedro de
Borja
3 daught
(2 nun
Francesco
6th Duke [1551–95]
m. Juana de Velasco
Pedro
m. Leonor de Borja
Luis Alonso
3 daughters
(all nuns)
Carlos
7th Duke
[died 1632]
Gaspare
[1582–1645]
Cardinal,
1611
Melchior
[died 1656]
Viceroy of
Sicily
Fernando
Viceroy of
Aragon
Magdalena
nun
Francesco III

-HE DUKES OF GANDIA

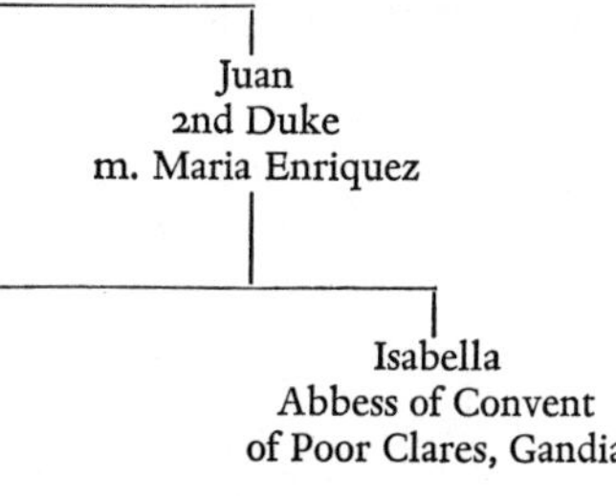

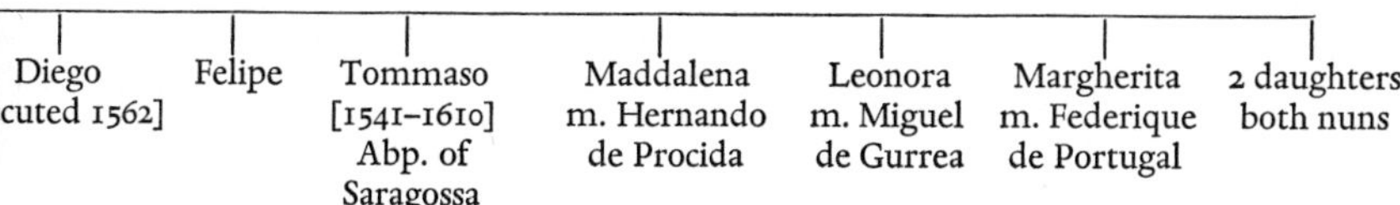

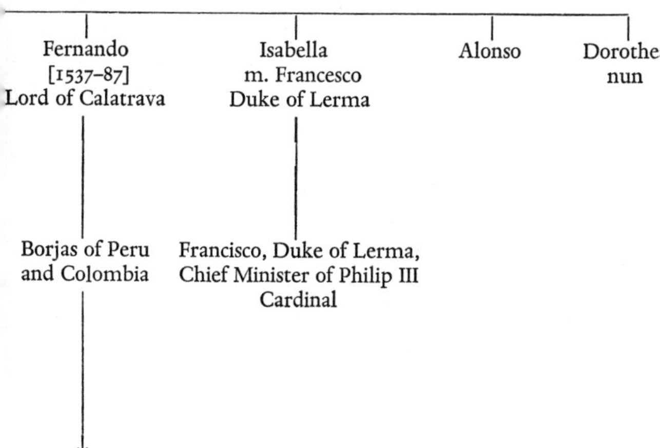

LATER DUKES OF GANDIA FROM THE MID-SEVENTEENTH CENTURY

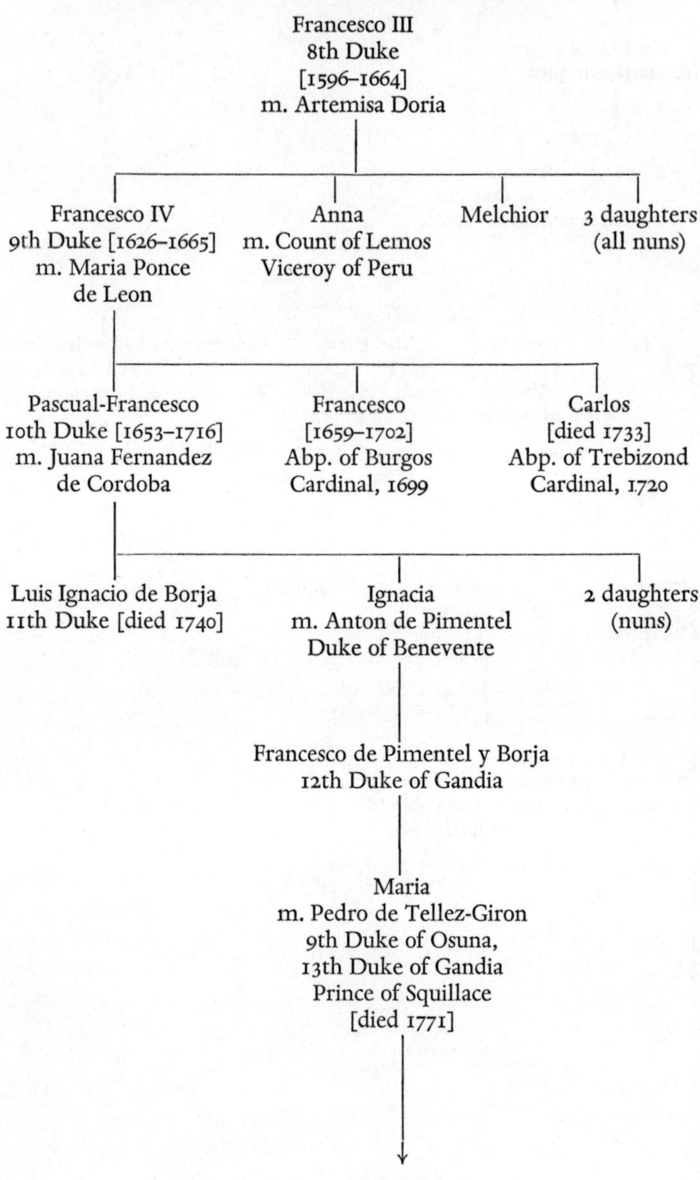
Francesco III
8th Duke
[1596–1664]
m. Artemisa Doria
Francesco IV
9th Duke [1626–1665]
m. Maria Ponce
de Leon
Anna
m. Count of Lemos
Viceroy of Peru
Melchior
3 daughters
(all nuns)
Pascual-Francesco
10th Duke [1653–1716]
m. Juana Fernandez
de Cordoba
Francesco
[1659–1702]
Abp. of Burgos
Cardinal, 1699
Carlos
[died 1733]
Abp. of Trebizond
Cardinal, 1720
Luis Ignacio de Borja
11th Duke [died 1740]
Ignacia
m. Anton de Pimentel
Duke of Benevente
2 daughters
(nuns)
Francesco de Pimentel y Borja
12th Duke of Gandia
Maria
m. Pedro de Tellez-Giron
9th Duke of Osuna,
13th Duke of Gandia
Prince of Squillace
[died 1771]

TABLE IV THE COLONNA FAMILY

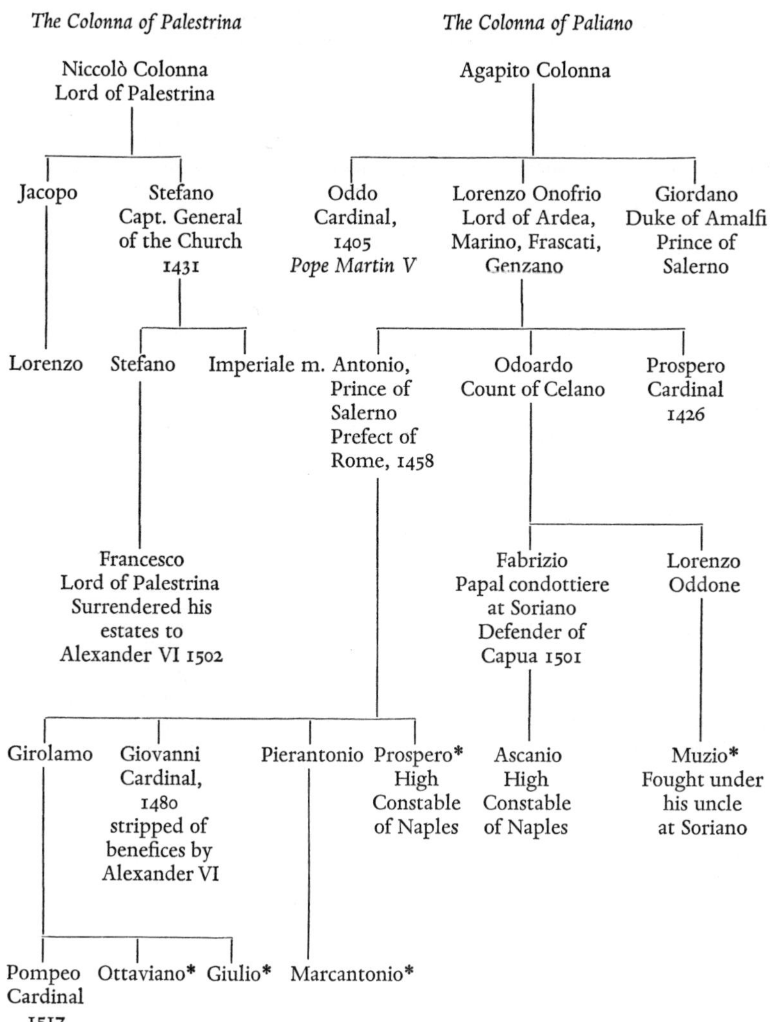

* These members of the family were excommunicated by Alexander VI in 1501.

TABLE V TH

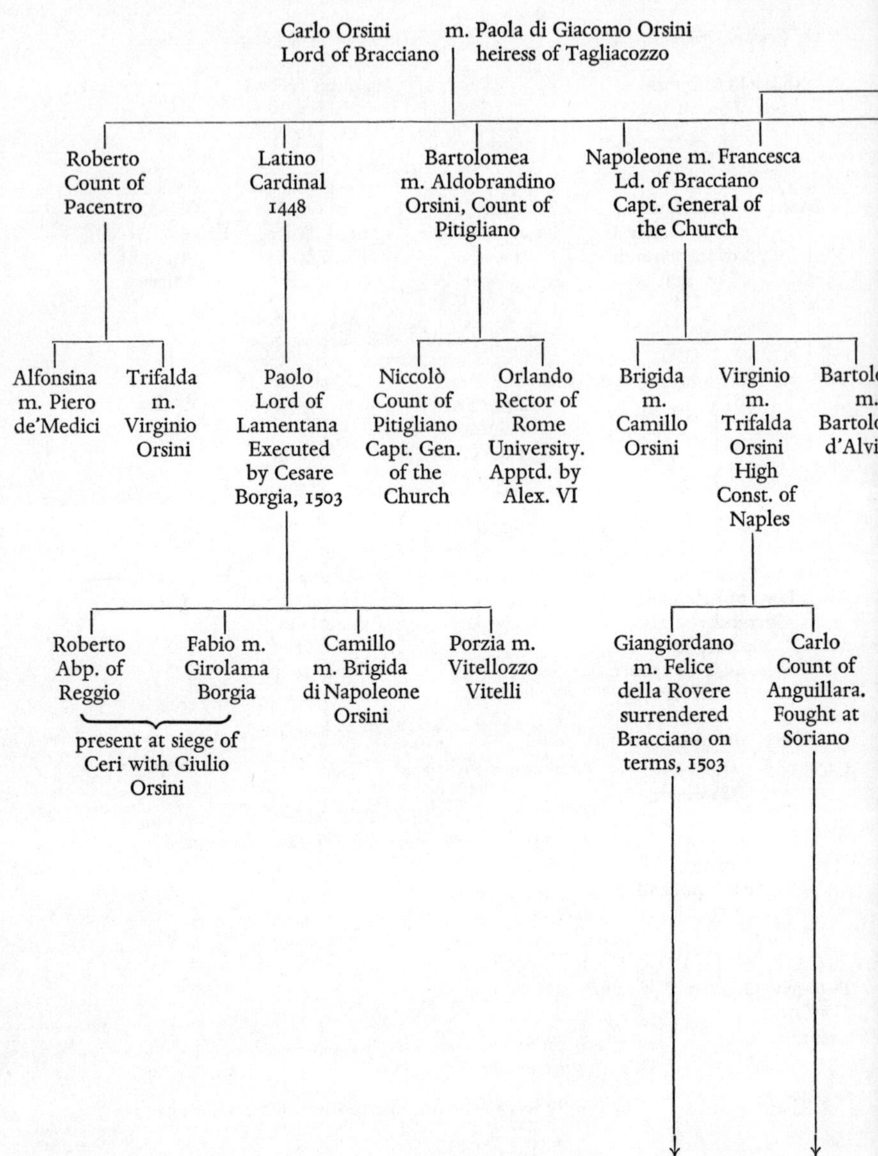

N.B. These are only the Roman branches of the Orsini family who came into conflict with Borgias.

RSINI FAMILY

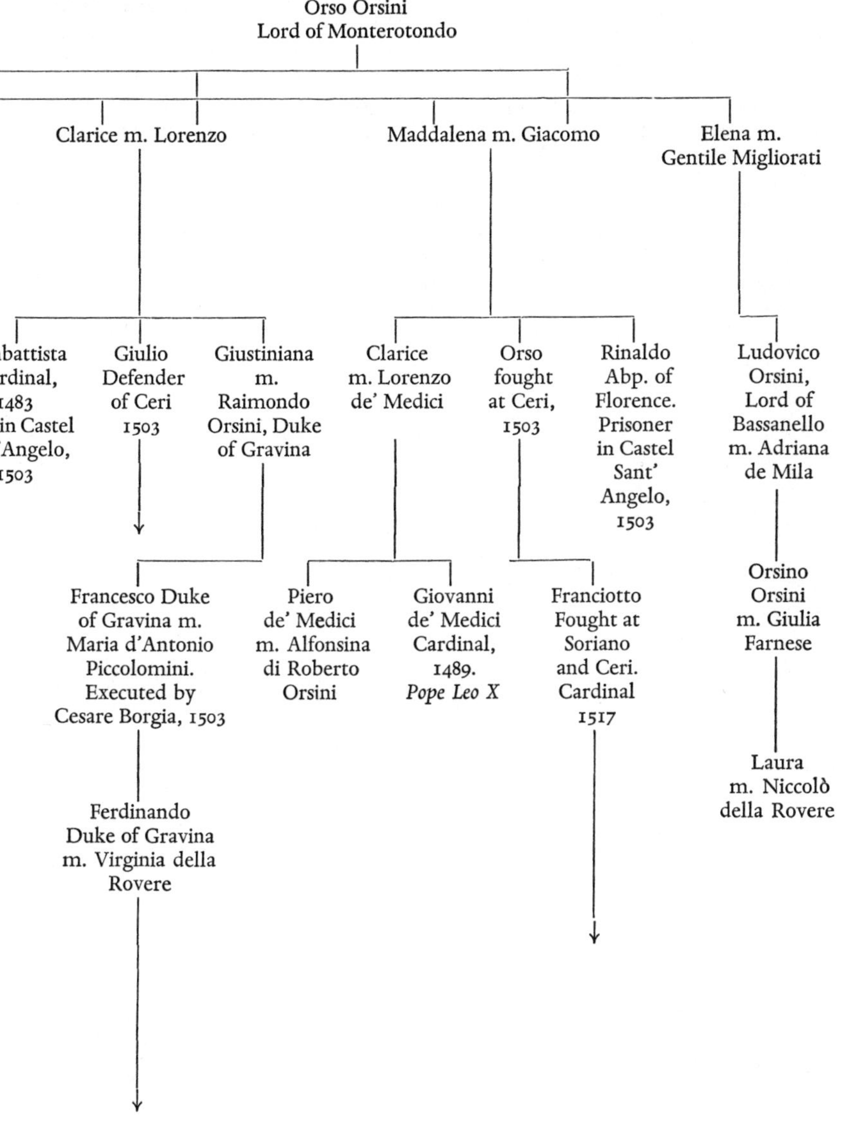

Orso Orsini
Lord of Monterotondo
Clarice m. Lorenzo
Maddalena m. Giacomo
Elena m. Gentile Migliorati
ianbattista Cardinal, 1483 ed in Castel nt'Angelo, 1503
Giulio Defender of Ceri 1503
Giustiniana m. Raimondo Orsini, Duke of Gravina
Clarice m. Lorenzo de' Medici
Orso fought at Ceri, 1503
Rinaldo Abp. of Florence. Prisoner in Castel Sant' Angelo, 1503
Ludovico Orsini, Lord of Bassanello m. Adriana de Mila
Francesco Duke of Gravina m. Maria d'Antonio Piccolomini. Executed by Cesare Borgia, 1503
Piero de' Medici m. Alfonsina di Roberto Orsini
Giovanni de' Medici Cardinal, 1489. Pope Leo X
Franciotto Fought at Soriano and Ceri. Cardinal 1517
Orsino Orsini m. Giulia Farnese
Laura m. Niccolò della Rovere
Ferdinando Duke of Gravina m. Virginia della Rovere

TABLE VI THE DELL

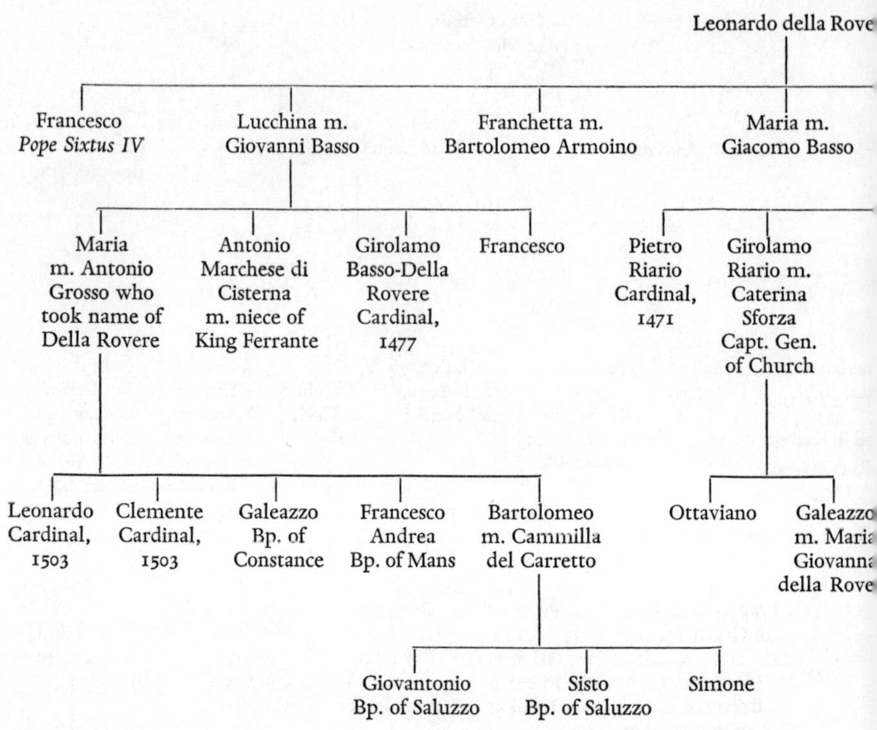

N.B. Cristoforo and Domenico della Rovere, who were brothers and made cardinals by Sixtus in 1477 and 1478, were described as *nipoti* and were probably descended from a brother of Leonar della Rovere.

ROVERE FAMILY

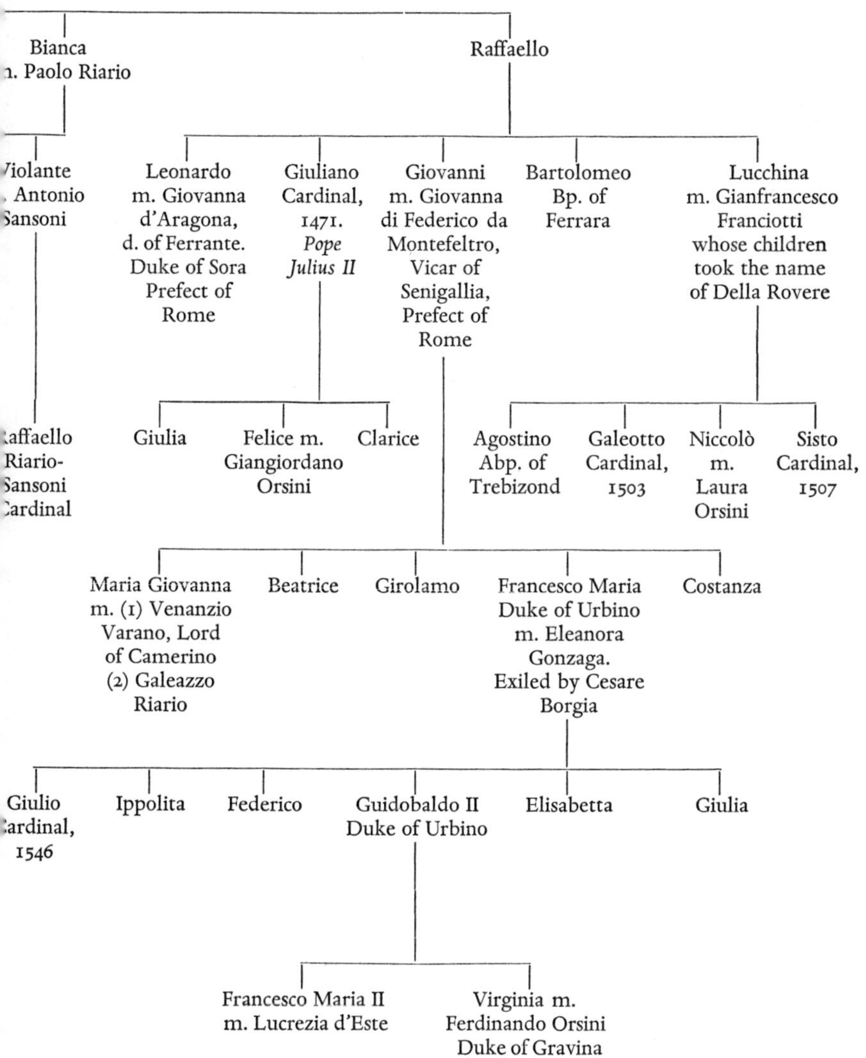

Bianca
m. Paolo Riario
Raffaello
Violante
m. Antonio
Sansoni
Leonardo
m. Giovanna
d'Aragona,
d. of Ferrante.
Duke of Sora
Prefect of
Rome
Giuliano
Cardinal,
1471.
Pope
Julius II
Giovanni
m. Giovanna
di Federico da
Montefeltro,
Vicar of
Senigallia,
Prefect of
Rome
Bartolomeo
Bp. of
Ferrara
Lucchina
m. Gianfrancesco
Franciotti
whose children
took the name
of Della Rovere
Raffaello
Riario-
Sansoni
Cardinal
Giulia
Felice m.
Giangiordano
Orsini
Clarice
Agostino
Abp. of
Trebizond
Galeotto
Cardinal,
1503
Niccolò
m.
Laura
Orsini
Sisto
Cardinal,
1507
Maria Giovanna
m. (1) Venanzio
Varano, Lord
of Camerino
(2) Galeazzo
Riario
Beatrice
Girolamo
Francesco Maria
Duke of Urbino
m. Eleanora
Gonzaga.
Exiled by Cesare
Borgia
Costanza
Giulio
Cardinal,
1546
Ippolita
Federico
Guidobaldo II
Duke of Urbino
Elisabetta
Giulia
Francesco Maria II
m. Lucrezia d'Este
Virginia m.
Ferdinando Orsini
Duke of Gravina

NOTES

List of abbreviations for frequently cited sources:

AV. Archivio Vaticano.
ASR. Archivio di Stato, Rome.
ASRSP. *Archivio della Società romana di storia patria.*
ASI. *Archivio storico italiano.*
Archivi *Archivi d'Italia e rivista internazionale degli archivi.*
AMR. *Atti e memorie della deputazione di storia patria per la Romagna.*
BRAH. *Boletin de la Real Academia de la Historia.*
RSCI. *Rivista di storia della Chiesa in Italia.*
RIS. *Rerum Italicarum Scriptores*, new series.
Pastor L. von Pastor, *History of the Popes from the Close of the Middle Ages*, trans. F. L. Antrobus (London, 1923) 5th edition.

CHAPTER ONE

1. On the Avignonese Popes *see* G. Mollat, *Les papes d'Avignon, 1305–78* (Paris, 1949; English translation, Edinburgh, 1963) and B. Guillemain, *La cour pontificale d'Avignon (1309–76): Étude d'une société* (Paris, 1962). Theories of papal sovereignty in the fourteenth century are clearly covered by M. J. Wilks, *The Problem of Sovereignty in the Later Middle Ages* (Cambridge, 1963) and B. Smalley, 'Church and State 1300–1377; Theory and Fact', *Europe in the Late Middle Ages*, ed. J. R. Hale *et al.* (London, 1965).

2. For the period of the Renaissance Papacy the main guide is still the magisterial L. von Pastor, *Geschichte der Päpste*, translated into English by F. L. Antrobus; there is a useful supplement to the Italian edition, vols. I–III (ed. A. Mercati, Rome, 1931). Other useful general accounts are M. Creighton, *A History of the Papacy from the Great Schism to the Sack of Rome* (London, 1897); E. Delaruelle, E.-R. Labande and P. Ourliac, *L'Église au temps du Grand Schisme et de la crise conciliare* (Paris, 1962); R. Aubenas and R. Ricard, *L'Église et la Renaissance* (Paris, 1951); A. C. Flick, *The Decline of the Medieval Church* (London, 1930); L. Elliott Binns, *The History of the Decline and Fall of the Medieval Papacy* (London, 1934); E. F. Jacob, *Essays in the Conciliar Epoch* (Manchester, 1943); N. Valois, *La crise religieuse du XV siècle; le pape et le concile* (Paris, 1909).

3. P. Richard, 'Les nonciatures apostoliques permanentes; la representation pontificale au XVe siècle, 1450–1513', *Revue d'histoire ecclésiastique*, vii, 1906; H. Biaudet, *Les nonciatures apostoliques permanentes jusqu'en 1648*

(Helsinki, 1910), pp. 14–17; G. Mattingley, *Renaissance Diplomacy* (London, 1962), p. 154.

4. On crusades and the crusading ideal in the late Middle Ages, *see* D. M. Vaughan, *Europe and the Turk* (Liverpool, 1954); A. S. Atiya, *The Crusade in the Late Middle Ages* (London, 1938); R. Schwoebel, *The Shadow of the Crescent; the Renaissance Image of the Turk (1453–1517)* (Nieuwkoop, 1967); S. Runciman, 'The decline of the crusading idea', *Relazioni del X Congresso internazionale di scienze storiche* (Florence, 1955), vol. III.

5. A bibliography of the part played by the Papacy in Italian fifteenth century politics would be endless, but for general background *see* particularly L. Simeoni, *La storia politica d'Italia: Le Signorie* (Milan, 1950), 2 vols, and E.-R. Labande, *L'Italie de la Renaissance* (Paris, 1954). On relations with Naples *see* also J. Ametller y Vinyas, *Alfonso V de Aragon y la crisis religiosa del siglo XV* (Gerona, 1903); on Florence *see* P. Partner, 'Florence and the Papacy in the earlier Fifteenth Century', *Florentine Studies*, ed. N. Rubinstein (London, 1968).

6. L. Celier, 'L'idée de réforme à la cour pontificale du concile de Bâle au concile du Latran', *Revue des questions historiques*, lxxxvi, 1909; P. Imbart de la Tour, *Les origines de la Réforme* (Paris, 1946); H. Jedin, *The History of the Council of Trent* (London, 1957), I, pp. 117–38.

CHAPTER TWO

1. For the early history of the Papal States, *see* P. Partner, *The Papal State under Martin V* (London, 1958), pp. 1–41; D. P. Waley, *The Papal State in the Thirteenth Century* (London, 1961); A. de Boüard, *Le régime politique et les institutions de Rome au Moyen Age* (Paris, 1920); J. Guiraud, *L'État Pontifical après le Grand Schisme* (Paris, 1896).

2. J. Larner, *The Lords of the Romagna* (London, 1965), pp. 89–91.

3. For the work done by Martin V, the first of the Renaissance Popes, in restoring papal authority in the Papal States, *see* Partner, *The Papal State under Martin V*.

4. The most recent account of the career of Caterina Sforza is E. Breisach, *Caterina Sforza* (Chicago, 1967); *see* also the centenary articles in *AMR*. ns., xv–xvi, 1963–5.

5. I. Robertson, 'The return of Cesena to the direct dominion of the Church after the death of Malatesta Novello', *Studi romagnoli*, xvi, 1965.

6. On the Malatesta *see* P. J. Jones, 'The vicariate of the Malatesta of Rimini', *English Historical Review*, lxvii, 1952, and *idem*, 'The end of Malatesta rule in Rimini', *Italian Renaissance Studies*, ed. E. F. Jacob (London, 1960).

7. N. Machiavelli, *The Discourses*, trans. L. J. Walker (London, 1950), Bk. III, chap. 29: 'The Romagna, before Alexander VI got rid of the lords

who ruled it, exemplified the very worst types of behaviour, for it was apparent to everyone that every least occasion was followed by killings and wholesale rapine. It was the wickedness of princes that gave rise to this, not the wicked nature of man, as people said.'

8. For an account of the financial organs of papal government, *see* Partner, *The Papal State under Martin V*, pp. 111–23 and 131–47. Older works are A. Gottlob, *Aus der Camera apostolica des 15. Jahrhunderts* (Innsbruck, 1889) and C. Bauer, 'Studi per la storia delle finanze papali', *ASRSP.*, l, 1927.

9. J. Delumeau, *L'alun de Rome, XVe–XIXe siècle* (Paris, 1962), pp. 23–51.

10. P. Partner, 'The "Budget" of the Roman Church in the Renaissance period', *Italian Renaissance Studies*, p. 263.

11. A. de Boüard, 'Lettres de Rome de Bartolomeo da Bracciano à Virginio Orsini (1489–94)', *Mélanges d'archéologie et d'histoire*, xxxiii, 1913, p. 269.

12. E. Rodocanachi, *Les institutions communales de Rome sous la Papauté* (Paris, 1901), pp. 51–143.

13. T. Mommsen, *History of Rome*, vol. IV (London, 1911), p. 471.

14. There are many descriptions of Rome in the late Middle Ages of which one of the most evocative is that of Pier Paolo Vergerio quoted by P. Paschini, *Roma nel Rinascimento* (Bologna, 1940), pp. 6–7. *See* also F. Gregorovius, *History of the City of Rome in the Middle Ages*, vol. vii, 2 (London, 1900–2), pp. 726–93; T. Magnuson, *Studies in Roman Quattrocento Architecture* (Rome, 1958), pp. 3–51.

15. Magnuson, *Studies in Roman Quattrocento Architecture*, pp. 217–349 and P. Tomei, *L'architettura a Roma nel Quattrocento* (Rome, 1942), *passim*.

16. E. Rodocanachi, *Histoire de Rome de 1354 à 1471* (Rome, 1922), p. 247.

CHAPTER THREE

1. Lorenzo de' Medici's letter to his son was published by A. Fabroni, *Laurentii Medicis Magnifici Vita* (Pisa, 1784), II, pp. 308 ff.

2. Rodocanachi, *Histoire de Rome de 1354 à 1471*, p. 340.

3. Pastor, V, pp. 269–70.

4. F. Gregorovius, *Lucrezia Borgia*, English translation by J. L. Garner (London, 1948), p. 190. Gregorovius' assertion is fully refuted by Pastor, VI, pp. 199–200.

5. G. Gaida (ed.), *Platynae historici Liber de vita Christi ac omnium pontificum*, *RIS*, III, pt. 1 (Bologna, 1923).

6. The main account of the patronage of the early Renaissance Popes is still E. Müntz, *Les arts à la cour des papes pendant le XVe et XVIe siècle* (Paris, 1878–82); but *see* also Paschini, *Roma nel Rinascimento, passim;*

E. Rodocanachi, *Histoire de Rome; une cour princière au Vatican pendant la Renaissance. Sixte IV, Innocent VIII, Alexandre VI* (Paris, 1925), *passim.*

7. Pastor, II, pp. 166–7.

8. Magnuson, *Studies in Roman Quattrocento Architecture*, pp. 55–214, discusses in detail the projects of Nicholas V.

9. R. Rubinstein, 'Pius II's Piazza S.Pietro and St. Andrew's Head', *Essays in the History of Architecture presented to Rudolf Wittkower* (London, 1967).

10. L. D. Ettlinger, *The Sistine Chapel before Michelangelo* (Oxford, 1965).

11. D. Redig di Campos, 'Il Belvedere di Innocenzo VIII in Vaticano', *Triplice ommaggio a S. S. Pio XII* (Rome, 1958); W. Sandström, 'The Programme for the Decoration of the Belvedere of Innocent VIII', *Konsthistorisk Tidskrift*, xxix, 1960.

12. Imbart de la Tour, *Origines de la réforme*, p. 15. For other accounts of the Curia administration *see* Partner, *The Papal State under Martin V*, pp. 131–58; P. Richard, 'La monarchie pontificale jusqu'au Concile de Trente', *Revue d'histoire ecclésiastique*, xx, 1924; Gottlob, *Aus der Camera apostolica.*

13. P. Partner, 'Camera Papae; Problems of papal finance in the later Middle Ages', *Journal of Ecclesiastical History*, iv, 1953.

14. L. Celier, *Les Dataires du XVe siècle et les origines de la Daterie Apostolique* (Paris, 1910).

15. In addition to the main works on papal history already quoted, for the electoral capitulations *see* W. Ullmann, 'The legality of the Papal Electoral Pacts', *Ephemerides Iuris Canonici*, xii, 1956.

16. Two recent articles on the College of Cardinals in the late fifteenth century make important points about their economic position: D. S. Chambers, 'The Economic Predicament of Renaissance Cardinals', *Studies in Medieval and Renaissance History*, iii, 1966 and A. V. Antonovics, 'A late Fifteenth Century Division Register of the College of Cardinals', *Papers of the British School at Rome*, xxxv, 1967.

17. Pastor, IV, pp. 409–15.

18. Chambers, 'The Economic Predicament of Renaissance Cardinals', p. 291.

CHAPTER FOUR

1. The best summary of the controversy about Borja origins is still P. De Roo, *Materials for a History of Pope Alexander VI, his Relatives and his Times* (Bruges, 1924), vol. I, pp. 35–47.

2. On the early career of Alonso de Borja *see* J. B. Altisent Jove, *Alonso de Borja en Lerida (1408–23) despues papa Calixto III* (Lerida, 1924); J. Sanchis y Sivera, 'El obispo de Valencia, don Alfonso de Borja', *BRAH.*, lxxxviii,

1926; J. Rius Serra, 'Alfonso de Borja', *Analecta Sacra Taraconensia*, vi, 1930. The most recent serious publication on the Borgias, S. Schüller Piroli, *Die Borgia; die Zerstörung einer Legende; die Geschichte einer Dynastie* (Freiburg, 1963), pp. 80–9, provides a useful summary of this material.

3. The usual authorities on Naples under Alfonso V make very little mention of Alonso de Borja; *see* R. Moscati, 'Le cariche generali nella burocrazia di Alfonso d'Aragona', *Miscellanea in onore di Roberto Cessi*, vol. II (Rome, 1958); P. Gentile, 'Lo stato napolitano sotto Alfonso I d'Aragona', *Archivio storico delle provincie napolitane*, ns., xxiii–iv, 1937–8; A. J. Ryder, 'The evolution of imperial government in Naples under Alfonso V', *Europe in the Late Middle Ages*.

4. For a new look at Cardinal Scarampo and a possible correction of his family name, *see* P. Paschini, *Ludovico Cardinale Camerlengo* (Rome, 1939). On the treaty of Terracina *see* Pastor, I, pp. 330–2.

5. ASR. Camerale I, *appendice* 25. This volume is an account of the income and expenses of the diocese of Valencia in 1452. Income totalled, in theory, just over 10,000 Aragonese pounds; but only 6460 were sent to Alonso in Rome. This was a good deal less than the usual estimates and reports of the value of the Valencian bishopric.

6. A. Ciaconius, *Vitae et Gesta Romanorum Pontificum* (Rome, 1677), vol. III, p. 190.

7. Francesco Borgia was probably born about 1432 and the Borgia genealogies in the Osuna family archives describe his father as one of Rodrigo's paternal uncles (*see* De Roo, *Materials for a History of Pope Alexander VI*, I, pp. 59–65). The Pinturicchio portrait in the fresco of the *Assumption of the Virgin* in the Borgia Apartments is usually thought to be Francesco despite the fact that it seems a very youthful portrayal of a man of sixty-three. It has also been suggested that this may be a portrait of Ascanio Sforza (Schüller Piroli, *Borgia*, p. 402) or Cardinal Juan Borgia-Lanzol, the younger (M. Menotti, *I Borgia; storia e iconografia*, Rome, 1917, p. 231).

8. One of the best accounts of this conclave comes in the Commentaries of Pius II, trans F. A. Gragg (Northampton, Mass., 1936–57), I, pp. 75–6.

9. Pastor, II, p. 338.

10. The story that the ringing of the church bells was linked to a fear of, and indeed the excommunication of, Halley's comet which had appeared at this time has been abundantly disproved. The story, which seems to have originated from Platina, was an attempt to discredit Calixtus and prove his superstition and intellectual limitations. *See* J. Stein, *Calixte III et la comète de Halley* (Rome, 1909).

11. Pastor, II, pp. 389–413; P. Brezzi, 'La politica di Callisto III; equilibrio italiano e difesa dell'Europa alla metà del secolo XV', *Studi romani*,

vii, 1959. For a good survey of Calixtus' crusading activity, *see* Schwoebel, *The Shadow of the Crescent*, pp. 37–57.

12. Calixtus' fleet has been studied by P. Paschini, 'La flotta di Callisto III (1455–58)', *ASRSP.*, liii–v, 1930–2; additional material on Catalans employed in the fleet appears in J. Rius Serra, *Regesto iberico di Calixto III* (Barcelona, 1948 and 1958), *passim*.

13. L. Banchi, 'Il Piccinino nello stato di Siena e la lega italica (1455–6)', *ASI.*, 4th. ser., iv, 1879, p. 58: 'Avete un papa affezionatissimo alla vostra repubblica; sappiate profitarne, però che in lui è grande l'animo quanto la carità, nè altro gli sta a cuore che la giustizia.'

14. Ibid., p. 230.

15. W. H. Woodward, *Cesare Borgia* (London, 1913), p. 7. There were rumours circulating about plans to marry Pedro Luis to the daughter of the King of Cyprus, and even to make him Emperor of Constantinople.

16. Pastor, II, pp. 337–40.

17. Luis Juan de Mila is often mistakenly described as Bishop of Segovia, but his see remained Segorbe, near Valencia, until 1459 when he was translated to Lerida.

18. J. Rius Serra, 'Catalanes y Aragoneses en la corte de Calixto III', *Analecta Sacra Taraconensia*, iii, 1927, pp. 227–9.

19. Pastor, II, p. 469.

20. Ibid., II, p. 329: 'Regnano i catalani e sa Dio come la loro natura ci si confa.'

21. Rius Serra, 'Catalanes', pp. 220 ff.; 1 out of 27 scriptors was a Catalan, 3 out of 5 auditors of the Rota, 2 out of 23 secretaries, and 12 out of 30 abbreviators.

22. Typical of the appointments held by Catalans were those of Berengario Clavell as Treasurer of Perugia, Pedro Climent as Governor of Frascati, Estaban Planas as castellan of Civitavecchia, and Galceran de Ribes as Senator of Rome (Rius Serra, 'Catalanes', pp. 220 ff.).

23. Vespasiano da Bisticci, *Vite di uomini illustri del secolo XV*, ed. P. Ancona and E. Aeschlimann (Milan, 1951), pp. 167–8.

24. J. Rius Serra, 'Un inventario de joyas de Calixto III', *Analecta Sacra Taraconensia*, v, 1929, pp. 8–9.

25. Pastor, II, p. 387 and E. Müntz, *Les arts à la cour des papes*, I, pp. 213–217.

26. These rough figures are based on an examination of the household accounts for 1454, 1455 and 1456 in ASR. Camerale I, *spese minute*, 1469 and 1470. Gregorovius examined this material (*see* his brief description of it in 'Das Römische Staatsarchiv', *Historische Zeitschrift*, xxxvi, 1876), but failed to notice the pre-1458 volumes.

27. R. Rubinstein, 'Pius II's Piazza S.Pietro and St. Andrew's Head', p. 22.

28. Pastor, II, pp. 332–6 and A. Albareda, 'Il bibliotecario di Callisto III', *Studi e testi*, CXXIV (*Miscellanea Mercati*, IV) (Vatican City, 1946), particularly pp. 206–8.

CHAPTER FIVE

1. Jacopo Gherardi da Volterra, *Diario Romano*, ed. E. Carusi, *RIS.*, XXIII, 3 (Città di Castello, 1904), pp. 48–9: 'Vir est ingenii ad quecumque versatilis et animi magni, sermo ei promptus est et in mediocri literatura valde compositus. Natura est calidus, sed ante omnia mire ad res tractandes industrie. Claret mirum in modum opibus; regum et principum plurimorum clientelis admodum clarus.'

2. The long established tradition, originating with Platina, that Rodrigo's father was Jofrè Borgia-Lanzol and that his real name was therefore Borgia-Lanzol has been conclusively disproved; *see* Woodward, *Cesare Borgia*, pp. 3–4 and De Roo, *Materials for a History of Alexander VI*, I, pp. 1–16.

3. F. Giorgi, 'Rodrigo Borgia allo studio di Bologna', *AMR.*, viii, 1890.

4. De Roo, *Materials for a History of Alexander VI*, I, pp. 548–9. In 1492 when the Milanese ambassador Jason del Maino delivered his congratulatory oration he referred to the 44 years which Alexander had spent in Italy.

5. Gaspare da Verona, *Le vite di Paolo II*, ed. G. Zippel, *RIS.*, XVI, 3 (Citta di Castello, 1904), p. 39: 'Formosus est, laetissimo vultu aspectuque iocundo, lingua ornata atque melliflua, qui mulieres egregias visas ad se amandum gratior allicet et mirum in modum concitat, plusquam magnetes ferrum.'

6. Don Jaime was the Cardinal of Portugal who died in Florence in 1459 and to whose memory a chapel is dedicated in San Miniato; *see* F. Hartt, G. Corti and C. Kennedy, *The Chapel of the Cardinal of Portugal (1434–59) in San Miniato in Florence* (Philadelphia, 1964).

7. F. La Torre, *Del Conclave di Alessandro VI, Papa Borgia* (Florence, 1933), pp. 46–7.

8. *Commentaries of Pius II*, VIII, pp. 535–6.

9. Jacopo Gherardi da Volterra, *Diario Romano*, p. 48.

10. Pastor, V, pp. 366–7 and 528–9.

11. Magnuson, *Studies in Roman Quattrocento Architecture*, pp. 230–40. The palace was restored and embellished by Galeotto della Rovere when he was Vice-Chancellor after 1507. When it ceased to be the Chancellery about 1517 it passed back to the Sforza family, and then by marriage in 1554 to the Cesarini. *See* F. Cancellieri, 'Notizie del Palazzo della Cancelleria Vecchia', *Effemeride letterarie*, Dec. 1821.

12. Among the more extravagant of the apologetic theses are those of M. J. H. Olivier (*Le Pape Alexandre VI et les Borgia*, Paris, 1870) who held that Alexander's children were the offspring of an early marriage with Giulia Farnese before he took up an ecclesiastical career, and De Roo (*Materials for a History of Alexander VI*, I, *passim*) who saw the children as being those of a nephew Guillen Ramon Borja-Lanzol.

13. A. Leonetti, *Papa Alessandro VI secondo documenti e carteggi del tempo* (Bologna, 1880), I, p. 106.

14. Pastor, II, pp. 452–4.

15. Ibid., II, pp. 454–5.

16. A. Luzio, 'Isabella d'Este e i Borgia', *Archivio storico lombardo*, xli–xlii, 1914–5, pt. I, p. 471. The episode has been examined in some detail by La Torre, *Conclave di Alessandro VI*, pp. 6–18.

17. It was at this moment that the other notorious incident of his career as cardinal took place when it was reported that he had not slept alone during his stay in Ancona. For comments on this *see* Pastor, II, p. 455; O. Ferrara, *The Borgia Pope Alexander VI* (London, 1942), pp. 63–5; G. B. Picotti, 'Ancora sul Borgia', *RSCI.*, viii, 1954, pp. 324–5.

18. Schüller Piroli, *Borgia*, p. 182; F. Gori, 'Residenza, nascite e fortificazioni dei Borgia nella rocca di Subiaco', *Archivio storico, artistico e letterario della città e provincia di Roma*, iv, 1880.

19. The Spanish legation has been described by J. Sanchis y Sivera, 'El cardinal Rodrigo Borgia en Valencia', *BRAH.*, lxxxiv, 1924; Schüller Piroli, *Borgia*, pp. 169–76; J. Fernandez Alonso, *Legaciones y nunciatures en Espana de 1466 a 1521*, Monumenta Hispaniae Vaticana, II (Rome, 1963).

20. J. Villanueva, *Viage literario a les iglesias de España* (Madrid, 1803), IV, pp. 306–7.

21. De Roo, *Materials for a History of Alexander VI*, II, pp. 180–6.

22. The marriage had already been celebrated on the basis of a forged Bull of dispensation; it was this that now had to be put right.

23. A. Garcia de la Fuente, 'Le legacion del cardinal Rodrigo de Borja y la cuestion monetaria de Enrique IV', *Religion y Cultura*, 1933.

24. State Archives, Florence. Missive della Seconda Cancelleria, 5, ff. 173–4; 6, ff. 1v, 2v, 16r, 44v, 45r, 87v.

25. L. Thuasne (ed.), *Johannis Burchardi Diarium* (Paris, 1883), I, p. 507: 'ma è tenuto si superbo et di mala fede che non se ne ha paura. . . .'

26. P. Paschini, 'Prodromi all'elezione di Alessandro VI', *Atti del I° Congresso nazionale di studi romani* (Rome, 1929), vol. I, *passim*.

27. P. Paschini, *Il carteggio fra il cardinale Marco Barbo e Giovanni Lorenzi*, (*Studi e testi*, CXXXVII, Rome, 1948), pp. 211–13.

28. G. B. Picotti, 'Nuovi studi e documenti intorno a papa Alessandro VI', *RSCI.*, v, 1951, p. 181.

29. De Roo, *Materials for a History of Alexander VI*, II, doc. 86.

30. G. Gasca Quierazza, *Gli scritti autografi di Alessandro VI nell'Archivum Arcis* (Turin, 1959); M. Batllori, 'La llengua catalana a la cort d'Alexander VI; in *Vuit segles de cultura catalana a Europa* (Barcelona, 1958). Batllori has also announced a forthcoming edition of the Catalan correspondence of the Borgias.

31. E. Carli, *Pienza: die Umgestaltung Corsignanos durch die Bauherrn Pius II* (Basle, 1964); G. B. Manucci, 'I quattro cardinali fedeli a Pio II nelle costruzioni pientine', *Bollettino senese di storia patria*, 3rd. ser., xiv–xv, 1955–6.

32. J. R. Hale, 'The early development of the bastion: an Italian chronology (c. 1450–c. 1534)', *Europe in the Late Middle Ages*, pp. 480–1 The fortress of Civita Castellana which is perhaps the best known of Rodrigo's fortifications was the work of his papal period; *see* below p. 237.

33. The chapel of Vanozza was that to the right of the main altar now known as the chapel of Santa Lucia. It was restored and redecorated by Alexander VII in the seventeenth century. The Bregno altarpiece is now in the sacristy.

34. A Ferrua, 'Ritrovamento dell'epitaffio di Vanozza Cattaneo', *ASRSP.*, lxxi, 1948.

35. F. Fita, 'Don Pedro Luis de Borja, Duque de Gandia', *BRAH.*, x, 1887.

36. U. Gnoli, 'Una figlia sconosciuta di Alessandro VI', *L'Urbe*, ii, 1937.

37. M. Menotti, 'Vanozza Cattanei e i Borgia,' *Nuova Antologia*, clxxxi, 1916.

38. The much disputed question of whether Cesare or Juan was the older now seems to be clearly resolved in favour of Cesare; *see* L. Celier, 'Alexandre VI et ses enfants en 1493', *Mélanges d'archéologie et d'histoire*, xxvi, 1906, pp. 330–4; Woodward, *Cesare Borgia*, pp. 24–6; Picotti, 'Ancora sul Borgia', p. 336.

39. For an extended discussion of the relationship between Alexander and Giulia Farnese, *see* G. Soranzo, *Studi intorno a papa Alessandro VI* (Milan, 1950), pp. 92–129; idem, 'Orsino Orsini, Adriana de Mila, sua madre, e Giulia Farnese, sua moglie, nei loro rapporti con papa Alessandro VI', *Archivi*, 2nd. ser., xxvi, 1959; Picotti, 'Nuovi studi e documenti intorno a papa Alessandro VI', pp. 207–40. Soranzo's thesis that Giulia was merely a hostage for the good behaviour of her husband seems hard to maintain.

CHAPTER SIX

1. F. Guicciardini, *Storia d'Italia*, ed. C. Panigada (Bari, 1929), I, p. 2. The translation is that of C. Grayson, *F. Guicciardini: the History of Italy and the History of Florence* (London, 1966), p. 86.

2. The main accounts of the election of Alexander VI are: Pastor, V,

pp. 375–96; La Torre, *Del Conclave di Alessandro VI*; W. Schweitzer, 'Zur Wahl Alexanders VI', *Historisches Jahrbuch*, xxx, 1909; Soranzo, *Studi intorno a papa Alessandro VI*, pp. 1–33.

3. The 200,000 ducats was at one time thought to be French money but historical opinion on this has changed: *see* Soranzo, *op. cit.*, p. 12.

4. Soranzo, *op. cit.*, p. 13.

5. The report is that of Giovanni Boccaccio, the Ferrarese ambassador, quoted by Pastor, V, pp. 533–4.

6. This report, which figures largely in many accounts, comes from the notoriously inaccurate chronicler Stefano Infessura, *Diario della città di Roma*, ed. O. Tommasini (Rome, 1890), p. 282.

7. The scrutiny lists were discovered by Schweitzer ('Zur Wahl Alexanders VI',) and analysed with a useful diagram by La Torre (*Del Conclave di Alessandro VI*, pp. 88–106).

8. Guicciardini, *Storia d'Italia*, I, p. 6.

9. G. Soranzo, 'Documenti inediti o poco noti relativi all' assunzione al pontificato di Alessandro VI', *Archivi*, xix, 1952, emphasises the extent of the satisfaction expressed by Italian powers at the election of Alexander.

10. G. B. Picotti, 'Giovanni de' Medici nel conclave per l'elezione di Alessandro VI', *ASRSP.*, xliv, 1921, pp. 138–51. In this article and in his more recent writings Picotti paints the opposite picture to Soranzo, one of widespread alarm and concern at Alexander's election.

11. The best descriptions of the coronation are those of Filippo Valori and Bernardino Corio printed in L. Thuasne (ed.), *Burchardi Diarium*, (Paris, 1883–5), II, pp. 615 ff.

12. A. Lisini, 'Cesare Borgia e la repubblica di Siena', *Bullettino senese di storia patria*, vii, 1900, pp. 91–2, argues for an immediate journey of Cesare to Rome in August 1492, but this seems to be on the basis of a misdated letter and all the other authorities oppose the view.

13. Pastor, V, pp. 398–9.

14. ASR. Camerale I, *mandati camerali*, 855, ff. 30r and 49. Rodrigo Borgia-Lanzol had 150 infantry and 24 mounted crossbow men under his command. He was later succeeded in the post by Guillen Ramon Borjia-Lanzol.

15. De Boüard, 'Lettres de Rome', p. 324.

16. The affair of the Cibo castles is fully discussed by E. Pontieri, *Per la storia del regno di Ferrante I d'Aragona, Re di Napoli* (Naples, 1946), pp. 351–94; and I. Dell'Oro, *Papa Alessandro VI (Rodrigo Borgia); appunti per chi vorrà scrivere la vera storia della famiglia Borgia* (Milan, 1940), pp. 46–82.

17. ASR. Camerale I, *mandati camerali*, 855, is full of payments to *condottieri* in 1493. *See* also De Roo, *Materials for a History of Alexander VI*, *IV*, pp. 278–9.

18. More lurid accounts of these ceremonies are derived from Infessura

(*Diario della città di Roma*, p. 287), but all other reports agree in describing a courtly but not outrageously immoral occasion. *See* Johannes Burchardi, *Liber notarum*, ed. E. Celani, *RIS*, XXXII, pt. 1 (Città di Castello, 1906) pp. 443–6; Boccaccio's report in Gregorovius, *Lucrezia Borgia*, pp. 37–8; a Mantuan report in Luzio 'Isabella d'Este e i Borgia', III, pp. 119–20; and L. Pescetti, 'Le prime nozze di Lucrezia Borgia in una lettera inedita di Jacopo Gherardi', *Rassegna volterrana*, 1955.

19. F. Trinchera (ed.), *Codice Aragonese in Napoli riguardanti l'amministrazione interna del Reame e le relazioni all'estero* (Naples, 1866), II, 2, pp. 41–8. The charges in this letter are refuted at length by Dell'Oro, *Papa Alessandro VI*, pp. 11 ff.

20. H. Vanderlinden, 'Alexander VI and the demarcation of the maritime and colonial domains of Spain and Portugal', *American Historical Review*, xxii, 1917; L. Weckmann, *Las bulas alejandrinas de 1493 y la teoria politica del papado medieval* (Mexico City, 1949); M. Battllori, *Alejandro VI y la Real Casa de Aragon* (Madrid, 1958), pp. 24–5.

21. J. Sanchis y Sivera, *Algunos documentos y cartas privadas que partenecieron al segundo Duque de Gandia, don Juan de Borja* (Valencia, 1919), pp. 23–30.

22. Luzio, 'Isabella d'Este e i Borgia', IV, pp. 415.

23. Sanchis y Sivera, op. cit., pp. 132–47.

24. Gasca Quierazza, *Gli scritti autografi di Alessandro VI*, docs. I, II and VII.

25. *Ibid.* doc. XVIII.

26. L. Fumi, *Alessandro VI e il Valentino in Orvieto* (Siena, 1877), pp. 6 ff.

27. Lisini, *Cesare Borgia e la Repubblica di Siena*, pp. 91–2. Lisini places these events in 1492 but Cesare's letter of protest from Caprarola should be dated 1493.

28. On this wedding ceremony *see* Burchard, *Liber notarum*, I, pp. 504–505, and the letter of Cardinal Juan Borgia-Lanzol, the elder, printed in R. Chabas, 'Don Jofrè de Borja y Dona Sancha de Aragon', *Revue hispanique*, ix, 1902.

29. De Boüard, 'Lettres de Rome', p. 330.

30. AV. AA I–XVIII, 5024, ff. 126–9. These documents have also been studied by M. Bellonci, *Lucrezia Borgia; la sua vita e i suoi tempi* (rev. ed., Milan, 1960), pp. 91–2.

CHAPTER SEVEN

1. Gasca Quierazza, *Gli scritti autografi di Alessandro VI*, doc. IX, X and XI.

2. The desultory campaign in the Romagna in 1494 has been carefully studied by G. L. Moncallero, 'Documenti inediti sulla guerra di Romagna del 1494', *Rinascimento*, iv–vi, 1953–5.

3. P. Negri, 'Le missioni di Pandolfo Collenuccio a papa Alessandro VI (1494–1498)', *ASRSP.*, xxxiii, 1910, p. 379.

4. One of the letters captured from Bocciardo was said to contain details of the 300,000 ducats offered by the Sultan for the murder of his brother, but this was probably a forgery. For detailed discussion of this, *see* Pastor, V, pp. 428–30; on the death of Djem the evidence has been well assessed by J. H. Whitfield, 'New views upon the Borgias', *History*, xxviii, 1943, pp. 77–8.

5. F. Matarazzo, 'Cronaca della città di Perugia dal 1492 al 1503,' ed. A. Fabretti, *ASI.*, xvi, pt. 2, 1851, pp. 37–9.

6. On the importance of Pisa to Florence, *see* M. E. Mallett, 'Pisa and Florence in the fifteenth century', *Florentine Studies*, ed. N. Rubinstein.

7. The conflict between Savonarola and Alexander VI has been discussed recently by G. Soranzo, *Il tempo di Alessandro VI papa e di Fra Girolamo Savonarola* (Milan, 1960) and G. B. Picotti, 'Alessandro VI, il Savonarola ed il cardinale Giuliano della Rovere in una pubblicazione recente', *ASRSP.*, lxxxiii, 1960.

8. G. Zurita, *Anales de la Corona de Aragon* (Zaragossa, 1610), V, p. 123.

9. F. Sansovino, *L'Historia di casa Orsini* (Venice, 1565), pp. 123–4; Sigismondo de'Conti, *Le storie dei suoi tempi dal 1475 al 1510* (Rome, 1883), II, pp. 166–72.

10. G. Ouy, 'Le pape Alexandre VI a-t-il employé les armes chimiques?', *Receuil de travaux offerts à C. Brunel* (Paris, 1955), II.

11. Burchard, *Liber notarum*, II, p. 19.

12. B. Feliciangeli, *Un episodio nel nepotismo borgiano; il matrimonio di Lucrezia Borgia con Giovanni Sforza, signore di Pesaro* (Turin, 1901), p. 11.

13. There are many accounts of the murder of the Duke of Gandia of which the most valuable are M. Sanuto, *Diarii* (Venice, 1879 ff.), I, cols. 650–63; Burchard, *Liber notarum*, II, pp. 42–5; A. Luzio and R. Renier, 'Relazione inedita sulla morte del Duca di Gandia', *ASRSP.*, xi, 1888. The best assessment of the evidence is still Pastor, V, pp 493–511.

14. Sanuto, *Diarii*, I, cols. 653–4.

15. For the text of the Bull, see Pastor, V, pp. 558–63, and M. Tangl, *Die päpstlichen Kanzleiordnungen von 1200–1500*, (Innsbruck, 1894), pp. 402–421.

16. See below pp. 240–1.

17. Dell'Oro, *Papa Alessandro VI*, pp. 302–3.

18. The more lurid reports of the death of Calderon clinging to the robes of the Pope while Cesare stabbed him emerge from Venetian sources more than two years after the event (Sanuto, *Diarii*, III, cols. 842 ff.), and are denied by Burchard's account of the unexplained discovery of his body floating in the Tiber. For suggestions that the child born to Lucrezia was the *Infans Romanus*, see below p. 181.

CHAPTER EIGHT

1. *See* the Mantuan ambassador Cataneo's report in Luzio, 'Isabella d'Este e i Borgia', IV, p. 420, and F. R. De Uhagon, *Relacion de los festines que se celebraron en el Vaticano con motivo de las bodas de Lucrecia Borgia con Alonso de Aragon* (Madrid, 1896).

2. Sanuto, *Diarii*, III, col. 846.

3. L. G. Pélissier, 'Sopra alcuni documenti relativi all' alleanza tra Alessandro VI e Luigi XII, 1498–9', *ASRSP.*, xvii–xviii, 1894–5, is still the best account of these negotiations although inclined to be unduly hostile towards the Borgias.

4. G. Breisach, *Caterina Sforza*, pp. 172–4.

5. Sanuto, *Diarii*, I, col. 753.

6. J. Larner, 'Cesare Borgia, Machiavelli and the Romagnol militia', *Studi Romagnoli*, xvii, 1966; also *see* below pp. 215–6.

7. A. Bernardi, *Cronache forlivesi dal 1476 al 1517* (Bologna, 1895–7), I, pt. 2, p. 265.

8. Many of these capitulation agreements are printed in the appendix of E. Alvisi, *Cesare Borgia, duca di Romagna* (Imola, 1878).

9. B. Feliciangeli, 'Le proposte per la guerra contro i turchi presentate da Stefano Taleazzo, vescovo di Torcello, a papa Alessandro VI', *ASRSP.*, xxxix, 1916.

10. Sanuto, *Diarii*, III, col. 845.

11. Ibid., III, col. 671. Only B. Buonacorsi (*Diario dei successi dall'anno 1498 fino all'anno 1512*, Florence, 1568, p. 51) of all the main sources for these events saves Cesare's name by saying that Alfonso died of his earlier wounds.

12. Gregorovius, *Lucrezia Borgia*, pp. 124–5. The Bulls are published in full in the original German edition of Gregorovius.

13. A. Giustinian, *Dispacci*, ed. P. Villari (Florence, 1876), I, p. 108 (7 Sept. 1502).

14. Gregorovius, *Lucrezia Borgia*, p. 125.

15. Ibid., p. 106 quotes a report by Pandolfo Collenuccio on Cesare's suite at the time of the occupation of Pesaro. Many were the same men who had accompanied him to France in 1498.

16. B. Feliciangeli, *Sull'acquisto di Pesaro fatto da Cesare Borgia* (Camerino, 1900), p. 52.

17. Gregorovius, *Lucrezia Borgia*, pp. 122–5.

18. I am indebted to Mr. John Larner for making this point to me.

19. Bernardi, *Cronache forlivesi*, I, pt. 2, pp. 324–9. Bernardi's account intermingles details of occasional fracas between the townsfolk and Cesare's troops on the one hand, with those of the stern discipline meted out to ill disciplined troops on the other.

20. See below pp. 210–19.

21. Many of the reports of the sack of Capua make no mention of Cesare's part in it; see Burchard, *Liber notarum*, II, p. 293; Sigismondo de'Conti, *Storie dei suoi tempi*, II, p. 239. It was the French chronicler Jean d'Auton (*Chroniques de Louis XII*, Paris, 1834–5, II, p. 62) who attached all the blame to Cesare.

22. Burchard, *Liber notarum*, II, p. 320.

CHAPTER NINE

1. Gregorovius, *Lucrezia Borgia*, p. 106.

2. Guidobaldo's letter to Cardinal Giuliano della Rovere giving his version of these events was published by Alvisi, *Cesare Borgia*, pp. 528–33.

3. N. Machiavelli, *Le legazioni e commissarie di Niccolò Machiavelli*, ed. S. Bertelli (Milan, 1964), I, pp. 267–8 (26 June 1502).

4. Ibid., I, pp. 386–7 (23 Oct. 1502).

5. Ibid., I, p. 392 (27 Oct. 1502).

6. Giustinian, *Dispacci*, I, p. 298.

7. Ibid., I. p. 238 (30 Nov. 1502).

8. Ibid., I, pp. 242–3 (2 Dec. 1502).

9. Ibid., I, p. 150 (13 Oct. 1502).

10. R. Cessi, *Dispacci degli ambasciatori veneziani alla corte di Roma presso Giulio II* (Venice, 1932), p. xiii.

11. For a careful analysis of the sources of the events at Senigallia, *see* G. Pepe, *La politica dei Borgia* (Naples, 1946), pp. 299 ff.

12. G. Volpe, 'Intorno ad alcune relazioni di Pisa con Alessandro VI e Cesare Borgia (1499–1504),' *Studi storici*, vi–vii, 1897–8, II, p. 89.

13. Giustinian, *Dispacci*, II, p. 91 (31 July 1503).

CHAPTER TEN

1. For many points in the discussion which follows I am particularly indebted to Mr. John Larner who very kindly showed me the manuscripts of two forthcoming articles: 'Cesare Borgia, Machiavelli and the Romagnol militia', *Studi romagnoli*, xvii, 1966, and 'Cesare Borgia and the "Buon Governo" of the Romagna'.

2. N. Machiavelli, *Il Principe*, chap. VII.

3. F. Guicciardini, *Storie fiorentine*, ed. R. Palmarocchi (Bari, 1931), p. 266.

4. Alvisi, *Cesare Borgia*, p. 391; Woodward, *Cesare Borgia*, pp. 313–8.

5. Matarazzo, 'Cronaca della città di Perugia', p. 219; G. Priuli, *I Diari*, *RIS.*, XXIV, pt. 3 (Città di Castello, 1921–41), II, p. 300. Pepe (*Poli-*

tica dei Borgia, pp. 185–8) states the strongest case against the tradition of the '*buon governo*' of Cesare Borgia.

6. The terms offered to the city of Fano are set out in a letter of Cesare of 5 Nov. 1501 now to be found in Biblioteca Comunale 'Aurelio Saffi' (Forlì), Raccolta Piancastelli. My attention was drawn to this letter, which escaped the notice of Alvisi, by Dr. Ian Robertson who very kindly showed me a microfilm of it.

7. Among the multiplicity of studies devoted to Leonardo, see particularly for his activities in the Romagna; C. Pedretti, *A Chronology of Leonardo da Vinci's Architectural Studies after 1500* (Geneva, 1962), p. 32; L. Beltrami, *Leonardo e il Porto di Cesenatico* (Milan, 1903); Nando de Toni, 'Leonardo da Vinci e i rilievi topografici di Cesena', *Studi romagnoli*, VIII, 1957; M. Baratta, 'La pianta di Imola di Leonardo da Vinci', *Bolletino della Società geografica italiana*, 1911.

8. C. H. Clough, 'The Chronicle (1502–12) of Girolamo Vanni of Urbino', *Studi urbinati*, ns. xxxix, 1965, p. 342.

9. Machiavelli, *Legazioni e commissarie*, I, p. 348 (11 Oct. 1502).

10. See the analysis of Cesare's armies in Larner, 'Cesare Borgia, Machiavelli and the Romagnol militia.'

11. Gregorovius, *Lucrezia Borgia*, p. 106.

12. C. Cansacchi, 'Agapito Gheraldini', *Bollettino della deputazione di storia patria per l'Umbria*, lviii, 1961.

13. V. Cian, part of a review of Pastor in *Giornale storico della letteratura italiana*, xxix, 1897, p. 432.

14. G. Soranzo, 'Il clima storico della politica veneziana in Romagna e nelle Marche nel 1503', *Studi romagnoli*, v, 1954.

15. ASR. Camerale I, *depositarius generalis*, 1758, f. 121 v, and *tesorerie provinciali*, Marca, 53.

16. De Roo, *Materials for a History of Alexander VI*, III, pp. 375–6.

17. F. Mancini, 'Lucrezia Borgia, governatrice di Spoleto', *ASI.*, cxv, 1957, pp. 183–4.

18. Matarazzo, 'Cronaca della città di Perugia,' pp. 37–9.

19. Lord Acton, 'The Borgias and their latest historian', *Historical Essays and Studies*, ed. N. Figgis (London, 1907), pp. 73: 'è molto necessario la provisione de le genti d'arme contro questi demonii che non fugono per acqua santa.'

20. Matarazzo, *op. cit.*, pp. 4–5.

21. The provincial treasurers' accounts in the Archivio di Stato, Rome, have been little studied for this period and are a mine of information for the administration of the Papal States under Alexander VI. For Spannochi's accounts, *see* ASR. Camerale I, *tesorerie provinciali*, Marca, 53 and 54.

22. Ferrara (*The Borgia Pope*, p. 131) describes the *reformationes Alexandri*

as 'the most far sighted and complete document upon public law in the whole history of papal Rome'; but this judgment is scarcely borne out by Rodocanachi's (*Institutions communales*, p. 207) broader view of Roman municipal government.

23. Pepe, *Politica dei Borgia*, p. 252; Luzio, 'Isabella d'Este e i Borgia', IV, p. 448.

24. Pepe, *op. cit.*, p. 256.

25. Giustinian, *Dispacci*, I, p. 297 (31 Dec. 1502); Machiavelli, *Legazioni e commissarie*, I, p. 455 (26 Nov., 1502).

26. According to Giustinian 182,800 ducats were sent by Alexander to Cesare between June 1502 and February 1503. For further information on Cesare's expenses in the Romagna, *see* D. Dal Re, 'Discorso critico sui Borgia con l'aggiunta di documenti inediti relativi al pontificato d'Alessandro VI', *ASRSP.*, iv, 1881, pp. 114–9 and M. Menotti, *Documenti inediti sulla famiglia e la corte di Alessandro VI* (Rome, 1917), pp. 43–7.

27. ASR. Camerale I, *mandati camerali*, 855, ff. 43v–44r.

28. Ibid. *passim.*

29. Giustinian, *Dispacci*, II, p. 30 (31 May, 1503): 'in modo che questo Pontefice, con i modi suoi, ha fatto certo cadauno che le intrade di un Papa sono tante quante lui medemo el vuol farlc csscr.'

30. Delumeau, *L'alun de Rome*, pp. 97 ff.

31. Pastor, VI, pp. 91–2.

32. Luzio, 'Isabella d'Este e i Borgia', IV, p. 418.

33. G. Soranzo, 'Giovanni Battista Zeno, nipote di Paolo II, cardinale di S. Maria in Portico (1468–1501)', *RSCI.*, xvi, 1962, p. 269.

34. Alexander made a personal visit to Porto to collect up Michiel's possessions from the cardinal's palace (Giustinian, *Dispacci*, II, p. 485).

35. Pastor, after considering all the accusations of poisoning (see particularly VI, pp. 126–8) comes to the conclusion that only Cardinal Michiel was probably poisoned on the orders of the Borgias. For discussion of the nature of the *cantarella*, see Ferrara, *The Borgia Pope*, pp. 313–27 and F. W. Rolfe, *Chronicles of the House of Borgia* (London, 1901) pp. 214–40.

36. Ricard, 'La monarchie pontificale', p. 434.

37. Giustinian, *Dispacci*, I, p. 453.

38. Gottlob, *Aus der Camera apostolica*, pp. 259–65.

39. Gregorovius, *Lucrezia Borgia*, p. 59 and Luzio, 'Isabella d'Este e i Borgia', I, pp. 477–8.

40. Three volumes of the household accounts of Alexander VI for 1501–3 are to be found in ASR. Camerale I, *spese minute*, 1484–6. Excerpts from these were published by Menotti, *Documenti inediti sulla famiglia e la corte di Alessandro VI*, pp. 120–35.

41. ASR. Camerale I, *spese minute*, 1485, ff. 30v and 47v

42. Gregorovius, *Lucrezia Borgia*, p. 122.

43. Matarazzo, 'Cronaca della città di Perugia,' p. 189; Burchard, *Liber notarum*, II, p. 303. For the Savelli letter *see* Burchard, II, pp. 312–15.

44. For the most recent assessments of Burchard's reliability, *see* Soranzo, *Studi intorno a papa Alessandro VI*, pp. 34–75 and Picotti, 'Nuovi studi e documenti intorno a papa Alessandro VI', pp. 173–80.

45. Giustinian, *Dispacci*, I, p. 404 (21 Feb. 1503).

46. This assessment of the papal household is based on G. Bourgin, 'La "famiglia" pontificia sotto Eugenius IV', *ASRSP.*, xxvii, 1904, and P. Piccolomini, 'La "famiglia" di Pio III', *ASRSP.*, xxvi, 1903, as well as the household accounts of Alexander VI.

47. L. Onori, 'Un maggiordomo di Alessandro VI', *Rivista del Collegio Araldico*, 1914.

48. A. Albareda, 'Il vescovo di Barcellona Pietro Garsias, bibliotecario della Vaticana sotto Alessandro VI', *Bibliofilia*, lx, 1958.

49. The most complete account of Alexander's artistic patronage is still E. Müntz, *Les arts à la cour des Papes Innocent VIII, Alexandre VI, Pie III (1484–1503)* (Paris, 1898).

50. For recent comments on Pinturicchio and the Borgia Apartments, *see*: F. Saxl, 'The Appartamento Borgia', *Lectures* (London, 1957) and J. Schulz, 'Pinturicchio and the Revival of Antiquity', *Journal of the Warburg and Courtauld Institutes*, xxv, 1962.

51. J. S. Ackermann, 'Bramante and the Torre Borgia', *Rendiconti della Pontificia Accademia romana di archeologia*, xxv–xxvi, 1949–51, pp. 247–8.

52. E. Rodocanachi, 'Le Chateau Sant-Ange sous le pontificat d'Alexandre VI', *Revue des questions historiques*, lxxxv, 1909.

53. F. Sanguinetti, 'La fortezza di Civita Castellana e il suo restauro', *Palladio*, ns. ix, 1959.

54. For the best accounts of the literary circle at the Borgia court, *see* Gregorovius, *Lucrezia Borgia*, pp. 79–84 and Cian, in *Giornale storico della letteratura italiana*.

55. Pico della Mirandola's letter was published by L. Dorez, in *Giornale storico della letteratura italiana*, xxv, 1895, p. 361.

CHAPTER ELEVEN

1. Pastor, VI, p. 131.

2. Ibid., pp. 135–6 examines very fully the theory that the Pope was poisoned, and convincingly rejects it. Those who were most influential in propagating the rumour were almost all not in Rome at the time, whereas the reports of eyewitnesses all suggest natural causes for Alexander's death.

3. Ibid., VI, p. 187. Some historians have argued that Cesare had control of Castel Sant'Angelo at this stage, but this was not the case.

4. Machiavelli, *Legazioni e commissarie*, II, pp. 599–600 (4 Nov. 1503).

5. Pastor, VI, p. 235 quoting the report of Beltrando Costabili, the Ferrarese envoy.

6. Machiavelli, *op. cit.*, II, pp. 631–2 (14 Nov. 1503).

7. Ibid., II, p. 709 (3 Dec. 1503).

8. For the most complete statement of Gonsalvo's supposed duplicity and treachery, *see* Pastor, VI, pp. 243–4; Woodward, *Cesare Borgia*, pp. 364–8 takes the opposite view.

9. C. Yriarte, *Cesar Borgia; sa vie, sa captivité et son mort* (Paris, 1889), pp. 215–77 gives the most complete account of the last days of Cesare.

10. Pastor, VI, p. 200.

11. F. Trinchera (ed.), *Codice Aragonese*, II, 2, p. 46.

12. Sigismondo de'Conti, *Le storie dei suoi tempi*, p. 282.

CHAPTER TWELVE

1. Pastor, VI, p. 138.

2. Ferrua, 'Ritrovamento dell' epitaffio', pp. 140–1.

3. Bellonci, *Lucrezia Borgia*, pp. 355–6 and 475–8.

4. Gregorovius, *Lucrezia Borgia*, pp. 219–20.

5. G. Soranzo, 'La più grave accusa fatta a papa Borgia', *Archivi*, 2nd. ser., xxviii, 1961.

6. Bellonci, *op. cit.*, p. 475 and Woodward, *Cesare Borgia*, p. 391.

7. On Charlotte *see* G. L. Schlumberger, *Charlotte d'Albret, femme de César Borgia, et le château de la Motte-Feuilly* (Paris, 1913) and E. L. Miron, *Duchess Derelict; a Study of the Life and Times of Charlotte d'Albret, Duchesse de Valentinois* (London, 1911).

8. Schlumberger, *op. cit.*, p. 38.

9. Quoted by Miron, *op. cit.*, pp. 323–4.

10. A. De la Chenaye-Debois and Badier, *Dictionnaire de la Noblesse* (Paris, 1863), III, pp. 778 ff.

11. The apparent dichotomy is most clearly expressed in Gregorovius, and G. Campori, 'Una vittima della storia: Lucrezia Borgia', *Nuova Antologia*, ii, 1866. For a more balanced account see Bellonci of which there is a translation of the older edition by B. Wall (*Life and Times of Lucrezia Borgia*, London, 1953). I am indebted to Professor Nicolai Rubinstein for showing me the manuscript of his account of Lucrezia for the forthcoming volume of *Dizionario biografico degli Italiani*.

12. Bellonci, *op. cit.*, pp. 205 and 540–3.

13. This is the often quoted description of Cagnolo da Parma; for the translation see Gregorovius, *op. cit.*, p. 159.

14. Beside the main biographies, *see also* B. Morsolin, 'Pietro Bembo e Lucrezia Borgia', *Nuova Antologia*, xv, 1885.

15. Bartolomeo Veneto is often credited with painting a number of portraits of Lucrezia; on Bartolomeo's period in Ferrara *see* G. Swarzenski, 'Bartolomeo Veneto und Lucrezia Borgia', *Städel-Jahrbuch*, 1922, and A. De Hevesy, 'Bartolomeo Veneto et les portraits de Lucrezia Borgia', *The Arts Quarterly of the Detroit Institute of Arts*, ii, 1939. Bellonci, *op. cit.*, pp. 525–7 identifies another possible Bartolomeo portrait in the National Gallery, London.

16. Gregorovius, *op. cit.*, p. 213.

17. For the Squillace line *see* L. N. Cittadella, *Saggio di albero genealogico e di memorie su la famiglia Borgia* (Ferrara, 1872), pp. 54–5; De Roo, *Materials for a History of Alexander VI*, I. p. 299; Schüller Piroli, *Die Borgia*, pp. 315 and 536.

18. C. A. Gonzalez Palencia, 'Noticias biograficas del Virrey poeta, Principe de Esquillache, 1577–1658', *Annuario de estudios americanos*, vi, 1949, pp. 79–93.

CHAPTER THIRTEEN

1. F. Cervos and J. M. Sola, *El palacio ducal de Gandia* (Barcelona, 1904).

2. Luzio, 'Isabella d'Este e i Borgia', IV, p. 421.

3. E. Bertaux, 'Monuments et souvenirs des Borgias dans le royaume de Valencia', *Gazette des Beaux Arts*, 1908, pp. 204–10.

4. L. Amoros, 'El monasterio de Santa Clara de Gandia y la familia ducal de los Borjas', *Archivo ibero-americano*, xx-xxi, 1960–1.

5. The best biography of St. Francis Borgia is still P. Suau, *L'histoire de S. François de Borgia* (Paris, 1910); but *see also* O. Karrer, *Der heilige Franz von Borja, General des Gesellschaft Jesu, 1510–72* (Freiburg, 1921); M. Yeo, *The Greatest of the Borgias* (London, 1936); C. C. Martindale, *In God's Army*, Vol. II. St. Francis Borgia (London, 1916).

6. Lady Moreton, *A Playmate of Philip II, Don Martin of Aragon* (London, 1915), p. 30; this work contains some details of the life of Luisa de Borja.

7. Loyola was in Alcala in 1426, but it was actually in Salamanca in the next year that he was a prisoner of the Inquisition. The legend has therefore obviously been embroidered but it is not impossible that Francis caught a glimpse of St. Ignatius at this stage.

8. J. Brodrick, *The Origins of the Jesuits* (London, 1940), pp. 190–4.

9. Suau, *S. François de Borgia*, p. 130; Schüller Piroli, *Die Borgia*, p. 540.

10. Rolfe, *Chronicles of the House of Borgia*, p. 298.

11. Gonzalez Palencia, 'Noticias biograficas del Virrey poeta, Principe de Esquilache', *passim*.

12. F. Panesso Posada, 'Las familias Borja y Zulueta', *Boletin de historia y antiquedades* (Bogota), xliv, 1957.

13. T. D. Kendrick, *Mary of Agreda; the Life and Legend of a Spanish Nun* (London, 1967), pp. 21 and 116.

14. A. Dominguez Ortiz, *La sociedad espanola en el siglo XVII* (Madrid, 1963), pp. 227–8 and 304.

15. *Lord Beaconsfield's Letters, 1830–52*, ed. A. Disraeli (London, 1887), p. 139.

SELECT BIBLIOGRAPHY

1. Printed sources

In this section are mentioned only the more important narrative sources for Borgia history, and the larger collections of documents. Many of the works subsequently quoted in the later sections publish individual, and small groups of, documents.

M. Batllori, *La correspondencia d'Alexandre VI amb els seus familiars i amb els reis catolics* (Saragossa, 1956). A collection of much of the Spanish correspondence of Alexander VI.

A. Bernardi, *Cronache forlivesi dal 1476 al 1517* (Bologna, 1895–7). An important Romagnol diary.

Sebastiano di Branca Tedallini, *Diario romano dal maggio 1485 al 6 giugno 1524*, *RIS.*, XXIII (Città di Castello, 1907). Tedallini was a relatively uncultivated priest whose disordered collection of oral tradition, although contemporary, contains nothing which does not appear in other accounts.

G. Brom, Einige Briefe von R. Brandolinus Lippus', *Römische Quartalschrift*, ii, 1888. Latin letters of the Roman humanist who was friend and tutor of Alfonso d'Aragona, Duke of Bisceglie.

Johannes Burchard, *Diarium*, ed. L. Thuasne (Paris, 1883–5). Although a much criticised edition of Burchard's diary, this contains a good deal of useful material in appendices.

Johannes Burchard, *Liber notarum*, ed. E. Celani, *RIS.*, XXXII, 2 (Città di Castello. 1907 ff.). This is a more careful edition of the same work but still does not take account of all available manuscripts. *See* above p. 231 for recent comments on the reliability of Burchard, and see also G. B. Picotti's review of the edition in *ASRSP.*, xxxviii.

Philippe de Commines, *Memoires*, ed. J. Calmette (Paris, 1924).

Sigismondo de' Conti, *Le storie dei suoi tempi dal 1475 al 1510* (Rome, 1883). An important contemporary account by a Curia official with a strong interest in military events and a sympathy for papal aims.

P. De Roo, *Materials for a History of Pope Alexander VI, his Relatives and his Times* (Bruges, 1924), 5 vols. A vast collection of Vatican documents in appendices.

Michaelis Firnus, *Historia nova Alexander VI ab Innocenti VIII obitu* (Rome 1493). A source for the election and coronation of Alexander VI.

G. Gasca Qiuerazza, *Gli scritti autografi di Alessandro VI nell'Archivum Arcis* (Turin, 1959). A selection from the important collection of Vatican documents on Borgia policy 1493–5.

Gaspare da Verona, *Le vite di Paolo II*, ed. G. Zippel, *RIS.*, XVI, 3 (Città di Castello, 1904).

Jacopo Gherardi da Volterra, *Diario romano*, ed. E. Carusi, *RIS.*, XXIII, 3 (Città di Castello, 1904).

P. Giovio, *Gli elogi* (Florence, 1554). Contains an early life of Cesare Borgia.

A. Giustinian, *Dispacci*, ed. P. Villari (Florence, 1876), 3 vols. Venetian reports from Rome in 1502–3; for a review see M. Brosch in *Historische Zeitschrift*, xxxvii, 1877.

F. Guicciardini, *Storia d'Italia*, ed. C. Panigada (Bari, 1929).

F. Guicciardini, *Storie fiorentine*, ed. R. Palmarocchi (Bari, 1921).

Stefano Infessura, *Diario della città di Roma*, ed. O. Tommasini (Rome, 1890). Infessura as one of the last upholders of the Roman republican tradition was critical of the Popes and particularly of Alexander. His account ends in 1494.

A. Luzio, 'Isabella d'Este e i Borgia', *Archivio storico lombardo*, xli–xlii, 1914–5. The work is in four parts and draws heavily on Mantuan and Ferrarese archives. The reports of the Mantuan ambassador in Rome, Giovanni Cattaneo, are in part IV.

N. Machiavelli, *Le legazioni e commissarie*, ed. Sergio Bertelli (Milan, 1964).

N. Machiavelli, *Il Principe*, ed. G. Sasso (Florence, 1963).

N. Machiavelli, 'Descrizione del modo tenuto dal Duca Valentino nello ammazzar. Vitellozzo Vitelli, Oliverotto de Fermo, il signor Paolo e il duca di Gravina Orsini, in *Tutte le opere di Niccolò Machiavelli*, ed. G. Mazzoni e M. Casella (Florence, 1929) and many other editions. For the most recent interpretation of Machiavelli's attitudes towards Cesare Borgia, see G. Sasso, *Machiavelli e Cesare Borgia; storia di un giudizio* (Rome, 1966).

F. Matarazzo, 'Cronaca della città di Perugia dal 1492 al 1503', ed. A. Fabretti, *ASI.*, xvi, 2, 1851. Matarazzo was a partisan of the Baglione family and strongly anti-Borgia.

M. Menotti, *Documenti inediti sulla famiglia e la corte di Alessandro VI* (Rome, 1917). Vast collection of documents from the Vatican archives on the Borgias and their circle.

Monumenta Historica Societatis Jesu, S. Franciscus Borgia (Madrid, 1894). The correspondence of St. Francis.

P. Negri, 'Le missioni di Pandolfo Collenuccio a Papa Alessandro VI (1494–8)', *ASRSP.*, xxxiii, 1910. Appendix of letters includes 19 written during the crisis of Charles VIII's invasion.

L. G. Pélissier, 'Sopra alcuni documenti relativi all'alleanza tra Alessandro VI e Luigi XII, 1498–9', *ASRSP.*, xvii–xviii.

B. Platina, *Liber de vita Christi ac omnium pontificum*, ed. G. Gaida, *RIS.*, III, 2 (Bologna, 1923). Includes life of Calixtus III.

H. Porcius, *Commentarius*, ed. L. Thuasne in *Burchardi Diarium*, *op. cit.* Source for election and coronation of Alexander VI.

G. Priuli, *I Diari*, *RIS.*, XXIV, 3 (Città di Castello, 1921–41). A Venetian account.

J. Rius Serra, *Regesto iberico de Calixto III* (Barcelona, 1948 and 1958).

A. Ronchini, 'Documenti borgiani dell' Archivio di Stato in Parma', *Atti e memorie della R. Deputazione di storia patria per le provincie dell'Emilia*, ns. i, 1877. Documents on Giovanni Borgia, *Infans Romanus*.

J. Sanchis y Sivera, *Algunos documentos y cartas privadas que partenecieron al segundo Duque de Gandia, don Juan de Borja* (Valencia, 1919). Publication of documents from the Archivo de la Catedral de Valencia, including letters of Juan and account books.

M. Sanuto, *Diarii* (Venice, 1879 ff.). A vast collection of Venetian reports and rumours starting in 1496.

Ser Tommaso di Silvestro, *Diario*, ed. L. Fumi, *RIS.*, XV, 5. Contains details of Alexander's activities in Todi and Orvieto in 1494–5.

A. Theiner, *Codex diplomaticus temporalis S. Sedis*, vol. III (Rome, 1862).

F. Trinchera (ed.), *Codice Aragonese in Napoli riguardante l'amministrazione interna del Reame e le relazioni all'estero* (Naples, 1866).

Vespasiano da Bisticci, *Vite di uomini illustri del secolo XV*, ed. P. Ancona and E. Aeschlimann (Milan, 1951). Comments on Calixtus III and his circle.

G. Zurita, *Anales de la corona de Aragon* (Saragossa, 1610).

2. *The Borgias—General*

Most works dealing with the Borgias are concerned entirely with Alexander VI and his immediate family, and these are discussed in section 4 of this bibliography. A few writers have however taken a broader view of the family:

L. N. Cittadella, *Saggio di albero genealogico e di memorie sulla famiglia Borgia, specialmente in relazione a Ferrara* (Ferrara, 1872). An early attempt to solve the problems of Borgia genealogy, but the main conclusions have been largely discredited by later writers and particularly by the discovery of the Osuna genealogies.

L. Collison-Morley, *The History of the Borgias* (London, 1932). A readable and, within its limitations, reasonably accurate account of the family.

C. Fusero, *I Borgia* (Milan, 1966). This is the most recent Italian contribution to the subject, but it contains nothing new and takes no account of many of the more recent studies.

M Menotti, *I Borgia; storia e iconografia* (Rome, 1917). Contains a good deal of scattered information, particularly on the iconography, much of which is highly controversial.

S. Schüller Piroli, *Die Borgia. Die Zerstörung einer Legende; der Geschichte einer Dynastie* (Freiburg, 1963). A valuable and very full account, somewhat vitiated by an attempt to prove a connection between the Borgias and witchcraft.

C. Yriarte, *Autour des Borgias* (Paris, 1891), largely concerned with iconography. Other accounts of the same type but of less value are:

J. Fyvie, *The Story of the Borgias* (London, 1912); V. Pascual, 'Notas para la historia de los Borjas', *Saitabi*, i, 1940; F. W. Rolfe, *Chronicles of the House of Borgia* (London, 1901); V. von Schubert Soldern, *Die Borgia und ihre Zeit* (Dresden, 1902).

3. Calixtus III

There is no full scale biography of Calixtus III but for short accounts readers can consult: *Catholic Encyclopedia*, III and *Dictionnaire d'histoire et de géographie ecclésiastique* IX

On his early life there are:

J. Rins Serra, 'Alfonso de Borja', *Analecta sacra Taraconensia*, vi, 1930; J. B. Altisent Jove, *Alonso de Borja en Lerida (1408–23) despues papa Calixto III* (Lerida, 1924); J. Sanchis y Sivera, 'El obispo de Valencia, don Alfonso de Borja', *BRAH.*, lxxxviii, 1926.

On Calixtus' policies as Pope, *see*:

P. Paschini, 'La flotta di Callisto III (1455–8)', *ASRSP.*, liii–lv, 1930–2; P. Brezzi, 'La politica di Callisto III; equilibrio italiano e difesa dell' Europa alla metà del secolo XV', *Studi romani*, vii, 1959; L. Fumi, 'Il disinteresse di Francesco I, Sforza, alla crociata di Callisto III contro i Turchi', *Archivio storico lombardo*, 4th. ser., xvii, 1912; C. Marinescu, 'Le Pape Calixte III (1455–58), Alfonso V d'Aragon, roi de Naples, et l'offensive contre les Turcs', *Bulletin de la section historique; Académie Roumaine*, xix, 1935.

See also L. Banchi, articles on the wars in Siena and the northern Papal States in which Calixtus became involved:

L. Banchi, 'La guerra de'senesi col Conte di Pitigliano', *ASI.*, 4th ser., iii, 1879; 'Il Piccinino nello stato di Siena e la lega italica (1455–6)', *ASI.*, 4th ser., iv, 1879; 'Ultime relazioni dei Senesi con papa Callisto III', *ASI.*, 4th ser. v, 1880.

Other works on Calixtus as Pope are:

J. Rius Serra, *Catalanes y Aragoneses en la corte de Calixto III* (Analecta sacra Taraconensia, iii, Barcelona, 1927); A. Albareda, 'Il bibliotecario di Callisto III', *Miscellanea Mercati*, vol. IV (*Studi e testi*, cxxiv, 1946), an account of the career of Cosimo de Montserrat; F. Martorelli, 'Biblioteca di Callisto III', *Miscellanea Ehrle*, vol. V (*Studi e testi*, xli, 1924), publishes an inventory of Calixtus' manuscripts; J. Rius Serra, 'Un inventario de joyas de Callixto III', *Analecta sacra Taraconensia*, v, 1929; G. F. Chambers, 'Halley's comet in 1456 and the Pope',

Journal of the British Astronomical Association, xviii, 1908; R. A. Sampson, 'Halley's comet and Pope Calixtus', *ibid.*, xix, 1909; J. Stein, *Calixte III et la comète de Halley*, Rome, 1909.

4. Alexander VI

The controversy about the Borgias and the Borgia legend has now raged intermittently for a century. Most of the early accounts were denunciations based on the narrative sources described in my introduction, and of these accounts the most influential were:

A. Gennarelli (ed.), *Giovanni Buchardi Diarum* (Florence, 1854).

A. Gordon, *The Lives of Pope Alexander VI and his son Cesare Borgia* (London, 1729).

The reaction to this phase was led by:

D. Cerri, *Borgia ossia Alessandro VI papa, e suoi contemporanei* (Turin, 1858). An entirely uncritical defence.

M. J. H. Ollivier, *Le Pape Alexandre VI et les Borgia* (Paris, 1870).

V. Nemec, *Papst Alexander VI* (Klagenfurt, 1879).

A. Leonetti, *Papa Alessandro VI secondo documenti e carteggi del tempo* (Bologna, 1880). This is the most soundly based of the vindications which appeared at this time.

The immediate counters to the theories put forward in these works were:

H. Matagne, 'Une rehabilitation de Alexandre VI et le cardinal Rodrigo Borgia', *Revue des questions historiques*, ix and xi, 1870–2. A reply to Ollivier.

H. de L'Épinois, 'Alexandre VI', *Revue des questions historiques*, xx, 1881. A reply to Leonetti.

Successive authors have tended to take one or the other line:

D. Dal Re, 'Discorso critico sui Borgia con l'aggiunta di documenti inediti relativi al pontificato di Alessandro VI', *ASRSP.*, iv, 1881.

E. Gebhart, 'Une problème de morale et d'histoire: les Borgia', *Revue des deux mondes*, lxxxiv, 1887.

Lord Acton, 'The Borgias and their latest historian', in *Historical Essays and Studies* (London, 1907).

A. H. Mathew, *Life and Times of Rodrigo Borgia, Pope Alexander VI* (London 1912).

G. Portigliotti, *The Borgias. Alexander VI, Cesare and Lucrezia* (translated from the Italian, London, 1928). An extravagant account in the best, mid-19th. century tradition.

P. De Roo, *Materials for a History of Alexander VI, His Relatives and his Times* (Bruges, 1924). A vast apologetic work in which useful material is often almost undetectable under the coat of whitewash.

I. Dell'Oro, *Il segreto de'Borgia* (Milan, 1938).

G. Truc, *Rome et les Borgias* (Paris, 1939).

O. Ferrara, *The Borgia Pope* (translated from the Spanish, London, 1942). Another extravagant vindication the interesting points in which are marred by a multiplicity of minor inaccuracies.

J. H. Whitfield, 'New views upon the Borgias', *History*, xxviii, 1943.

D. Elias Olmos y Canalda, *Revindicacion de Alejandro VI* (Valencia, 1954).

This long controversy has been carried into recent years by two Italian historians in a series of publications:

G. Soranzo, *Studi intorno a papa Alessandro VI* (Milan, 1950). This work includes essays on the election, on Burchard's diary, the Archivum Arcis documents, the position of Giulia Farnese, and on Alexander's policies as a whole.

G. B. Picotti, 'Nuovi studi e documenti intorno a papa Alessandro VI', *RSCI.*, v, 1951. Refutes Soranzo's defence of the Borgias with the publication of some new documents.

G. Soranzo, 'Documenti inediti o poco noti relativi all'assunzione al pontificato di Alessandro VI', *Archivi*, 2nd ser., xix, 1952.

G. B. Picotti, 'Ancora sul Borgia', *RSCI.*, viii, 1954. A scathing review article on Ferrara's book.

G. Soranzo, 'Orsino Orsini, Adriana de Mila, sua madre, e Giulia Farnese, sua moglie, nei loro rapporti con papa Alessandro VI', *Archivi.* 2nd ser., xxvi, 1959.

G. Soranzo, *Il tempo di Alessandro VI e di Girolamo Savonarola* (Milan, 1960). These studies include an essay on anti-Borgia literature, on Alexander's response to the French invasion in 1494, on Alexander and Savonarola, and Alexander and Giuliano della Rovere.

G. B. Picotti, 'Alessandro VI, il Savonarola ed il cardinale Giuliano della Rovere in una pubblicazione recente', *ASRSP.*, lxxxiii, 1960. A further refutation of Soranzo's views.

G. Soranzo, 'La più grave accusa fatta a papa Borgia', *Archivi*, 2nd ser., xxviii, 1961. The accusation is that of having fathered children while Pope.

Inevitably some authors have seen the controversy as a sort of trial and have written their books in this manner:

R. de Maricourt, *Le Procès des Borgia* (Paris, 1882).

E. Moreu-Rey, *El pro i el contra dels Borja* (Palma, 1958).

A. Del Vita, *Processo ai Borgia* (Arezzo, 1959).

For the early career of Alexander, see:

F. Giorgi, 'Rodrigo Borgia allo studio di Bologna', *AMR.*, viii, 1890; J. Sanchis y Sivera, 'El cardinal Rodrigo Borja en Valencia', *BRAH.*, lxxxiv, 1924; J. Fernandez Alonso, *Legaciones y nunciatures en Espana de 1466 en 1521*, vol. I, 1466–1486 (Rome, 1963); A. Garcia de la Fuente, 'La legacion del cardinal Rodrigo de Borja y la cuestion monetaria de Enrique IV', *Religion y cultura*, 1933; P. Paschini, 'Il cardinale

Rodrigo Borgia, vice-cancelliere, e le trotte dell'Aniene', *Roma*, II, 1924, with details of Rodrigo's illness at Subiaco in 1485.

The election of Alexander is covered by:

W. Schweitzer, 'Zur Wahl Alexanders VI', *Historisches Jahrbuch*, xxx, 1909, the first publication of the complete scrutiny lists; J. Schnitzer, 'Zur Wahl Alexander VI', *Zeitschrift für Kirchengeschichte*, xxxiv, 1913; G. B. Picotti, 'Giovanni de'Medici nel conclave per l'elezione di Alessandro VI', *ASRSP.*, xliv, 1921; P. Paschini, 'Prodromi all'elezione di Alessandro VI', *Atti del I° Congresso nazionale di studi romani*, I, 1929, concerned with Alexander's advance preparations for the conclave in the preceding years; F. La Torre, *Del conclave di Alessandro VI, papa Borgia* (Florence, 1933).

On Borgia policy there are:

I. Dell'Oro, *Papa Alessandro VI, Rodrigo Borgia; appunti per chi vorrà scrivere la vera storia della famiglia Borgia* (Milan, 1940). An outline of Alexander's diplomacy making him out to be one of the most intelligent and astute Popes of all.

G. Pepe, *La politica dei Borgia* (Naples, 1946). A harsh indictment of Borgia policies.

E. Pontieri, 'Alessandro VI, Ferrante I d'Aragona e Virginio Orsini', in *Per la storia del regno di Ferrante I d'Aragona, Re di Napoli* (Naples, 1946).

G. B. Picotti, 'Per le relazioni fra Alessandro VI e Piero de'Medici', *ASI.*, lxxiii, 1915.

H. F. Delaborde, 'Alexandre VI et Charles VIII', *Bibliothèque de l'École des Chartes*, xlvii, 1886.

H. Heidenheimer, 'Die Korrespondenz Sultan Bayazet II mit Papst Alexander VI', *Zeitschrift für Kirchengeschichte*, 1882.

J. Calmette, 'La legation du cardinal de Sienne, 1494', *Mélanges d'archéologie et d'histoire*, xxii, 1902. Publishes the reports of Piccolomini to Alexander.

C. Maumene, 'Une ambassade de Alexandre VI au roi Charles VIII', *Revue des deux mondes*, lii, 1909.

E. Vecchi Pinto, 'La missione del cardinale Piccolomini legato pontificio presso Carlo VIII', *ASRSP.*, lxviii, 1945. Publishes the oration which Piccolomini prepared to deliver to Charles VIII.

M. Maulde de la Clavière, 'Alexandre VI et le divorce de Louis XII', *Bibliothèque de l'École des Chartes*, lvii, 1896.

G. Volpe, 'Intorno ad alcune relazioni di Pisa con Alessandro VI e Cesare Borgia (1499–1504)', *Studi storici*, vi–vii, 1897–8.

M. Batllori, *Alejandro VI y la Casa Real de Aragon* (Madrid, 1958). Publishes some documents including letters of King Ferdinand.

H. Vanderlinden, 'Alexander VI and the demarcation of the maritime and colonial domains of Spain and Portugal', *American Historical Review*, xxii, 1917.

E. Staedler, 'Die Urkunden Alexanders VI zur westindischen Investitur der Krone Spaniens von 1493', *Archiv für Urkundenforschung*, xv, 1938.

M. Giminez Fernandez, 'Las bulas alejandrinas de 1493 referentes a las Indias', *Annuario de estudios americanos*, i, 1944.

L. Weckmann, *Las bulas Alejandrinas de 1495 y la teoria politica del papado medieval* (Mexico City, 1949).

Miscellaneous aspects:

L. Fumi, *Alessandro VI e il Valentino in Orvieto* (Siena, 1877). Particularly in 1493–5; G. Ouy, 'Le pape Alexandre VI a-t-il employé les armes chimiques?', *Receuil de travaux offerts à C. Brunel*, II (Paris, 1955), publishes a report of the French commander at the siege of Ostia in 1497; L. Celier, 'Alexandre VI et la réforme de l'Eglise', *Mélanges d'archéologie et d'histoire*, xxvii, 1907, is concerned with the reform capitulations of 1497; B. Feliciangeli, 'Le proposte per la guerra contro i turchi presentate da Stefano Taleazzi, vescovo di Torcello, a papa Alessandro VI', *ASRSP.*, xxxix; R. Garnett, 'A Contemporary oration on Alexander VI', *English Historical Review*, 1892, being the oration by the Bishop of Gallipoli at the opening of the conclave after the death of Alexander.

On Vanozza there are: P. Fedele, 'I gioielli di Vanozza', *ASRSP.*, xxviii, 1905; F. Pasini-Frassoni, 'Lo stemma di Vanozza Borgia', *Rivista araldica*, 1909; A. Ferrua, 'Ritrovamento dell'epitaffio di Vanozza Cattaneo', *ASRSP.*, lxxi, 1948.

5. Cesare Borgia

The best biographies of Cesare are:

E. Alvisi, *Cesare Borgia, Duca di Romagna* (Imola, 1878).

C. Yriarte, *César Borgia, sa vie, sa captivité, son mort* (Paris, 1889).

W. H. Woodward, *Cesare Borgia* (London, 1913).

These three works, and particularly Alvisi, broke away from a traditional view of Cesare as an unpleasant and worthless villain which the earliest biography, G. Leti (pseud. Tomaso Tomasi), *La Vita del Duca Valentino* (Monte Chiaro, 1655) had been largely influential in creating.

Most subsequent biographers have reproduced to some extent the almost heroic proportions given to Cesare by Alvisi without adding any significant new dimensions to the portrait. They include:

Sir Charles G. Robertson, *Caesar Borgia* (The Stanhope Essay, Oxford, 1891); J. Richepin, *Les debuts de César Borgia* (Paris, 1891); J. L. Garner, *Caesar Borgia. A Study of the Renaissance* (London, 1912); R. Levy, *César Borgia* (Paris, 1930); P. Rival, *César Borgia* (Paris, 1931); C. Beuf,

Cesare Borgia, the Machiavellian Prince (Toronto, 1942), which propounds the strange thesis that Cesare was the son of Vanozza and Giuliano della Rovere; A. J. Onieva, *Cesar Borgia; su vida, su muerte y sus restos* (Madrid, 1945); G. Sacerdote, *La vita di Cesare Borgia* (Milan, 1950), the most reliable of the recent biographies; C. Fusero, *Cesare Borgia* (Milan, 1958), a very slight compilation.

On Cesare in France, *see*:

P. Ferrato, *L'entrata del Valentino nel 1499 al Chinone* (Venice, 1866); A. de Gallier, 'César Borgia. Documents sur son séjour en France', *Bulletin de la Société d'Archéologie de la Drôme*, xxix, 1895; E. L. Miron, *Duchess Derelict. A Study of the Life and Times of Charlotte d'Albret, Duchesse de Valentinois* (London, 1911), a romantic account of Charlotte which tells us little about Cesare; G. L. Schlumberger, *Charlotte d'Albret: femme de César Borgia, et la château de La Motte-Feuilly* (Paris, 1913).

Cesare in the Romagna is also covered by:

G. Chierici, 'L'idea di Roma nel ducato della Romagna di Cesare Borgia', *Istituto di studi romani: sezione emiliana*, ii, 1944; R. Mariotti, 'Breve sunto di alcuni documenti riferibili al governo di Cesare Borgia conservati nell' archivio notarile di Fano', in *Le Marche illustrate nella storia*, I (Fano, 1901); A. A. Bernardy, *Cesare Borgia e la Repubblica di San Marino, 1500–1504* (Florence, 1905); A. Bonardi, 'Venezia e Cesare Borgia', *Nuovo archivio veneto*, ns, xx, 1910; R. De la Sizeranne, *César Borgia et le duc d'Urbino* (Paris, 1924); B. Feliciangeli, *Sull'acquisto di Pesaro fatto da Cesare Borgia* (Camerino, 1900); P. E. Vecchione, *La rocca di Senigallia e la tragica casa del Valentino* (Senigallia, 1934); G. Castelloni, 'Il Duca Valentino; due documenti inediti', *AMR.*, 3rd ser., xiv, 1896, provides evidence that Cesare's *census* as vicar was never paid; L. Beltrami, *Leonardo da Vinci e Cesare Borgia* (Milan, 1916).

Machiavelli and Cesare Borgia; inevitably discussion of the part allotted to Cesare Borgia in *The Prince* occupies a major place in the vast literature of commentaries on Machiavelli. I cite here only those works in which interest in Cesare occupies the forefront of the argument.

H. Heidenheimer, *Machiavellis erste römische Legation: ein Beitrag zur Beleuchtung seiner gesandt schaftlichen Thätigkeit* (Darmstadt, 1878); A. Medin, 'Il duca Valentino nella mente di Niccolò Machiavelli', *Rivista europea*, xxxix, 1883; M. Brosch, 'Machiavelli, Cesare Borgia und Alexander VI', *Zeitschrift für Kirchengeschichte*, xxiii, 1902; C. Benoist, 'César Borgia; l'original du Prince', *Revue des deux mondes*, xxxvi, 1906; G. Sasso, 'Sul VII capitolo del Principe', *Rivista storica italiana*, lxiv, 1952; C. Clough, 'Niccolò Machiavelli, Cesare Borgia and the Francesco Troche episode', *Medievalia e umanistica*, xvii, 1966; G. Sasso, *Machiavelli e Cesare Borgia; storia di un giudizio*

(Rome, 1966); C. Dionisotti, 'Machiavelli, Cesare Borgia e Don Michelotto', *Rivista storica italiana*, lxxix, 1967; J. Larner, 'Cesare Borgia, Machiavelli and the Romagnol militia', *Studi Romagnoli*, xvii, 1966).

Miscellaneous aspects:

A. Caracciolo, *Un ratto di Cesare Borgia* (Naples, 1921), concerns the abduction of Dorotea Caracciolo; A. Francesco, *Cesare Borgia e il sacco di Capua* (S. Maria di Capua Vetere, 1954); R. Garnett, 'Contemporary Poems on Cesare Borgia', *English Historical Review*, i, 1886; T. Hagen, 'Caesar Borgia und die Ermordung des Herzogs von Biselli', *Zeitschrift für Katholics Theologie*, x; A. Lisini, 'Cesare Borgia e la Repubblica di Siena', *Bulletino senese di storia patria*, vii, 1900; G. Perez, 'Cesar Borgia, obispo de Pamplona', *Razon y Fe*, 1934.

6. Lucrezia Borgia

Two biographies stand out from the vast literature on Lucrezia:

F. Gregorovius, *Lucrezia Borgia* (Stuttgart, 1874) with English edition (London, 1948).

M. Bellonci, *Lucrezia Borgia; sua vita e suoi tempi* (rev. ed. Milan, 1960) with abridged English edition (London, 1953).

Other biographies are:

C. Zucchetti, *Lucrezia Borgia* (Mantua, 1860); G. Campori, 'Lucrezia Borgia; una vittima della storia', *Nuova Antologia*, 1866; M. Brosch, 'Alexander VI und Lucrezia Borgia', *Historische Zeitschrift*, xxxiii, 1875; L. Cappalletti, Lucrezia Borgia e la storia (Pisa, 1876); A. Ademollo, 'Lucrezia Borgia e la verità', *Archivio storico, artistico, archeologico e letterario della città e provincia di Roma*, ii, 1877; M. Catalano, *Lucrezia Borgia, Duchessa di Ferrara* (Ferrara, 1920), published many documents in connection with Lucrezia's Ferrarese period; W. Ramirez de Villa-Urrutia, *Lucrezia Borja* (Madrid, 1922); F. Funck-Brentano, *Lucrèce Borgia* (Paris, 1930); M. Buggelli, *Lucrezia Borgia* (Milan, 1931); F. Berence, *Lucrèce Borgia* (Paris, 1951); A. J. Onieva, *Lucrezia Borgia* (Barcelona, 1957).

On Lucrezia's marriages *see*:

B. Feliciangeli, *Un episodio nel nepotismo borgiano; il matrimonio di Lucrezia Borgia con Giovanni Sforza, Signore di Pesaro* (Turin, 1901); L. Pescetti, 'Le prime nozze di Lucrezia Borgia in una lettera inedita di Jacopo Gherardi', *Rassegna volterrana*, 1955; F. R. De Uhagon, *Relacion de los festines que se celebraron en el Vaticano con motivo de las bodas de Lucrecia Borgia con Alonso de Aragon* (Madrid, 1896); L. A. Gandini, 'Lucrezia Borgia nell'imminenza delle sue nozze con Alfonso d'Este', *AMR.*, 1902; C. Errera, 'Il passaggio per Forlì di Lucrezia Borgia sposa di Alfonso d'Este', *ASI.*, 5th ser., x, 1892.

Miscellaneous aspects:

F. Mancini, 'Lucrezia Borgia, governatrice di Spoleto', *ASI.*, cxv, 1957; B. Morsolin, 'Pietro Bembo e Lucrezia Borgia', *Nuova antologia*, xv, 1885; L. Beltrami, *La guardaroba di Lucrezia Borgia* (Milan, 1903); R. Davidsohn, 'Lucrezia Borgia suora della penitenza', *ASI.*, 5th ser., xxviii, 1901; A. De Hevesy, 'Bartolomeo Veneto et les portraits de Lucrezia Borgia', *Arts Quarterly of the Detroit Institute of Arts*, ii. 1939.

7. Other children of Alexander VI

General surveys:

L. Celier, 'Alexandre VI et ses enfants en 1493', *Mélanges d'archéologie et d'histoire*, xxvi, 1906; M. Olivier y Hurtado, 'Don Rodrigo Borja (Alejandro VI), sus hijos y descendientes', *BRAH.*, ix, 1886.

Pedro Luis:

C. R. von Hoefler, 'Don Rodrigo de Borja und seine Sohne, Don Pedro Luis I and Don Juan II, Herzöge von Gandia aus dem Hause Borja', *Denkschriften der kaiserliche Akademie der Wissenschaften*, xxxvii, 1889; F. Fita, 'Don Pedro Luis de Borja, Duque de Gandia', *BRAH.*, x, 1887.

Juan:

R. Chabas, 'Alejandro VI y el Duque de Gandia', *El Archivo*, vii, 1893, documents published here are reprinted by Sanchis y Sivera, *Algunos documentos y cartas privadas*, *op. cit.* (see Section 1); A. Knöpfler, 'Der Tod des Herzogs von Gandia', *Theologische Quartalschrift*, xlix; A. Luzio and R. Renier, 'Relazione inedita sulla morte del Duca di Gandia', *ASRSP.*, xi, 1888, being the account of Gian Carlo Scalona, the Mantuan ambassador.

R. Chabas, 'Don Jofre de Borja y Dona Sancha de Aragon', *Revue Hispanique*, ix, 1902.

U. Gnoli, 'Una figlia sconosciuta di Alessandro VI', *L'Urbe*, ii, 1937, concerns Isabella Borgia-Matuzzi.

C. Ricci, *Anime dannate: Ginevra Sforza, Il figlio di Cesare Borgia, ecc.* (Milan, 1918) on Girolamo Borgia.

A. Gilioli, 'La legittimazione di Camilla Borgia', *Atti e memorie della deputazione provinciale ferrarese di storia patria*, 1946–9.

N. Cionini, 'Angela Borgia o una pagina di storia sassolese del secolo XVI', *Atti della deputazione di storia patria per le provincie modenesi*, vi, 1910.

8. The later Dukes of Gandia and St. Francis Borgia

For Gandia itself, see:

E. Bertaux, 'Monuments et souvenirs des Borgias dans le royaume de

Valencia', *Gazette des Beaux Arts*, 1908; F. Cervos and J. M. Sola, *El palacio ducal de Gandia* (Barcelona, 1904).

On Juan, the 3rd Duke:

C. R. von Hoefler, 'Die Katastrophe des herzoglichen Hauses der Borjas von Gandia', *Denkschriften der kaiserliche Akademie der Wissenschaften*, xli, 1892; M. Batllori, 'De ortu Johannis, tertii ducis Gandiensis, sancti Francisci Borgiae patris', *Archivum Historica Societatis Jesu*, xxvi, 1957.

St. Francis Borgia: the almost contemporary biography of P. Ribadeneira, *S. Francis Borgia* (Rome, 1596) provided a picture of almost unbelievable asceticism and sanctity on which all early accounts were based. This picture was decisively changed to reveal a more understandable and sympathetic character, by the best of all the biographies of St. Francis, that of P. Suau, *Histoire de S. François de Borgia* (Paris, 1910) which utilised the vast correspondence of the saint.

Later accounts have all drawn largely on Suau's work:

C. C. Martindale, *In God's Army*, vol. II, St. Francis Borgia (London, 1916); O. Karrer, *Der heilige Franz von Borja, General der Gesellschaft Jesu, 1510–72* (Freiburg, 1921); M. Yeo, *The Greatest of the Borgias* (London, 1936); F. Garzon, *Vida de San Francisco de Borja* (Madrid, 1953); Saint-Paulien, *Saint Francois Borgia; l'expiateur* (Paris, 1959).

For particular aspects of the life of St. Francis Borgia, there are:

C. M. Abad, 'Carlos V y san Francisco Borja', *Miscellanea Comillas*, xxxi, 1959; P. J. Blanco Trias, '*El virreinado de san Francisco de Borja en Cataluna* (Barcelona, 1921); L. Lopetegui, 'San Francisco de Borja y el plan misional de San Pio V', *Archivum historica Societatis Jesu*, xi, 1942; A. Xavier, *El Duque de Gandia* (Madrid, 1943) concerned with the period before 1550.

On later Borjas:

L. Amoros, 'El monasterio de Santa Clara de Gandia y la familia ducal de los Borjas', *Archivo Ibero-Americano*, xx–xxi, 1960–1; C. A. Gonzalez-Palencia, 'Noticias biograficas del Virrey poetal Principe de Esquilache, 1577–1658', *Annuario de estudios americanos*, vi, 1949; F. Panesso Posada, 'Las familias Borja y Zulueta', *Boletin de Historia y Antiquedades* (Bogota), xliv, 1957, on the Borjas in Peru and Colombia.

9. The Borgias and the Arts

General:

E. Müntz, *Les arts à la cour des Papes Innocent VIII, Alexandre VI, Pie III (1484–1503)* (Paris, 1898); E. Rodocanachi, *Histoire de Rome. Une cour princière au Vatican pendant la Renaissance: Sixte IV, Innocent VIII, Alexandre VI* (Paris, 1925); A. Ademollo, *Alessandro VI, Giulio II e Leone X nel carnevale di Roma; documenti inediti* (Florence, 1886).

On Borgia building programmes:

F. Cancellieri, 'Notizie del Palazzo della Cancelleria Vecchia', *Effemeride Letterarie*, 1821; F. Gori, 'Residenza, nascite e fortificazioni de'Borgia nella rocca di Subiaco', *Archivio storico, artistico, archeologico e letterario della città e provincia di Roma*, iv, 1880; E. Rodocanachi, 'Le château Saint-Ange sous le pontificat d'Alexandre VI', *Revue des questions historiques*, lxxxv, 1909; F. Sanguinetti, 'La fortezza di Civita Castellana e il suo restauro', *Palladio*, ns. ix, 1959.

On the Borgia Apartments:

F. Ehrle and H. Stevenson, *Les fresques du Pinturicchio dans les salles Borgia au Vatican* (Rome, 1898); F. Hermanin, *L'appartamento Borgia in Vaticano* (Rome, 1934); F. Saxl, 'The Appartamento Borgia', *Lectures* (London, 1957); J. Schulz, 'Pinturicchio and the Revival of Antiquity', *Journal of the Warburg Courtauld Institutes*, xxv, 1962.

Other Borgia patronage:

J. Lopez Rey, 'On Velasquez portraits of Cardinal Borja', *Art Bulletin*, 1946; T. Crombie, 'The Portrait of Cardinal Borja by Velasquez', *Connoisseur*, cxlvii, 1961.

Borgia heraldry: A. van de Put, *The Aragonese Double Crown and the Borja or Borgia device* (London, 1910); G. Biasiotti, 'Araldica Borgiana nel soffitto della Basilica di Santa Maria Maggiore', *Rivista del Collegio Araldico*, 1915.

The Borgias and letters:

V. Cian, review of Pastor in *Giornale storico della letteratura italiana*, xxix, 1897, pp. 424–35

10. The Borgia circle

Many of the figures who surrounded Alexander VI and his family have emerged as shadowy personalities, and it seems fitting to conclude these bibliographical notes with some indication of biographical material available on these men:

M. Batllori, 'Bernardino Lopez de Carvajal, legado de Alejandro VI en Anagni, 1494', *Saggi storici intorno al Papato dai professori della Facoltà di storia ecclesiastica* (Rome, 1959).

P. Paschini, 'Leonello Chieregato, nunzio d'Innocenzo VIII e di Alessandro VI', *Lateranum*, ns., i, 1935.

J. Schnitzer, *Peter Delfin, General des Camaldulenserordens. Ein Beitrag zur Geschichte der Kirchenreform, Alexander VI und Savonarola* (Munich, 1926).

B. Feliciangeli, 'Ingresso del cardinale Ippolito d'Este nel mondo cortigiano di Roma', *Miscellanea per nozze Crocioni-Ruscelloni* (Reggio, 1908).

E. Filippini, 'Liverotto Euffreducci', *Atti della deputazione di storia patria per le Marche*, 1895.

G. Ferrari Moreni, 'Vita di cardinale Ferrari', *Atti e memorie della deputazione modenese e parmensi di storia patria*, viii.

A. Albareda, 'Il vescovo d Barcellona, Pietro Garsias, bibliotecario della Vaticana sotto Alessandro VI', *Bibliofilia*, lx, 1958.

C. Cansacchi, 'Agapito Gheraldini', *Bollettino della deputazione di storia patria per l'Umbria*, lviii, 1961.

B. Feliciangeli, 'Agapito Gheraldini', *Storia ed arte* (Florence, 1916).

L. Michelini Tocci, 'Agapito Gheraldini', *Collectanea Vaticana in honorem Anselmi M. Cardinale Albareda* (Vatican, 1962).

A. Albareda, 'Intorno alla fine del bibliotecario apostolico Giovanni Lorenzi', *Miscellanea Pio Paschini* (*Lateranum*, ns., xv, 1949).

L. Onori, 'Un maggiordomo di Alessandro VI; Pedro Melendez de Valdes', *Rivista del Collegio Araldico*, 1914.

D. Zauli-Naldi, *Dionigi e Vincenzo Naldi in Romagna* (*1495–1504*) (Faenza, 1925).

A. Gottlob, 'Der Legat Raimund Peraudi', *Historische Jahrbuch*, vi.

J. Fernandez Alonso, 'Don Francesco de Prats, primer nuncio permanente en Espana (1492–1503),' *Anthologica annua*, i, 1953.

J. Llanodosa Pujol, *El cardinal Remolins* (Lerida, 1956).

F. Spanu Satta, *Memorie sarde in Roma* (Sassari, 1962) with information on Jaime Serra.

L. Piccioni, *Di Francesco Uberti umanista cesenate* (Bologna, 1903).

INDEX